BEYOND POPULISM

BEYOND POPULISM

Angry Politics and the Twilight of Neoliberalism

Edited by Jeff Maskovsky
and Sophie Bjork-James

WEST VIRGINIA UNIVERSITY PRESS
MORGANTOWN

ISBN
Cloth 978-1-949199-45-1
Paper 978-1-949199-46-8

Library of Congress Cataloging-in-Publication Data is available
from the Library of Congress

Cover design by Than Saffel / WVU Press
Book design by Copperline Book Services

CONTENTS

ACKNOWLEDGMENTS

This anthology developed from two workshops held to explore rising authoritarian, nationalist, and populist politics across the world and came together as a collaborative effort involving the editors and the contributors. The first workshop took place at Vanderbilt University in March 2017. The second was at the CUNY Graduate Center in October 2017. These workshops materialized thanks to financial support from the National Science Foundation and the Wenner-Gren Foundation for Anthropological Research. The opinions, findings, and conclusions expressed here are those of the editors and authors and do not necessarily reflect the views of the National Science Foundation or the Wenner-Gren Foundation. At Wenner-Gren we thank Mary Beth Moss, Laurie Obbink, and Danilyn Rutherford. At NSF, we thank Deborah Winslow and Jeff Mantz. At Vanderbilt University, we thank the Anthropology Department, especially department chair Beth Conklin. At the Graduate Center, we thank the PhD Program in Anthropology and the Advanced Research Collaborative, especially ARC director Don Robotham.

Our greatest debts go to the contributors who sustained an open, intellectually generous, and kind collective conversation with us for the two years during which this project came together. We also thank Alyson Cole, Beth Conklin, Chelsey Dyer, Nadja Eisenberg-Guyot, Leith Mullings, Ida Susser, Anand Taneja, and Gary Wilder. Although they did not contribute chapters to the anthology, their participation in the workshops shaped our collective conversation in important ways. The administrative support provided by Merrit Corrigan, Chelsey Dyer, Nadja Eisenberg-Guyot, and Anze Zadel at various stages of this anthology's completion was also essential and much appreciated.

We are very grateful to Derek Krissoff at West Virginia University Press, who welcomed this project enthusiastically. His superb editorial guidance made this anthology much better. At West Virginia University Press, we also thank Charlotte Vester for her editorial work. Thanks also to Julian Aron Ross and Paulo Suarez for compiling the index.

Introduction

This book is about the political forms of anger that have emerged across the globe in the last decade, and what they tell us about the conjunctural shifts taking place as neoliberalism exhausts itself as a set of ruling projects, ideologies, and rationalities. Exasperated publics routinely express their disdain for the political and economic status quo and the prioritization of finance-led globalization, free trade, structural adjustment, and austerity. At first it appeared that the left would successfully channel this public anger, as the Arab Spring, Indignados movement, Occupy Wall Street, #BLM, and other uprisings criticized neoliberal austerity, challenged the legitimacy of authoritarian regimes, condemned economic inequality, opposed environmental destruction, protested racialized state violence, and innovated radically democratic governing forms. Yet, very quickly, right-wing nationalist movements also flourished. In the United States and among the countries in the European Union, angry publics delivered xenophobic political outcomes such as the Brexit vote and Donald Trump's presidency. And political leaders in Russia, India, the Philippines, Turkey, and in parts of Latin America and Africa also mobilized public anger into attacks on cosmopolitan elites and outsiders.

Populism is the key term that typically is used to describe these political developments, and for good reason: it directs our attention to the brutal effectiveness of political mobilizations channeling popular disdain for established governing norms, forms, ideas, and values, replacing democratic ideals of inclusion with nationalist movements advocating the power of "the people" against outsiders and the elites who allow them in. Yet conventional academic debates over populism's exact form and the kinds of politics that are covered by the term do little to help us understand the ways that popular disdain, disillusionment, and disenchantment are taking political form in the world today. Nor does the term *populism* capture the full scope of popular misgivings about the status quo that are expressed in current political formations. This book thus does not attempt to intervene in the academic discussion around populism's proper definition or to isolate its organizational or ideological features in current movements. Our focus is instead the kinds of disturbances and dislocations that are created by today's popular political passions.

In a broad sense, we locate what we are calling *angry politics* within the political-economic regime of neoliberalism and its failures as a viable project. Indeed, we make the anthropological case that angry politics in many ways point to the decline, limits, and failures of various neoliberal projects as they have been enacted across the globe. Yet our point is not simply that new political forms emerge mainly as a popular expression of dismay over the kinds of dispossession, inequality, and disenfranchisement that have accompanied neoliberalism's rise, though they are sometimes that. Rather, we argue that new destructive projects of resentment have surfaced in the political spaces opened up by neoliberalism's recent failures, faults, and retreats. These projects, the book demonstrates, enact retrograde politics around race, class, gender, sex, ethnicity, migration, and inclusion and help to consolidate harder edged forms of authoritarian rule.

The Twilight of Neoliberalism

The collapse of the global financial sector in 2007–8 is one of many signs of strain in a global neoliberal order that has sought, since the 1980s, to tie US-led globalism with a revived form of nineteenth-century liberalism. In truth, the form of capitalist political economy since the 1980s that is frequently glossed as neoliberal globalization has never been fully secure, just like the Keynesian order before it (Harvey 2007, 2018). It nonetheless succeeded on many fronts: anointing a new group of transnational elites, restoring profitability and growth in the metropolitan centers of global capitalism after they had declined in the 1960s and 1970s, enabling the rise of China, India, and Brazil as economic powerhouses, and facilitating the emergence and expansion of the entrepreneurial middle classes in parts of Latin America, the Caribbean, Africa, Asia, and in some of the countries in the former Soviet orbit. Yet neoliberal policies and projects also introduced greater competition, financialized volatility, and economic polarization, poverty, and precarity. For example, the introduction of a billion new workers into the global capitalist system devalued labor on a global scale, producing new patterns of class division, uneven development, and dispossession (Kalb and Halmai 2011). Far from a laissez-faire system, governments—especially central banks—have had to intervene repeatedly to stabilize an increasingly volatile economy. Indeed, long before the 2008 financial meltdown, neoliberal globalization was plagued by recurrent crises, from the US savings and loan disaster of the 1980s and the collapse in the late 1990s of the technology boom, to the 1997 Asian financial crisis. In these moments of crisis, and beyond them, economic policy makers seldom asked for, or were given, popular support or approval for the technocratic reforms they proposed and implemented. The liberal democratic ideals that are at the ideological core of neoliberalism were thus chronically under strain, and a long-term crisis in political authority and legitimacy was, in fact, endemic to neoliberal globalization from the start.

The twenty-first-century rise of authoritarian regimes is not merely an expression of neoliberalism's core political contradiction, however. A variety of contingencies have reshaped global, regional, and national politics in the post–Cold War period. The United States attempted to position itself in the aftermath of the Cold War as the unrivaled global hegemon with neoliberalism as the core ideology of its global ambitions. Yet it failed to consolidate global power on precisely these terms in the wake of 9/11. Indeed, the Bush-era war on terror, far from helping to consolidate a new global order, failed at every level, including militarily. What was supposed to mark a new phase of privatist, free market globalism cum US-styled democracy (which is what the neocons envisioned for both Afghanistan and Iraq) marked instead the beginning of the end of global American imperialism (Smith 2005). Russian interventions in the Middle East and elsewhere further offered up an alternative to US geopolitical power and demonstrated the United States' declining influence. And China's ascent onto the global stage occurred without the democratizing political reforms that pundits in the West predicted for decades as the inevitable consequence of its integration into the global capitalist system (Mann 2008). In parts of the Global South, during the same period, popular mobilizations surfaced against the erosion of the economic and social benefits previously available to the popular classes during the period of state-led development (Almeida 2007; Brenner et al. 2010). Although these mobilizations exposed the limitations of the neoliberal development model and its attendant pattern of inequality, the leaders who rode the wave of these protests into political office had to rely mostly on China and the Global North for investments, rarely broke with global trade accords, and faced considerable obstacles in the crafting of heterodox development models as a result.

With US-led globalism in decline, liberalism itself, and neoliberalism in particular, have weakened in several senses. The neoliberal orthodoxies of unfettered international competition, flexible and deregulated labor markets, and the noninterventionist state, for example, no longer hold sway even if the global economy continues to be organized with a neoliberal architecture. At the level of policy and ideology, neoliberalism has become a form of zombie economics, a set of dead ideas and policies that walk the earth in search of vulnerable people to feed on (Peck 2010; Quiggin 2012). Further, democracy itself is no longer seen as vital to economic growth and prosperity. Indeed, for many, the very idea of a global order organized around human rights and liberal democratic principles is no longer as compelling as it once was, as issues of safety, security, and stability take popular priority over the liberal freedoms that were traditionally valued or aspired to. This is not to say that the ideals and rationalities associated with liberalism, neoliberal or otherwise, were unproblematic. The actually existing liberal order has left a great deal to be desired and was built on systems of colonialism, slavery, exploitation, oppression, war, and violence at a scale that had never been seen in human history. But, as Don Robotham argues in his essay in this volume, the liberal movement also served productively as a counterpoint to more radical experiments in economy, democracy, and inclusion, which now must find different footing in a world where liberalism is no longer taken for granted (cf., Chatterjee 2016). In short, the ideological and political terms of popular struggle and sovereignty have changed dramatically since the Cold War ended, first with the demise of the Soviet model and now apparently with the demise, or at least the dramatic weakening, of the liberal model that was expected to ascend unrivaled after its collapse. Taken together, these developments are suggestive that faith in the idea of representative democracy and cosmopolitan liberalism as the longstanding political and governmental correlates of capitalism itself has been severely undermined.

It is no surprise, in this situation, that the forces of reaction and authoritarianism have grown steadily, frequently in the form of angry politics on the right. The political elite in the United States, for example, lost legitimacy in the aftermath of the 2008 financial collapse, when both neoliberals and neoconservatives alike offered adequate bailouts only to the banks, not to the millions of people who faced home ownership foreclosure, mortgage default, job loss, and social precarity. Donald Trump exploited this legitimacy crisis to make his political ascent. The imposition of austerity worked similarly in Europe, at both its core and edges, where frustration with technomanagerial rule became linked in some political quarters to longstanding skepticism about the European Union and about its stance on open borders and migration. Right-wing populist parties gained electoral ground in Italy, the Netherlands, France, Germany, Hungary, Finland, Bulgaria, and elsewhere. In contrast, Latin America returned to some extent to the neoliberal fold as the antineoliberal "pink tide" receded in the late 2000s. Across the region, the limitations of neoextractivist growth models, or, in Brazil, the "Lula model," hamstrung left-leaning governments, which backtracked on their redistributive promises. This created new tensions between leaders and the social movements that brought them to power, and several governments have taken unexpected authoritarian turns, as in Venezuela, as a means to "protect" the Bolivarian revolution against incursions from the right. In Brazil, a coup toppled the left-leaning president and a far-right populist won the presidency. Meanwhile, in the former Soviet sphere, authoritarian regimes have gained broad popular support as people express their disappointments with the politicians who steered the postsocialist transition and who championed European market integration schemes that weakened worker protections. In Turkey, the Philippines, and India, political entrepreneurs stoke nationalist sentiments to encourage popular outrage at "outsider" privileges, meddling, and control. Meanwhile, since 2017, eleven African countries have experienced coups, popular uprisings, or other forms of nonelectoral political change to oust longstanding dictators, although several have been replaced with equally authoritarian leadership.

What precisely is meant by the term *populism* in the current conjuncture? Clarifying how we use the term—and the limits we see to its uses—is important in a moment when the term is frequently used as a gloss for a variety of political configurations and forms. Benjamin Arditi (2007) defines populism as primarily about disrupting "politics as usual," a definition focused on a difference in style, where populists engage in provocative rhetoric that unsettles the usual order of political discourse. A different approach, influenced by Ernesto Laclau (2005), proposes that populism should be understood as a particular political form, not an ideology, which unites disparate elements as equivalent while critiquing some form of power. Accordingly, Francisco Panizza usefully defines populism's core element as "the notion of the *sovereign people* as an actor in an antagonistic relation with the established order" (Panizza 2005: 4).

Further, populism's appearance is typically associated with distinct social, political, and economic conditions: a breakdown in the political order, the failure of a political system to respond adequately to economic crisis, the loss of legitimacy by political parties, popular outrage over a lack of accountability by political elites, widespread social turmoil, and the rise of new forms of political identification and representation outside of establishment norms (Panizza 2005). These circumstances abound in the current conjuncture, and scholars today use the term to trace a wide variety of political developments, from populist efforts to empower marginalized groups in Africa, Southeast Asia, and Latin America, to populist efforts against them in Europe, the United States, and Australia (see, e.g., Torre 2015, 2018). Yet, as with Panizza and many other scholars, we do not find it especially useful to pin down too precisely what is meant by populism. Indeed, a survey of populist politics across the globe would not find among them a common ideology, constituency, or set of demands. Nor are today's populists unified by their political strategies or tactics or by a shared sense of who "the people" or their antagonists are. Indeed, as Chantal Mouffe insists in her call for a populism of the left to rise as a counterweight to its right-wing form (Mouffe 2018), a variety of populisms with different political coordinates are possible. Along these lines, we note in the literature the proliferation of populisms, popularly describable in terms of nationality, region, or scale (Asian populism, Russian populism, Latin American populism, Italian populism, global populism, and so forth), and in terms of particular kinds of people or politics (Islamic populism, agrarian populism, authoritarian populism, populist parties, and so forth).

Despite this variety, it is important to note the frequent organization of right-wing populism around a specific kind of antagonism: that between "the people" and an internal or external "other." And, in the right-wing populist playbook, the established political order is frequently attacked for its tolerance of, or ineffectuality in purging, the enemies of "the people." This dynamic is clearly at play today in the angry expression of anti-immigrant politics that have arisen in the United States, the United Kingdom, Italy, France, Germany, Sweden, Denmark, Hungary, and elsewhere in Europe, in Duterte's war on drugs in the Philippines, and Modi's political project and crackdown on dissent in India. These dynamics are significantly different than those at play in Africa, Latin America, and Asia, where authoritarian leaders are sometimes challenged by populist revolts and where populist parties governed.

Furthermore, there is no unitary explanation for right-wing populism's rise, political form, or popularity. Indeed, scholars emphasize different political forces, characteristics, and contexts. For example, Kalb and Halmai (2011) see right-wing populism's appearance in Europe as the "return of the repressed," an expression of working-class neonationalism borne from decades of dispossession and disenfranchisement under neoliberal rule. John Judis (2016), in contrast, places greater emphasis on the political instabilities unleashed by the Great Recession of 2007–8 (see also Tooze 2018). Pankaj Mishra (2017) locates current political trends within an even longer historical trend, as a backlash by modernity's losers, a widely disparate group that is susceptible to demagoguery because it is unable to enjoy the freedoms and prosperity that modernity has offered only to its elites (Mishra 2017). We appreciate these approaches for putting populism in its place within wider cultural, political, and economic contexts. Yet we note as well, as does Éric Fassin (2018), a failure to take race seriously at the level of theory in many of these accounts. Despite the centrality of racism and xenophobia in right-wing movements across the globe, rare is the account that places race at the center of the analysis. One result is that racist violence and animosity is figured in many accounts as a displacement of some other, more fundamental class-based political grievance.

We see politics around race—and around gender, sex, and class—as of equal importance in the making of right-wing populist politics. Indeed, "the people" is almost always constituted as a raced, classed, and gendered political subject. In the United States, for example, we have seen in recent years a mad-dash scramble to formulate workable political programs in defense of the ever-ambiguous category of "the middle class." Trumpism is one such attempt that articulates the middle class in largely racial—and racist—terms, and in terms also of retrograde gender and sex politics as well (Cole and Shulman 2018; Maskovsky this volume; see also Maskovsky 2017). Pundits have tried hard to insist that the roots of the flagrant racism and sexism of Trumpism is not racism or sexism but displaced anger at economic precarity. But polling data contradicts this assertion, which is frequently made by pundits who support various forms of economic populism from the left. In the vote for Trump, the single most powerful indicator was race, not class or gender, and most Trump voters were, in fact, middle class (Schaffter et al., 2018). Across Europe, coverage of the refugee crisis and anti-immigrant politics in Italy's 5-star movement, among anti-Brexit Remainers in the United Kingdom, in Marine Le Pen's National Front in France, and in increasingly visibly and politically effective far-right groups in Germany, Hungary, Poland, Sweden, Denmark, and elsewhere, may suggest a "return of the repressed" among many who were adversely affected by Europeanization and austerity politics (Kalb and Halmai 2014). But the politics of these groups also signal the return of long simmering racial and other resentments. In Latin America, popular politics has a complex relationship with the politics of indigeneity, gender, and race, and with populist traditions, which themselves are complicated and cannot be reduced to simple class dynamics (Laclau 2005). These are but a few examples that suggest a more complicated approach is needed that takes class seriously but that also goes beyond class in or for itself.

This brings us to the major theoretical orientation of this volume, which emphasizes conjunctural analysis over a singular or unitary account of the current global populist wave. Following Stuart Hall and others who have developed conjunctural analysis (Clarke 2014; Hall et al., 2013 [1976]; Hall 1986, 1987, 1989), we are interested in the complexity of the current moment and of the multiplicity of forces, antagonisms, conflicts, and emergent political forms that mark the present as a moment of crisis. With this approach in mind, we explore angry politics in different social, geographical, cultural, governmental, and economic contexts, asking what social, economic, governmental, political, and historical forces coalesce in the making of angry politics today. Central to this inquiry is attention to the forms of nationalism, populism, racism, and xenophobia that have emerged from the current conjuncture. As cracks widen in the neoliberal order, new political possibilities have arisen. We are seeing the evidence that angry politics from the right are particularly persuasive at this moment; however, as the essays in this volume collectively assert, they do so in geographically and historically specific ways. Their forms may, of course, follow similar patterns or influence each other, but projecting resentments and grievances onto others is always a matter of local politics and history.

Angry Politics

Along these lines, we need to consider the different kinds of anger that are at play in the politics of the present. We wish to highlight in particular three kinds of anger that have taken on political form in various contexts. Although there are many forms of angry politics, we highlight *neoliberal disenchantment, racialized resentments,* and the *rage of the downtrodden and repressed* as particularly salient and durable today. Taken together, these three kinds of anger do some of the work that is necessary to instantiate popular support for more authoritarian forms of politics across vastly different political contexts.

First is the disenchantment with neoliberalism itself. Recently a different form of angry politics led to a set of very different social movements. We can think back to the rallying cry of the Occupy movement, "We are the 99%," as a movement articulating an anger against class-based inequality. This deeply democratic framing of a people jointly oppressed by a small economic elite channeled this anger into an important form of popular insurgency around the world, but it did not coalesce into a durable form of popular or transformative politics. Similarly, the Arab Spring utilized a politics of anger to mobilize hundreds of thousands across several countries. According to Wendy Pearlman, across the Arab Spring multiple citizens used the same expression to describe their participation: "*inkasar hajez al-khawf*—The barrier of fear has broken" (Pearlman 2013: 388). Replacing a legacy of fear, anger helped to mobilize tens of thousands to risk their lives and demand democracy. Though these mobilizations toppled several long-term dictatorships, the anger at authoritarianism and economic exploitation that inspired most of these protests has led to only tenuous or temporary victories.

Across the Global North, the new discourse of economic exploitation provided by Occupy, and the anger it both cultivated and created, translated into few policy changes. Instead, the global economic consensus since 2010 has been an emphasis on austerity, leading to increased stratification. Extreme class inequality continues to define our economic reality. In 2017 the top 1 percent of global wealth holders received 82 percent of all wealth generated, while the poorest 50 percent of the global population received none of the generated wealth (Pimentel, Aymar, and Lawson 2018). The elite now get to fantasize about more extreme forms of luxury (the booming luxury yacht and private jet industries are now accompanied by an emerging private space travel line), leaving the multitudes faced with the challenges of meeting their basic needs. It has now become clear that the neoliberal promise of prosperity serves only as a "cruel optimism," to use the words of Lauren Berlant (2011), for everyone but the wealthy. In the present, the desire for the "good life" of economic prosperity is expressed mostly in contexts where the possibilities for achieving this life of economic success and stability is impossible for most. In the crucible of neoliberal fantasies, which promises that as the wealthy get wealthier and as the welfare state is shrunk, all will rise, the realities of economic stratification, precarity, debt, and stagnating wages now produce widespread disaffection, distrust, and disenchantment. Importantly, in the Global South, the coordinates of angry politics are somewhat different. In many Global South contexts, neoliberalism's demise is viewed less as a "crisis" in the "global economy" and more as a diminishment of US and European imperial economic, political, and cultural power. Further, the popular classes in the Global South learned the lessons of neoliberalism's limitations and often expressed their anger and frustration against it through left-leaning mobilizations, and they did so long before their counterparts in the Global North. The angry turn in the Global South is thus not so much targeted against neoliberal rationality exclusively, though that anger still abounds. It is also now frequently asserted politically against those who promised—but failed—to offer a persuasive way out of the neoliberal quagmire.

This disaffection between the promise of prosperity and the reality of precarity can serve as a political resource for various forms of politics, but there are reasons why it leans so readily toward right-wing authoritarianism. Wendy Brown (2018) places these varied moves toward authoritarian right-wing movements as an outgrowth of neoliberal rationality itself. Brown writes, "As neoliberal rationality becomes our ubiquitous common sense, its principles not only govern through the state but suffuse workplaces, schools, hospitals, gyms, air travel, policing, and all manner of human desire and decisions" (Brown 2018: 62). Here the personal sphere is expanded and freedom is defined by personal pursuits and not collective protections or the collective exercise of democracy. In this logic democracy becomes a threat to freedom, in that the collective—any collective—may limit the freedom of the individual to pursue their own private economic interests. This shrinking of democratic values and state welfare leaves only private interest and family values, which are themselves deeply antidemocratic. Brown thus sees neoliberal economic privatization as subversive of democracy in two senses: first because the kind of inequality it produces enacts a "profoundly dimmed democratic imaginary" and second because "it wages familial rather than market warfare on democratic principles and institutions. It positions exclusion, patriarchalism, tradition, nepotism, and Christianity as legitimate challenges to inclusion, autonomy, equal rights, limits on conflicts of interest, secularism, and the very principle of equality" (Brown 2018: 66). Brown sees the "personal, protected sphere" that is created in this situation as "empowered against the social" in such a way that it "expands to envelop the nation itself, securing and protecting it requires increasingly robust statism in the form of law, policing, and defense" (Brown 2018: 66). In line with scholars such as Ben Anderson (2016), who cautions against totalizing accounts of neoliberal affects, we take Brown's analysis as an entry point into the ways that anger, disillusionment, disaffection, and other affects condition and are conditioned by neoliberal rationality in specific contexts. Our analysis thus places many of these thrusts toward authoritarianism as an outgrowth of the conditions of neoliberalism and the particular structures of feelings and atmospherics it produces.

This leads us to racialized resentments and their connection to the new authoritarian turn. Across multiple national contexts, it is populations historically privileged by race—and gender, ethnicity, or religion—that are now defining themselves as victims, launching their fury at others, and challenging the political establishment. Indeed, in the liberal democracies, a new wave of anger is cultivated through framing privileged groups—especially those that are privileged along racial lines—as imperiled. Political rage is thus an expression of victimhood, which is one type of anger that helps to animate right-wing politics and to undermine the political and institutional bases of liberal democracy itself. As Brown writes, "the displacement suffered by whites, and especially white men, is not mainly experienced as economic decline but as lost entitlement to politically, socially, and economically reproduced supremacism," and the salve to this feared loss of supremacy is not economic equality but a shoring up of this privileged identity (Brown 2018, 69). Perhaps then the real source of these angry politics is not the people left behind by modernity, or the working class who are angry at economic exploitation, but rather the fear by those holding racially supremacist positions that their supremacy might be slipping.

Third is the anger of the downtrodden, expelled, exploited, oppressed, and repressed. This is typically the kind of anger associated with resistance, revolution, or militant reformism in both liberal democratic and authoritarian contexts, and it was widely in evidence not so long ago during the Arab Spring, Occupy Wall Street, the Indignados, and in popular political movements in Latin America and elsewhere. However, as we note above, the antidemocratic impulses of neoliberal reason and racialized resentments are bolstered by the fact that leftist alternatives are weak or foreclosed in most contexts today. There are many reasons for this: the end of the Cold War; high-tech surveillance and the repression of political groups on an unprecedented scale; the capture of militancy by consensus politics; the pervasive elaboration of technocratic governing projects; and the failures of left social movements to gain popular support. One result is that the anger of the dispossessed and repressed is more easily channeled in antidemocratic directions (Kalb and Halmai 2011). As Gerald Creed and Mary N. Taylor write in this volume, "with the left foreclosed, restricted, or 'postpolitical,' there seems nowhere for the dissatisfied citizen to go but further right."

These three kinds of angry politics work frequently in tandem to create a form of authoritarian populism that has a harder edge than the form described famously by Stuart Hall and his colleagues in *Policing the Crisis* (Hall et al., 2013 [1976]). Hall and his colleagues described the reorganization of British society via the populist mobilization against a racialized criminal "enemy"—the mugger—that was conceived as the counterpoint to a white, classed British "people." And this facilitated extension of the law and order society in one sphere and the rise of a new technocratic elite enabled via Thatcher's deregulation of the financial sector in another. In the years since Thatcherism and its governing correlates elsewhere were put into effect, the principles of liberal democracy have withered even further. It is not just a case that nationalist economic principles have gained popularity and political legitimacy in many places where they had once been vanquished. (And it is still too soon to tell what effect the protectionist games orchestrated by Trump and the isolationist moves such as Brexit will have on the global economy.) What is clear is that the axis of power now pivots between a neoliberal authoritarianism that seeks to regain its legitimacy and a harder edged, regressive nationalist authoritarianism from the right. In this situation, Modi, Bolsonaro, Putin, Orbán, Erdogan, and Trump thrive while leaders such as Evo Morales in Bolivia become increasingly distanced from their original missions. In short, popular sovereignty in whatever form is more difficult to achieve in the face of a global political polarity that pits an increasingly illiberal form of authoritarianism against another that seeks to remain cloaked in neoliberal consensus politics.

Beyond Populism

In calling this anthology "Beyond Populism," we do not mean to suggest that populist politics do not exist or that the populist right has not gained ground in many contexts. But to call populism a political trend is not as essential, in our view, as is placing it and other forms of angry politics in their broader contexts and in disaggregating angry politics, so that the complexity and plurality of its sources and its multiple political coordinates become legible. It is essential, in other words, to use conjunctural thinking to make sense of the angry politics that are in play across the globe. We organize the essays collected here in three parts: "The Roots of Rage," "Multiplicities of Anger," and "Unsettling Authoritarian Populisms."

In part I, "The Roots of Rage," four essays locate the roots of new angry politics in shifting global and regional capitalist political economy and in the elaboration of novel political rationalities that emerge in the context of a deepening critique of neoliberalism. Don Robotham's contribution to this volume describes the dynamics we see at the heart of today's angry politics in the Global North or West. In his essay, he places the recent turn toward populism, and its "the people" versus "the other" dynamics, in the context of neoliberalism's decline. For Robotham, people in the Global North are not just dismayed by the effects of recent economic policies. They are also rejecting neoliberalism's globalist cultural imperatives, and, in particular, in their embrace of populism, whites in the Global North are expressing their dismay and dissatisfaction that they can no longer take their global hegemonic positionality for granted (Robotham, this volume). Sophie Bjork-James takes a slightly different angle on the roots of anger in the Global North with an analysis of current-day diversity within the category of "white" within white conservative and far right social movements in the United States. By comparing the millennial visions of the religious right and white nationalists, she shows how a unified racial ideology worked to bring these groups into an uneasy and tentative coalition. Her essay highlights the roots of anger in white supremacist rationality but also explores the limits and limitations of this convergence and is suggestive of a political fragmentation that is perhaps yet to come.

Several essays also explore the ways that angry politics fuels and disrupts authoritarian forms in the Global South. In her essay, Preeti Sampat analyzes the rise of Hindutva in India, drawing a connection between the emergence of "jobless growth" in the Indian economy and the rise and consolidation of power by Modi and Hindu nationalist forces. Modi's and the Rashtriya Swayamsevak Sangh's politics reconfigures the Indian economy as both spectacle and as an implicit signifier for Hindutva. Lesley Gill takes up the case of Colombia, where an organized far right resisted the pink tide sweeping through the region and transformed the country into a narcostate. This authoritarian configuration formed to resist demands for redistribution, building an alliance between drug traffickers, politicians, the military, and the economic elite, who together held antipathy for social movements and guerilla insurgencies. Through establishing a unique economic/political alliance rooted in the trade of cocaine, a far-right coalition reestablished political power in the face of both guerillas and popular social movements. In these cases, we see dramatically different examples of the strategies and tactics that political elites use to quell or channel popular anger and repress left-wing popular politics.

Part II, "Multiplicities of Anger," gathers essays that go beyond popular and academic explanations of the global populist rise by tracing the multiple and complex political forces that converge to forge new and unexpected political alignments and outcomes. John Clarke makes clear the importance of conjunctural thinking in his analysis of the anger expressed in the Brexit vote in Britain. This vote, he argues, is multiply motivated as frustrations with politics as usual and globalism were linked with anti-immigration and anti-European sentiments in the Leave campaign. Acknowledging these multiple sources of anger is essential for understanding the political ambiguities and contradictions that shape moments like Brexit and their aftermath. Indeed, overlapping constituencies with various disaffections and multiple ideas for how they might be remedies went into the Brexit vote. An important lesson from Clarke's analysis is thus that if we ignore these ambiguities, if we ascribe instead simple or unitary explanations for events that are shaped by multiple perspectives and multiple political forces of disaffection, we ignore the new lines of political danger and possibility that open up in the aftermath of moments such as the vote for Brexit. In a similar vein, two essays—Gerald Creed and Mary N. Taylor's on eastern Europe and Lilith Mahmud's on Italy—show how the present-day use of labels such as "populism" and "fascism" unsettle politics and have unexpected political effects themselves. Creed and Taylor, for example, trace the history of appeals to "the people" according to different paradigms in Eastern Europe and point to the political analytical dilemmas that ensue when commentators use the term *populism* exclusively to reference right-wing, nationalist, and authoritarian movements. Drawing from case studies of Hungary and Bulgaria, they argue that liberal antipopulism reads people's legitimate, longstanding economic and political concerns out of the political scene, reproducing a widespread sense of resentment and political disaffection. They show also how this politics disables the resurfacing of the socialist critique of the unequal distribution of resources. Mahmud takes a similar approach to her analysis of the use of the term *fascism* in contemporary Italian politics. Focusing on the constitutional referendum of 2016, she analyzes the political effects of the term's use by a ruling neoliberal center-left party to characterize their political opponents. One effect of this is to obscure the multiple social and political bases of opposition to the referendum, some of which were indeed nationalist and xenophobic while others were rooted in left-wing concerns over mounting inequality and the elitism of technocratic rule. Fascism is thus, Mahmud shows, a specter that haunts Italian politics today in ways that ironically obscure the active resistance of antifascists against both the neoliberalism of the centrist left and the nationalist and xenophobic rage of the far right. Jeff Maskovsky discusses the race politics that adhere in Trump-era white nationalism and in the liberal response to it in the United States. Contrasting white nationalism's attempts to solve America's "race problem" with that of their liberal antagonists, his essay points to a political impasse in which a variety of political forces converge in politics that seeks, unlike white nationalism, to make politics in the United States about anything other than race. Noah Theriault posits the phrase "green authoritarianism" to explain the connection of environmental concerns to the Duterte regime's consolidation in the Philippines. Theriault shows how climate-change adaptation, disaster management, and environmental enforcement became central promises and premises in Duterte's politics, and how he used his engagements in ecopolitics to defuse opposition and to consolidate his authoritarian rule. Taken together, these essays point to the multiplicity of liberal projects that operate in different political contexts and to the various kinds of anger—at multiculturalism, privatization, immigration, environmental destruction, and so forth—that converge to move politics toward illiberal and authoritarian ends.

The third and final part, "Unsettling Authoritarian Populisms," highlights the ways that populist and popular politics unsettle authoritarian regimes. Carwil Bjork-James again looks at Latin America, where frustrations with neoliberal economics inspired widespread social movements two decades ago largely stemming from the left. This so-called pink tide changed several national governments and mobilized a critique of globalization. In the Bolivian case, as C. Bjork-James shows, the leftist antiglobalization movement that brought Morales to power succeeded in providing material advances and symbolic power to the formerly marginalized indigenous majority. To do so it had to overcome a form of technocratic authoritarianism that suppressed popular movements and marginalized and punished indigenous and peasant groups. These groups, in turn, formed movements that mobilized in anger about marginalization to achieve both symbolic and structural changes. C. Bjork-James shows how the MAS (Movement Towards Socialism) that brought Morales to power embraced extractivism and mass export of raw materials and put off its socialist and plurinational goals. It was one of the more durable pink-tide regimes in a region that is moving rapidly to the right, although Morales was recently forced to resign amid an electoral scandal. Jennifer Riggan takes on the case of populist politics in Ethiopia, where, as with cases in Latin America, the Philippines, and elsewhere, the contradictions of neoliberalism have led the country's leaders to blur right and left political ideologies as well as authoritarian and liberal governance strategies. Popular protests that began in 2015 as an ethnic conflict coalesced a few years later in a challenge to state authoritarianism, putting a progressive prime minister in place in 2018. In the final essay in the volume, Nazia Kazi links the anti-immigrant politics of Trump to the post-9/11 rise in Islamophobia in the United States. She also directs attention to the varieties of political responses forged by Muslim American groups, highlighting the limited effects of efforts to promote multicultural "tolerance" for Muslims and its ineffectual response to the Trump administration's imposition of anti-immigrant policies. Kazi contrasts this approach with the more militant, and effective, forms of popular pro-immigrant activism that erupted spontaneously in reaction to Trump's "travel ban" in February 2017. These essays point to the limits and limitations of right-wing populism and authoritarian rule and are suggestive of the ways out of the current political quagmire.

This anthology is not intended to be a comprehensive ethnographic overview of the most salient kinds of angry politics and public outrage that have emerged across the globe since 2010. Rather, it is a collection of critical essays, inspired by ways of knowing in cultural studies and anthropology, by scholars with deep knowledge of places where different kinds of angry politics have surfaced recently. We see the rise of angry nationalisms, right-wing populisms, racist xenophobia, and various forms of authoritarianism as connected directly to the fraying of the global order of the last four decades. We eschew any simple, unitary, or reductionist explanation for the fraying of this order or for the turns to authoritarianism in the spaces that have opened as the neoliberal order weakens and exhausts itself. Our approach is collectively animated by the explanatory power of political economic analysis and the critical investigation of new and extant patterns of inequality and domination (Maskovsky and

Susser 2015), while we seek as well to unsettle disciplinary thinking in ways that can help to imagine new political possibilities in this dangerous moment of authoritarian ascent.

References

Almeida, Paul D. 2007. "Defensive Mobilization: Popular Movements against Economic Adjustment Policies in Latin America." *Latin American Perspectives* 34 (3): 123–139.

Anderson, Benedict R. 1991. *Imagined Communities: Reflections on the Origin and Spread of Nationalism.* London: Verso.

Anderson, Ben. 2016. "Neoliberal Affects." *Progress in Human Geography* 40 (6): 734–753.

Arditi, Benjamin. 2007. *Politics on the Edges of Liberalism: Difference, Populism, Revolution, Agitation.* Edinburgh: Edinburgh University Press.

Bederman, Gail. 1995. *Manliness and Civilization: A Cultural History of Gender and Race in the United States, 1880–1917.* Chicago: University of Chicago Press.

Berlant, Lauren. 2011. *Cruel Optimism.* Durham, NC: Duke University Press.

Boyer, Dominic. 2016. "Introduction: Crisis of Liberalism." Hot Spots, Cultural Anthropology website, https://culanth.org/fieldsights/986-introduction-crisis-of-liberalism.

Brenner, Neil, Jamie Peck, and Nik Theodore. 2010. "After Neoliberalization?" *Globalizations* 7 (3): 327–345. https://doi.org/10.1080/14747731003669669

Brown, Wendy. 2018. "Neoliberalism's Frankenstein: Authoritarian Freedom in Twenty-First-Century 'Democracies.'" *Critical Times* 1(1).

Brubaker, Rogers. 2005. *Nationalism Reframed: Nationhood and the National Question in the New Europe.* Cambridge: Cambridge University Press.

Chatterjee, Partha. 2016. "Nationalism, Internationalism, and Cosmopolitanism: Some Observations from Modern Indian History." *Comparative Studies of South Asia, Africa and the Middle East* 36 (2): 320–334.

Clarke, John. 2014. "Conjunctures, Crises, and Cultures: Valuing Stuart Hall." *Focaal* 70: 113–122.

Cole, Alyson, and George Shulman. 2018. "Donald Trump, the TV Show: Michael Rogin Redux." *Theory & Event* 21 (2): 336–357.

Fassin, Éric. 2018. "Left-Wing Populism: A Legacy of Defeat." *Radical Philosophy,* June.

Hall, Stuart. 1986. "Gramsci's Relevance for the Study of Race and Ethnicity." *Journal of Communication Inquiry* 10 (5): 5–27.

Hall, Stuart. 1987. "Gramsci and Us." *Marxism Today* (June): 16–21.

Hall, Stuart. 1989. *The Hard Road to Renewal*. London: Verso.

Hall, Stuart, Chas Critcher, Tony Jefferson, John Clarke, and Brian Roberts. 2013. *Policing the Crisis: Mugging, the State, and Law and Order*. New York: Palgrave Macmillan.

Harvey, David. 2007. *A Brief History of Neoliberalism*. Oxford: Oxford University Press.

Harvey, David. 2018. *Marx, Capital, and the Madness of Economic Reason*. New York: Oxford University Press.

Herzfeld, Michael. 2005. *Cultural Intimacy: Social Poetics in the Nation-State*. New York: Routledge.

Holmes, Douglas R. 2000. *Integral Europe: Fast Capitalism, Multiculturalism, Neofascism*. Princeton, NJ: Princeton University Press.

Kalb, Don, and Gábor Halmai. 2011. *Headlines of Nation, Subtexts of Class: Working-class Populism and the Return of the Repressed in Neoliberal Europe*. New York: Berghahn Books.

Mann, Jim. 2008. *The China Fantasy: Why Capitalism Will Not Bring Democracy to China*. New York: Penguin.

Judis, John B. 2016. *The Populist Explosion: How the Great Recession Transformed American and European Politics*. New York: Columbia Global Reports.

Laclau, Ernesto. 2005. *On Populist Reason*. London: Verso.

Maskovsky Jeff. 2017. "Toward the Anthropology of White Nationalist Postracialism: Comments Inspired by Hall, Goldstein, and Ingram's 'The Hands of Donald Trump.'" *HAU: Journal of Ethnographic Theory* 7 (1): 433–440.

Maskovsky, Jeff, and Ida Susser. 2015. "Critical Anthropology for the Present." In *Anthropology in Crisis*, ed. James Carrier, 154–174. London: Berg.

McClintock, Anne. 1995. *Imperial Leather: Race, Gender, Sexuality in the Colonial Contest*. New York: Routledge.

Mishra, Pankaj. 2017. *Age of Anger: A History of the Present*. New Yok: Farrar, Straus & Giroux.

Mosse, George L. 1985. *Nationalism and Sexuality: Middle-Class Morality and Sexual Norms in Modern Europe*. Madison: University of Wisconsin Press.

Mouffe, Chantal. 2018. *For a Left Populism*. London: Verso.

Muehlebach, Andrea. 2016. "Time of Monsters." Hot Spots, Cultural Anthropology website, https://culanth.org/fieldsights/9.

Peck, Jamie. 2010. "Zombie Neoliberalism and the Ambidextrous State." *Theoretical Criminology* 14 (1): 104–110. https://doi.org/10.1177/1362480609352784

Puri, Jyoti. 2004. *Encountering Nationalism*. Malden, MA: Blackwell.

Panizza, Francisco. 2005. *Populism and the Mirror of Democracy*. London: Verso.

Pearlman, Wendy. 2013. Emotions and the Microfoundations of the Arab Uprisings. *Perspectives on Politics* 11 (2): 387–409.

Pimentel, Diego Alejo Vázquez, Iñigo Macías Aymar, and Max Lawson. 2018. *Reward Work, Not Wealth: To End the Inequality Crisis, We Must Build an Economy for Ordinary Working People, Not the Rich and Powerful*. Oxfam International.

Quiggin, John. 2012. *Zombie Economics: How Dead Ideas Still Walk among Us*. Princeton, NJ: Princeton University Press.

Schaffner, Brian F., Matthew MacWilliams, and Tatishe Nteta. 2018. "Understanding White Polarization in the 2016 Vote for President: The Sobering Role of Racism and Sexism." *Political Science Quarterly* 133 (1): 9–34.

Shoshan, Nitzan. 2016. The Management of Hate: Nation, Affect, and the Governance of Right-Wing Extremism in Germany. Princeton, NJ: Princeton University Press.

Shryock, Andrew, ed. 2004. *Off Stage/On Display: Intimacy and Ethnography in the Age of Public Culture*. Stanford, CA: Stanford University Press.

Smith, Neil. 2005. *The Endgame of Globalization*. New York: Routledge.

Tooze, Adam. 2018. "Balancing Act." *Dissent* 65 (4): 104–109.

Torre, Carlos de la. 2015. *The Promise and Perils of Populism: Global Perspectives*. Lexington: University Press of Kentucky.

Torre, Carlos de la. 2018. *The Routledge Handbook of Global Populism*. New York: Routledge.

Yuval-Davis, Nira. 1997. *Gender and Nation*. Thousand Oaks, CA: Sage.

PART ONE

The Roots of Rage

Populism and Its Others

After Neoliberalism

For much of the past decade, neoliberalism and in particular neoliberal globalization has been the focus of anthropological concern. Now a new phenomenon is taking center stage: the political movement being characterized as populism. Previously, the rise of and opposition to neoliberalism was the issue at stake. Now, however, it is the failure of neoliberalism and what seems to be succeeding it that is becoming a principal concern of the discipline.

What seems to be succeeding neoliberalism are various forms of populism. But populism is only the political expression of a much deeper civilizational malaise that includes economics, morality, and culture. Previously, populist movements had only gained control of the state in weaker countries in the world system. But this was when the crisis of neoliberalism was local or confined to select regions of the world. With the election of Donald Trump this has clearly changed. Neoliberalism had undermined its own "performance legitimacy" and the crisis had become global. Populism had now captured the pinnacle of political power in the global system and it is hardly possible to open the media today without seeing an article or hearing a discussion on its rise. Generally, this refers to the rise of Trump and other political leaders like Erdogan in Turkey, Orban in Hungary, Duterte in the Philippines, the Five Star movement in Italy, and Le Pen in France. As is apparent, this is applied principally to political leaders and movements on the right but not exclusively so. As Kofi Annan has pointed out, there is much room for the rise of populism in the developing world (Annan 2018).The late Hugo Chavez in Venezuela and Evo Morales are also frequently instanced as examples of left-wing populism, while in France, Jean-Luc Melenchon and his *La France insoumise* movement are placed in the same category. How are we to understand these developments and what do they portend (Fieschi 2012; Hawkins August 2009; Weyland July 2013)?

Populism and Neoliberalism

The point of note is that all these movements in one way or the other, whether right or left, focus on one thing: the crisis in the economy, society, and culture created by neoliberal globalization. And all are claiming that they and only they have found a way of rectifying the failures of neoliberal globalization and of developing a distinctive (right-left) approach to public policy in order to protect all the various social strata, cultural, and national interests threatened by its juggernaut-like expansion. Not much analysis is needed to realize that this turn to new political movements on the right and the left has coincided with the failure of neoliberal globalization to deliver on the promises it held out for large parts of the population of Europe and the United States, setting aside the Global South. Neoliberalism never claimed to be a social program—on the contrary it was opposed to the "tax and spend" welfare state and championed an ethic of self-reliance. But it did promise to deliver the economic goods: privatization and deregulation would release large-scale investments that would expand employment and lead to an overall increase in wages (Robotham 2009). Nothing of the sort has happened—the rising tide only lifted the yachts at the very top. The "stagflation" of the 1960s has been replaced by a runaway capitalism in which there is no such thing as "inclusive growth" (El-Erian 2017; Whitehouse 2018). While providing untold wealth for the 1 percent of the 1 percent, neoliberalism has led to median wage stagnation and relative decline, and the expansions in the labor market that have occurred have been largely at the lower end—in the fast food sector and other temporary forms of service employment.

The issue before us when we discuss the rise of populism, therefore, is really the issue of the failure of neoliberalism, in a broad civilizational sense. And, what is to replace it?

In answering this question it is critical to note that this is a very Western way of posing the question. This is not at all how the situation appears in Asia, and for good reason. Having devastated the Global South (outside of Asia) for decades, neoliberalism has now had severe social and economic consequences in the Global West in which one may include central, eastern, and southern Europe. But, generally speaking, this has not been the result in Asia. China, India, Bangladesh, Vietnam, Thailand, Malaysia, Indonesia, Myanmar, Cambodia, and the Philippines are all experiencing rapid economic growth that is lifting hundreds of millions out of poverty even as it has produced a new and prosperous Asian middle class (Iskyan 2016). This is typical of the longstanding tendency of capitalism to uneven development in which first the economy of one region, then another, expands, often at the expense of the other (Van Bavel 2016).

In Asia, the issue of doing away with neoliberal globalization does not arise and, when it does, is greeted with a shrug. It is the domestic economies of Western nations that are now on the receiving end of the tendency to uneven development as neoliberal globalization has undermined the standing of large sections of society. It is also upturning the global political system and giving Asian countries a centrality to the global order that they have not had in several centuries (Dadush and Shaw 2011). One researcher estimates that "by 2030, Asians will constitute two-thirds of the global middle-class population" (Kharas 2017). This too is an important factor in the rise of populism in the West: ressentiment at the rise of Asia and a vague sense that white people can no longer take their global hegemony for granted. At the same time, it is worth noting that complacent assumptions that this rise of an Asian middle class would be accompanied by an inevitable turn to liberal democracy have so far proven unfounded: none of the above Asian states show much sign of becoming paragons of liberalism. Rather, these seem to be political cultures in which varying brands of authoritarianism and populism have no difficulty in flourishing—which is not to say that liberal constitutionalism is a lost cause in Asia. What is more, as many scholars have noted, the posture of the Chinese seems to be changing. The role of the state and the Chinese Communist Party in controlling the economy and the entire society seems to be growing significantly (Hornby 2018). They no longer see their political and economic system as something peculiar to China. Increasingly, unlike in the days of Deng Xiao Ping, the current regime sees "the Chinese model" as exportable and of high general relevance, especially in the Global South. It is in its early days yet so this economic buoyancy and political assertiveness has yet to produce a cultural renaissance. But, in time, this too may come.

Not Only Economics

It was only to be expected that the deep socioeconomic and cultural transformations wrought by neoliberalism would be bound to evoke a strong political response, especially in strata of the Global North, which have long taken its economic prosperity and social status nationally and in global society for granted as simply a given part of reality. But this should not be understood narrowly as a purely economic process. On the contrary, neoliberalism and the aims of populism too are civilizational: alongside neoliberalism's economic effects are its moral and cultural effects, which, among other things, include an assault on homophobia, sexism, racism, and national chauvinism, the expansion of abortion and other rights for women, combined with a far-reaching relativism of values. This is why it makes no sense, as N. Gidron, P. A. Hall, and A. J. Cherlin point out, to ask whether the support for populism is due to economic pressures, a loss of social status, or resentment at new cultural norms as D. C. Mutz seems to argue (Mutz 2018). It's all of the above. The areas in which the cosmopolitan "flyover" mindset prevails are strongly identified with the East and West Coasts of the United States, which are also the bastions of neoliberal globalization (Cherlin 2018; Gidron and Hall 2017).

Neoliberal globalization in this broad civilizational sense has now made it clear that neither the traditional cultural norms nor economic and social status nor the political institutions of postwar capitalism can be taken for granted. There is a real prospect of the West being surpassed by Asia and its rising middle class, especially as the increasingly rapid application of artificial intelligence and other automation technologies to the production process gathers speed. It should not escape our notice that the first group to experience these processes in the United States was the black working class in the steel and auto industries of the 1960s. Even as the civil rights movement was rising to a crescendo and the Civil Rights Act of 1964 and the Voting Rights Act of 1965 were becoming law, Japanese competition (followed later by the South Koreans) was already leading to a harsh deindustrialization in places such as Gary, Indiana—the home of US Steel and a longstanding stable black working-class community. Detroit was ground zero: here the entire social base of the black community collapsed as the automobile industry came under Japanese competitive pressure. The descent into crack cocaine and repressions via mass incarceration led to the collapse of black community life and was the first casualty in the expansion of the global economy. The destruction of the black working class in the first round of deindustrialization in the United States, which followed until restrictions were imposed on Japan with the Plaza Accord of 1985, was thoroughgoing. This is why it makes little sense to oppose race to class—it is both race *and* class. The black working class has suffered and is suffering far more than its white counterpart. Today the lower and middle strata of the black population are in a very different position from the members of the top quantile of black income earners. The latter have experienced substantial improvements in their economic and social positions relative to their white counterparts, although with a considerable way to go (Bayer and Charles 2016).

From the point of view of Europe, the story is similar though with its own specifics. There the question has been the austerity imposed by Germany on southern and eastern Europe considerably complicating the transition from state socialism to capitalism in the former socialist bloc. The experience of Greece, Italy, and France has been critical and continues to be so. At the same time, economic and sociopolitical developments toward right-wing populism in Hungary, Poland, Italy, and other states have been even more crucial. Where all this will end is anyone's guess. It suffices to note that we are only in the very earliest stages of this sociopolitical, cultural, and economic upheaval that is unlikely to be concluded any time soon—act I, scene I, so to speak. The transformations in question are deep and far reaching and are likely to have the most profound impact on particular social strata; local, regional, and national cultures and nation-states; and the global system as a whole. Many twists and turns are to be expected with the final outcome being determined by the social and political forces and movements that prove able to resolve the contradictions of our time. That is why it is a mistake to expect populism to simply fall victim to its own contradictions—or for its supporters to abandon the movement because of outrageous behavior by its leadership. The roots of the turn to populism are deep and if, as is quite possible, their economic policies seem to achieve some short-term success (as is the case in the United States, Poland, and Hungary) then their "performance legitimacy" will certainly increase, strengthening the turn to the right nationally and globally.

The rise of what is being called "populism" is an immediate political reaction to such challenges. Chavez in Venezuela and Lula in Brazil, within the framework of their individual nation-states, mounted a defense against the neoliberal onslaught. In Greece, Syriza also tried to resist neoliberal austerity but in 2015 was coerced into surrender by the superior forces of German finance capitalism. The consequences for all these regimes and their populations have been unforgiving. Social strata and political movements observing these crises from their vantage points in Spain, Portugal, and elsewhere have to be forgiven for concluding that there is simply no way to resist neoliberalism within the normal framework of liberal democratic parliamentary politics. Hence the rise of new political movements outside of the liberal framework that are being categorized as populist.

Immediately the problem arises of what is meant by populism and how are we to understand its political consequences. In particular, what are the consequences of populism for liberal democracy—is it a *prefascism* with all the dire implications of such a term? Many definitions of populism focus on its political style and its consequences for liberal democracy (Abts and Rummens 2007; Mudde and Kaltwasser 2013). Populist leaders are said to use a highly emotive demagogic vernacular designed to keep the populace in a permanent state of political mobilization and semihysteria. Indeed, one body of research in the Philippines could be taken as confirming that view: a sense that the former populist Estrada and the current president Duterte, both at home in the urban vernacular, are "men of the people" is an important source of their political support especially with working-class voters in Manilla (Garrido 2017).

Another common approach—not mutually exclusive—stresses the tendency of populists to draw a sharp distinction between those who belong to "the people" and those who belong to "the elite." According to this line of analysis, populist claims to mobilize a homogenous "people" against a treacherous "elite" further defines those who "truly" belong to the people in moralistic and essentialist cultural terms. Thus from this viewpoint, populism abhors and attempts to erase the heterogeneity of society and is inherently opposed to pluralistic liberal political systems that seek to tolerate the widest possible public and personal diversity consistent with public order. Therefore, those who use the term *illiberal democracy* are held to be conceding too much to populism since, according to this view, liberalism is an inherent part of democracy and to constrain liberal pluralism is itself to attack democracy (Muller 2016).

But this approach still focuses too much on political styles and culture rather than on ideological substance. Stephen Bannon, for example, conscious of the specifics of the United States and always harboring the thought of recruiting more Hispanics and African Americans to the populist cause, insists that he is no ethnonationalist. Rather, he argues that he formulates his populism in purely political terms: if you are an American citizen then you are eligible to join, is what seems to follow from his approach, a claim that many find completely unconvincing.

There is indeed a phenomenon properly designated as populism that looks behind the stylistics and discourse or the political moralism identified by Muller. This is a politics that rejects a class (or interest group) approach to politics, which was the norm in Europe for many decades, including in the postwar period. In the United States, this class-based politics was less clear but in general it was the case that big business and establishment conservatives led the Republican Party and that the working and middle class and the black and Hispanic populations as a whole, found a home among the Democrats. As in Europe, these distinctions are no longer firm as substantial sections of the white male working class have gone over to populism and critical sections of the establishment are alienated from a Trump-dominated Republican Party. Concurrent with this has been the political realignment in Europe and the United States that Thomas Piketty has described as the rise of a "Brahmin Left vs a Merchant Right" (Piketty 2018). This is the idea that social democratic parties now cater to the well-off, culturally cosmopolitan professionals in the big cities while the establishment conservatives are thoroughly neoliberal. As a result, it is argued, large sections of society—working and middle class, and especially, rural society—now find that none of the established parties represent their interests. But it is unclear that such sweeping generalizations are supported by the data.

Ideological Eclecticism

They argue that it is possible to find economic, social, and political solutions to the problems of the day that do not privilege a particular section of society and that are neither left nor right (or are both) but serve "the people" as a whole. One nation, under God, indivisible, so to speak, but minus the succeeding words "with liberty and justice for all." Further, this populist position argues that the everyday existing common sense of the people provides a template for public policy, the success of which is above all to be measured by its popularity, that is, the extent to which policies meet with public acclaim. From this point of view, populism is a particular type of extreme nationalism and is not primarily about attacking a national elite, except and insofar as that elite becomes *comprador*—agents of a foreign power—or is promoting an alien metrosexual culture. Populism is about addressing the economic, social and political problems created by neoliberal globalization.

Although most political scientists seem to argue that the opposition between "the people" and an alien domestic elite is at the core of populism, this is not necessarily so. Often "the elite" in question is presented as an external one—Eurocrats or Jewry, rootless cosmopolitans or immigrants—profoundly alien to the "true people"—*La France profonde*. The internal problem arises, according to this view, when immigration threatens cultural identity and when some minorities of the people become contaminated by these external influences and become alien viruses in the body politic. Then, drastic surgery is justified to remove "the cancer" and to restore the body to its pristine state. But the key point is not so much the demagogic attack on an elite, whether internal or external, but this political, cultural, and economic conviction: that there is in reality such a thing as "one nation, indivisible" (the original formulation), that the nation-state is the political expression of this entity, and that therefore there are solutions that exist for "the people as a whole," despite the existence of diverse individual and class interests in society. And, indeed, this kind of inclusive growth was the case in many capitalist countries in both the Global North and South during the postwar period of expansion. Now, outside of Asia and the central European populist regimes, the benefits of economic growth overwhelmingly accrue to the 1 percent especially in the United States. (Piketty, Saez et al., 2016; Whitehouse 2018).

Populists, whether in advanced capitalist countries like the United States, or in Turkey, Hungary, or Venezuela, face this contemporary crisis and claim that they have rediscovered solutions that are solidary, once "the elite" is excluded. In the United States, given the hegemonic position over the entire global neoliberal system, the position is necessarily different. Here the global neoliberal elite coincides with the national elite, hence, in this case there is a particular focus on the need to combat this powerful cosmopolitan group and "the deep state" that protects it.

Thus the critical point for this account is the left-right nature of populism. Sometimes this outlook is rationalized moralistically, at other times ethnically or racially, or economically and politically. In other words, populist movements are particular types of cross-class alliances that deny that they are an alliance of conflicting interests. Where they recognize diversity of interests at all, they argue that these are fundamentally harmonious and that only they have developed the formula to reconcile these interests. This reconciliation is achieved by the concept of "the people" meaning that the enormous class differences between the 1 percent and the middle and working classes are inconsequential since they all belong to the same race or nation. Populists do not argue, as is the norm under free market capitalism, that giving precedence to the interests of the capitalist class serves the interests of all of society. Instead they claim to be seeking to arrive at a line of policy that serves all members of "the people" as a collective whole, which is neither capitalist nor socialist, not upper, middle, or working class, neither left nor right. Given that in practice diverse interests exist within this collective, which classes, strata, and ethnic groups constitute what is in fact an alliance (as recognized by Fidesz in Hungary where their secondary title is "The Hungarian Civic Alliance"), and which dominate the leadership, is therefore crucial. This will determine who "the people" are understood to be and will often determine whether this is a left or a right populism. If the dominant forces in the movement are from segments of the urban lower-middle and working class and their main sociopolitical opponents are the upper strata on the right, then populists naturally turn left, as in Venezuela. On the other hand, if the movement is led by conservative segments of the provincial middle classes and rural society and the political-cultural opponents are on the left, then populists unhesitatingly hew to the right, as in Poland, Hungary, and Turkey.

Given the actual socially heterogeneous composition of "the people"—ideological protestations of "indivisibility" notwithstanding—policies being pursued will necessarily defy a clear ideological designation, except in one respect: populists all operate within the framework of a market economy and, most important, on the basis of the nation-state. Indeed, behind the rhetorical smoke one can often detect the crassest interests of particular upwardly mobile groups striving to climb to the top of the economy. Fidesz in Hungary, with its widespread practice of cronyism is a case in point, as argued by Gerald Creed and Mary N. Taylor (this volume). Indeed, this is part of their popular appeal, especially in societies like the United States in which capitalist ideology is profoundly rooted in all social strata, including the working class. This is also why protectionist economic policies that curb free trade always arise in populist movements, wherever possible. Protectionism appeals both to sections of the right ("unfair competition") as well as to sections of the left ("deindustrialization") and has as its stated goal to strengthen particular strata of the national economy even if it means to some extent undermining the global neoliberal free trade order and replacing it with some form of "managed trade." State intervention in the economy via large infrastructure programs to help the populist base will therefore be combined with private outsourcing of construction contracts to sweeten the pot for particular groups in the business elite. In other words, we arrive at this conclusion: populism is the ideology of particular strata in capitalist society—the weaker segments of the capitalist class, the middle and working classes—who are unable to maintain (or improve) their position in society under the conditions of neoliberal globalization. These groups embrace the nation-state as their only bulwark—against Asian competitiveness, in the case of the United States, or against German dominance of Europe, in the case of Italy, the United Kingdom, Poland, and Hungary. Given their position in society and their outlook, they remain firmly within the framework of a market economy and oppose any attempt to encroach on the rights of property. Populists, out of necessity, reject the idea that the nation-state is powerless in today's neoliberal global world or that the only way to combat the ills of globalization is to pursue reforms at the international economic level, for example, via reforms of rules of the World Trade Organization (Scheuerman 2011).

The eclectic combinations of left and right policies pursued by Fidesz in Hungary under Orban are classic examples. Sharp reductions in the budget deficit and other standard neoliberal policies have been combined with a public works and jobs program (particularly beneficial to particular strata in rural society). This has reduced unemployment in Hungary more rapidly than in any other eastern European country—750,000 jobs have been created in a country of ten million people. Relatively generous social benefits—free school books and lunches—complete the picture. Much has been funded by the European Union's "cohesion" budget and is directed on a cronyist basis to shore up the political base of Orban and his supporters, as Creed and Taylor point out (this volume). At the same time, great emphasis has been placed upon entrenching respect for private property rights and the rule of law at the level of the lower courts. The government claims to have redistributed 3 percent of annual GDP from capital to wages since 2011 (Bershidsky 2018). Writing in *Bloomberg View*, Bershidsky stated further: "When I asked Gyorgy [a presidential advisor] if he saw a contradiction between such a leftist, redistributive economic policy and Orban's resolutely right-wing political stance, he protested. 'It's not a leftist policy, it's a balance-setting pro-capitalist one,' he said. 'We don't want to give money to the poor unconditionally, we want to create a balance between capital and wage earners to give people a decent salary and enable them to consume more'" (Bershidsky 2018).

So, it is this procapitalist balance that is being sought—capitalism with Hungarian (or Italian, or Polish) capitalist characteristics—a point to which I shall return. With these achievements, no one should be surprised that Orban has been able to increase his electoral and popular support. He has achieved what the liberal Hungarian left with its dutiful adherence to European Union pure neoliberalism failed hopelessly at—temporarily stabilizing the Hungarian economy, especially the well-being of parts of rural society, but without securing any deep structural advances (Szombati 2018). Consequently, the liberal left in Hungary has been discredited for the foreseeable future. Despite railing against the European Union, Orban is careful not to tread on the toes of German investors with whom he enjoys excellent relations and who act as a restraining influence on any potentially punitive policies that may emerge from the German state and from Brussels. He is also careful to maintain close ties with the Bavarian-based Christian Social Union—his recent rebranding as a Christian Democrat speaks volumes. This also serves to protect the regime from political pressure emanating from Brussels. Paradoxically then, a certain type of Keynesianism turns out to be far from incompatible with populism or authoritarianism, as many historians of Nazi autobahn construction policies after 1933 have pointed out (Tooze 2006).

Thus, the core claim of populism is that it has found the solution to the challenges posed by neoliberal globalization, including the cultural dilemmas posed by cosmopolitanism. The ethnonation as both a culturally homogenous entity and a unified economic unit is the magic signifier. The solution is a combination of economic and social policies that are neither left nor right or, more accurately, are both left and right, justified with ethnocultural chauvinism and a strong anti-immigrant demagogy, all within the framework of capitalist economic relations. Indeed, populists would argue that it is the ideological dogmatism on both the left and the right that is preventing them from arriving at a solution to the economic, social, and cultural crisis: one wants social democracy and the other hypercapitalism; but they both seek "balance." Indeed, some may go further and argue that this is the only way to rescue capitalism from a left-wing critique of the sort mounted by Bernie Sanders in the United States and that they are ultimately helping to secure the social positions of the more cosmopolitan sections of capitalism—ethnonationalism being the necessary and only tool. By abandoning this search for ideological consistency and not hesitating to combine positions traditionally held to be ideologically and economically incompatible, populism claims to have arrived at the solution for the central problem of our time. Ethnonationalism, eclecticism, and pragmatism are their watchwords. At the same time, they firmly uphold the rights of private property. One of the purposes of right-wing populism is precisely to pull the popular classes away from any socially progressive politics. It deploys appeals to ethnonationalism to weld working-class people more solidly to existing elites. From this viewpoint, demagogic and inflammatory rhetoric are a necessary requirement for populist regime stability and is the price that the cosmopolitan finance elites in the big cities have to pay in order to survive, no matter how much they may privately deplore such tactics.

Thus in the very nature of the populist case, there will be slippage from right to left—an ever-present tendency for a right course to (occasionally) veer left and vice versa—the so-called quer-left phenomenon. In the course of its life, as different groups struggle for supremacy, one tendency will become more prominent than the other, but this is not likely to last. At the end of the day, one tendency wins out and while the other doesn't completely disappear in policy terms, it becomes a secondary feature of the regime. It was not for nothing that there were "left" Nazis like the Strasser brothers who had to be purged. Nor is it wishful thinking for those on the right in the United States to plan how they can pull large numbers of the libertarian left or even parts of the Hispanic and black community over to their side: *Links ist da, wo der Daumen rechts ist!*[1]

This feature springs from the fact that populist movements invariably have a working-class component in its political base even though the leadership and large part of the membership originate higher up in the social order.

Populism, Liberal Democracy, and Social Democracy

As already mentioned, one of the most important issues that has arisen concerns the nature of the threat that populism poses to liberal democracy and whether the term *illiberal democracy*—coined by Orban to describe his regime—has validity. Cas Mudde's and Jan-Werner Muller's argument that the term *illiberal democracy* should be rejected, since there can be no democracy without liberalism, is problematic. Here we run up against the well-known problem of liberalism: that it tries to draw a sharp line between itself and any other form of democracy—whether of the right or the left, illiberal or social. In order to do this, political theorists who champion liberalism often present constitutions as arising out of a rationalistic, pluralist, convention, as was the case in the United States. What this obscures is that liberal constitutions, in fact, often arose out of armed struggle and war and mass movements that bear a striking resemblance to mass populist movements. Liberal constitutionalism prevails in Germany and Japan today because it was imposed by the bayonets of the victors in World War II. Likewise, liberal constitutionalism is nonexistent in China and Vietnam because the Chinese and Vietnamese communist-led movements won those wars, not the forces backed by the West. The fact that India is a liberal constitutional democracy is due to a moment of unprecedented turbulence and mass destruction (at Partition). Moreover, unlike in China (and later in Malaysia and Indonesia) the Marxist left in India was incomparably weaker and in no position to dictate political terms at the time of independence in 1947. In the case of the American Constitution, the precondition for the deliberations in Philadelphia in 1787 and the later amendments of the Bill of Rights was the defeat of Cornwallis at Yorktown in 1781. The Thirteenth Amendment abolishing slavery, the Fourteenth Amendment establishing citizenship and due process, and the Fifteenth Amendment establishing the right to vote irrespective of race and color required a civil war—arguably a highly populist affair. Likewise the Nineteenth Amendment, giving women the right to vote in 1920, arose out of a mass nonparliamentary movement. The Voting Rights Act did not emerge from a graduate seminar in law. It took intense popular mobilizations such as the civil rights movement in which society was sharply divided and people were killed. In other words, many if not all of the civil rights celebrated by liberal constitutionalism arose from struggles principally outside of the parliamentary arena and framework, in which liberalism was only one ideological tendency—the one that triumphed. It is therefore quite evident that liberal constitutionalism has been both a help and a hindrance not just to the extension of democracy but to the formal-legal entrenchment of civil rights themselves. Liberal parliamentary constitutionalism by itself would never have been able to establish a liberal constitutional order.

Additionally, as has been commonly argued, one of the purposes of liberal constitutions is precisely to constrain an unrestricted democracy. Much has been written about the US Constitution and its thrust to prevent "mob rule" and to protect minority rights. The late Christopher Hill also wrote at length of how (in the United Kingdom) a more democratic concept of liberty was undermined and in effect captured by men of property with the result that private property became the supreme "liberty" (Hill 1996). The most forceful recent statement about the conflictual relation of liberalism to democracy is contained in the work of Yascha Mounk. Writing about "the democratic myth that has long underwritten the stability of the American republic," he states:

> The political systems of countries like Great Britain and the United States were founded not to promote, but to oppose, democracy; they only acquired a democratic halo in retrospect, thanks to more recent claims that they allowed the people to rule. . . .
>
> The undemocratic roots of our supposedly democratic institutions are clearly on display in Great Britain. Parliament was not designed to put power in the hands of the people; it was a blood-soaked compromise between a beleaguered monarch and the upper echelons of the country's elite. . . .
>
> For the Founding Fathers, the election of representatives, which we have come to regard as the most democratic way to translate popular views into public policy, was a mechanism for keeping the people at bay. Elections were, in the words of James Madison, meant to "refine and enlarge the public views, by passing them through the medium of a chosen body of citizens, whose wisdom may best discern the true interest of their country." That this radically curtailed the degree to which the people could actually influence the government was no accident. "The public voice, pronounced by the representatives of the people," Madison argued, "will be more consonant to the public good than if pronounced by the people themselves, convened for the purpose." In short, the Founding Fathers did not believe a representative republic to be second best; they found it far preferable to the factious horrors of a true democracy." (Mounk 2018)

None of which is to be taken to mean that liberal rights are unimportant to advocates of social democracy and socialism—on the contrary. Altogether we must reject the critique of liberal democracy deriving from Carl Schmitt that some on the left seem to find so appealing (Bernstein 2011; Scheuerman 1999; Schmitt 1976; Schmitt 1985). This is the idea that because the rights of liberal democracy are formal rights under the law, therefore, such rights are empty, hypocritical, and of no value. This, indeed, is a criticism from the right not the left. Who can seriously deny that, all their limitations notwithstanding, the Voting Rights and Civil Rights Acts, not to mention the earlier *Brown v. Board of Education*, represent extremely important achievements for the black population in particular and, indeed, for all people around the world. All of these are achievements of liberal democratic constitutionalism—of the legal system in particular. They need to be safeguarded at all costs and extended not scoffed at as vacuous expressions of formal bourgeois law—the notorious "empty chatter of the bourgeois liberal." Likewise for the Bill of Rights and the Nineteenth Amendment. Critiques such as Schmitt's look backward to an age when authoritarianism was unquestioned and its legitimacy uncontested. They critique the formal nature of liberal rights as "hollow" and they expose the concrete power differentials that it conceals. By espousing a seductive realism the aim is to reconcile us to accepting the inevitability of such power inequities and the authoritarian, "decisionistic" regime of the right, which is its inevitable corollary. The left viewpoint is actually the opposite of this: it recognizes the power differentials that liberal rights conceal but with a view to the removal of these socioeconomic and political (and not purely legal) impediments to democracy. It looks forward to building a new society and seeks not to do away with liberal rights but to extend them into the substantive socioeconomic and political realms. What this highlights is that a purely defensive posture with respect to the preservation of liberal democracy is unlikely to be effective. Liberalism has to demonstrate that it is open to being extended to more social forms of democracy and that it is capable of resolving the economic, social, and cultural crises of our time. Liberalism will not be preserved from within a purely liberal position by itself. In order to protect liberalism, it will be necessary to go beyond it.

Conclusion

The argument presented here is that the rise of populism (left or right) is a direct result of the principal challenge of the day: the crisis of neoliberal global capitalism as it assaults not only the economic and status conditions of millions of people around the globe, but as its cosmopolitanism shatters long-held moral and cultural assumptions. At the end of the day, the economic, status, and moral-cultural challenges are one unified whole insofar as every way of life and moral universe requires certain economic foundations for it to be viable and to have a future. But neoliberal globalization has brought precisely this into question and in a particularly brutal and unforgiving manner. In a previous essay I discussed the rise of neoliberalism and argued that this was not a voluntaristic event but arose out of the recovery of the postwar capitalist economy (Robotham 2009). By the 1960s, this recovery had led to the economic and political strengthening of capital, putting an end to its thirty-year postwar subordination to social democratic tax and spend policies. This capitalist restoration, which is what neoliberalism represented, culminated in what it has always culminated in: a financial crisis. This time, in 2008, with the Great Recession only escaping the total collapse of 1929 because of the existence of the Chinese economy and the resort to extreme Keynesian reflation of the Western economies, led by the United States. All of this has further intensified the basic crisis of our time: the conflict between globally developed productive forces on a hitherto unheard of scale (global supply chains, robotics, artificial intelligence) and the private ownership of these ultramodern, global means of production. This remains the fundamental contradiction. From this point of view the rise of extreme inequality, documented by Piketty and others, remains but a symptom: before the 1 percent could accumulate such wealth, it first had to be produced and they first had to have an ironclad entitlement to the fruits of the entire global production/financial system.

What this means is that, ultimately, this conflict can only be solved by the transformation of production relations—in other words by encroaching on the rights of private property. This is the problem of liberal democracy, from the angle of political economy. Because, the crucial feature of liberal democracy is rightly seen as its emphasis on individual rights, the rule of law, and the protection of minority rights against the dangers posed by an overbearing majoritarian rule. But what upholders of liberal democracy are clear on is that the foundation of this system of rights, especially the rights of the individual, rest on one basic cornerstone right: the deeply entrenched and uncontested right to private property. This Lockean "possessive individualism" is at the core of the system of rights that is liberal democracy and any encroachment on it necessarily poses a challenge to liberal democracy itself (Macpherson 1968). What then happens when the economic and social problems posed by advanced global capitalism raise above the prospect of an encroachment on private property rights—either through restrictions on free trade, increased taxation, more social provision, re-nationalizations, or through policies that separate income and social status from economic relations such as an effective guaranteed minimum income or extensive job programs? This is a conundrum to which liberal and social democracy, not to mention socialism with Chinese characteristics, have yet to find a convincing answer, although there is considerable historical and contemporary experience to go by (Caldwell 2000; Fraenkel 2010).

Into this void comes right-wing populism and various forms of authoritarian liberalism (Scheuerman 2015). They declare, with their ideological eclecticism, that they have found the solution to the economic and cultural dilemmas of our time. All that is needed is to curb the extremes of neoliberal globalization and to return to a form of national capitalism dominated by the nation-state, and which seeks to strengthen the global position of national capital—the classic "strong state, strong economy" formula championed in the authoritarian prefascist jurisprudence of Carl Schmitt but now adapted to an immeasurably higher development of the productive forces (Dyzenhaus 2003). It naturally follows that this approach must justify these policies in terms of extreme forms of nationalism, including ethnonationalism, and far more aggressive stands have to be taken by the Great Powers both vis-à-vis each other and smaller nations, in a manner reminiscent of nineteenth-century Europe. It would be the height of folly to think that this approach is incapable of achieving certain short-term results. The example of Hungary discussed above shows this is far from being the case. Nonetheless, this populist eclecticism resolves nothing and ultimately will result in the further immiseration and subordination of its working-class base and an even greater enrichment of the 1 percent. Those who wish to preserve the hard-won rights of liberal democracy as well as those on the left who struggle for more social and cultural rights need to take heed.

Note

1. Left is, [the hand] where the thumb is on the Right.

References

Abts, Koen, and Stefan Rummens. 2007. "Populism versus Democracy." *Political Studies* 55: 405–424.

Annan, Kofi. 2018. Interview with Nathan Gardels. "The Developing World Is an Easy Target for Populists." *The WorldPost: Berggruen Institute/The Washington Post*. Washington, DC: The Washington Post.

Bayer, Patrick, and Kerwin. K. Charles. 2016. "Divergent Paths: Structural Change, Economic Rank, and the Evolution of Black-White Earnings Differences, 1940–2014." *NBER Working Paper Series: Working Paper 22797*. Cambridge, MA: National Bureau of Economic Research, 53.

Bernstein, Richard J. 2011. "The Aporias of Carl Schmitt." *Constellations* 18 (3): 403–430.

Bershidsky, Leonid. 2018. "Orban's Economic Model is Trump's Dream." *Bloomberg View*. New York: Bloomberg Finance L.P.

Caldwell, Peter C. 2000. "Is a 'Social *Rechtstaat*' Possible? The Weimar Roots of a Bonn Controversy." In *From Liberal Democarcy to Fascism*, ed. P. C. Caldwell and W. E. Scheuerman, 136–153. Boston: Humanities Press.

Cherlin, Andrew J. 2018. "You Can't Separate Money from Culture." *New York Times*, May 6.

Dadush, Uri, and Wiliam Shaw. 2011. *Juggernaut: How Emerging Powers Are Reshaping Globalization*. Washington, DC: Carnegie Endowment for International Peace.

Dyzenhaus, David 2003. *Legality and Legitimacy: Carl Schmitt, Hans Kelsen, and Hermann Heller in Weimar*. New York: Oxford University Press.

El-Erian, Mohammed A. 2017. "Beware of the Consequences of Low, Non-Inclusive Growth: The Benefits of Weak Expansion Have Accrued to the Rich." *Bloomberg View*. New York: Bloomberg L.P.

Fieschi, Catherine 2012. "A Plague on Both Your Populisms." Accessed August 28, 2019. Opendemocracy.net/en/plague-on-both-your-populisms/.

Fraenkel, Ernst 2010. *The Dual State: A Contribution to the Theory of Dictatorship*. Clark, NJ: The Lawbook Exchange.

Garrido, Marco. 2017. "Why the Poor Support Populism: The Politics of Sincerity in Metro Manilla." *American Journal of Sociology* 123 (3): 647–685.

Gidron, Noam, and Peter A. Hall. 2017. "The Politics of Social Status: Economic and Cultural Roots of the Populist Right." *British Journal of Sociology* 51: 1–44.

Hawkins, Kirk A. August 2009. "Is Chavez Populist: Measuring Populist Discourse in Comparative Perspective." *Comparative Political Studies* 42 (8): 1040–1067.

Hill, Christopher. 1996. *Liberty Against the Law: Some Seventeenth-Century Controversies*. Harmondsworth: Allen Lane.

Hornby, Lucy. 2018. "Living Marxism: The Chinese Communist Party Reasserts Control." *Financial Times*, May 6.

Iskyan, Kim. 2016. "China's Middle Class Is Exploding." *Business Insider*, August 28.

Kharas, Homi. 2017. "The Unprecedented Expansion of the Global Middle Class: An Update." *Global Economy and Development*. Washington, DC: The Brookings Institution, 27.

Macpherson, Crawford B. 1968. *The Political Theory of Possessive Individualism: Hobbes to Locke*. Oxford: Oxford University Press.

Mounk, Yascha. 2018. "Can Liberal Democracy Survive Social Media?" *The New York Review of Books*, April 30.

Mudde, Cas, and Cristobal R. Kaltwasser. 2013. "Populism." In *The Oxford Handbook of Political Ideologies*, ed. M. Freeden and M. Stears, 1–23. New York: Oxford University Press.

Muller, Jan-Werner. 2016. *What Is Populism?* Philadelphia: University of Pennsylvania Press.

Mutz, Diana C. 2018. "Status Threat, Not Economic Hardship, Explains the 2016 Presidential Vote." *Proceedings of the National Academy of Sciences* 115 (19): E4330–E4339.

Piketty, Thomas 2018. "Brahmin Left vs. Merchant Right: Rising Inequality and the Changing Structure of Political Conflict (Evidence from France, Britain and the US, 1948–2017)." WID.world Working Paper Series.

Piketty, Thomas, Emmanuel Saez et al., 2016. *Economic Growth in the United States: A Tale of Countries*. Washngton, DC: Washington Center for Equitable Growth.

Robotham, Don. 2009. "Liberal Social Democracy, Neoliberalism, and Neoconservatism: Some Genealogies." In *Rethinking America: The American Homeland in the 21st Century*, ed. J. Maskovsky and I. Susser, 213–233. New York: Routledge.

Scheuerman, Wiliam E. 1999. *Carl Schmitt: The End of Law*. Lanham, MA: Rowman & Littlefield.

Scheuerman, William E. 2011. "Realists Against the Nation State." *Transnational Law and Contemporary Problems* 20 (67): 67–105.

Scheuerman, William E. 2015. "Hermann Heller and the European Crisis: Authoritarian Liberalism Redux." *European Law Journal* 21 (3): 303–312.

Schmitt, Carl. 1976. *The Concept of the Political*. New Brunswick, NJ: Rutgers University Press.

Schmitt, Carl. 1985. *The Crisis of Parliamentary Democracy*. Cambridge, MA: MIT Press.

Szombati, Kristof. 2018. *The Revolt of the Provinces: Anti-Gypsyism and Right-Wing Politics in Hungary*. New York: Berghahn.

Tooze, Adam. 2006. *The Wages of Destruction: The Making and Breaking of the Nazi Economy*. New York: Penguin.

Van Bavel, Bas. 2016. *The Invisible Hand? How Market Economies Have Emerged and Declined Since AD 500*. New York: Oxford University Press.

Weyland, Kurt. July 2013. "The Threat from the Populist Left." *Journal of Democracy* 24 (3): 18–32.

Whitehouse, Mark. 2018. "Tax Cuts Still Don't Seem to Be Helping Workers." *Bloomberg View*. New York: Bloomberg Finance L.P.

Americanism, Trump, and Uniting the White Right

During the 2016 Republican National Convention, Donald Trump outlined his nationalist agenda, offering a neologism and the proclamation: "Americanism, not globalism, will be our credo." This credo provided the framework for much of the campaign's message, articulated in its final video ad in which dramatic images of shuttered factories and an ominously dark sky over the US capital are contrasted with bright images of Trump campaign rallies. In the ad, "the global special interests" are blamed for supporting trade, immigration, and foreign policies over national interests. Despite a global scientific consensus of the increasing public health, economic, and ecological threats posed by climate change, this topic remained either ignored or ridiculed on the campaign trail. Instead, a consistent focus on borders framed immigrants and the "special interests" that supported immigration as the most significant threats facing the United States. Continually emphasizing this nationalist credo worked to unite disparate elements of the US right, including drawing support from the white nationalist and white evangelical movements.

Despite his ability to galvanize various aspects of the US right, much of the popular liberal response to Trump's victory focused on the issue of economic disenfranchisement. Despite its popularity, this analysis of class resentment as a driver of Trump's success did not match the evidence. Exit polls showed that Trump did not have particular appeal among the white working class. In fact only around 35 percent of his supporters had incomes below $50,000 (Carnes and Lupu 2017). His support didn't cluster around a class demographic, but did cluster around a racial one. He won every demographic of white Americans, with the one exception of college-educated white women. The resentment fueling his success is then both racial and economic (Brown 2018).

If Trump was the answer, then what was the question? This is important to ask because how we understand the appeal of this nationalist credo leads to very different analyses. The narrative of a working-class white revolt centers the crisis of class inequality as the key problem. From this, the coastal and college-educated elites, increasing class-stratification, and stagnating wages are the culprits fueling these roots of rage. In contrast, thinking about the Trump victory as centrally about race raises a different set of questions about what allowed for such widespread support among white Americans across class, regional, and educational demographics.

This isn't to argue that class is irrelevant to the politics that brought Trump to the White House. As we discuss in the introduction, all authoritarian movements stem from a unique conjuncture of factors endemic to neoliberal economics. The shuttered factory in Trump's final campaign ad signaled a broader critique of economic disenfranchisement that attended the shift from a manufacturing economy to a service economy. While not wanting to deny the relevance of this critique in the campaign, I show the ways that we cannot separate out race and class in our analysis of this movement. Rather, they must be understood together.

Trump's rhetoric fits within a broader pattern of authoritarian and populist leaders engaging in what I am calling an economic critique for some. This pattern tends to involve a combination of economic critique embedded in a critique of the loss of another form of power. In Trump's case, the campaign successfully merged fear of economic and racial change. If this was a revolt, then, it articulated a racial logic. This is a challenging argument to make as white people are seldom looked at as a cohesive group with their own interests. There is a long history of whiteness standing in for the norm and as the norm, whiteness is often conceptualized as an absence of identity, an absence that does not lend itself to any kind of self-conscious interest (cf., Carter 2007; Dyer 1997; Frankenberg 1994).

In this essay I seek to explore the racial dimensions of this nationalist credo, focusing specifically on the white evangelical and white nationalist movements, two groups that have remained some of Trump's most loyal supporters. While white nationalists are overtly organized around defending white racial privilege, white evangelicals understand themselves as defending Christian interests, not racial ones. However, evangelical churches and political movements are deeply divided by race (Edgell and Tranby 2002; Emerson, Smith, and Sikkink 1999; Emerson and Smith 2000; Jones and Francis 2012). For decades white evangelicals have remained one of the largest voting blocs in the United States, making up roughly a quarter of the electorate voting around 80 percent Republican. The white nationalist movement is minuscule in both numbers and influence compared to the religious right. They remain very different movements. Despite these important differences, both groups are animated by many similar hierarchies and ideologies. There is much to be said about the gendered politics of these movements as both movements are organized around defending patriarchal gender relations, something I write about elsewhere (S. Bjork-James n.d.). Here, I focus on the ways that these two movements share a breadth of similar ideas and values.

In this essay I will compare two iconic texts that help to define these movements: the white nationalist *Turner Diaries* (Macdonald 1996), broadly known as the Bible of the racist right, and the white evangelical Left Behind series (LaHaye and Jenkins 1995), a sixteen-book franchise that includes several movies and a stand-alone children's book series. Through showing the similarities of these texts—particularly their views on international governing bodies, a distinction between grievable and ungrievable life, and understandings of the environment—I show the underlying ideologies that structure these movements and how they resonate with Trump's Americanism. These texts demonstrate the ideology that animates these movements and how this ideology primed movement members to support Trump's campaign.

Each text frames their protagonists as victims of an aggressive enemy and thus does the difficult work of reframing a privileged identity (Christian and/ or white) as a persecuted group. Turning dominant groups into victims justifies a wide variety of violence, something I explore in detail in this analysis. It also produces a sense of justified anger. In effect, both texts rest on the idea of a chosen people who are threatened by groups that are immoral, inferior, and evil. The political thrust of these novels is found not in their advocacy of a particular political position, but in their construction of this notion of a chosen people who are imperiled and thus whose violence is justified. In these constructions class is not a concern, rather group similarities are stressed, and problems stem from either outsiders or in-group members who don't defend the group. Democracy here, including global democratic institutions, becomes a dangerous obstacle, for why would one want to share political power with a foreign enemy focused on destruction?

I explore how this stoking of anger and false sense of persecution relates to Trump's rhetorical Americanist credo. For, just as in each text, the Trump campaign framed an implicitly raced nation as persecuted by foreign enemies harboring ill will and threatening plans. And cultivating this sense of victimhood on the campaign trail procured a paired anger against these imagined threats.

I have researched these two movements for more than ten years, having studied an online white nationalist website with over 300,000 members since 2004 and white evangelical megachurches in Colorado since 2008. During the 2016 presidential campaign I was caught off guard seeing both movements so completely rally around the same candidate. These movements tend to support different political actors, largely over divergent perspectives on US foreign relations with Israel. White evangelicals are deeply committed to US military support for Israel and white nationalists are equally committed to anti-Semitism.[1] In my decade studying these movements I have never seen them rally support for the same candidate, although the Tea Party movement did galvanize both groups in different ways. However, analyzing these texts points to the unifying principles shared by these movements that the Trump campaign worked to mobilize.

Both texts were written by movement leaders intent on converting new members and encouraging their movements. Tim LaHaye described his goal with the novels as helping people to "be prepared." A 2007 *Time* magazine article quotes an evangelical stating, the novels "helped me to look at the news that's going on about Israel and Palestine," seeing it as "just ushering in the End Times, and it's exciting for me" (quoted in McAlister 2007, 213). Pierce similarly wrote *The Turner Diaries* with the hope of inspiring converts and movement members. Pierce went so far as to say that Timothy McVeigh's bombing, clearly inspired by his book, overall helped the movement. These texts are also wildly popular within these movements. Though not everyone in each movement ascribes to all ideas in these texts, they have had significant real-world effects in shaping how members of these movements understand the world around them.

In many ways these are very different texts. William Luther Pierce first published *The Turner Diaries* in serial form in the racist magazine *Attack!*, of the National Alliance, using the pseudonym Andrew Macdonald. The novel became central to white supremacist circles in the 1980s and 1990s, coming to national attention when McVeigh brought photocopies of the novel in a manila envelope and a massive homemade bomb to the federal building in Oklahoma City. The bombing closely resembles a bombing described in the novel. The book is also linked to dozens of bank robberies and over two hundred murders in forty terrorist attacks (Berger 2016). While it is popular among the racist right it is far from a commercial success. It is not widely available, but used copies can be purchased online and are circulated among recruits. It is, however, widely revered in nationalist and neo-Nazi online forums. It can also be delivered via interlibrary loan, where I received a copy. The Anti-Defamation League describes the novel as "probably the most widely read book among far-right extremists."[2] Aside from McVeigh, a number of white nationalist groups have formed over the last forty years inspired directly by the novel.

In contrast, the Left Behind series is the most popular Christian fiction franchise of the past thirty years. Total sales for the series are estimated around 80 million copies and seven books made it to the number one spot on the *New York Times* bestseller list. For some measure, this is more sales than either the *Little House on the Prairie* franchise or the *Hunger Games* books. Religious right leader Jerry Falwell commented on the first book, "In terms of its impact on Christianity, it's probably greater than that of any other book in modern times, outside the Bible." Several prequel books supplemented the original twelve-book series, a separate set of Left Behind novels were published for children, and several feature films based on the books have come out. The novels were written by Bob Jones university graduate and theologian Tim LaHaye and the novelist Jerry B. Jenkins. LaHaye, along with his wife Beverley, were longtime religious right activists. He was widely regarded as a theologian, minister, and an expert in prophesy within conservative Christian circles. He founded the Tim LaHaye School of Prophecy at Falwell's Liberty University. His standing as a well-known theologian and expert in prophesy provided the novels with a sense of theological legitimacy so that many read them not merely as fiction but as a prophetic blueprint. The novels are credited as widely inspiring a fascination with eschatology within evangelicalism. One can still go to leftbehind.com to find a piece by LaHaye and Jenkins stating, "Many are asking, 'How long can it be until the end of history, the end of life as we know it?'" Indeed, in my research among megachurches in Colorado Springs, Sunday morning sermons frequently involved some form of prayer asking for Jesus's speedy return and praying for the end of days to be upon us soon.

Similarities

Let me next outline the similarities between these texts, which are substantial.

Each text is authored by an activist who has crafted their narrative with the goal of recruiting new members. Each focuses on a small revolutionary group of white male leaders fighting a morally corrupt global governmental force, although *Left Behind* includes several people of color in the larger military group, and both groups include white women as subordinate members. Each narrative is premillennial, in that the goal of the group is to achieve a utopian society birthed out of apocalyptical destruction (Brodie 1998). Creating the utopian society requires the death of the majority of people on the planet, and the destruction of all or most of the world's environment. Each tells the story of a government set on confiscating guns, which is followed by widespread repressive actions by the state. Each involves a successful love interest for a protagonist, and each book ends with a heroic white male leader dying in battle, in whose death he secures immortality. Israel and Jewish people are a focus of each, although in different ways. In one, victory is achieved through the destruction of the nation of Israel, whereas in the other victory is achieved through the destruction of the whole of the world except for Jerusalem, when a third of Israel enters heaven. In each, war creates a lasting peace, and the world is clearly divided between grievable and ungrievable life. Both novels glorify violence, both going so far as to describe a key battle as creating "rivers of blood," and violence is described in gory detail in each text.

Despite celebrating death, the authors of each book frame their armies as engaging in moral work. Death and destruction, including the destruction of the environment, are necessary steps in achieving this utopia. And the enemy lines are always crystal clear, with the protagonists always and only on the side of good. Violence here is both moral and necessary. To understand this seeming contradiction we can turn to historian Claudia Koonz's work on Nazi Germany. Koonz argues that morality is rooted in an agreement of reciprocity that is exclusive. As she writes, the "universe of moral obligation, far from being universal, is bounded by community" (Koonz 2003, 5). Thus, each narrative divides humanity very clearly into an us and them, with morality defining the us, and evil defining the them, and military might, war, and death become requirements for winning against evil.

Despite their differences, these novels show that white evangelicalism and white nationalism are organized around similar apocalyptical narratives. Each text adheres to a premillennial apocalyptic belief, where achieving the group's goals will result in both an apocalypse and a long period of peace for the victors. And for our topic, both prioritize a moral order worth dying for. Both see global forces as evil, and frame the destruction of the earth as a utilitarian requirement for achieving utopia. Exploring these understandings of the future, the nation, and the environment help to show how Trump's Americanism credo fostered such widespread support among these two movements. Comparing these texts shows that despite their differences, they share similar apocalyptical narratives, ideologies, ontologies, and understandings of the future.

The Turner Diaries

On the first page of *The Turner Diaries* the US government bans all guns for private citizens. The government is controlled by "the System," a group of Jewish politicians supported by people of color, with white liberals in subordinate positions; the banning of guns is an act of aggression against white power. The novel is organized around diary entries from the protagonist, Earl Turner, who joins a white nationalist military force—the Organization—that forms to challenge the Jewish-led government. Led by a secretive group of men called the Order, it engages in a variety of military actions, eventually creating a white enclave in Southern California.

In establishing this racist utopia, Pierce lays out a map of the types of political murder and ethnic cleansing that are required for creating such a society. One of the most violent examples is described as the "Day of the Rope," in which tens of thousands of race traitors are hung from lampposts across LA. Describing the gruesome violence Turner writes, "It is frighteningly clear now that there is no way to win the struggle in which we are engaged without shedding torrents—veritable rivers—of blood" (79).

Unlike the *Tribulation Force*, the militia leading the fight against the antichrist in *Left Behind* focuses on the importance of conversion to Christianity. The Organization introduces its readers to both a racial conspiracy and instructions on building a militarized force, from storing caches of weapons to building bombs. A theme of the book is the conversion of former white liberals into activists espousing the importance of a white racial identity. Katherine, the love interest in the novel, is described in this way, moving from an apolitical worker into a dedicated white supremacist activist after encountering a conspiracy that Jews control society. In this claiming of a racial identity, characters find a profound sense of meaning and peace in the world. Katherine's conversion is described in this way: "Most important, she began acquiring a sense of racial identity, overcoming a lifetime of brainwashing aimed at reducing her to an isolated human atom in a cosmopolitan chaos" (29).

The environment becomes a useful tactic in this race war. The Organization eventually secures several nuclear bombs, detonating them in New York City, Detroit, and Baltimore. The Southeast United States becomes uninhabitable after being hit by several nuclear bombs. Puerto Rico is described as a new all-white colony populated by whites fleeing the radioactive Southeast.

Alongside this widespread destruction we learn that members of the System have killed Katherine. This is the only death in the book that is mourned, and Turner goes through a devastating depression after her death. This is contrasted to the coldness with which the destruction of whole cities, including widespread radiation sickness among the white people in these regions, is justified as necessary and deserving.

In a passage explaining that tolerating the System is just as bad as supporting it, Turner writes, "talk of 'innocents' has no meaning. We must look at our situation collectively, in a race-wide sense. We must understand that our race is like a cancer patient undergoing drastic surgery in order to save his life. There is no sense in asking whether the tissue being cut out now is 'innocent' or not" (198). Innocence and suffering are not concerns of this movement, moral righteousness is instead the focus. And death is portrayed as cleansing.

Eventually Turner joins the Order, the elite military cabal that leads the Organization, where he is offered a suicide mission to deliver a nuclear bomb to the Pentagon, thereby sounding the death knell of the System. Through this suicide bombing he achieves everlasting life. The eventual global success of the System is accomplished through widespread environmental destruction. After Europe is taken over by the Organization, China attempts to invade "European Russia," to which the Organization responds with "chemical, biological, and radiological means" so that "some 16 million square miles of the earth's surface, from the Ural Mountains to the Pacific and from the Arctic Ocean to the Indian Ocean, were effectively sterilized" (210). This destruction is celebrated in the text as part of a global victory for white supremacy. Again, carnage is portrayed as cleansing.

The novel ends with an epilogue in which a future society reflects back on the importance of Turner in ensuring that "the Order would spread its wise and benevolent rule over the earth for all time to come" (211). Millennial themes are central to the structure of the text (Brodie 1998).

The Left Behind Series

The novels in the Left Behind series begin when millions of people around the world are raptured to heaven as a sign of the beginning of the end of days. In the wake of the disappearance, a group of primarily white Americans begin to unite and form a secretive militia called the Tribulation Force. The core group is made up of European Americans, with significant interactions with African Americans (first appearing in book four), a Native American, Muslim American converts, and several Israelis. Just as in the broader white evangelical culture, the leaders of this book series are all white, American men (see Frykholm 2004).

In the aftermath of the chaos caused by the disappeared, the fictional former president of Romania, Nicolae Carpathia, begins a rise to global power. He first becomes the secretary general of the United Nations, and it is in his workings in the UN that the nationalist vision of the series is laid bare. As the newly appointed secretary general, Carpathia puts forward several positions that fit within a leftist agenda, but in this telling they are part of a sinister plot to persecute Christians and to achieve satanic global domination. As head of the UN, Carpathia convinces world governments to abolish 90 percent of their weapons and to donate the remainder to the UN. He calls for a "global village," wants to end hunger, and asserts his goal is world peace. Carpathia then disbands the UN and replaces it with a new global government called the Global Community. It soon becomes clear that Carpathia is actually the antichrist incarnate. A prominent Muslim character, the Pakistani Suhail Akbar, becomes Carpathia's chief of security.

The Global Community disbands old nation-states and establishes new territories, including the United North American States. While the apocalyptical story begins in the United States, with characters from California and Illinois, Israel quickly becomes a key site of the story. In the twelfth book, Carpathia, who was killed in an earlier book, is resurrected as Satan himself and wages a battle against Christ.

In the graphic depictions of this battle, the Global Community—the rebranded UN—serves as an agent of evil, working to implement Satan's goals. In this text the death and murder of Carpathia's army, known as the Global Community Peacekeepers, is understood as the work of God. In one passage, the death of a carload of Global Peacekeepers is described in gruesome detail as they are turned into skeletons, made no longer human through a gruesome death. These deaths are not mourned but glorified. The authors write, "The declared enemies of God were being decimated around the world" (279).

In this series, death is the requirement for creating peace. In book three, 25 percent of the world's population dies after an earthquake, after which the sun goes red. In book six, horsemen destroy another 25 percent of the world's population, although Christian lives are spared in this battle. In the final apocalyptical skirmish, Jesus has returned and the antichrist's army is experiencing defeat. The authors describe this as a celebratory carnage. They write, "The great army was in pandemonium, tens of thousands at a time screaming in terror and pain and dying in the open air. Their blood poured from them in great waves, combining to make a river that quickly became a swamp" (249). Such death and suffering is celebrated in the text. In a subsequent scene Jesus appears, and the writers have Jesus condemn those who have died.

The narrative then quickly turns from a celebration of carnage to exaltations of love. The authors cite extensively from 1 John 4, with no recognition of the overt shift in tone from the former scenes of carnage, quoting: "Beloved, love one another, for love is of God; and everyone who loves is born of God and knows God. He who does not love does not know God, for God is love" (259). The text is portrayed as if there is no contradiction between celebrating murder and commandments to love, as Carpathia's army is portrayed as outside the bounds of moral reciprocity.

Similar to *The Turner Diaries*, the destruction of the earth serves a utilitarian function in this cosmic war, and it is in these descriptions that life is clearly divided between grievable and ungrievable. Just before Jesus wins this battle with Satan, a global earthquake occurs: "Islands disappeared. Mountains were leveled. The entire face of the planet had been made level, save for the city of Jerusalem itself" (275). Here the rendering of the earth as unlivable is not a cause for concern but for celebration. For the Lord appears in the sky celebrating Jerusalem, and the faithful Tribulation Force who have all long converted to Christianity are joyously awaiting their conversion into martyrs. They wait impatiently in a cosmic queue to meet their loved ones in heaven. In this story the earth is no longer relevant and heaven is promised and is found elsewhere.

Themes

There are several lessons that stem from exploring the similar themes that span these narratives, particularly in comparing their millennial understandings about war, the earth, and the future. These similarities demonstrate a wide array of objectives that unite these two disparate movements, showing how this ideological training can direct their supporters in a similar political direction.

While both texts are structured around millennialist narratives, millennial movements vary significantly. The Christian Identity movement, a white supremacist movement that is rooted in Christian beliefs, rejects the understandings of the rapture promulgated by much of the white evangelical movement (see Barkun 1997, 103–105). The Turner Diaries is not officially a part of the Christian Identity movement, but it has been widely read within it. Nazism itself was structured around a millennial narrative, employing both apocalyptical plans and the promise of a "Thousand-Year Reich" (Redles 2008). Millennial movements can lead to very different political outcomes, but this analysis points to a variety of similarities that cross these movements.

The Nation against the World

Both texts renounce international obligations and portray global governing bodies as resolutely evil. And, in each, destroying these bodies is a key strategy for achieving movement goals. In The Turner Diaries "the System" is an international Jewish cabal. In Left Behind, the UN and its efforts to alleviate hunger and reduce conflict become strategies of the antichrist to establish global domination and to attack Christianity. Thus, in both texts international bodies are conduits of evil.

Given that global bodies are portrayed in these texts in such a negative light, it should not be surprising that these political movements also tend to oppose international obligations and organizations. For the white nationalist movement, international governing agencies are frequently derided for supporting the state of Israel and are seen as an anti-white effort to challenge the rule of European countries and people of European decent. In conservative evangelicalism, the discourse of American exceptionalism inspires a focus on the nation form, and a disavowal of international obligations.

In 2007, Richard Cizik, the then vice-president of the National Association of Evangelicals (NAE), the largest evangelical body, invited Ban Ki-moon, the secretary general of the UN, to a meeting to discuss climate change. Cizik said of the meeting, "My joke is, some people will say the evangelical Christians have invited the Antichrist to the Last Supper" (quoted in Milbank 2007). The popularity of Left Behind among evangelicals has inspired a broad disdain for the UN, for obvious reasons. Cizek's leadership focused on shifting the culture of evangelicalism to support environmental protections, garnering the nickname the "green evangelist." His efforts to expand evangelical politics beyond a religious right agenda made him increasingly unpopular within the NAE. He eventually left the NAE in 2008, due to increasing conflicts, particularly over his stances on same-sex marriage and climate change.

Given the wide disdain for international governing bodies in these novels, it is clear why Trump's nationalist message might be appealing to these movements. Trump's criticism of global special interests fits well within each narrative. White nationalists can read this as a critique of a Jewish-run system and white evangelicals can understand it as a critique of a liberal order susceptible to evil.

Grievable and Ungrievable Life

Another theme that unites these texts is a very clear demarcation of grievable from ungrievable life. As Judith Butler (2016) reminds us, this distinction is not the exclusive domain of these movements, but it remains a central theme in them. And in these narratives death and destruction are required for establishing utopia and are thus celebrated, and are not full of grief or mourning. Tim LaHaye described the bloodshed found in his books in this way: "The Rapture is a time of incredible mercy and grace. If you only look at the people who defy God, it's a negative time. But if you look at the whole population, it's a blessed time" (*BeliefNet* 2003). And as the interpreters of this biblical story, LaHaye and Jenson revel in this death. Death is cleansing and offers immortal life.

In both texts it is not only that certain lives are worth living, but also that death and destruction are necessary steps to creating a utopian end goal. This understanding is part of a modern, European, and European American understanding of the regenerative properties of war. In *Society Must Be Defended*, Foucault (2003, 257) writes, "In the nineteenth century—and this is completely new—war will be seen not only as a way of improving one's own race by eliminating the enemy race . . . but also as a way of regenerating one's own race." This theme is also found in Richard Slotkin's (1973) far-reaching history of the role of the idea of the frontier in US culture. Slotkin argues that the frontier serves as a space for a particular type of American masculinity to be formed based on what he calls "regeneration through violence." Through venturing out into the perceived space outside of civilizing influences, white men achieved a form of masculinity through the enactment of violence on others dubbed uncivilized. Through spatializing this violence, white masculinity was defined as virile and strong, while simultaneously innocent and morally pure. The frontier and the uncivilized living on it became the source of violence, whereas white masculinity only travels there temporarily, returning to civilization pure and cleansed. This spatialization of violence did the crucial work of justifying colonial expansion as morally necessary, and the violence perpetrated by European American men was deemed justified and provoked.

Both texts perpetuate this notion in extraordinarily similar ways. In each, excessive violence enacted by white male protagonists is projected as stemming from their enemies and is thus always already justified. Their violence then acts as a source of moral action, and the concept of celebrating love alongside destruction is not contradictory. Indeed, the excessive violence outlined in gory detail in these texts is understood by readers as attributable to these evil others and not an explicit product of the imagination of their white male authors. Thus, both LaHaye and Pierce can describe their imagined rivers of blood as securing moral purity for their protagonists, perpetuating a long history of understanding violence as regenerative. Cruelty, pain, and despair are understood as promulgated by those deemed other, even as the violence is generated from their respective author's imaginations. Both texts thus prime their readers to justify war, to disregard the harm caused by military actions, and to disregard the suffering of others, so long as the harm is perpetrated against those outside of the moral community. And in each, the destruction of the earth and resulting human suffering are understood as acts of a moral force not a cause for grieving.

Again, Koonz's (2003) work is important in understanding how moral communities justify violence through defining who belongs and who remains outside the community. Koonz writes,

> Conscience, as we usually think of it, is an inner voice that admonishes "Thou shalt" and "Though shalt not." Across cultures, an ethic of reciprocity commands that we treat others as we wish to be treated. Besides instructing us in virtue, the conscience fulfills a second, and often overlooked, function. It tells us to whom we shall and shall not do what. It structures our identity by separating those who deserve our concern from alien

"others" beyond the pale of our community. Our moral identity prompts us to ask, "Am I the kind of person who would do that to this person?"

With this moral demarcation in mind, we can see that both texts are teaching their movements to similarly see the world as divided between a moral "us" and an immoral "them." In this way love is an appropriate emotion for those recognized as belonging to the shared community. Outside of those bounds, evil awaits and requires violence.

Platonized Theology

A final theme undergirding both texts involves a particular aspect of their millennial visions: each portrays the destruction of the environment in utilitarian terms. In each, it is not only violence against humans that is portrayed as regenerating. This idea is actually extended to include the natural environment, so that the destruction of nature involves cleansing properties. In each, achieving utopia is only possible through the destruction of the earth.

These ideas relate to what scholars of religion and race describe as platonized theology. Kelly Brown Douglas (2006) refers to this theological tradition as a separation of body from mind so that, "The body is condemned as a source of sin." This European tradition shapes much of North American Christianity and manifests, as Douglas argues, in an understanding that sexual desires are a primary source of sin. Through this division the body becomes the site and source of evil, while the spirit alone is the site of potential purity. In these texts we can see the operationalization of these ideas onto a broader environmental ethic. Understanding this division helps to elucidate far more than why sexuality is so prevalent in contemporary Christian politics.

In both *The Turner Diaries* and the Left Behind series we can see this platonized cultural logic from the denigration of the human body to the denigration of nature. What then becomes important is found beyond the confines of life on earth. Corporeality itself loses significance in contrast to a separated and pure moral realm that is elsewhere. In this way, the place where one lives, the broader ecosystem that one resides within, the networks that ensure drinkable water and food, become insignificant. Instead the apotheosis of their movements is elsewhere, or nowhere.

This occurs in different ways in these two narratives, and in thinking about these texts through this lens it is the Left Behind series that is far more violent.

For in Left Behind the earth is merely a holding cell where battles occur between good and evil so that those who prevail receive the real reward, a heaven elsewhere. This understanding is shared widely by white evangelicals and speaks to why white evangelicals remain fairly politically silent on matters of environmental protection. As an example, a 2014 PEW poll found that only 28 percent of white evangelicals believe that climate change is caused by human activity (Funk and Alper 2015). This makes white evangelicals the single largest demographic group in the United States to doubt the reality of human-caused climate change.

In my research on evangelicalism in the United States, I rarely saw evidence of concern for the environment. Evangelicals who do advocate for environmental protections, such as the Young Evangelicals for Environmental Action, refer to this broader evangelical eschatalogical tradition as an "escape ship theology." They critique the idea put forward by LaHaye and Jenkins and many others that the end of times will lead to the end of the earth. Many evangelical environmentalists offer a competing theological interpretation that believes that heaven instead will be made here on earth. This framing challenges the platinized theological stance and thus centers a need to care for the environment.

This separation of body and earth from spirit is also placed on a grid that deems the present as less significant than a future end goal, thus the planet and planetary suffering are not causes of concern but are steps for securing an end goal. *The Turner Diaries* poses a different understanding of the earth and the end times, so that not only is the future paradise placed on the earth but it also is contained to the areas not sacrificed by nuclear war. And to achieve this, the land worth living on is the property of whites and much of the world becomes uninhabitable in the process.

Conclusion

In conclusion let me go back to the Trump campaign and to one of the questions guiding this volume, specifically the role sentiments play in shaping contemporary nationalist movements. Many have commented on the centrality of anger associated with the Trump campaign. I argue that part of the appeal of Trump's Americanist credo is that it portrayed the nation as both persecuted and dominant. This is embedded in the promise to "Make America Great Again!" The *again* is the crucial word in the phrase in that it contains the promise of American dominance alongside a narrative of decline. The ambiguousness of the term *great* is also part of the appeal, in that its meaning is dependent on each listener. The unifying message is one of decline and a promised ascendance, the causes and consequence of the decline and the ascendance can vary based on constituent interpretation. Just as in the novels, this message primarily reframes the nation as persecuted, and the anger rallied about this decline remained a driving force of the campaign.

In relation to the question of emotion and politics, we can narrow this to ask: How does emotion shape understandings of truth? And what are the political effects of this epistemological and affective training?[3] In a discussion of the role of anger in feminist politics, Sara Ahmed writes: "It is not that anger at women's oppression 'makes us feminist': such anger *already* involves a reading of the world in a particular way" (2004, 171). In this way Ahmed directs the analysis away from emotion as the primary site of political mobilization and instead directs us to the interpretive training that allows us to understand political messages in particular ways, eliciting particular feelings. Ahmed continues, "emotions are what move us, and how we are moved involves interpretation of sensations and feeling not only in the sense that we interpret what we feel, but also in that we might be dependent on past interpretations that are not necessarily made by us, but that come before us" (2004, 171). Thus, even in seemingly nonpolitical arenas, emotional-ethical interpellations shape the possibilities of political behavior in significant ways, largely through forming interpretive frames to shape specific emotional responses.

Thinking about interpretive framing in relation to the content of the novels analyzed here helps to show how the very different movements of white nationalism and white evangelicalism could so clearly be mobilized by the same message. A primary focus of these novels is the cultivation of a justified anger and a sense of persecution, a reframing of dominant identities as victims. This message of both moral superiority and victimhood maps well onto the MAGA credo, particularly when we also consider the gendered politics of these texts, which center the actions of white men.

We can also see in the Americanist credo elements of each of the three dominant themes from the novels, specifically: the denunciation of international obligations; the construction of a moral national community where some lives matter, some lives are welcome, and others should be sacrificed; and a trivialization of the physical places where we reside and that nurture us.

Framing conservative politics as rooted solely in working-class anger ignores the centrality of race and gender in conservative mobilizations. It denies the broader ideological training that is fostered by various conservative movements that work to reframe whiteness, and white Christianity, as a persecuted identity and not one benefiting from a variety of institutionalized privileges. Class inequality is indeed a significant problem, and the deindustrialization of the United States has had wide-ranging negative impacts. However, class and race are difficult to separate in the US context, and class alone is not the main factor shaping Trump's political success. It seems clear from the analysis here that he was successful at mobilizing conservative agendas that frame white masculinity or white Christian masculinity as threatened. And, just as in *Left Behind* and *The Turner Diaries*, the threats stem from a morally inferior other. And, just as in the novels, environmental destruction remains ungrievable.

Locating Trump's appeal in a class critique misses much of the causes of anger that fueled his campaign's success. Trump's campaign was able to frame the racially privileged in the United States as though they are under threat. Thinking through Trump's authoritarian bent alongside these novels, we can also see a deeply antidemocratic tradition sponsored by these movements. Recent research shows an inverse relationship between white racial prejudice and support for democratic values (Miller and Davis 2018), a concern made clearly visible in these works of fiction and made manifest in Trump's campaign success.

Notes

1. A common believe in white evangelicalism is that Israel, as a Jewish state, will play an important role in the return of Jesus and that US support for Israel needs to be strong (for context see Spector [2008]; Wilkinson [2007]).

2. See https://www.adl.org/education/resources/backgrounders/turner-diaries.

3. Affect theory breaks down into two basic camps. One understanding, articulated in Massumi's (2002) work, argues that bodily sensations are autonomous from thought and will determine the possibilities of action. Another camp, articulated in the work of Ahmed (2010) and Berg and Zayas (2015), instead understands affect as something closer to a "structure of feeling" (Williams 1977). My approach to affect follows this latter understanding, which recognizes affect as intersubjective and produced through material encounters.

References

Ahmed, Sara. 2004. *The Cultural Politics of Emotion*. New York: Routledge.

Ahmed, Sara. 2010. *The Promise of Happiness*. Durham, NC: Duke University Press.

Barkun, Michael. 1997. *Religion and the Racist Right: The Origins of the Christian Identity Movement*. Chapel Hill: University of North Carolina Press.

BeliefNet. 2003. "'Be Not Afraid': Interview with Tim LaHaye," 2003.

Berg, Ulla D., and Ana Y. Ramos-Zayas. 2015. "Racializing Affect: A Theoretical Proposition." *Current Anthropology* 56 (5): 654–677.

Berger, J. M. 2016. "The Turner Legacy: The Storied Origins and Enduring Impact of White Nationalism's Deadly Bible." The Hague: ICCT.

Brodie, Renee. 1998. "The Aryan New Era: Apocalyptic Realizations in *The Turner Diaries*." *Journal of American Culture* 21 (3): 13–22.

Brown, Wendy. 2018. "Neoliberalism's Frankenstein: Authoritarian Freedom in Twenty-First Century 'Democracies.'" *Critical Times* 1 (1).

Butler, Judith. 2016. *Frames of War: When Is Life Grievable?* New York: Verso.

Carnes, Nicholas, and Noam Lupu. 2017. "It's Time to Bust the Myth: Most Trump Voters Were Not Working Class." *Washington Post*, June 5.

Carter, Julian. 2007. *The Heart of Whiteness: Normal Sexuality and Race in America, 1880–1940*. Durham, NC: Duke University Press.

Douglas, Kelly Brown. 2006. "Black Church Homophobia: What to Do About It?" *Reflections: A Magazine of Theological and Ethical Inquiry from Yale Divinity School*. Accessed August 3, 2019. http://reflections.yale.edu/article/sex-and-church/black-church-homophobia-what-do-about-it.

Dyer, Richard. 1997. *White*. London: Routledge.

Edgell, Penny, and Eric Tranby. 2002. "Religious Influences on Understandings of Racial Inequality in the United States." *Social Problems* 54 (2): 263–288.

Emerson, Michael O., and Christian Smith. 2000. *Divided by Faith: Evangelical Religion and the Problem of Race in America*. New York: Oxford University Press.

Emerson, Michael O., Christian Smith, and David Sikkink. 1999. "Equal in Christ, but Not in the World: White Conservative Protestants and Explanations of Black-White Inequality." *Social Problems* 4 (3): 398–417.

Foucault, Michel. 2003. *Society Must Be Defended: Lectures at the Collège de France, 1975–76*. London: Penguin.

Frankenberg, Ruth. 1994. "Whiteness and Americanness: Examining Constructions of Race, Culture, Nation in White Women's Life Narratives." In *Race*, ed. S. Gregory and R. Sanjek, 62–77. New Brunswick: Rutgers University Press.

Frykholm, Amy Johnson. 2004. "What Social and Political Messages Appear in the Left Behind Book? A Literary Discussion of Millenarian Fiction." In *Rapture,*

Revelation, and the End Times: Exploring the Left Behind Series, ed. B. Forbes and J. Kilde, 167-195. New York: Palgrave.

Funk, Cary, and Becka A. Alper. 2015. "Religion and Views on Climate and Energy Issues." PEW. October 22.

Jones, Robert P., and Robert D. Francis. 2012. "The Black and White of Moral Values: How Attending to Race Challenges the Mythology of the Relationship between Religiosity and Political Attitudes and Behavior." In *Faith and Race in American Political Life,* ed. Nancy Wadsworth and Robin Dale Jacobson, 127–148. Charlottesville: University of Virginia Press.

Koonz, Claudia. 2003. *The Nazi Conscience.* Cambridge, MA: Harvard University Press.

LaHaye, Tim, and Jerry Jenkins. 1995. *Left Behind.* Carol Stream, IL: Tyndale House.

Macdonald, Andrew. 1996. *The Turner Diaries.* New York: Barricade Books.

Massumi, Brian. 2002. *Parables for the Virtual: Movement, Affect, Sensation.* Durham, NC: Duke University Press.

McAlister, Melani. 2007. "Left Behind and the Politics of Prophecy Talk." In *Exceptional State: Contemporary U.S. Culture and the New Imperialism,* ed. Ashley Dawon and Malini J. Schueller. Durham, NC: Duke University Press.

Milbank, Dana. 2007. "Guess Who Came to the Evangelicals' Dinner." *Washington Post,* October 12.

Miller, Steven V., and Nicholas T. Davis. 2018. "White Outgroup Intolerance and Declining Support for American Democracy" (blog).

Redles, David. 2008. *Hitler's Millennial Reich: Apocalyptic Belief and the Search for Salvation.* New York: New York University Press.

Slotkin, Richard. 1973. *Regeneration Through Violence: The Mythology of the American Frontier, 1600–1860.* Middletown, CT: Wesleyan University Press.

Spector, Stephen. 2008. *Evangelicals and Israel: The Story of American Christian Zionism.* Oxford: Oxford University Press.

Wilkinson, Paul Richard. 2007. *For Zion's Sake: Christian Zionism and the Role of John Nelson Darby.* Eugene, OR: Wipf & Stock.

Williams, Raymond. 1977. *Marxism and Literature.* Oxford: Oxford University Press.

Make in India

Hindu Nationalism, Global Capital, and Jobless Growth

P rime Minister Narendra Modi led the Hindu-right Bharatiya Janata Party (BJP) to a winning majority in the 2014 general elections in India, and once again in 2019. In 2014, 33 percent of the national vote-share enabled a strong BJP-led coalition government in the center.[1] In 2019 this was further improved to 37.4 percent. Both elections have marked a turning point in India's multiparty political system after three decades of weak coalition governments. The last such national majority was enjoyed by the Congress Party with a "sympathy wave" for Prime Minister Rajiv Gandhi after the assassination of his mother, Prime Minister Indira Gandhi, in 1984. A "Modi-wave" swept the BJP to power in 2014 and again in 2019.

Modi's election campaigns, which are financially supported by powerful Indian business houses, are nothing short of spectacular. Many domestic capitalists publicly endorsed Modi as an ideal prime ministerial candidate as early as 2009. Indian capital consistently received favorable treatment in Gujarat, where Modi was chief minister for nearly fourteen years before his 2014 elevation to prime ministership. Indian capitalists praised him for facilitating a business-friendly environment with easy access to land, resources, and other concessions in the state. Their endorsements of Modi also followed from their souring relationship with the Congress Party–led coalition government in power until 2014, especially in its second term from 2009 to 2014.[2] Corruption, coalition politics, and a fundamentally divided policy and political dispensation under the Congress Party–led United Progressive Alliance (UPA) government then in power for ten years, created the political opening for the Modi-led National Democratic Alliance (NDA) government in 2014, and the peculiar convergence of capitalism and Hindu nationalism it has since configured.

Endorsement by big capital was crucial for Modi's makeover from a deeply controversial leader implicated in overseeing a pogrom against Muslims in

Gujarat in 2002. Over two thousand Muslims were killed under his watch that year, resulting in international condemnation and pressure from the global human rights community. Modi was consistently refused visas to travel to the United States and Europe as the chief minister of Gujarat for twelve years; the "travel ban" against him was finally relaxed in 2014 after he became the prime minister of India. Indian tycoons such as the Ambani brothers, Ratan Tata and Gautam Adani, were special invitees for Modi's swearing-in in 2014.

"Development for all" was Modi's mantra in 2014, augmented to "Solidarity for all, Development for all, Trust of all" by 2019. His public relations teams carefully curated a presidential-style election campaign highlighting his personality and oratorical skills over and above his party in both elections. In 2014, private jets to attend election rallies and motor vans projecting holograms of his speeches in small towns and villages across the country sponsored by his wealthy supporters carried his message widely. The cadres of the Rashtriya Swayamsevak Sangh (RSS; National Patriots Organization) also threw themselves into election campaigns nationally. Invoking *Hindutva*, or Hindu nationalism, the cultural nationalist ideology propagated by V. D. Savarkar and his Hindu-right followers since the early twentieth century, they successfully garnered a broad range of Hindu sympathies.

In characteristic flourish, slogans like "Make in India," "Minimum Government, Maximum Governance," "Start Up India," "Smart Cities," and several other catchy phrases have peppered Modi's policy rhetoric for the Indian economy. Deals with global and domestic capital on infrastructure projects are signed with fanfare, as strong-arm economic policy decisions such as the dismantling of the Planning Commission; the demonetisation of currency notes; and the arbitrary introduction of a goods and services tax regime are presented as a government unafraid to take action. As chilling violence against Muslims is executed with numbing regularity in an alarming growth of violent Hindu nationalism, state institutions responsible for upholding the rule of law are steadily undermined. Rationalists and other vocal critics of Hindutva are murdered.[3] Critical regional and national voices in the press are continually heckled, harassed, and sought to be suppressed. Hindu-right online troll armies style themselves as Modi-*bhakts* (devotees) on social media, intimidating and threatening critical voices with rape, murder, and other brutal violence, narrowing freedom of expression and speech with impunity. More alarming, Hindutva vigilante groups carry these threats out to the streets, with little legal redress for their victims or punishment for their crimes.

This essay explores the current historical conjuncture of the rise of Hindutva in India; its relations with global and domestic capital (and their crises); and the emergence and implications of jobless growth in the Indian economy for the Hindu nationalist project. How has Hindu nationalism seized the current conjuncture of capitalist development in India with the aid of global and domestic capital? What lessons do the attempts to institute a strong Hindu nation-state—by targeting minorities, Muslims in particular; war jingoism with Pakistan and China; and the suppression of political dissent—offer for studies of contemporary authoritarianism? How may the allied forces of global and domestic capital and Hindutva in India come to impasse?

India is witnessing an attempt to transition from a weak liberal Congress Party leadership to a strong Hindu nationalist state. Systematic dismantling of the liberal secular democratic political order and institutions of the post-Independence period is accompanied with a simultaneous emphasis on capitalist development, albeit in an unpredictably contingent trajectory. Recent analyses of political developments and policy in India tend to treat political economy and Hindu nationalism as disconnected domains.[4] In this essay I am interested in analyzing the cultural nationalism of Hindutva in relation to the economic policies of what is being termed *Modi-nomics*. Policy emphases on capitalist growth follow an older liberal trajectory of economic liberalization from the 1980s in India, but Hindutva forces also rely on big capital for support.[5] This historical, cultural, and political economic conjuncture requires further interrogation and analysis.

I begin with a brief history of Hindutva as an ideology and a political movement. I then discuss the "economy as spectacle" under Modi-nomics; I am particularly interested in examining the work that spectacular infrastructural investments do (or not) for Hindutva under Modi. The final section follows up with the phenomenon of jobless growth and other dissatisfactions brewing across the country and concludes with the possibilities of impasse, or hegemony, in the consolidation of the Hindu *rashtra* (nation-state) in India.

A Brief Genealogy of Hindutva

According to M. S. Golwalkar,

> The foreign races in Hindustan must either adopt the Hindu culture and language, must learn to respect and hold in reverence Hindu religion, must entertain no idea but those of the glorification of the Hindu race and

culture, i.e., of the Hindu nation and must lose their separate existence to merge in the Hindu race, or may stay in the country, wholly subordinated to the Hindu nation, claiming nothing, deserving no privileges, far less any preferential treatment not even citizen's rights. (Golwalkar 1939, as quoted in Bal 2017)

Hindutva was a term coined in the early 1920s by V. D. Savarkar, a *brahmin* from Maharashtra state who expounded the notion of a *Hindu Rashtra* (nation-state) premised on a common Hindu identity. Savarkar himself was an atheist and argued that Hindu religion was only one aspect of the Hindu nation-state—a shared race, culture, language, and territory forming other crucial elements. The slogan "Hindu, Hindi, Hindustan" referenced a common religion (or culture), language, and territory drawn from a Hindu revivalist reaction to the Khilafat movement and a deep-rooted hostility to Islam. Muslims were considered a threat to Hindus because of their allegiance to Mecca and Istanbul, because of their better organization as a community, and greater aggression. Muslims and other religious minorities (notably Christians, given that Buddhists, Sikhs, and Jains were seen as closely linked to Hinduism) were thus outsiders, who must pay allegiance to Hindutva (see Jaffrelot 2017).[6]

K. B. Hedgevar, another brahmin from Maharashtra (although with origins in Andhra Pradesh), subsequently founded the Rashtriya Swayamsevak Sangh (RSS; National Volunteer Corps) in 1925 and created local *shakhas* (branches) across towns and villages to propagate Hindutva and reform Hindu society from below. The RSS soon became the most powerful Hindu nationalist movement with as many as 600,000 volunteers at the time of India's independence in 1947. In the meantime Savarkar went on to found the Hindu Mahasabha as a political party in the late 1930s. But it was only after independence when the RSS was banned after the assassination of M. K. Gandhi by a former RSS member, that the RSS, then led by M. S. Golwalkar, decided to join negotiations with the Hindu Mahasabha, then led by S. P. Mookerjee. The Bharatiya Jana Sangh (predecessor to BJP) was thus formed in 1951, just before the first national elections in independent India (see Jaffrelot 2017).

In the post-Emergency elections of 1977, the Jana Sangh allied with the socialists, merging into the Janata Party to defeat Indira Gandhi. However, the alliance soon broke because the Jana Sangh refused to break ties with the

RSS, and Indira Gandhi sailed back to power in the national elections held in 1980. The BJP was formed the same year, with a more moderate approach of soft Hindutva. Through the 1980s, as the BJP's national presence grew, the VHP and the RSS supported a more militant Hindutva, mobilizing for a Ram temple at Ayodhya.[7] The militancy of the Ram *Janmabhoomi* (birthplace) movement yielded further political dividends to the BJP and by 1999, it led the coalition government under the National Democratic Alliance (NDA) for the first time, holding its tenure for five years until 2004 under a moderate prime minister, A. B. Vajpayee. The NDA failed to return to power in 2009; the moderate Hindutva line under Prime Minister Vajpayee was held responsible for the defeat of the NDA (Jaffrelot 2017).

Under Golwalkar's leadership, the RSS established a number of organizations to work with diverse social groups, such as the student-wing Akhil Bharatiya Vidya Parishad (Indian Student's Association); the Bharatiya Mazdoor Sangh (Indian Worker's Union); the Vanavasi Kalyan Ashram (Center for Tribal Welfare); and the religious-wing Vishwa Hindu Parishad (VHP). Together, these organizations formed the Sangh Parivar (RSS family) and proliferated over the years; the VHP, for instance, created the youth wing, Bajrang Dal, and a women's wing, Durga Vahini. The cultural work of the RSS has continued apace. Sangh Parivar organizations train young members for combat; and male members wear khaki trousers (recently changed from knee-length shorts), white shirts with black caps, and *lathis* (long batons) in all official conclaves and demonstrations.

VHP members have been implicated in instigating the violence against Muslim and *adivasi* (indigenous) Christian minorities in Gujarat and Odisha respectively, that resulted in thousands dead in both states. The Australian Christian missionary Graham Staines and his two sons were burned alive in Odisha in 1999 with a BJP-led government in power at the central and state level. More recently, the ABVP has overseen the vitiated atmosphere in the Jawaharlal Nehru University in Delhi where duly-elected student leaders were arrested on charges of sedition for attending an event on Kashmir. The ongoing killings of ordinary Muslims on suspicion of possession of beef and of cattle transporters by cow vigilantes mirror the trend of terrorizing religious minorities, notwithstanding the fact that substantial populations of the country consume beef as an integral part of their diet.[8]

The Hindu right has historically alternated violent religious majoritarianism and nationalist jingoism with Pakistan to foment Hindutva. Under Prime Minister Vajpayee nuclear tests were carried out to send a nationalist message internationally, and a series of cease-fire violations along the Indo-Pak border allegedly by Pakistan escalated into diplomatic belligerence between the two countries. Since Modi's ascent to power, these strategies continue.

S. Corbridge and J. Harriss (2000) argue that Hindu nationalism's rise (or popularity) in the twenty-first century constitutes an elite reaction to the democratization of the political forces in India as subaltern classes threaten entrenched social and political orders. The rise of the *dalit* and *bahujan* parties in recent decades, especially in politically significant northern states, is particularly noteworthy in this regard.[9] Recent unrest from dalit and bahujan formations protesting caste atrocities in UP and in Gujarat are indicative of ongoing caste strife. However, the BJP has previously mobilized a range of actors from across the social spectrum brokering an alliance with the Bahujan Samaj Party.

Prime Minister Modi was a dedicated activist of the RSS before he was moved to the BJP by the Sangh in the early 1980s. RSS activists hold key BJP and government positions and are openly represented as political stakeholders in all national debates by the news media. The current turn to the Hindu right in India is decidedly populist,[10] riding on Prime Minister Modi's charismatic, authoritarian, and, following C. Schmitt (1985), *decisionist* personality. But it must be emphasized that Hindu nationalism in India is a product of a dedicated historical, cultural, nationalist movement rather than a more contingent authoritarian populism sustained by the popularity of a charismatic leader alone. To put it plainly, authoritarian populism under Modi is fundamentally tethered to a historically emergent protofascist movement committed to creating a profoundly exclusionary *Hindu Rashtra*. If fascism is: (1) fundamentally illiberal and antidemocratic; (2) supports dictatorship and a mythical idea of the leader; (3) promotes social-nationalist capitalism; and (4) promotes a radical idea of the enemy (cf. Finchelstein 2017); the Hindutva forces in India point to a potent mix of these elements working toward their avowed goal of the creation of a Hindu nation by steadily hollowing out rule of law and democratic institutions (albeit without explicitly espousing these latter aims), and in this sense are protofascist.[11]

Political Opening

Toward the latter half of its second term from 2009–14, the Congress-led UPA government was widely represented as corrupt, inefficient, and in a state of policy paralysis. Land acquisition controversies over industrial and infrastructure projects and policies, such as Special Economic Zones (SEZs), were significant sources of distress for big business. What irked most however, were a series of corruption scams implicating some of the big domestic capitalists in a series of litigations. A number of major corruption scandals implicating the then-ruling Congress Party–led UPA government and high-profile Indian capitalists struck national headlines by 2010 and caused much resentment among the business classes (see Varadarajan 2014).

In 2009, the Central Bureau of Investigation filed a charge-sheet over serious irregularities in an official spectrum allocation auction by the central government. The comptroller and accountant general (CAG) of India reported a loss of USD 27 billion to the exchequer in these allocations. The Supreme Court of India ruled in 2012 that the allocations were unconstitutional and cancelled all 122 spectrum licenses to corporates (DNA 2012). In 2010, another massive controversy broke out when a corporate lobbyist was investigated for influencing deals and a number of big corporate houses, including Ratan Tata, were implicated in the "Radiagate" scandal (Varadarajan 2014). Next followed the arrest of tycoon Suresh Kalmadi in 2011 over allegations of corruption in construction projects in the national capital region of Delhi during the international Commonwealth Games in 2010 (Kumar 2011). A scam with respect to coal mining allocations was next unearthed by the CAG in 2012, with an estimated windfall gain for the companies worth approximately USD 28 billion (*Economic Times* 2012).

A retroactive tax net for Vodafone and the application of a new minimum alternate tax over SEZs and other similarly privileged industrial clusters raised the pitch against the UPA. Land acquisition–related reversals of projects on account of local popular resistance to land-grabs added to the sense of paralysis. The new land acquisition law in 2013 that replaced the colonial law of 1894 was seen as particularly difficult for land consolidation for large investment projects, as it required establishing consent from a majority of landowners and social impact assessments of projects. With land and real estate emerging as extremely lucrative investments in India's growing rentier economy (see

Sampat 2018), the difficulties of obtaining consent from landowners and social impact assessments of projects were seen as cumbersome by domestic capital. Deep dissatisfaction was reported in the business press leading up to the national general elections in 2014.

In this backdrop, Modi's promise of "ease of doing business" beckoned. As his record in Gujarat demonstrated, environment, labor, and land regulations were repeatedly diluted to accommodate business interests. Contestations were dealt with with authoritarian repression (except when political expediency forced his hand; see below), and Hindu-right forces were strengthened within the state administration, judiciary, and police to quell dissent (see Jaffrelot 2012).

The Economy as Spectacle

Recent controversies around demonetization, the goods and services tax, or the earlier attempts at amending land acquisition regulations and the dismantling of the Planning Commission of India are indicative of Modi's decision-ism (cf. Schmitt 1985).[12] Policy decisions and consequently power are increasingly located in the prime minister's office (PMO). Decisions are made by the PMO in consultation with the RSS and are often announced dramatically, without prior public intimation or wider consultation.

In November 2016, in an unprecedented move of massive proportions, the government demonetized Rs. 500 and Rs. 1000 currency notes in circulation in the country, amounting to 86 percent of all currency notes then in circulation. The aim was to bring the large flows of illegal or so-called black money in circulation into the formal economy through the banks and to promote digital monetary transactions. Neither of these claims have borne out. With 86 percent of the currency no longer valid, people had to exchange these currency notes in banks within a stipulated period of a few months. As a result, cash flows of the large majority of people dependent on the so-called unorganized or informal sectors of the economy, nearly 80 percent of the working population, including small traders, took a big hit. This had an immediate fallout on the demand for goods and services, putting people out of work for lack of adequate cash and resulting in a large-scale recession that the economy is still negotiating (see Kohli 2018; Nigam and Balaji 2017; PTI 2017a).

The 2017 Goods and Services Tax (GST) was announced in a special midnight session of the Parliament on June 30, 2017 by the finance minister, and served another blow to the informal economy. Ostensibly introduced to create a "rational" one-tax regime across the country (previously taxes varied across commodities and states), it has been criticized for slotting various commodities arbitrarily into four different tax slabs, and the exempt and additional cess categories. Petroleum and other energy products have been left out of its ambit altogether, in order to allow the government to tinker with their taxes to regulate budget deficits (*The Wire* 2017). This complex system has been further confounded by frequent changes in the tax slabs of goods and services.[13] Reports after one year of implementation suggest dampened exports and manufacturing. The informal economy is reeling from the twin impact of demonetization and GST, leading to a crisis on the supply side. There seems little rise in tax revenue as well, with the direct tax–GDP ratio at 5.9 percent in 2017–18, lower than the 6.9 percent in 2007–8 (Mehra 2018).

Spectacular investment promises in infrastructure have been another recurrent feature of Modi-nomics. Every advanced capitalist country's leader coming to the country signs some "iconic" business deal with the government, more recently one signed by Japanese prime minister Shinzo Abe to introduce a bullet train from Mumbai to Ahmedabad in Gujarat, an international partnership rhetorically claimed to counter the global economic heft of China. Despite grand announcements and inauguration of these projects in the presence of the two prime ministers, actual investment flows and implementation are shaped by electoral political expediency in a region, rather than a consistent economic liberalization agenda. The project envisages land acquisition of 850 hectares, affecting 192 villages in Gujarat and 120 villages in Maharashtra, even as resistance gathers strength within the two states (see Gupta 2018; Newsclick 2018; PTI 2018).

Similarly, infrastructure projects along the much-touted Delhi Mumbai Industrial Corridor (DMIC) are in a state of limbo, either because resistance to land acquisition is strong or there is a paucity of investors. The Dholera Smart City project along the DMIC is one such project where ongoing resistance from twenty-two villages has stalled the project for nearly a decade, with local residents also challenging the state government in the Gujarat High Court (see Sampat 2016, 2018).[14] The contingency of resistance leads to an ad hoc and politically expedient infrastructure investment strategy. In Gujarat where millions of dollars' worth of investments have been reportedly signed in the decade and half of Modi's chief ministership, few have materialized on the ground.

As the global economy seems to slowly show greater growth rates, there is little evidence of commensurable investments into the Indian formal economy. The more recent global recovery is largely skipping India, as even Indian big capital prefers investments abroad (see Mundle 2017). The politics of expediency and contingent economic policy are creating dissatisfactions among varied social forces. The economic agenda under Hindutva is politically contingent, and curates spectacle through high-profile decisionism.

And yet, while Modi's popularity hollowed out with state assembly elections in early 2019 swinging in favor of the Congress (if somewhat precariously), the BJP did manage to retain majority in significant states such as UP and Gujarat in 2017. Some argue that the political spin given to these spectacular decisions by the Modi government, of making sacrifices for higher gain, and of leveling the plane for rich and poor alike by making everyone stand in line to exchange the demonetized currency for instance, has paid off. Banerjee and Kala (2017) suggest that the traders in UP, for instance, read these decisions as a signal of Modi's intentions, making them feel better about the country's prospects. Or that there was a politics of resentment against the rich at work, making the poorer feel better that people with large amounts of cash (the "corrupt") suffered losses. There is no reason to believe that the corrupt indeed suffered heavy losses, and this perception can be attributed to BJP's effective perception management.

Walter Benjamin is instructive here. Drawing on the theory of perception (aesthetics), he points out:

> Fascism attempts to organize the newly proletarianized masses while leaving intact the property relations which they strive to abolish. It sees its salvation in granting expression to the masses—but on no account granting them rights. The masses have a *right* to changed property relations; fascism seeks to give them *expression* in keeping these relations unchanged. *The logical outcome of fascism is an aestheticizing of political life....* [Humankind's] self-alienation has reached the point where it can experience its own annihilation as a supreme aesthetic pleasure. *Such is the aestheticizing of politics, as practiced by fascism.* (2008, 41–42)

It is sobering to consider that the "aestheticizing of politics" with demonetization, GST, and spectacular investment promises may presage a self-alienation of profound proportions in India.

Jobless Growth and Other Dissatisfactions

While some figures show greater economic activity in manufacturing and exports, the recovery is too little to draw conclusions (*The Wire* 2018). Small farmers continue to commit suicides in states across the country and agrarian distress remains acute with support prices being less than sustainable for what is produced. Agitations by famers are on the rise. Unemployment is at an all-time high, investment sentiment is very low, and the two unilateral decisions of demonetization and the introduction of the GST have brought large parts of the economy to a standstill. Large portions of the Indian economy are showing alarming signs of crisis and dissatisfactions are growing.

The Gujarat state assembly elections in December 2017 were illustrative. The BJP won a total of ninety-nine assembly seats in the state, with the Congress winning seventy-seven (fourteen more from the previous state elections), from a total of 182 seats in the state assembly (seats in the state assemblies of India vary according to the state's population). However, out of 140 total rural assembly seats BJP won sixty-one, while the Congress secured seventy-one. The BJP won with a majority of barely 7 percent votes more than the Congress (see PTI 2017b). Dalit votes also went against the BJP as a result of widespread protests against recent instances of caste violence in the state under BJP's watch, but the dalit population of the state is 6.7 percent so it could not have exerted a significant influence on the result (see Sethi 2017). In December 2018 three key states, Rajasthan, Madhya Pradesh, and Chhattisgadh went to the Congress Party, buoying the center-liberal opposition party's hope for at least a weaker NDA government in 2019.

However, the Hindu right has historically alternated violent religious majoritarianism (Muslims are about 13 percent of the Indian population) and nationalist jingoism with Pakistan to foment Hindu supremacism. Frequent attacks on Pakistan's territory since 2014, the most recent in February 2019, following a suicide attack killing forty Indian soldiers in Pulwama in the Kashmir valley, have had powerful results. While the state assembly elections in 2018 had indicated widespread discontent, the strike on Pakistan in the aftermath of the Pulwama attack turned the narrative to the "strong" leadership of Modi before the general elections in April–May 2019.

In the mix of looming crises and structural economic conditions, Hindu nationalism offers a tactical maneuver to counter deep frustrations welling up in farmers' protests, dalit uprisings, and shows of solidarity from diverse citizens' groups for freedom of press, expression, and association. Modi has historically dealt with contestations with authoritarianism and repression and has strengthened Hindu-right forces within state apparatuses to quell dissent (see Jaffrelot 2012 for an analysis of the "saffronization" of state apparatuses in Gujarat). However, the BJP will find itself constrained to distract from the unfolding economic crisis with war jingoism and communal hatred against religious minorities over the longer term. While opposition parties put together tenuous coalitions and fail to counter the Hindu right's tactical manouevers, the most promising coalitions have emerged from new dalit uprisings and a younger political left (see Chaudhary 2019; PTI 2019). It is difficult to gauge if any substantive political alternative can emerge from these solidarity coalitions and how long it may take to challenge the Hindutva project. Indeed Kanhaiya Kumar, a Communist Party of India candidate representing these solidarity coalitions lost by a large margin in the 2019 general elections. But the political churning in the wake of a powerful Hindu right points to nascent reimagining of progressive politics. Regardless, that an explicit turn to political violence targeting especially religious minorities and dissenters is the new political norm in India under the Modi-RSS combine is clear. Modi-nomics, in the meantime, performs a dual function; on the one hand it serves to *aestheticize politics*, and, on the other, it acts as an *empty signifier* for Hindutva.[15]

Notes

1. National-level general elections are held every five years in India and elect a national government to the center (federal), whereas state elections are held on separate schedules. This is in keeping with the federal nature of India's constitution. Since the Modi government came to power in 2014, however, there has been discussion on a controversial proposal to have simultaneous central and state government elections. Critics argue that this is not only unfeasible given the large and diverse Indian population, but it undermines the federal nature of the constitution and would allow the ruling majority party to capture votes and power at the center and in the states by persuading the electorate to vote for the same party (Pai 2016).

2. The Congress Party–led United Progressive Alliance (UPA) coalition government had defeated the BJP-led National Democratic Alliance government in the 2004 general elections and was reelected for a second term in the 2009 general elections. A series of corruption scandals implicating several Indian corporate houses erupted in the second term of the UPA, leading to resentment among the business classes (see Varadarajan 2014).

3. The Indian rationalist movement draws its roots from the early nineteenth century from the works of Jotiba Phule, followed by Periyar Ramasamy and Gora into the twentieth century. Members of the more recent Indian Rationalist Association, Narendra Dabholkar and M. M. Kalburgi, as well as Communist Party of India leader Govind Pansare and journalist Gauri Lankesh have been assassinated in a series of high-profile murders by unidentified gunmen, allegedly for their vocal challenges to the rise of Hindu nationalism (Firstpost 2017; Johnson et al. 2015).

4. For historically detailed analyses linking dominant shifts in India's political economy with the growth of Hindutva, see Corbridge and Harriss (2000).

5. See Don Robotham (this volume) for the cultural civilizational project of neoliberalism and the failure of its promises. Here, I bring the critique of liberalism (see also Lilith Mahmud, this volume) in relation with the cultural nationalist project of Hindutva.

6. A. Skaria (2016) argues that Hindutva is a secularity that rejects secularism. It draws on immanent causes without invoking divine power, and it does not have transcendental goals for its citizens and hence is secular. But citizenship, or belonging, is strictly defined in relation to belonging to land, culture, language, and race, and hence rejects secularism, which renders such belonging private and irrelevant for public life.

7. Ayodhya is a small town in the northern Indian state of Uttar Pradesh, believed to be the birthplace of the Hindu god Ram. The Hindutva forces maintain that the Mughal emperor Babar demolished a temple at the holy site of Ram's birthplace and erected the Babri Mosque in its place. The Ram Janmabhoomi movement sought to demolish the mosque and erect a Ram temple at the same spot. In December 1992, after months of mobilization that saw violence against minorities across the country, the mosque was demolished by a massive Hindu mob of over 150,000 Hindu volunteers, instigated by prominent Hindu-right leaders. The matter is currently being adjudicated by the Supreme Court of India (Rajagopal 2017).

8. The slaughter of cows and the consumption of beef are banned in India except in a few states as the cow is considered a holy animal under Hinduism.

9. Under the Hindu caste system, *dalit* communities fell outside the hierarchy of the four main caste groups (*brahmin, kshatriya, vaishya,* and *shudra*) and were considered untouchable. *Dalit* implies oppressed or broken and refers to a political identity. *Bahujan* refers to the broader alliance of *dalit* and so-called lower castes.

10. F. Finchelstein (2017) distinguishes populism and fascism but argues that they are genealogically connected and belong to the same history. He argues that a new populist modernity was born with the defeat of fascism and offered a third way between liberalism and communism. While postwar populism comprises a diverse set of authoritarian experiments in democracy, unlike fascism, populism's supporters want authoritarianism to be a democratic choice. Populism speaks in the name of a single

people expressed in the leader, and democracy under populism is defined in terms of the desires of the populist leader(s).

11. Discussing the rise of the Hindu right historically, leading up to and in the aftermath of the Babri mosque demolition and shortly before the BJP's emergence as the ruling party in the 1999 general elections, T. Raychaudhuri (1999) argued for a recognition of their absolutist and fascist project but did not distinguish between protofascism and fascism conceptually. Lilith Mahmud (this volume), asks, "Can fascism be named, before it *is*?"; protofascism in this vein, offers a plausible conceptual category for the current authoritarian conjuncture in India.

12. Within months of coming into power, the NDA government attempted to dilute consent and social impact assessment provisions of the 2013 land acquisition law, initially through an ordinance and subsequently through an amendment to the law tabled in the Indian Parliament. The consent and social impact assessment provisions of the 2013 land acquisition law were a major grouse against the UPA government and fueled accusations of policy paralysis as they were seen as cumbersome measures making large-scale land acquisition difficult for private infrastructure investments. The proposed amendments were in keeping with the promises made by Modi to big capital for the ease of doing business. As they faced nationwide agitations that brought together peasants, big farmers, social activists, environmentalists, journalists, lawyers, academics, other concerned actors, political parties, and trade unions, the amendment bill was eventually withdrawn (Sampat 2018).

13. P. Mehra (2018) points out that the GST has been used as a populist scheme for political gains. For instance, the GST on Gujarati savories was reduced prior to the assembly elections in the state. Similarly, in another populist move, government employees have been given a pay hike under the Seventh Pay Commission, and the decontrol of petrol and diesel prices was stalled at the time of the Karnataka state elections (Mehra 2018). All these indicate the populism of Modi-nomics and its departures from classic liberal priorities.

14. An illustrative case of political expedience in infrastructure policy is the erstwhile Mandal Becharaji Special Investment Region close to Dholera where similar agitation resulted in the removal of the land of thirty-six out of forty-four villages from the project by then chief minister Modi in 2014, presumably as a result of the political sensitivity of the national election year.

15. E. Laclau (2007) elaborates that an empty signifier can only emerge if there is a structural impossibility in signification and this impossibility signifies itself as an interruption of the structure of the sign. As Laclau reminds us, the presence of empty signifiers is the very condition of hegemony.

References

Bal, H. 2017. "The Instigator: How MS Golwalkar's Virulent Ideology Underpins Modi's India." *Caravan*, July 1. Accessed August 1, 2019. https://caravanmagazine .in/reportage/golwalkar-ideology-underpins-modi-india.

Banerjee, A. and Namrata Kala. 2017. "The economic and political consequences of India's demonetisation." VoxDev, June 21. Accessed August 10, 2018. https:// voxdev.org/topic/institutions-political-economy/economic-and-political -consequences-india-s-demonetisation.

Benjamin, W. 2008 [1936]. *The Work of Art in the Age of Its Technological Reproducibility, and Other Writings on Media*. Cambridge: Harvard University Press.

Chaudhury, A. 2019. "Millennials Shaking Up This Election: Doctorate, Rhodes Scholar, Law Grad." *NDTV*, May 15. Accessed May 25, 2019. https://www.ndtv .com/india-news/atishi-kanhaiya-kumar-jignesh-mevani-millennials-shaking-up -this-election-2037825.

Corbridge, S., and J. Harriss. 2000. *Reinventing India*. New Delhi: Polity.

DNA. 2012. "Supreme Court Quashes 122 2G Licences Awarded in 2008." *DNA*, February 3.

Economic Times. 2012. "Government Suffered Loss of Rs 1.86 Lakh Crore from Coal Block Allocation." August 17. Accessed August 7, 2019. https://economictimes .indiatimes.com/industry/indl-goods/svs/metals-mining/cag-government -suffered-loss-of-rs-1-86-lakh-crore-from-coal-block-allocation/printarticle /15529730.cms (accessed August 7, 2019).

Finchelstein, F. 2017. *From Fascism to Populism in History*. Berkeley: University of California Press.

Firstpost. 2017. "Gauri Lankesh Murder Was Worryingly Similar to Govind Pansare, Narendra Dabholkar and MM Kalburgi Killings." *Firstpost*, September 7. Accessed April 29, 2018. https://www.firstpost.com/india/watch-gauri-lankesh -murder-was-worryingly-similar-to-dabholkar-pansare-and-kalburgi-killings -4013161.html.

Golwalkar, M. S. 1939. *We or Our Nationhood Defined*. Nagpur: Bharat Publications.

Gupta, S. 2018. "Adivasi Farmers Protest Over Land Acquisition for Bullet Train Project." *NDTV*, May 3. Accessed May 25, 2019. https://www.ndtv.com/india -news/adivasi-farmers-protest-over-land-acquisition-for-bullet-train-project -1846836.

Jaffrelot, C. 2017. *Hindu Nationalism: A Reader*. New Delhi: Permanent Black. 2012.

Jaffrelot, C. 2012. "Gujarat 2002: What Justice for the Victims? The Supreme Court, the SIT, the Police and the State Judiciary." *EPW* 47(8): 75–87.

Johnson, T. A., E. Roy, and D. Goyal. 2015. "The Risk of Reason." *Indian Express*, September 21.

Kohli, R. 2018. "Cash Signals: Trend Reversion Questions Formalisation of the Economy after DeMo and GST." *Financial Express,* March 6.

Laclau, E. 2007. *Emancipation(s).* New York: Verso.

Mehra, P. 2018. "Passing Off Politics as Economics." *The Hindu Center for Politics and Public Policy.* Accessed May 29, 2018. https://www.thehinducentre.com /the-arena/current-issues/article24012281.ece.

Mitra, S. 2016. "India's Demonetisation Drive: Politics Trumps Economics." *Ideas for India.* Accessed May 29, 2018. http://www.ideasforindia.in/topics/money -finance/india-s-demonetisation-drive-politics-trumps-economics.html.

Mundle, S. 2017. "Sliding Economic Growth: What Is to Be Done?" *Livemint,* September 15.

Newsclick. 2018. "Farmers in Maharashtra Protest Against Bullet Train Land Acquisition in Palghar." *Newsclick,* May 3. Accessed June 1, 2018. https://newsclick.in /farmers-maharashtra-protest-against-bullet-train-land-acquisition-palghar.

Nigam, A., and R. Balaji. 2017. "Big Trouble for the Small and Informal Sector." *BusinessLine,* November 7.

PTI. 2019. "General Elections 2019: Jignesh Mevani Campaigns for Kanhaiya Kumar in Bihar." *CNBC TV18,* April 9. Accessed May 29, 2019. https://www.cnbctv18 .com/politics/general-elections-2019-jignesh-mevani-campaigns-for-kanhaiya -kumar-in-bihar-2767251.htm.

PTI. 2018. "Gujarat Farmers Protest against Bullet Train Land Acquisition Process." *Hindustan Times,* April 9.

PTI. 2017a. "Demonetisation Impacts India's Informal Sector: UN Report." *TimesNow News,* September 15. Accessed January 6, 2018. http://www.times nownews.com/business-economy/economy/article/demonetisation -impacts-india%E2%80%99s-informal-sector-un-report/91269.

PTI. 2017b. "Urban Voters Still with BJP, Rural Gujarat Behind Congress." *NDTV,* December 20. Accessed June 9, 2018. https://www.ndtv.com/india-news/gujarat -election-results-2017-urban-voters-still-with-bjp-rural-gujarat-behind-congress -1789883.

Pai, S. 2016. "Why Modi's Idea of Holding State, Parliamentary Elections Together May Not Work." *The Wire,* September 10.

Rajagopal, K. 2017. "What Is the Babri Masjid Case All About?" *The Hindu,* December 2.

Raychaudhuri, T. 1999. "Hindu Nationalism or Proto-fascism: The Nature of Hindu Communal Politics in India." In *Wissenschaftscolleg: Jahrbuch 1997/98.* Berlin: Wissenschaftscolleg zu Berlin.

Sampat, P. 2018. "India's Land Impasse: Infrastructure, Resistance and Rent." In *Relational Poverty Politics: Forms, Struggles, and Possibilities,* ed. V. Lawson and S. Elwoood, 95-112. Athens: University of Georgia Press.

Sampat, P. 2016. "Dholera: The Emperor's New City." *Economic and Political Weekly* 51 (17): 59–67.

Schmitt, C. 1985. *Political Theology: Four Chapters on the Concept of Sovereignty.* Chicago: University of Chicago Press.

Sethi, G. 2017. "Gujarat Election Results 2017: Why the Dalit Vote Went against BJP." *Hindustan Times*, December 18.

Skaria, A. 2016. "The Death and Rebirth of Gandhi." *Outlook*, November 7.

The Wire. 2018. "Fact Check on Jaitley: The Fact-Checker Paints Unflattering Picture of Economy." *The Wire*, June 7.

The Wire. 2017. "Explained: The Short, Medium and Long-Term Fallout of India's GST." *The Wire*, June 30.

Varadarajan, S. 2014. "The Cult of Cronyism." *Seminar* (April): 60–63.

Blue Bloods, Parvenus, and Mercenaries

Authoritarianism and Political Violence in Colombia

The failure of governments around the world to deal with the problems generated by neoliberalism has opened the door for the far right to exploit working-class anger and disillusionment in the aftermath of the 2008 financial collapse (e.g., Kalb and Mollona 2017). The election of Trump and the passage of Brexit signal that racial dog whistles and imperial privilege no longer satisfy broad segments of the white working class in the United States and Great Britain, where anxieties about economic decline and terrorism have bolstered anti-immigrant nationalism and support for strongman rule. In Latin America, after falling global commodity prices revealed the limits of "twenty-first-century socialism," the ebb of the so-called pink tide of progressive governments has set the stage for the resolution of crises in favor of the right. Depleted commodity rents from minerals, oil, natural gas, and other export products have made uplifting the poor, without challenging the power of capital, impossible, and left-leaning regimes have lost one election after another while Venezuela unravels.

Colombia, however, diverges from its neighbors, as well as from the experiences of North America and Europe. A leftist government has not held power since the 1930s, and counterinsurgent violence made the neoliberal reconfiguration of society and economy bloodier than elsewhere. Just as popular demands for national sovereignty, economic equality, and limits on corporate power began to sweep in left-leaning governments in Venezuela, Ecuador, Bolivia, Brazil, and Argentina, Colombia became a narcostate. Its decades-long civil war reached a blood-drenched climax at the end of the twentieth century, as the emergence of a violent, far-right political alliance led by a rising group of cocaine entrepreneurs crushed revolutionary and reformist political projects, forestalled the enactment of redistributive policies, and ushered a new group of far-right political leaders to power.

Explaining the rise of authoritarian regimes around the world is an important task for scholars. This essay places the rise of a powerful right-wing political bloc in Colombia within a materialist history of state formation, class antagonism, regional differences, and shifting international conjunctures. It asks how the Colombian far right emerged, how it carried out a violent counterrevolution, and how it then forged a political movement that tried to reconcile wartime violence with liberal democracy. To do so, it explores how an emergent alliance of drug traffickers, neoliberal entrepreneurs, landowners, merchants, military personnel, and conventional politicians manipulated hierarchical networks of local power and advanced a distinct form of authoritarian state formation based in the production and export of cocaine. The essay argues that nowadays, the far right is not only concerned with protecting what it won in the war but is also hostile to equality and the redistribution of power. It is also a forward movement that has succeeded by reaching outward to the United States and by extending downward to harness the energy of the middle class and subalterns. And although it emerged as a reaction to challenges from below, the far right is more than an expression of retrograde nostalgia. It is a vital force that has arisen at the juncture of international fields of power and regional configurations of capital accumulation and has drawn in recruits and revitalized its worldview to meet new challenges (see also Grandin 2010; Mayer 2000; Robin 2018).

The first section of this essay focuses on the emergence of the illegal cocaine traffic in the 1970s and 1980s and the growth of a far-right alliance of blue-blooded aristocrats and narco parvenus comprised of drug traffickers, politicians, landowners, cattle ranchers, merchants, and sectors of the security forces. Because it initially sought to defend the status quo rather than transform society, the far right, like other counterrevolutionary movements in Latin America, was less attuned to history and did not lay out a strategy for victory. It emerged in reaction to the left, even imitating it in certain ways, and took shape as praxis rather than theory (see Grandin 2010, 22; Robin 2018, 3–38). The analysis turns to how, beginning in the 1980s, this far-right alliance supported the creation of paramilitary militias that crushed the opposition and established regimes of "parcellized sovereignty" (Hylton 2006, 12) where it controlled territory and regulated social life. It then became more politically aware of itself and emerged as a force for regional and national social change with a revitalized message that attempted to appeal to the masses, while simultaneously protecting the class-based inequalities deepened by its counterinsurgent violence and enabling its continued accumulation of wealth.

The Narco Nexus

The enormous profits of the illegal cocaine industry generated a tectonic shift in the configuration of power in Colombia, replacing an older form of import-substitution industrialization with gangster capitalism anchored in the production and export of an illegal narcotic. Beginning in the 1970s, the rise of cocaine displaced older industries, such as coffee and textiles, and propelled a violent group of narcoentrepreneurs into the leadership of a far-right political bloc that included regional combinations of landowners, merchants, traditional politicians, and members of the security forces who were animated by an impulse to accumulate and defend wealth, power, and privilege. Reactionary to the core, the politics of the new right were rooted in regional configurations of power, patronage, and clientelism, marinated in Catholic conservatism, steeped in notions of victimhood, loss, and self-defense, and forged in violent opposition to peasants, indigenous working people, and guerrilla insurgencies who demanded the redistribution of wealth, greater political participation, and the involvement of the state in the provision of social welfare.

According to historian David Bushnell, Colombia is "a nation in spite of itself," a country divided by deep regional antagonisms and lacking "a true national identity and proper spirit of nationalism" (Bushnell 1993, xii), at least compared to neighboring countries. Until the 1980s, the Colombian bourgeoisie was divided between, on the one hand, regionally based landowners who derived their wealth from cotton, sugar, cattle, tobacco, and coffee and ruled with considerable autonomy within their provincial spheres of influence, and, on the other hand, a Bogotá-based bourgeoisie based in light manufacturing, banking, media, and food and beverage distribution and that controlled national political power. Although there was overlap between these groups, no faction of the bourgeoisie ever united the others, along with subalterns, to represent its interests as those of the nation (Hylton 2006, 8–9). Rather, sovereignty was regionally circumscribed, operating through two dominant political parties—the Liberals and Conservatives—that were characterized by weak central administration and strong, regionally based, clientelistic relationships between the population and political bosses, who were typically landlords with large landholdings. Party loyalties passed from generation to generation, constituting the equivalent of national allegiances in other countries.

Import substitution policies—the development model adopted by Latin American countries, except Cuba, after World War II—protected traditional landlords and manufacturers with high tariffs on imported goods, until they entered a permanent crisis in the 1970s. The government then turned to sources of foreign investment, and new export enclaves in oil, bananas, coal, gold. Coca/cocaine opened in remote frontier regions, reconfiguring the spatial coordinates of class power around regional poles of development and aggravating Colombia's already pronounced regionalism. Cocaine was the most important of these commodities. A rising group of narcoentrepreneurs used organized violence to create circuits of commodity production and distribution that undergirded the creation of enormous fortunes and reorganized the Colombian bourgeoisie, regionally and nationally.

The cultivation of coca leaves from which pure cocaine is derived, and the manufacture and sale of cocaine, linked peasant settlers in the southeastern lowland frontier and the Pacific and Atlantic coasts to networks of traffickers based in the highland cities of Calí and Medellín. The traffickers, known as the Calí and Medellín cartels, then connected these cities to major North American and European centers where cocaine was consumed. At the height of their power in the 1980s and 1990s, the networks became multi-billion-dollar enterprises that invested heavily in legitimate businesses—from pharmacies and discos to soccer clubs and banks—and controlled most of the world cocaine market. Cocaine replaced coffee as Colombia's primary export commodity, and the new industry integrated more of Colombia's regions than any of the older ones. It drew on a labor pool of un- or underemployed labor freed up by the decline of import-substitution industrialization, distributed wealth through money laundering, patronage, and corruption, and resolved conflicts with violence. The disruptive spatial, social, and economic dynamics of cocaine capitalism created the conditions of possibility for far-right alliances and politics to emerge (e.g., Hylton 2006).

With some notable exceptions, the new cocaine entrepreneurs hailed from humble social backgrounds. Men like the infamous Pablo Escobar, who perched atop the Medellín cartel, cut their teeth on an older contraband trade in cigarettes, clothing, and cars smuggled from the duty-free Panama Canal Zone, as well as in marijuana, exported from the Guajira peninsula since the 1960s (Brito 2015). Cocaine, however, was a far more lucrative commodity. As men of modest means became fantastically wealthy, a new narcobourgeoisie displayed its wealth in garish forms of luxury consumption, such as multiple mansions, flashy automobiles, helicopters, expensive jewelry, and exotic animals, and through the purchase of rural land. The drug lords amassed vast landholdings for several reasons. The precariousness of rural property rights, especially in frontier regions, enabled them to launder money more easily through land acquisitions than through urban real estate and other businesses more closely monitored by the state (Richani 2012, 64), and monopolizing land along trafficking routes facilitated the clandestine movement of cocaine. Land purchases also had speculative value and enabled the narcos to carve out places for their opulent mansions, acquire social status, and elbow their way into the long-established agrarian bourgeoisie.

Although the established rural oligarchs despised the crass cocaine parvenus whom they referred to disparagingly as lice, and only slightly more charitable as the *clase emergente*, the rising threat of guerrilla insurgencies in the 1980s fed oligarchic fears of chaos and stimulated a sense of self-preservation that prompted a deeper integration of the two groups. Like the agrarian old guard, drug-traffickers-turned-landlords quickly fell victim to insurgent demands for "war taxes." Yet because their vast financial resources were useful in the fight against the guerrillas, a marriage of convenience blossomed between opportunistic oligarchs and the narcos, especially in regions, such as the North Coast, the Middle Magdalena, Urabá, Antioquia, and Caquetá, where peasants and insurgents contested the power of these increasingly intertwined groups.[1] The infusion of new blood enabled rural patricians to protect their interests at a time when many landlords were growing wary of venturing into the countryside to visit their properties because of guerrilla extortion demands and kidnapping attempts.

Regional powerholders (e.g., landlords, machine politicians, merchants) and the new cocaine capitalists also shared a fundamental hostility to social movements and popular demands for a more equitable apportionment of wealth, whether peasant appeals for land and credit, urban movements' calls for housing, public education, and infrastructure, or workers' petitions for better wages and working conditions. These demands grew louder in the 1970s and 1980s. In addition to radicalized peasants, oil workers and shantytown dwellers staged a "civic strike" in the oil town of Barrancabermeja to protest the lack of social services and the event became a prototype for similar strikes in other cities (Giraldo and Camargo 1985). The Colombian labor movement also united in 1986, when workers created the *Central Unitaria de Trabajadores*— the nation's largest trade union federation. Among the founding members were two banana workers' unions from the Urabá region that won landmark labor agreements that established the eight-hour day, raised wages, and promised urban housing (Chomsky 2008, 181–221). The experience of having their wealth and power threatened drove regional blue-bloods and narcos into an alliance that spread death and destruction to any person or organization whose words and actions were deemed "subversive," especially if they could be linked to guerrilla insurgencies.[2] In addition to guerrilla harassment, what most irritated the far right was the self-organization and agency of the lower orders. Imagining working people freeing themselves from the shackles of their presumed betters disturbed patricians and parvenus alike, because it threatened what Corey Robin calls "the private life of power" and conjured a social world in which the ruling class was irrelevant (Robin 2018, 3–38).

The Revolutionary Armed Forces of Colombia (FARC) was Colombia's largest and oldest guerrilla movement. Formed in 1964 as the armed wing of the Colombian Communist Party, its stronghold was the southeastern lowlands, a remote region where peasant refugees settled during a devastating civil war (1948–64) between the Liberal and Conservative parties that produced massive loss of life and became known simply as *La Violencia*.[3] Because of the absence of markets, bad roads, and the lack of viable alternatives, frontier peasants turned to the cultivation of coca leaves. When demand for cocaine escalated in the United States in the 1970s, coca cultivation exploded, and the FARC, after initial uncertainty, facilitated peasant participation into the cocaine economy on favorable terms. Taxes on coca paste[4] provided the guerrillas with a new source of revenue that strengthened their military power relative to the Colombian security forces and local cattle ranchers and allowed them to protect peasants from military repression, encroachment from ranchers, and exploitation from the emissaries of the major drug traffickers who came to the region to buy coca paste (Hough 2011). Buoyed by a war chest fattened on cocaine, the FARC then expanded out of its stronghold and established a presence in many of Colombia's municipalities during the 1980s and 1990s.

Colombia's second largest insurgency—the National Liberation Army (ELN)—formed at approximately the same time as the FARC but was less immersed in the drug economy. Tied to middle-class university students and the liberation-theology wing of the Catholic Church, the ELN drew inspiration from the Cuban revolution, Christian humanism, and regional experiences of collective struggle in the oil-rich Middle Magdalena region, where it put down deep roots. The guerrillas remained largely a regional phenomenon until the 1980s, when, like the FARC, the ELN began to grow and reach beyond its regional power base. The increasing shift of the Colombian economy to new export enclaves in remote regions, where a single commodity predominated, presented them with new material possibilities. As sectors of the national bourgeoisie and multinational corporations invested in gold mining in northeast Antioquia department, bananas in the northwest Urabá region, coal in the Guajira peninsula, and oil in North Santander and Arauca departments, they became targets of ELN and FARC extortion and kidnapping for ransom, which financed the insurgent military build-up and geographic expansion.

Guerrilla harassment alarmed regional entrepreneurs who demanded that the state do more to protect them. Anxieties intensified when, in 1982, the government of Belisario Betancur opened a peace process with the FARC that ended in a 1985 ceasefire agreement. As part of the accord, President Betancur decentralized certain governmental decision-making powers to municipal authorities and allowed the direct election of mayors, previously appointed by the president. The decision was motivated, in part, by a strategic calculus that political decentralization would pacify the FARC and coopt the insurgents into the electoral process (Castro 1998). The FARC, in turn, agreed to participate in elections through the formation of a new party called the *Unión Patriótica* (UP), and similar electoral fronts—*A Luchar* and *Frente Popular*—represented the ELN and the Popular Liberation Army (EPL), another insurgency active at the time.

Betancur's peace initiative and the political opening renewed hope and raised expectations among peasants, workers, and poor urbanites that the enactment of broad democratic reforms, such as land reform, public services, infrastructure, and public education, might be around the corner (Romero 2003). For the first time in decades, a broad electoral left tied to the insurgencies but not coterminous with them organized and performed well in elections. Many insurgents laid down their arms and put their faith in the peace process, and hundreds of ordinary people bet on peace as well. They were trade unionists, peasants, teachers, and students who had previously given up on politics, because they believed all politicians were corrupt, or because they felt that the Liberals and Conservatives ignored their concerns. Unfortunately, their optimism was short lived.

No sector of the bourgeoisie or the army had ever supported a negotiated peace, and the peace process itself unfolded in a bellicose international context. Following the 1980 election of Ronald Reagan, US counterinsurgency wars intensified in Central America, and the US ambassador to Colombia,

Louis Tambs, signaled the hardline US policy by labelling the FARC "narco-guerrillas," a concept that simultaneously called forth Cold War anxieties and delegitimized the guerrillas as a political movement. Fearful entrepreneurs, landlords, and sectors of the security forces, who worried that peace and political decentralization would tip the balance of power in favor of the guerrillas and their supporters, backed Washington's bellicose stance toward the FARC. They united behind the banner of anticommunism, binding themselves to sectors of the middle class, as well as North American and Latin American ruling classes elsewhere, and justified the violent suppression of political reform.

The old-style agrarian bourgeoisie saw themselves as the victims of both guerrilla predation and of an absent state. These individuals suffered from a special kind of victimhood rooted in the threat of property loss rather than their association with people who owned very little,[5] and they sought protection for their investments from the traffickers, who armed and financed death squads that consisted of mostly poor young men.[6] Death to Kidnappers was an early group that emerged in the Middle Magdalena region with the financial backing of members of the Medellín cartel and the participation of local merchants, cattle ranchers, state security forces, and the Texaco Company. Integrated into military intelligence networks, Death to Kidnappers carried out the unsavory acts of dirty war in alliance with state security forces that denied any knowledge of their existence. Similar groups subsequently arose in other regions, targeting, through physical elimination or forcible displacement, organizations and individuals who supported radical social reforms or who simply impeded the emergent far right's accumulation of wealth.

What Arno Mayer describes as "the furies of revolution"—a fierce, merciless, and rising crescendo of violence—was driven by the feverish right-wing reaction to the growing power of the guerrillas and the resurgent legal left (Mayer 2000, xvi). As it gathered force, the emergent far-right alliance did not produce a roadmap to success but forged its thinking and its strategy in combat, in relation to the left and often copying it. For example, it located itself in a movement of the masses by christening death squads "self-defense" groups, a reference to the communist-controlled, peasant communities that resisted the military in southern Colombia during *La Violencia* and became the bases of the FARC. The Colombian Army—a key ally of the death squads—also tailored the notion of "human rights" to its counterinsurgent mission (Tate 2007). And, most lethally, it appropriated the guerrilla notion of "the combination of all forms of struggle," in which individuals acting on behalf of the insurgencies participate in popular organization, to deadly effect. Like right-wing movements elsewhere, the Colombian far right produced knowledge in reaction to the left by "read[ing] situations and circumstances" and preferring "adaptation and imitation" (Robin 2018). Mutilated bodies, displaced communities, and traumatized survivors initially sent the most important messages.

The peace process with the FARC and political decentralization served less to demilitarize and democratize Colombian society than to intensify an upward swirl of terror within an expanding counterinsurgency war. In only one year, 1987, mercenaries murdered forty labor leaders in the Urabá banana zone, bombed one union's headquarters, and forced many other workers into internal exile (Chomsky 2008, 181–221), and between 1987 and 1992, they assassinated eight hundred members of the recently formed *Central Unitaria de Trabajadores*. Most ominous for the left, right-wing mercenaries literally wiped out the UP, massacring several thousand activists, as well as unknown numbers of *A Luchar* and *Frente Popular* militants, between 1985 and 1991, and pulverizing the broadest electoral left coalition to emerge in more than forty years. The annihilation of the UP became known as a "political genocide." Many FARC members who had opted for peace did not survive, leaving a faction of the insurgency more committed to a military solution in control of the movement and not averse to financing its remilitarization through stepped-up kidnapping, extortion, and deeper involvement in narcotics (Dudley 2004). For the next two decades, the furies consumed much of Colombia in a dialectical maelstrom that solidified the alliances between drug traffickers, sectors of the security forces, and regional powerholders that first came together against the UP. This matrix of drug money, violence, and landed political power represented the crucible that came to define the extreme right. Yet even as it claimed to be preserving the established order, the far right became more aware of itself as a political force and developed into a power for social change.

Blood and Fire

Collaboration between cocaine traffickers and Colombia's regional powerholders reached unprecedented levels at the end of the millennium, when Colombia became a narcostate. The "self-defense groups" of the 1980s morphed into standing paramilitary armies that conquered and controlled territory, murdered and displaced tens of thousands of people, pushed the guerrillas out of their traditional strongholds, and accelerated the opening of the Colombian economy in the 1990s, which further enriched the narcos. The far right then moved to institutionalize its power by retooling its message, propelling previously unknown politicians to the center of national power, and in regions most ravaged by its violence, building a popular support base (e.g., Ballvé 2012). This was not a seamless process and it was full of contradictions. Yet the cumulative result went beyond the maintenance of the status quo. It rolled back reformist and revolutionary political movements, reterritorialized power, incorporated working people into new relationships of inequality, and created manageable spaces for the attraction of global capital. To understand how this happened, let us review how the far right became a fundamental force for social change in contemporary Colombia.

Paramilitary armies were second-generation drug trafficking organizations that lacked the centralized leadership of the Medellín and Calí cartels, which collapsed in the early 1990s. Regional "blocs" expanded under the cover of the Colombian state, which briefly authorized legal self-defense groups between 1997 and 1998, and they could act autonomously because their leaders' domination of the cocaine industry allowed them to finance military operations. They also possessed well-developed networks of local, regional, and national political support, a strong military structure, and the backing of numerous military officers, all of which enabled them to scale-up their power in 1997, when several regional armies federated under the umbrella of the United Self-Defense Forces of Colombia (AUC) (see Duncan 2006; López 2010; Romero 2007). Led by former Medellín cartel operative Carlos Castaño, the AUC defined itself as "an anti-subversive, political-military movement in exercise of the legitimate right to self-defense that demands the transformation of the state but does not attack it" (Valencia 2007, 22–23).

Paramilitary mercenaries and those they served amassed land through massacre, displacement, and illegal appropriation and created nodes of parcelized sovereignty (Hylton 2006), or "parastates," after they took over provincial towns and entire regions of the countryside. The paramilitaries became most powerful in frontier regions, such as the Urabá banana zone (Ballvé 2012), the oil and cattle region of the Middle Magdalena and North Santander (Gill 2016), the gold mining zone of northeast Antioquia, the cattle ranching planes of southern Cordoba, and the ranching and coca processing centers of the eastern plains (Hough 2011; Ramírez 2011; Tate 2007). In these areas, the paramilitaries operated alongside or in place of the institutional state. Landlords, businessmen, multinational corporations, and machine politicians who supported their advance depended on the mercenaries for security, enrichment, and their positions as regional power brokers vis-à-vis central government institutions and urban centers. Consequently, as paramilitaries formed strategic networks, exercised the power to regulate social, economic, and political life, and killed with impunity, the boundaries between public/private and legal/illegal blurred.

Paramilitarism was the violent, armed expression of the far-right bloc that took sharper form in 1990s Colombia. Yet neither the AUC nor the civilians that it represented were a seamless phenomenon. The AUC, for its part, never managed to articulate a national political vision nor did it solidify an alliance among all regional commanders, who were divided by personal rivalries, suspicions, and competition over control of the drug economy. As one Colombian magistrate stated, "each commandant did what he wanted in his zone with absolute autonomy, and declared unilateral war whenever he wanted to expand territorially, despite the efforts to create a confederation by the "Castaño house" (Verdadabierta 2017).

Centrifugal forces also tugged at intraclass solidarity among the narcos and the regional landlords, cattle ranchers, machine politicians, entrepreneurs, and merchants who allied with them. The drug lords benefited from the neoliberal restructuring of the economy that began under President César Gavíria (1990–94) far more than conventional large landowners, because the shift to free market policies lubricated the flow of capital (legal and illegal) and made trafficking and money laundering easier. The narcos became Colombia's uber-capitalists: economic liberals who, although opposed to the state's efforts to extradite them to the United States and dismantle their industry, benefited from free markets and private property rights. They also accelerated the neoliberal opening of the economy by drenching the country in a flood of contraband from Panama, which effectively undercut protectionist policies. Because they were not averse to mass murder, the traffickers took the lead in the destruction of the opposition, which cemented their position within the right-wing alliance. In contrast, traditional agriculturalists, who had long been shielded from the brute force of the international market by Latin America's highest tariff barriers, lost their protective cushion, and cheap imports displaced domestic production. Neoliberal agricultural policies favored new export commodities, such as African palm, which spread across lands illegally appropriated by the paramilitaries. They also undermined domestic food production by ruining peasant producers and energizing the spread of illegal coca cultivation—the only realistic solution to a deepening subsistence crisis for desperate peasant families—which in turn stimulated the explosive growth of the cocaine industry.

Peasants who did not cultivate coca leaves were driven to the city, where the narcos increasingly dominated the popular economy of the shantytowns that sprouted like mushrooms on urban peripheries. The children of displaced peasants and the urban poor became available as cheap labor for an expanding network of narco-controlled criminal activities, such as loan-sharking, extortion, low-level drug dealing, the sale of lottery tickets, and the theft of gasoline. As ever-larger swathes of the economy became integrated into the cocaine industry, the narcoentrepreneurs grew more powerful, becoming the leading force of a far-right alliance in a newly deregulated, anything-goes capitalist economy.

The far right then moved to institutionalize its rule by organizing an electoral project with populist appeal that addressed rich and poor alike. It did so by attacking indifferent Bogotá elites, railing against corruption, and promising to deliver Colombia's forgotten regions from the abandonment of the central state. Although this form of reactionary populism addressed concrete grievances, it made little mention of the state-backed political and economic processes that were reconfiguring Colombian society and deepening inequality and marginalization. It had even less to say about the narco-fueled violence that propelled this transformation. Yet the far right managed to pole vault previously unknown regional politicians to the center of national political power.[7] In areas under paramilitary domination, a raft of new, right-wing parties emerged and gained power at the expense of the traditional Liberal and Conservative parties. Convergencia Ciudadana, Colombia Viva, Cambio Radical, Movimiento de Integración Popular, and Alas represented some of the upstarts. In electoral contests between 1999 and 2003, previously unknown "outsider" politicians from these parties parachuted into local, regional, and national political office. In some cases, they ran unopposed because threats and violence had forced competitors out and created single electoral options; in other cases, paramilitary pressure moved voters to cast ballots for candidates approved by the mercenaries. And in still others, their populist message about the absent state resonated with voters and received popular support.

The results constituted an astonishing reconfiguration of Colombia's electoral map, which was "substantially modified" in twelve provinces and "partly transformed" in many others (Valencia 2007, 14; see also Lopez 2010). Even more important, the far right established a large, national congressional bloc in which, as paramilitary commander Salvatore Mancuso boasted in 2002, it controlled 35 percent of the delegates, and, in the same year, it elected one of its own—Álvaro Uríbe—to the presidency, a man who, according to AUC leader Carlos Castaño, "is the man closest to our philosophy" (Aranguren 2001, 177).

Uríbe's presidency (2002–10) marked a shift away from the Liberal-Conservative diarchy that had ruled Colombia for 150 years. A renegade Liberal from a prosperous ranching family in Antioquia province, Uríbe did not share a surname with the Bogotá bourgeoisie and cultivated a personal image that combined aggressive militarism with a paternalistic love of the countryside. After serving as governor of Antioquia province, he broke with the Liberal party over negotiations with the FARC and organized his own party to stand for election in 2002. He was welcomed by the United States, which saw an Uríbe administration as a bulwark against left-leaning governments coming to power elsewhere in Latin America, even though accusations of ties to drug traffickers and support for paramilitaries had dogged Uríbe throughout his career. As president, Uríbe pushed a hardline military strategy for which he was rewarded with funds from Plan Colombia, a multi-billion-dollar, mostly military aid program, that deepened US involvement in Colombia's civil war.[8] Although billed as a counternarcotics initiative, Plan Colombia targeted the FARC's southern coca fields, rather than moving against paramilitary-dominated areas on the northern coast, where cocaine was shipped to the United States. Not surprising, it did little to stem the flow of cocaine to the United States, but strengthened the security forces—paramilitaries' closest allies—and weakened the FARC.

As the far right gained an upper hand, regional paramilitary commanders realized that, with the guerrillas on the defensive and in disarray, the time had come to move beyond war and build a durable base for their revanchist political project and an enduring regime of accumulation. This realization came only after they had hammered the civilian population and discarded the importance of cultivating popular support because of the backing of the security forces. Not surprising, creating a stable social order through community organizing was a complicated and contradictory endeavor. Yet as Teo

Ballvé has demonstrated, paramilitaries flush with cash in Urabá basically succeeded. They organized local groups and worked through community organizations (*juntas de acción comunal*) on a variety of grassroots projects that unfolded alongside official development initiatives that promoted popular participation, environmental protection, and the empowerment of women. The paramilitaries articulated their base-building initiatives to the structures and practices of the municipal government and international development organizations, and what emerged, according to Ballvé, was compatible with capitalist development and liberal projects of institution building and political participation (Ballvé 2012). Yet the paramilitary base-building project was riven with contradictions.

Reconfiguring Rule and Legitimating the Illegitimate

The far right had difficulty resolving the tensions between the violence, population displacement, and death that had facilitated the restoration of capitalist power, on the one hand, and the trappings of Colombia's liberal democracy, on the other. After paramilitary armies converted vast extensions of rural Colombia into zones of resource extraction and export agriculture and pushed the guerrillas aside, they became a liability for their blue-blooded supporters and an embarrassment for a government that claimed to represent South America's oldest democracy. Forced to contain the violence unleashed to defeat the insurgencies and no longer able to deny the existence of paramilitaries, Uríbe announced a "peace process" in 2003 that culminated in the official demobilization of the AUC in 2006, when paramilitarism officially ceased to exist.

Because the government had never been at war with the armed right, the result of the negotiations was an amnesty program, condemned by human rights groups for institutionalizing impunity, that sought to incorporate the paramilitaries into mainstream politics. In exchange for demobilizing their troops, confessing their crimes, and dismantling their criminal operations, some paramilitary commanders who had committed crimes against humanity agreed to reduced prison sentences and laid down their arms. Others balked at the prospects of spending any time in jail, arguing that they had saved the country from the guerrillas, and threatening to expose their dealings with government officials and civilian collaborators. A perilous moment for the far-right bloc then ensued. In 2006, a public scandal over revelations about the connections between paramilitary commanders and politicians erupted, after a few mercenary leaders revealed their involvement in war crimes and political corruption schemes during public testimony. These revelations led to the jailing or investigation of dozens of governors and members of Congress, but when the paramilitaries threatened to get close to the president, Uríbe extradited them to the United States, where they were wanted on drug trafficking charges and less likely to be questioned about human rights violations.[9]

What all the scandals had in common was the location of paramilitarism in the past, implying a rupture between the violent late twentieth century and the post-2006 present in which paramilitarism officially no longer existed. Government officials ignored how political parties tainted by the scandals reorganized under new names to guarantee their continued influence and the local political power of the scandal's heirs. Neoparamilitary groups also reorganized in areas formerly dominated by the AUC, where they continued to use violence to suppress dissent, dispossess working people, and accumulate capital on behalf of a retooled right-wing alliance purged of its most noxious elements (Hristov 2010). A new official designation—*bandas criminales*—disappeared neoparamilitary groups into the realm of common thieves and youth gangs that were responsible for continuing violence. Such sleight of hand severed the connection between the narcos who used violence to accumulate capital and political leaders, the old bourgeoisie, and the security forces that supported them. It also reestablished the illusion of separation between the official state and the narcostate.

Conclusion: Behind the Veil of Peace

The specter of Colombia's turbulent past hangs over the present like a persistent nightmare. The emergence and consolidation of a reactionary right-wing bloc, tied to the rising power of cocaine capitalists has reordered Colombia's place in the global economy, transformed class relations, reworked relations between Bogotá and Colombia's regions, and ignited cocaine-fueled consumption booms. It has also served the broader interests of that faction of Colombia's ruling class resident in the major cities—Bogotá, Calí, Medellín, and Barranquilla—by marginalizing the guerrillas and providing "security and stability" for investment in extractive industries and the expansion of agroindustry in those regions once dominated by the guerrillas. It has done so by stifling criticism, criminalizing protest, and decimating the left (Hylton and Tauss 2016).

No longer confronting a powerful opponent on its left flank, the far right has faced less pressure to defend power and privilege than in the past, and, not surprising, the glue that held blue-bloods and narcos together has begun to dissolve. The fissures in the alliance erupted in the unexpected defeat, in 2016, of a national referendum meant to ratify an historic peace deal between the Colombian government and the FARC. Uríbe's former defense minister and then president Juan Manuel Santos negotiated the deal, which had the support of business associations, Colombia's largest conglomerates, and urban professionals, as well as the Colombian left, despite its distaste for Santos. Yet the accord could not withstand the force of former president and now senator Álvaro Uríbe's political machine and went down in a narrow defeat. Although Congress would ratify a modified version of the agreement, the far right reclaimed the presidency in 2018 with the election of Uríbe acolyte Iván Duque, who campaigned against the peace deal, which subsequently unraveled.

Nowadays, the targeting of social movement leaders who press for the return of stolen lands and the rights of war victims is ongoing. Some FARC guerrillas have rearmed after growing disillusioned with the peace process, while others cluster in demobilization campuses, still waiting for government assistance promised more than two years ago. Neoparamilitary groups continue to operate around the country at the service of a retooled right-wing alliance. They remain in control of urban peripheries, where a majority of Colombia's rural displaced and working class live, and although they are less ideologically driven than their predecessors, in part because the far right won the war, the mercenaries are still available to suppress demands for social justice or the equitable distribution of wealth. They are able to do so because seventeen years and $10 billion dollars after the United States launched Plan Colombia, the illegal cocaine traffic is enjoying boom times. Colombia's defense minister, Luis Carlos Villegas, told the *Washington Post* that "We've never seen anything like it" (Miroff 2016).

This essay has argued that the emergence of the Colombian far right was animated by a fundamental hostility to redistributive demands from below and a desire to protect the power and privilege of a shotgun marriage between regional oligarchs and an emergent group of narcocapitalists who led the attack on both revolutionary and reformist political movements. It has shown that the growth of this far-right alliance was a dynamic, violence-driven process, and it has demonstrated that far from being a conservative effort to maintain oligarchic privilege, the Colombian far right transformed the status quo that it had initially sought to defend, producing an extreme form of neo-liberal capitalism. Yet Colombia is also indicative of a much broader pattern of working-class setback, the recalibration of space for global commodity flows, and deepening inequality that we must understand to grasp the resurgence of the far right around the world.

Notes

1. See Zamosc (1986) for a discussion of the Asociación Nacional de Usuarios Campesinos, a national-level political movement whose radical faction invaded haciendas on the North Coast, a region where paramilitarism subsequently became deeply rooted.

2. Many foreign corporations participated in these alliances. Between 1997 and 2004, for example, Chiquita admitted to funneling nearly $2 million to right-wing paramilitary crops in the Urabá banana zone and paid a $25 million fine in 2007.

3. In addition to the massive loss of life, one of the consequences of La Violencia was the suppression of left populism through the murder of Jorge Eliécer Gaitán and the repression of the movement that bore his name. The prospect of Gaitán winning the presidency led to his assassination in 1948, a day that in popular memory marked the start of La Violencia.

4. Coca paste is a brownish mash manufactured from coca leaves that is an intermediate step in the production of pure cocaine.

5. Robin (2018) notes that victimhood has long been a talking point of right-wing movements.

6. The practice of privatizing security had already been established during La Violencia, when vigilante groups knows as pájaros and chulavitas violently suppressed popular demands with gruesome forms of terror.

7. Teo Ballvé (2012) provides a detailed description of how paramilitary populism succeeded in Urabá and elaborates further in a forthcoming book.

8. Congress enacted Plan Colombia in 1999, making Colombia the largest recipient of US military assistance after the Middle East.

9. During his two-term tenure as president, he shipped off 1,100 paramilitaries to the United States, far more than the 333 extradited prior to his presidency (Ramsey 2012).

References

Aranguren, Mauricio. 2001. *Mi Confesión: Carlos Castaño revela sus secretos*. Bogotá: Editorial Oveja Negra.

Ballvé, Teo. 2012. "Everyday State Formation: Territory, Decentralization, and the Narco Landgrabs in Colombia." *Environmental Planning D: Society and Space* 30: 603–622.

Brito, Lina. 2015. Hurricane Winds: Vallenato Music and Marijuana in Colombia's First Illegal Drugs Boom. *Hispanic American Historical* 95 (1): 71–102.

Bushnell, David. 1993. *Colombia: A Nation in Spite of Itself*. Berkeley: University of California Press.

Castro, Jaime. 1998. *Decentralizar para pacificar*. Bogotá: Editorial Ariel.

Chomsky, Aviva. 2008. *Linked Labor Histories: New England, Colombia, and the Making of a Global Working Class*. Durham, NC: Duke University Press.

Dudley, Steven. 2004. *Walking Ghosts: Murder and Guerrilla Politics in Colombia*. New York: Routledge.

Duncan, Gustavo. 2006. *Los señores de la guerra: De paramilitares, mafiosos, y Autodefensas en Colombia*. Bogotá: Planeta.

Gill, Lesley. 2016. *A Century of Violence in a Red City: Popular Struggle, Counterinsurgency, and Human Rights in Colombia*. Durham, NC: Duke University Press.

Giraldo, Javier, and Santiago Camargo. 1985. "Paros y movimientos cívicos en Colombia." *Controversia* 128: 11–42.

Grandin, Greg. 2010. "Living in Revolutionary Times: Coming to Terms with the Violence of Latin America's Long Cold War." *A Century of Revolution: Insurgent and Counterinsurgent Violence during Latin America's Long Cold War*, ed. Greg Grandin and Gilbert Joseph, 1–44. Durham, NC: Duke University Press.

Hough, Phillip. 2011. "Disarticulations and Commodity Chains: Cattle, Coca, and Capital Accumulation along Colombia's Agricultural Frontier." *Environment and Planning A* 43: 1016–1034.

Hristov, Jasmine. 2010. "Self-Defense Forces, Warlords, or Criminal Gangs? Toward a New Conceptualization of Paramilitarism in Colombia." *Labour, Capital, and Society* 43 (2): 14–56.

Hylton, Forrest. 2006. *Evil Hour in Colombia*. London: Verso Press.

Hylton, Forrest, and Aaron Tauss. 2016. "La paz en Colombia: Una nueva estratégia de crecimiento." *Nova et Vetera* 25: 116–122.

Kalb, Don, and Maximiliano Mollona. 2017. *The World-Wide Mobilizations: For an Anthropology of Urban Insurrection*. New York: Berghahn.

López, Claudia, ed. 2010. *Y refundaron la patria: De cómo mafiosos y políticos reconfiguraron el Estado Colombiano*. Bogotá: Debate.

Mayer, Arno. 2000. *The Furies: Violence in the French and Russian Revolutions.* Princeton, NJ: Princeton University Press.

Miroff, Nick. 2016. "A Side Effect of Peace in Colombia? A Cocaine Boom in the US." *Washington Post,* May 8. www.washingtonpost.com.

Ramírez, Maria Clemencia. 2011. *Between the Guerrillas and the State: The Cocalero Movement, Citizenship, and Identity in the Colombian Amazon.* Durham, NC: Duke University Press.

Ramsey, Geoffrey. 2012. "Colombia Reassesses Extradition in Anti-Drug Fight." *Insight Crime.* Accessed July 5, 2019. http://www.insightcrime.org/news-analysis/colombia-weighs-importance-of-extradition-in-anti-drug-fight.

Richani, Nazih. 2012. "The Agrarian Rentier Political Economy: Land Concentration and Food Insecurity in Colombia." *Latin American Research Review* 4 7(2): 51–78.

Robin, Corey. 2018. *The Reactionary Mind: Conservatism from Edmund Burke to Sarah Palin.* New York: Oxford University Press.

Romero, Mauricio. 2003. *Paramilitaries y Autodefensas, 1982–2008.* Bogotá: IEPRI.

Romero, Mauricio. 2007. *Parapólitica: La ruta de la expansion paramilitary y los acuerdos politicos.* Bogotá: Corporación Arco Iris.

Tate, Winifred. 2007. *Counting the Dead: The Culture and Politics of Human Rights Activism in Colombia.* Berkeley: University of California Press.

Valencia, León. 2007. "Los caminos de la alianza entre los paramilitares y los politicos." In *Parapólitica: La ruta de la expansion paramilitary y los acuerdos politicos,* ed. Mauricio Romero, 13–43. Bogotá: Corporación Arco Iris.

Verdadabierta. 2017. "Las AUC fueron una alianza criminal de ejércitos privados," June 16. www.verdadabierta.org.

Zamosc, León. 1986. *The Agrarian Question and the Peasant Movement in Colombia: Struggles of the National Peasant Association, 1967–1981.* New York: Cambridge University Press.

PART TWO

Multiplicities of Anger

Frustrations, Failures, and Fractures

Brexit and "Politics as Usual" in the United Kingdom

In June 2016, the United Kingdom voted in a referendum on continuing membership in the European Union. To the surprise of many, the "Vote Leave" campaign triumphed, winning 52 percent of the popular vote and triggering a complex and contested process of disengagement from the European Union, intended to be completed in 2019. The politics of the referendum, the result, and its consequences have remained controversial issues. Here I take up some questions about the "Brexit" (British exit) vote's implications for "politics as usual" in the UK. Both the Leave and Remain campaigns cut across party lines in significant ways, even though the referendum itself was called by then prime minister David Cameron primarily as a tactic to settle disputes within the Conservative Party. The following two years have seen considerable political turbulence across the leading political parties, plunging several into leadership elections (the Conservatives, Liberal Democrats, and UK Independence Party [UKIP]). As Watkins (2016) has argued, Europe and the European Union have a much longer history of contention within political parties in the UK (with only the Liberals/Liberal Democrats being consistently committed to the European "mission"). At the same time, the referendum was credited with reengaging many of those detached from politics as usual, with a turnout of 72.2 percent of eligible voters, compared to results ranging from 59 percent to 66 percent in the four general elections since the turn of the century (2001, 2005, 2010, and 2015). The subsequent general election called by the new Conservative prime minister, Theresa May, in 2017, was intended to shore up her authority and increase the Conservative majority in Parliament but backfired rather badly, with a Labour Party revival, led by Jeremy Corbyn, raising the possibility of a break from austerity-defined politics and policies and involving an unusual mobilization of younger voters (Edgar 2017b).

Brexit can be seen variously as a matter of intraparty discipline, as a setting for individual political ambition (Boris Johnson, Michael Gove, Theresa May), as disrupting established party formations, and as a significant dislocation of established party affiliations. It has also become associated with a variety of governmental and constitutional troubles as attempts are made to turn the campaign slogan "Take back control"—into international and national settlements (see, inter alia, Clarke forthcoming a). An alternative approach to Brexit has been to treat it as part of a wider series of disturbance and dislocations. Brexit has been variously viewed as part of a revolt against neoliberalism (Piketty 2016), as part of a populist revolt (Judis 2016; Müller 2016), as the revenge of a dispossessed working class (see the discussion in Khan and Shaheen 2017), as part of the return of nationalism in the face of globalization or Europeanization (Delanty 2019), or as part of antiglobal rage, expressing popular disaffection from elite projects (e.g., Mishra 2017). While each of these views identifies particular dynamics of popular disaffection and makes them part of a wider set of changes, I argue that the temptations of "epochal thinking" (Williams 1977) ought to be resisted in favor of a more differentiating *conjunctural* analysis of Brexit (what Williams called "actual historical analysis"). In particular, I suggest that this means thinking carefully about how aspects of popular disaffection, nationalism, racism, and the political repertoire of populism are being combined—or *articulated*—in specific ways in particular places. This does not make questions of globalization, neoliberalism, or antimodernism irrelevant, but asks that we think about their uneven and contradictory combinations rather than treating them as simple "prime movers" whose effects can be found everywhere.

Articulating Frustrations: Brexit and the Conjuncture

A conjuncture can be understood as a configuration of time and space in which many tendencies, forces, temporalities, and contradictions are condensed (this is argued at greater length in Clarke 2010, 2018, and forthcoming b). So, rather than a single motivating cause or driving force, a conjuncture condenses multiplicities—of forces, antagonisms, contradictions, and possibilities. Together these may crystallize in a point of rupture in which lines of possibility and potential new settlements between social forces emerge. However, such resolutions of the underlying pressures do not necessarily occur. In their absence, a conjuncture may become a long drawn-out nonresolution of the tensions in play; or different attempted resolutions may be developed—and fail. It may be helpful to think of such configurations of time/space as simultaneously overdetermined and underdetermined. They are overdetermined in the Freudian/Althusserian sense of condensing multiple causes and dynamics into one moment; while they are underdetermined in the sense that the multiplicity of forces and dynamics means that there is no single, necessary, or guaranteed resolution of the situation.

Brexit can be seen as a distinct moment within a longer conjuncture (Clarke and Newman 2017). The successful "Vote Leave" campaign appeared to speak effectively for many of those frustrated by the status quo and the prevailing Europhile political-cultural "elite." It was, as Jeremy Harding observed, a moment of vigorous popular disaffection: "The big guns of the international liberal order were wheeled out to stop us going headlong for the Puerto Rican option: the IMF, the WTO, the OECD. Ten Nobel economists added to the din; Obama wagged a finger; Clinton too. Then Soros. In reply, a forest of fingers was stuck in the air" (Harding 2016; see also Taylor 2017).

Much has been made of Brexit, and similar populist eruptions, as giving voice to popular anger. However, it may be important to view anger not as a generic affective condition but as both conjuncturally specific and multiply motivated. So we might want to think about the diverse frustrations that were bundled together in the act of voting to leave rather than assuming their unity. I suggest that they ranged from a sense of economic abandonment (built upon deindustrialization and disinvestment) to cultural dislocation, expressed as the loss of "our way of life" and often linked to immigration. But there was also explicit political disaffection, reflecting deepening mistrust and cynicism about politics, politicians, and the "political classes" seen as detached from "ordinary people." This was focused on the two main parties, acting as the national handmaidens of neoliberalization (albeit with different repertoires). Finally, there were undoubtedly forms of nationalist rage, in which anti-immigration, anti-European, and postimperial sentiments were uneasily bundled together. Nevertheless, these multiple frustrations found a common point of expression and promise of redress in the Leave campaign's claim that people could "take back control."

Such diverse frustrations, however, point to the multiple, and potentially contradictory, dynamics that made up the conjuncture. The national character of the political conflict, and the revitalization of nationalism as a political discourse, marks the confluence of several dynamics, particularly the tendency toward economic globalization and the related but different dynamic of Europeanization (that has both advanced and contended aspects of corporate globalization). These two dynamics intersect with the current trajectories of migration from south to north, and, particularly salient for the English/British discourse, from the peripheries of the EU to the UK. Together, these tendencies have exposed the nation as a contestable site—a potent imaginary that articulates a distinctive history, a vulnerable and victimized present, and a fantasized future of potential greatness. That is to say, we might need to think of nationalism as taking multiple and conjuncturally specific forms, rather than being a generic condition (Kalb and Halmai 2011; see also Clarke 2018). Thinking about these diverse frustrations raises further questions about Brexit as a politics of articulation.

The Leave campaign found ways of speaking for some of those multiple frustrations as if they formed a coherent and consistent unity—summed up in the potent figure of "the People." Like similar movements elsewhere, the Leave campaign found populist tropes a vital device for political mobilization, with Nigel Farage of UKIP celebrating the referendum vote as the UK's "Independence Day" and claiming that: "We have broken free from a failing political union. We have managed, the little people, the ordinary people who have ignored all the threats that have come from big business and big politics and it has been a huge, amazing exercise in democracy" (Dunn 2016).

But this populist repertoire raises problems about how we understand the process by which "the people" come to voice. John Judis, for example, sees the recent populist explosion as giving voice to the concerns of ordinary people at odds with dominant politics. He suggests that populist movements arise in "times when people see the prevailing political norms—put forward, preserved, and defended by the leading segments in the country—as being at odds with their own hopes, fears, and concerns. The populists express these neglected concerns and frame them in a politics that pits the people against an intransigent elite" (2016, 17).

Judis's argument that "populists express these neglected concerns" misses the *work* of politics, especially the practice of articulation between what Antonio Gramsci called "fragments" of common sense and a would-be hegemonic political project. Populist projects—like others—involve the *selective* voicing of elements of common sense (and the silencing or denial of others) by way of narratives, propositions, claims, images, and promises that appear to represent a coherent program grounded in the "good sense" of ordinary people.

The Leave movement selectively addressed popular frustrations in a variety of registers. For instance, the sense of economic dislocation, concentrated in the former industrial heartlands, was attributed to a double dynamic. On the one hand, people were suffering the effects of the UK being inserted into the European economy, undermining the possibility of "British jobs for British workers." The figures of both the "jobs" (not enough investment "at home") and the "workers" (migrants displacing or undercutting the British) explicitly connected this sense of loss to the EU and the dominant theme of "excessive" migration. However, the economic decline was also represented as a result of a distant and uncaring political elite, who had little interest in the lives and needs of ordinary people.

The sense of cultural dislocation—the loss of "our way of life"—was most directly associated with migration, with attention particularly focused on recent migration from eastern Europe within the EU, but inextricably entangled with two other dynamics: first, the demonization of refugees and would-be refugees, particularly those fleeing war zones in the Global South, and second, the longstanding and unfinished business of Britain's postcolonial condition (Gilroy 2004). The entangling of anxieties about migration, race, and nation was exemplarily condensed in Nigel Farage's use of a photograph of a long line of Syrian refugees queuing at a border (not the UK's), captioned "Breaking Point" (see Media Mole 2016). There is a further element to the Leave articulation of this sense of cultural dislocation that points a finger at the liberal elite, guilty of cosmopolitanism, multiculturalism, feminism, and a metropolitan isolation from the lives of ordinary people and their good sense (traditional virtues and decency). The traditional way of life (and the structures of real and imagined privilege and social authority in which it was enmeshed) also needed to be rescued.

It is, then, possible to see how the Leave campaign was able to articulate feelings of political detachment and disaffection. It should be clear that contemporary populism did not invent or discover sentiments of political scepticism, cynicism, and disaffection among subordinate groups. Indeed, they have probably been in circulation since the expansion of mass suffrage, but the moment of Brexit offered both a vocabulary for naming the causes of such disaffection (the elite/Europe) and a device (the referendum) that made voicing such disaffection possible. It was the culmination of three decades of growing suspicion about politics, politicians, and political classes—about the political management of neoliberalism, the recurrently revealed forms of

corruption and collusion among politicians (expense scandals, etc.), and varieties of governmental and party incompetence. As Jeremy Gilbert (2015)
has argued, we reached a point where "disaffected consent" (a grudging willingness to buy into the promises of neoliberal growth and progress) had become exhausted—and the Leave campaign found ways of articulating some
forms of that disaffection. Other, equally disaffected, elements voted Remain
sceptically.

Finally, the Leave movement brought to the fore a simmering cluster of nationalist sentiments, with unevenly and uneasily anti-European, antimigrant,
and racist orientations. In doing so, it drew on a long history of nationalist
rage, given political and cultural life by a stream of right-wing groupings, including the National Front, British National Party, Britain First, and English
Defence League. In the last decade, UKIP made a pitch for combining this nationalism with a strong anti-EU populism and was a significant force in bringing about the referendum. The Leave movement argued (as had UKIP) that
to be nationalist and antimigration is not necessarily racist. While this might
be true in the abstract, the animosity mobilized during the campaign certainly
was racist—working on what Stuart Hall (2017) called the "fateful triangle" of
race, nation, and ethnicity, such that hostility to Polish migrants (not the right
"white") oscillated with anti-Muslim themes, into which flickered a longer
colonial imagery of brown and black "dangers." The rise of racist crimes and
discourse (along with parallel violence around gender and sexuality) following the referendum suggests that these articulations made possible significant
changes in public discourse and conduct.

"Failing and Flailing Forwards": The Paradoxes of Actually Existing Neoliberalism

As Don Robotham's essay (this volume) makes clear, one of the crucial dynamics of the present conjuncture is the continuing contradictory development of neoliberalization. Alongside its global dominance as the common
sense of the age, internalized by diverse national governments and international organizations, it is important to give attention to two other features:
first, its shape-shifting character achieved through waves of intellectual and
political innovation; second, its chameleonlike quality as it enters into alliances and partnerships with a range of political forms—from social democracy to dictatorship—as the means of establishing its rule in specific

national and transnational spaces. Both of these dynamics point to an underlying feature of neoliberalism: its propensity to fail. Its grand plans—and grand promises—have proven difficult to realize, while its progress has been constantly crisis-ridden, disaster-prone, and contradictory, with each crisis requiring new rationales and new political blocs to implement them (ranging, for example, from 1970s Friedmanite monetarism to the post-2008 demand for fiscal austerity).

Although neoliberalization has certainly liberated capital from many of its former "shackles," it has proved difficult to stabilize as a settled regime of accumulation. This can be seen in its recurring economic and environmental crises but is also visible in the social and political consequences of neoliberal failures: the creation of more crisis-ridden, divided, unequal, contradictory, and antagonistic social formations. One critical issue here involves the problems and paradoxes of attempting to politically and governmentally manage neoliberalization and its effects. Jamie Peck has insisted that we pay attention not just to the grandiose discourses of neoliberalism but also the "turgid reality of neoliberalism variously failing and flailing forwards" (2010, 7). This forms the site of the recurring political contradictions of neoliberalization: despite its nominal antistatism, it has reformed, restructured, and exploited state capacities in attempts to manage the project, to build and secure popular consent for the regime of accumulation, and to organize the field of social relations and practices in appropriate ways, accentuating individualization (and, I would argue, familialization) as the necessary social correlates of neoliberalization (remember that Margaret Thatcher's famous dictum "there is no such thing as society" had a conclusion: "there are only individual men and women and there are families"). Neoliberalism has also looked to political parties—and conventional interparty competition—to develop innovative ways of managing the regime and its attendant contradictions and crises (while certainly not being averse to being embodied in noncompetitive forms of political regimes). It is at this point we encounter the fraught struggles of national governments to manage both the project and its economic, social, and political effects. These national political formations have attempted to manage the tensions between an unstable regime of accumulation (and its fundamentally transnational logic) while securing what Bob Jessop (1990) calls its "societalization"— the social and political arrangements necessary to enable its reproduction. Peck's phrase—"failing and flailing *forwards*"—points to the way in each resulting crisis, neoliberalism's protagonists have recurrently insisted that only a better, bigger neoliberalizing reform program can resolve the problems caused by its failures.

This is one critical nexus for understanding the current political moment. Although popular detachment from formal representative politics is not new, the conditions for Brexit marked the exhaustion of popular consent, even in its limited, passive, or what Jeremy Gilbert (2015) called its "disaffected" forms. The accumulating contradictions of neoliberal rule—especially the dynamics of deindustrialization and uneven development, the growth of low/no wage jobs and the more general stalling of wages, and the increasingly decaying public infrastructure—have contributed to the growing sense of frustration and disaffection. As Allan Cochrane (2017) has argued, the important role of the EU in driving these dynamics of uneven development was not forgotten by those voting Leave. Nonetheless, these accumulating antagonisms resulting from the recurring reinvention of neoliberalization were not the only forces. They are tied to other transnational/national dynamics with different temporalities and trajectories, most obviously the shifting dynamics of migration. The Migrant has been the focus of continuing postcolonial anxiety in the UK since the postwar generations arrived in the "mother country" from the Empire. This has been overlaid by recurring panics about the nation's others (shifting eventually from lawless African Caribbean youth to the threat of "radicalized" Muslims after 9/11 (Hall et al. 1978; Tyrer 2013), and it has mutated as other migrations took shape, particularly those from eastern Europe (after EU enlargement) and from the Global South after Western interventions into Iraq, Syria, Afghanistan, and more. The Migrant came to be represented in a double figure: on the one hand, the Migrant condensed many trajectories and embodiments (colonial subject, Romanian laborer, or Syrian asylum seeker), but all racialized and all projected as a threat to "our way of life." On the other hand, the Migrant was inseparably connected to the question of the EU and its founding principle of the free movement of labor, such that the apparent solution to the "problem of immigration" was to break with the EU and "take back control of our borders" (enabling in the process a last gesture of colonial disdain to the Republic of Ireland (see O'Toole 2018, for example).

In the UK context, then, the crises and contradictions of neoliberalization cannot be understood separately from the crises and contradictions of the postcolonial condition. These dynamics play out in a social landscape dominated by the combination of economic deindustrialization, wage stagnation, and the seemingly endless re/deconstruction of the state, not least the welfare state and the associated public realm. Despite rhetorical (and highly conditional) political commitments to "fairness," inequalities have deepened, insecurities have grown, and the promises of neoliberal "progress" have failed to materialize for growing numbers of the population. The politics and policies of "austerity" that followed the financial crisis (and the remarkable disbursing of public funds that followed to "save the system from itself") deepened these tendencies and the increasing detachment of many from conventional party politics (some of which was manifested in growing support for the populist politics of UKIP (see Ford and Goodwin 2014). These complex dynamics point to the significance of a conjunctural approach. Rather than tracing a singular line of descent from a prime mover (neoliberalization, globalization, or even neoliberal globalization) as a route to explaining local phenomena, conjunctural analysis insists on the way in which the concrete instance is produced by many determinations—different dynamics with different temporalities and trajectories that are condensed into the particular place and time. But it also means paying attention to the multiple social forces that are in play in this moment of space-time.

Building a Bloc? Social Fractures and the Moment of Brexit

Thinking about Brexit as a political moment poses significant questions about how we understand social forces and their mobilization/demobilization as political forces. For many commentators, Brexit was a moment in which the Leave campaign successfully spoke to, and for, disenchanted working class voters. The referendum result and its aftermath revealed a profoundly divided and contradictory "nation." This division has been mapped into some profoundly simplifying versions of political demography—of place, age, and, perhaps most strikingly, class. It might be more accurate to say that what has been evoked is a very British imagery of class and culture, an imagery both captured and contested in these comments by a trade union official in Sheffield:

> I am a branch officer of Unite the Union South Yorkshire Community branch who campaigned, as did my Union, for remain. As I type I am sitting on the fault line of the brexit debate. To the west lies the affluent suburbs of Sheffield where there has been much howling and gnashing about losing the vote. To the east lies the working class parts of the city

and the wider de-industrialised county of South Yorkshire which voted, with much anger, to leave. The two sides are glaring at each other through the fractures of English society, or so we are told. On one side the educated, liberal progressives, on the other the people who do not know any better; at least according to the likes of the guardian. This is dangerous myth. Most of our members live precarious lives, some are on the dole, some work in fast food joints, some at local universities. You would be hard pushed to tell the difference between the budding academic and the burger flipper, sometimes they are the same person. (James 2016)

This helpfully problematizes some assumptions about the "class divide" around Brexit (see also Edgar 2016; Khan and Shaheen 2017; Taylor 2017). It indicates above all the need for a historically dynamic understanding of class formation. The "rediscovery of class" in the moment of Brexit has too readily evoked an older image of the working class as though it—a male, factory-centered, industrial working class—was the universal form that the proletariat takes. However, the social and economic impacts of neoliberalization on class formation in the UK took place at the intersection of at least four dynamics. One is the process of regional and local uneven development, itself inextricably interwoven with processes of deindustrialization, decollectivization, and desocialization. The combination of these processes produced—and distributed— both joblessness and forms of precarity. The result is a highly fragmented working class in which collective identity, organization, and action have all become increasingly problematic.

The simplifying class/culture imagery of Brexit conceals a different problem—this time around the place of the middle classes. The assumption is that the middle classes were characterized by a cosmopolitan liberalism that prompted them to vote Remain. This ignores a substantial population of what might be called the "traditional" middle classes (an older petit bourgeoisie, in occupational, generational, and cultural terms). Indeed, Danny Dorling (2016) claims that some 59 percent of the middle class overall voted to quit the EU, compared to 24 percent of the working class. Brexit was strongly supported by this traditional(ist) middle class, at home in the suburbs and shires, which remained committedly noncosmopolitan. There it was also apparently fueled by immigration anxiety (despite such spaces typically not being occupied by many migrants). Attention to this particular class formation underscores the significance of the age/generation division around Brexit (those older than forty-five being much more likely to vote Leave). This is an aging population that feels "loss" in a variety of economic, social, and cultural registers and provided a potent audience for the Brexit version of the "national-popular." Loss proved to be a critical "structure of feeling" for the Brexit mobilization (Clarke, 2019).

The "rediscovery" of class via Brexit has also drawn on the problematic imagery of the "white working class"—a figure that has occupied a significant place in recent British academic, popular cultural, and political discourse (e.g., Collins 2004; Dench, Gavron, and Young 2006; Sveinsson 2009). Apparently abandoned by the Labour Party, unloved by a cosmopolitan middle class, and displaced from its indigenous rights by migrants, these representations of a white working class return us to troubling controversies about the relationships between race, place, and culture—and politics. These representations tend to silence other conceptions of class formation (see Bhambra 2017; Khan and Shaheen 2017). They exclude migrants and ethnic minority others, young graduate unemployed, carers, and volunteer workers who are, somehow, not *imaginable* as part of the working class. In the process, proponents of the "white working class" thesis articulate an understanding of antagonisms between class and its others (especially its racialized others), who are represented instead in politically diminutive terms as "communities," "minorities," or "identities" (rather than the "black working class," for example). This differentiation both reproduces—and contributes to—understandings of the relationship between place, race, and nation that were central to the Brexit campaign (there are interesting parallels with some of the debates about the racialization of politics in the United States, see the essays by Sophie Bjork-James and Jeff Maskovsky in this volume).

These issues point to a central question for conjunctural analysis: how are social groups mobilized as political forces? Answering the question demands two sorts of analysis—one that is attentive to the complex constitution of social groups (rather than broad brush and reductive characterizations of social classes) the other requires attention to the discourses, representations, and imaginaries through which people are invited to see themselves as political actors and through which they become mobilized (or demobilized). The Brexit campaign involved a skillful assemblage of populist, nationalist, antimigrant, and anti-European elements, linked by threads of xenophobia and racism, that promised to restore the nation—putting the "Great" back into "Great Britain." Leave voters were consistently summoned to see themselves as part of a nation, composed of "ordinary, decent people" who had been ignored, abandoned, and abused by the cosmopolitan elite, and whose goodwill had been exploited by migrants whose ability to enjoy the fruits of the United Kingdom (including picking them, as seasonal laborers) was being enabled by the EU's founding principle of the freedom of movement. As I have already argued, a critical element in this mobilization was the possibility of expressing frustration, anger, and rage. The referendum—a political form different from conventional local, national, and European election systems and their associated party affiliations—offered a way of saying no. Lilith Mahmud's essay (this volume) also points to the instability of the referendum as a political device, involving what Gerard Delanty has described as the "illusion of a constitutive moment" (2019, 102–104).

This points to the unstable mix of people and politics that was mobilized by the Vote Leave campaign, assembled under the leadership of some exceptionally idiosyncratic embodiments of capital (see Arron Banks, for example), populist leaders denied a leadership role (Nigel Farage of UKIP), and a strange cast of Conservative Party chancers (notably Boris Johnson and Michael Gove) who saw personal and political opportunities in the politics of the referendum. Around them was assembled a very contingent coalition of the frustrated, angry, and outraged. This coalition cut across classes in a strange way, nicely expressed in Cochrane's description of the "strange alliance" between the twin nostalgias emerging from the postimperial home counties and the postindustrial heartlands (2017). One of the strange effects of the Brexit moment is that most attention and analysis has been focused on the Brexiters. This is not the place to remedy that situation but it is important to note that those who voted Remain also formed a complex and contingent coalition—an equally temporary alliance built out of diverse social forces: leading fractions of industrial and especially financial capital; much of the broadsheet press, as opposed to most of the tabloids who supported Leave; core sections of most of the political parties; and the public sector–based and more socially liberal fractions of the middle classes and some sections of the working class. The Remain voter tended to be younger than the Leaver and the younger fractions were predominantly female: 80 percent of the Remain voters between 18–24 were female (Statista, n.d.). The Remain vote was also built from multiple motivations, from enthusiastic endorsement of the EU as marketplace to those inclined to more cosmopolitan "European" dispositions or attached to the increasingly residualized traces of the social dimension of the EU. It is perhaps most important to avoid a simplifying distinction that treats Brexit as the embodiment of visceral emotion (a politics of rage) and the Remain campaign as the continuation of normal (i.e., rational, considered, or even calculating) politics. On the contrary, the Remain campaign, dubbed "Project Fear" by its opponents, sought to evoke anxiety and anger about the risks of leaving the EU (and marshalled heavy weaponry to authorize such anxiety). The diverse attachments to Europe and the EU that motivated Remain votes were often, and explicitly, weighed against the problems of the actually existing EU (especially after the Greek crisis) and of entering into the unholy alliance that voting Remain involved. One recurring trope of the referendum campaign appeared in jokes about the horror of voting Remain with Conservative demons such as David Cameron and George Osborne; a prospect only made bearable by looking at whom one would be bundled with in voting Leave (Michael Gove, Boris Johnson, and Nigel Farage, in particular). And in the aftermath of the referendum, anxieties, anger, and despair have all been part of what Ben Anderson (2015) calls the "affective atmospheres" of current British politics (see Knight 2017).

In short, I suggest that conjunctural analysis demands attention to how blocs and coalitions are put together, not least the political practices through which groups of people come to be political actors (or not). It offers a way of avoiding the temptation to mistake these moments as epochal—as marking a structural change (from politics as usual to an era of populism or an age of rage).

Conclusion: Brexit and Politics as Usual?

Did the Brexit vote mark a permanent realignment of UK politics? Did it reconfigure political affiliations and attachments? Did it rework the internal elements of the UK, where both Scotland and Northern Ireland had majorities for Remain? The resurgence of British/English nationalism, a degradation of public culture (particularly around race/ethnicity and other "minority" identities), a socially conservative conception of a nation of "ordinary decent people," and a politically conservative inheritance of the Leave vote (as the then prime minister Theresa May insisted that "Brexit means Brexit") suggested that the referendum had indeed dramatically reshaped British politics. It could also be seen as part of a much wider dynamic toward a renewed right-wing nationalist and authoritarian populism in Europe and beyond:

Across the west, the postwar social democratic alliance between a left-behind working class and middle-class social liberals broke down. From Warsaw to Wisconsin, socially conservative anti-immigration populists devised interventionist economic policies, so as not to put off working class voters they wanted to attract. A new fault line was scored, pitting what was defined as a liberal cosmopolitan elite against the economic interests and conservative instincts of the majority. Values trumped (or Trumped) economics. The best identifier of *Homo Brexitus* was not class or income or age but a positive attitude to the death penalty. Being for public whipping of criminals was a pretty good indicator too.

In Britain and America, mainstream parties followed in the populist wake. The Republicans picked Trump, and the Conservatives anointed as prime minister a distinctly illiberal home secretary, with a dubious record on gay rights and a fuzzily interventionist economic programme, whose line on cosmopolitan liberalism was that a citizen of the world is a "citizen of nowhere." (Edgar 2017b)

But, as Edgar goes on to argue, in the UK context such pessimistic projections of a new political order were soon challenged when the incoming Conservative prime minister, Theresa May, called a general election in June 2017 with the ambition of establishing a substantially increased parliamentary majority. Instead, her majority shrank and the resulting Conservative government was sustained only by an expensive and complicated arrangement with the Democratic Unionist Party of Northern Ireland. Equally striking was the way that the votes for parties outside the "big two" (Conservative and Labour) eroded, returning us to a much older binary version of "politics as usual." However, this version differed in that the Labour Party was led by an aging left winger (Jeremy Corbyn) who had been the subject of leadership challenges and intraparty plotting since he took up the leadership in 2015. Denounced by the conventional media as the biggest of "no hopers," Corbyn led Labour on an anti-austerity, propublic services manifesto and successfully mobilized younger people to vote, and to vote Labour. The election thus saw a further reconfiguring of the political landscape, turning some of the frustrations mobilized in Brexit into an anti-austerity politics that challenged both the austerity narratives that had dominated after the financial crisis and the longer standing promarket or neoliberal consensus that had prevailed since the 1980s. David Edgar has developed the account from which the above quotation was taken into a larger argument about the possibilities of rebuilding progressive alliances across classes and across generations to challenge the declining appeal of the regressive bloc centered on the Conservative Party (Edgar 2017a). Meanwhile, Andrew Gamble (2019) has pointed to the difficult calculations facing all the major parties (and some smaller ones) in the unsettled conditions following Brexit, noting the particular paradoxical calculation facing Labour: that while two-thirds of Labour voters voted Remain, two-thirds of Labour-held parliamentary seats voted Leave.

For a time, the social and political fractures emerging from the UK's neoliberalization (and Conservative austerity) were given a terrible focus by the fire at Grenfell Tower in west London, which killed seventy-one people and has been seen as embodying the increasingly divided society generated by neoliberal politics and policies. The fire came to symbolize the degradation of the public realm, the marginalization of social housing tenants, and the increasing gap between rich and poor—in the country at large, but especially in the specific local authority, the borough of Kensington and Chelsea (e.g., Wismayer 2017). Here, too, anger and frustration, entangled with grief, came to voice and were articulated in challenges to the pro-austerity and antisocial policies prevailing at local and national levels. Even so, at the time of writing (March 2019), fragile Conservative rule continues, struggling toward a global "free trade" version of Brexit. The end of politics as usual—at least the managerial politics of the last thirty years—has established new lines of fracture and of possibility: how they will turn out is, as usual, the puzzle at the heart of conjunctural analysis.

References

Anderson, Ben. 2015. "Neoliberal Affects." *Progress in Human Geography* 30: 1–20.

Bhambra, Gurminder K. 2017. "Brexit, Trump, and 'Methodological Whiteness': On the Misrecognition of Race and Class." *British Journal of Sociology* 68 (S1): S214–S232.

Clarke, John. 2010. "Of Crises and Conjunctures: The Problem of the Present." *Journal of Communication Inquiry* 34 (4): 337–354.

Clarke, John. 2018. "Finding Place in the Conjuncture: A Dialogue with Doreen." In *Doreen Massey—Critical Dialogues*, ed. Marion Werner et al., 201–213. London: Agenda Publishing.

Clarke, John. 2019. "A Sense of Loss? Unsettled Attachments in the Current Conjuncture." *New Formations*, 96–97 (This Conjuncture): 132–146.

Clarke, John. Forthcoming a. "Re-imagining Scale, Space, and Sovereignty: The United Kingdom and "Brexit." In *Unsettled States, Movements in Flux, Migrants out of Place: The Tumultuous Politics of Scale,* ed. D. Nonini and I. Susser. New York: Routledge.

Clarke, John. Forthcoming b."Looking for the Conjuncture: Condensations of Time and Space. In *Cultural Studies/Etudes Culturelles: Au-delà des Politiques des Identités,* ed. E. Maigret and L. Martin. Lyon: Les Presses Universitaires de Lyon avec le Centre de Cerisy.

Clarke, John, and Janet Newman. 2017. "People in This Country Have Had Enough of Experts": Brexit and the Paradoxes of Populism. *Critical Policy Studies* 11 (1): 101–116.

Cochrane, Allan. 2017. "From Brexit to the Break-up of Britain." Paper presented to the *Audit UK* Workshop, Centre for British Studies, Humboldt University, Berlin, September 27–29.

Collins, Michael. 2004. *The Likes of Us: A Biography of the White Working Class.* Cambridge: Granta.

Delanty, Gerard. 2019. "What Does Self-determination Mean Today? The Resurgence of Nationalism and European Integration in Question." *Global Discourse* 9 (1): 93–107.

Dench, Geoff, Kate Gavron, and Michael Young. 2006. *The New East End—Kinship, Race and Conflict.* London: Profile Books.

Dorling, Danny. 2016. "Brexit: The Decision of a Divided Country." Accessed August 2, 2019. http://www.dannydorling.org/?p=5568.

Dunn, James. 2016. "Nigel Farage Calls for a New Bank Holiday to Mark UK's 'Independence Day' as His Life's Work Comes to Fruition as the Country Votes for Brexit." *Daily Mail.* Accessed August 2, 2019. http://www.dailymail.co.uk/news/article-3657627/What-Nigel-Farage-s-life-s-work-comes-fruition-stunning-Brexit-vote-lauds-new-dawn-Britain-outside-EU.html#ixzz4Cng17Zj9.

Edgar, David. 2016. "Labour Can Fight for Working People without Dumping Progressive Ideals." *The Guardian,* August 4. Accessed August 2, 2019. https://www.theguardian.com/commentisfree/2016/aug/04/labour-fight-for-working-people-progressive-ideas.

Edgar, David. 2017a. *Cosmopolitans, Communitarians and the New Fault-Line: How to Renew The Labour Alliance.* London: Compass Think Piece #87. https://www.compassonline.org.uk/wp-content/uploads/2017/09/D.E-Thinkpiece.pdf.

Edgar, David. 2017b. "We Thought Homo Brexitus Was the Future, but He Isn't Winning Anymore." *The Guardian,* June 28. Accessed August 2, 2019. https://www.theguardian.com/commentisfree/2017/jun/28/postwar-progressive-alliance-labour-corbynomics.

Ford, Robert, and Matthew Goodwin. 2014. *Revolt on the Right: Explaining Support for the Radical Right in Britain.* London: Routledge.

Gamble, Andrew. 2019. "The Realignment of British Politics in the Wake of Brexit." *The Political Quarterly.* Accessed August 2, 2019. https://onlinelibrary.wiley.com /doi/full/10.1111/1467-923X.12643.

Gilbert, Jeremy. 2015. "Disaffected Consent: That Post-Democratic Feeling." *Soundings: A Journal of Politics and Culture* 60: 29–41.

Gilroy, Paul. 2004. *Postcolonial Melancholia.* New York: Columbia University Press.

Hall, Stuart. 2017. *The Fateful Triangle: Race, Ethnicity, Nation.* Edited by Kobena Mercer. Cambridge, MA: Harvard University Press.

Hall, Stuart, Chas Critcher, Tony Jefferson, John Clarke, and Brian Roberts. 1978. *Policing the Crisis: Mugging, the State, and Law and Order.* Basingstoke: Macmillan (2nd ed., 2013).

Harding, Jeremy. 2016. "Contribution to "Where Are We Now? Responses to the Referendum." *London Review of Books* 38 (4): 12.

James, Mark. 2016. "Response to a Working Class Brexit." *Commentary on Working-Class Culture, Education, and Politics.* Accessed August 2, 2019. https://working classstudies.wordpress.com/2016/06/27/a-working-class-brexit/.

Jessop, Bob. 1990. *State Theory: Putting the Capitalist State in Its Place.* Cambridge: Polity Press.

Judis, John B. 2016. *The Populist Explosion: How the Great Recession Transformed American and European Politics.* New York: Columbia Global Reports.

Kalb, Don, and Gabor Halmai, eds. 2011. *Headlines of Nation, Subtexts of Class: Working Class Populism and the Return of the Repressed in Neoliberal Europe.* New York: Berghahn.

Khan, Omar, and Faiza Shaheen. 2017. *Minority Report: Race and Class in Post-Brexit Britain.* London: Runnymede Trust. Accessed August 2, 2019. http://www .runnymedetrust.org/uploads/publications/pdfs/Race%20and%20Class%20 Post-Brexit%20Perspectives%20report%20v5.pdf.

Knight, Daniel. 2017. "Anxiety and Cosmopolitan Futures: Brexit and Scotland." *American Ethnologist.* Accessed August 2, 2019. http://onlinelibrary.wiley.com /doi/10.1111/amet.12474/full.

Media Mole. 2016. "Nigel Farage's Anti-EU Poster Depicting Migrants Resembles Nazi Propaganda. " *NewStatesmanAmerica.* Accessed July 5, 2019. https:// www.newstatesman.com/2016/06/nigel-farage-s-anti-eu-poster-depicting -migrants-resembles-nazi-propaganda.

Mishra, Pankaj. 2017. *The Age of Anger: A History of the Present.* London: Penguin Books.

Müller, Jan-Werner. 2016. *What Is Populism?* Philadelphia: University of Pennsylvania Press.

O'Toole, Fintan. 2018. "A 'Precious Union'? The Brexiters Don't Care about Northern Ireland." *The Guardian*, October 19. Accessed August 2, 2019. https://www.theguardian.com/commentisfree/2018/oct/19/brexiters-theresa-may-northern-ireland.

Peck, Jamie. 2010. *Constructions of Neoliberal Reason*. Oxford: Oxford University Press.

Piketty, Thomas. 2016. "Reconstructing Europe after Brexit." *M Blogs* (Le Monde). Accessed August 2, 2019. http://piketty.blog.lemonde.fr/2016/06/30/reconstructing-europe-after-brexit/.

Sveinsson, Kjartan, ed. 2009. *Who Cares about the White Working Class*? London: Runnymede Trust.

Statista. N.d. Distribution of EU Referendum Votes in the United Kingdom (UK) in 2016, by Age Group and Gender. Accessed August 2, 2019. https://www.statista.com/statistics/567922/distribution-of-eu-referendum-votes-by-age-and-gender-uk/.

Taylor, J. D. 2017. "The Working Class Revolts." *New Statesman*, February 7. Accessed August 2, 2019. http://www.newstatesman.com/politics/uk/2017/02/working-class-revolts.

Tyrer, David. 2013. *The Politics of Islamophobia: Race, Power and Fantasy*. London: Pluto Press.

Watkins, Susan. 2016. "Editorial: Casting Off?" *New Left Review* 100: 5–31.

Williams, Raymond. 1977. *Marxism and Literature*. Oxford: Oxford University Press.

Wismayer, Henry. 2017. "Grenfell Was No Accident" *Citylab*, August 17. Accessed August 2, 2019. https://www.citylab.com/equity/2017/08/grenfell-was-no-ordinary-accident/536907/.

Postsocialist Populisms?

In the contemporary wave of angry politics shaking the globe, eastern Europe could be seen as the epicenter. While the countries involved may be small, the number of them is noteworthy. From Lithuania and Poland, across Slovakia and the Czech Republic, through Hungary, and down to Bulgaria, the region has seen one government after another come under the political sway of insurgent politicians and new parties capitalizing on (and some would say fomenting) a groundswell of popular discontent. While varied in character, timing, and specific policies, all have been designated as "populist" by observers and commentators, as well as by some politicians themselves. This has inspired journals dedicated to research on the region to devote special issues or sections to the rise of populism.[1] We want to trouble this label. In contemporary usage the term *populist* is almost always ascribed negatively. This not only delegitimizes the objectionable programs currently pursued by many so-called populist politicians (to wit, ethnonationalism and authoritarianism), but also diminishes the legitimacy of the motives and demands driving popular support for them and their programs, especially class-based agendas.[2] The label thus operates much like the notion of nostalgia in devaluing and dismissing what it purports to represent (Creed 2010). Indeed, the label of populism may say more about those deploying it than those described as such (D'Eramo 2013).

According to prevailing definitions, populism is a rhetorical technique used by politicians to distinguish a corrupt elite from a virtuous people. Many acknowledge that, as such, populism can be employed across the political spectrum. However, the recent and wholesale embrace of the technique by nationalist and authoritarian parties and politicians, and their relative success with it, has led to a conflation, whereby in many minds populism is assumed to be essentially nationalistic and authoritarian, as well as right wing. Particularly disturbing is the way that widespread contemporary uses of the term have the tendency to reduce all popular/elite binaries (contrasts) to rhetorical constructions, conspiracy, or manipulation. They also tend to cast populism (whether left or right) as "radical," in contrast to a "center," reinforcing the legitimacy of the latter and constraining, if not disqualifying, political debate.[3] Finally, current uses can obscure the specificities of the historical legacies of the terms "the people," "populist/popular," and of popular struggle itself. Our agenda here is to use two cases we know to flesh out the diversity of the application of the populist label and to provide an appreciation for why intelligent citizens might find the rather strident and extreme parties now in power palatable. We seek to look beyond the label of populism to examine what is happening and why, particularly in regard to the supposed role of the people (the demos) in postsocialist liberal democracy and the seeming equation of popular with accusations of populism in the political sphere. We argue that we must approach these questions with a sensitivity to historical and geographical processes and class formation. While we see what is happening in this region as part of a global trend, we focus on the specificities of this postsocialist and semiperipheral region.

Despite the introduction of representative democracy, the restructuring of the economies of former state socialist societies in the age of neoliberalization "turned out to be a nightmare for the overwhelming majority of people in the region" (Fabry 2015). As existing skills and infrastructure were made obsolete, and enterprises were transformed under the direction of (financial) transnational capital, class and regional inequalities opened and deepened. Large proportions of the industrial and agricultural sectors of the socialist economy simply crumbled and mass unemployment ensued (Fabry 2015). At the same time the population faced the loss of the social safety net and benefits that had been central to their well-being and their understanding of democracy. Disparities unimaginable in the socialist period came to mark society, while the supposed democracy that would contrast this period from that of party rule remained elusive.

Communist successor parties, now socialist in name and character, eventually emerged as strong contenders in the new system of electoral democracy across the region. Like other parties, when socialists came to power they too became overseers of the privatization process and advanced the neoliberal project. This was accompanied by "political capitalism" in which many former communist elites or late socialist technocrats were able to acquire wealth and power through the levers of privatization (King 2001). As privatization continued, these societies had less control over their assets (Böröcz 2016) and were forced to adjust their social commitments, often at the direction of foreign debt holders, the International Monetary Fund (IMF), or the World Bank. Membership in the European Union added to the list of overseers demanding that aspiring states limit deficit spending and indebtedness.

Disciples of liberalism would contest this summary with an equally long list of positive developments in the region since 1989. Without denying those achievements, we believe the trajectory we outline better explains the political developments currently shaking the region. We proceed with a brief description of these political events in two cases we know best, then turn to a collection of additional factors that we think help us make sense of these developments. With that in mind, we return to implicate antipopulism in obscuring and delegitimizing reasonable sources of popular discontent.

The Emergence of Antisystemic Politics in Bulgaria and Hungary

For a full decade after the collapse of communist rule in Bulgaria, the socialist successor to the Communist Party and a center-right coalition, known as the Union of Democratic Forces (UDF), oscillated in power, while the Turkish minority party, the Movement for Rights and Freedom (MRF), played spoiler (first allying with the Democrats, then later with the Socialists). Neither party managed to redress the devastation caused by the collapse of the socialist system, leaving the average Bulgarian disenchanted and frustrated. The first person to take advantage of this was the last tsar of Bulgaria, in exile since 1946. Just two months before the election of 2001 he formed the National Movement for Simeon the Second, and with virtually no party members, won a solid victory, receiving nearly 43 percent of the vote. His administration presented a government of experts to the right of the preceding UDF government. While he managed to stay in power for a full term, his party dropped to only 20 percent of the vote in the 2005 election.

The Socialists won again with 31 percent, but this did not restart the former oscillation with the UDF. Instead, the next election saw the ascent of Boyko Borisov and his party, Citizens for the European Development of Bulgaria (the Bulgarian acronym is GERB, which means coat of arms in Bulgarian). GERB received nearly 40 percent of the vote in 2009. Borisov was a former bodyguard of deposed communist leader Todor Zhivkov. He later served as secretary of the Bulgarian Ministry of Interior under Simeon the Second and then as mayor of Sofia. Borisov seized upon the fight against organized crime and corruption and superimposed it on all issues, including his characterization of parliamentarians as liars and losers. His party is ostensibly a center-right formation, but his government shows a personalization of politics increasingly centered on his personality and strongman image. Decisions appear to be made by him personally, with little regard for his Council of Ministers. He uses a combative vocabulary with dichotomous images of political opponents who need to be destroyed, especially the Socialists.

Borisov is now in his third term as prime minister, this time in coalition with the United Patriots (UP), an alliance of three nationalist parties, including the notorious Ataka. Ataka leader Volen Siderov rails against Roma crime, Turkification, and the theft of national resources by the corrupt political establishment, but advocates a leftist economic platform (Ganev 2017). The GERB and UP coalition are also supported by yet another newcomer, Trump-like businessman Veslin Mareshki, "who preaches patriotism, strict immigration controls, friendlier relations with Moscow, and, above all, the need to 'sweep away the garbage' of a corrupt political establishment" (Lyman 2017: A9). His party, Volya (Will), got 4.15 percent of the vote and twelve seats in Parliament. Together, GERB, the UP, and Volya make up 56 percent of the current Bulgarian Parliament, and the old liberal Democrats (UDF) are not even represented.

In 2006 anger erupted onto the streets of Hungary, triggered by the release of a recording in which Prime Minister Ferenc Gyurcsany (of the Hungarian Socialist Party—MSZP) admits lying about the state of the economy to get reelected. MSZP's 2006 campaign had promised "reform without austerity," but, once reelected, the party introduced radical austerity measures to stay within the boundaries of the Maastricht criteria (Fabry 2015). In return for an IMF (World Bank and EU) emergency loan in 2008, MSZP enacted public-sector cuts and other measures aimed at reducing the deficit. Fidesz, a liberal youth party in the early postsocialist era that morphed into a right-wing national conservative party, then in the opposition, countered with a wildly successful anti-austerity referendum.

The 2010 elections lodged Fidesz and its front man Viktor Orbán (in solid coalition with the Christian Democratic People's Party—KDNP) in power with a two-thirds majority and saw the far-right Jobbik party (Movement for a Better/Righter Hungary) enter Parliament. The most consistent warden of neoliberal dependent development since 1989 (by virtue of its number of terms in power), MSZP was now marked as an arrogant and elitist agent of neoliberal capital and liberal/antinational values along with foreign investors, funders of "civil society," and Brussels. By 2013, MSZP's prior coalition partner, the Alliance of Social Democrats (SZDSZ), had dissolved completely. The liberal left was in shambles.

As the global economic crisis was taking its long toll, poverty, homelessness, and unemployment spiraled upward. In the countryside, the welfare system and liberal projects aimed at helping minorities were seen by struggling "post-peasants" as favoring the "work shy," that is, Roma (Szombati 2018). Jobbik organized rallies (while its paramilitary arm, the Hungarian Guard, organized patrols) in depressed regions where ethnic tensions were growing, effectively suturing local experiences into a national rhetoric around "Gypsy crime" (Szombati 2018).

In 2011, the Fidesz government unilaterally rewrote the constitution, and in 2014, Orbán announced his pursuit of an illiberal state. State "capture" (Martin 2017) has funneled state funds (much of it from the EU) to loyalist oligarchs via multiple paths, paralleling Orbán's goal of replacing the "foreign-minded" bourgeoisie with a "national one."[4] The party's reelection is nearly assured by far-reaching changes to electoral law and a dual citizenship law passed in 2010 granting voting rights to "over-the-border Hungarians," which has secured new Fidesz supporters.[5]

With theatrical flair, Fidesz seems to upset neoliberal rules, but its class politics are not much different. The government's economic and monetary policies have lessened external vulnerability but are very friendly to German car companies, for example, at the expense of Hungarian workers (Koltai 2018). The government intervened in 2011 to aid households with mortgages in foreign currencies but targeted the most solvent households, aiding only 10 percent of the third of Hungarian households that had taken out these mortgages between 2005 and 2008. The government paid back the 2008 IMF loan early (in 2012), but this symbolic defiance of dependency came with less than transparent agreements with other lenders.

Fidesz's 2014 incumbent victory came despite assault on labor protections, shaming of the poor, criminalization of homelessness, and attacks on civil society and the media. The party offered a more moderate approach to Jobbik's "Gypsy crime," aided by an extended workfare regime (Hann 2016), while it took advantage of the "migrant crisis" (unfolding in 2015) to solidify an antiforeigner position. Jobbik made attempts to move to the center, dropping anti-Semitic language and courting Jewish leaders. The April 2018 elections awarded Fidesz a supermajority and confirmed Jobbik as the second largest party in Parliament.[6]

Clearly, Hungary and Bulgaria do not present identical scenarios. Ethnonationalism has held some purchase in electoral politics in Hungary since the early years of the transition, but it was not a notable factor in postsocialist Bulgarian politics until 2005. Orbán traffics more explicitly in the discourse of national protection against foreign-minded and foreign-bodied threats, whereas Borisov relies more on the rhetoric of corruption and crime, although the latter carries a resounding anti-Roma subtext. Borisov is generally considered a supporter of the EU, while Orbán is often described as a Euroskeptic. While both GERB and Fidesz have been affiliates of the EU's European People's Party, Fidesz's membership was suspended in March 2019. Borisov has been forced to resign twice as prime minster and returned each time with a different slate of coalition partners, whereas Fidesz's 2010 supermajority in Parliament began an unbroken period of single-party dominance. There are also clear authoritarian tendencies evident in the GERB government, most notably in the campaign and election processes that have gotten it reelected twice, but Borisov has not consolidated the extent of support or exerted the degree of control that Orbán has.

Both traffic, however, in the binary opposition between a virtuous people and a corrupt elite, and they seem to share a comparable, and apparently compatible, political style and character.[7] Rather than accounting for the obvious differences, we use the broader similarities as a provocation to think about what might account for parallels in two significantly different historical contexts, with the expectation that such factors may operate elsewhere in the region. We look at the historical and contemporary factors that help us understand why Fidesz's and GERB's appeal to the people resonates at the current conjuncture. By recovering the different meanings of "the people" and "nation," and different mobilizations around them, we not only show how resonance can be built but also why using the term *populism* in the way it is being used (or perhaps at all) may get in the way of understanding what is happening.

Understanding the Political Choices of the Demos

The first factor we need to attend to is the history of appeals to "the people," and their relationship to popular mobilizations in this region. The terms in

Bulgarian and Hungarian are *narod* and *nép*, respectively. Nancy Ries refers to narod, shared across most Slavic languages, as "the Key 'Key Word'" (1997, 27). As Raymond Williams's (1976) canonical text suggests, key words are usually riddled with multiple historical meanings that sometimes intertwine in present usage. In Slavic languages narod has many meanings, from simply the people in a place, to the citizens of a country, to an ethnic group or nation, to the peasantry/folk or working people generally. It is the same for the Hungarian cognate nép, as it is for the German *volk* and Italian *popolo*. Some of these meanings have been more ascendant in different eras.

The agrarian movement starting in 1899 was constitutive in modern Bulgarian history. The Bulgarian Agrarian People's Union, which developed into a political party in 1901, became the strongest agrarian party in the region and under the leadership of Alexander Stamboliiski gained control of the Bulgarian government from 1919 to 1923. In this iteration, narod referred explicitly to the peasant masses, which at the time constituted around 80 percent of the Bulgarian population. Stamboliiski supported the notion that land should belong to the people who work it and succeeded in bringing about land redistribution by setting limits to property holdings. Although certainly guilty of strongman/authoritarian tactics Stamboliiski was hardly your typical nationalist leader, famously referring to himself as a "south Slav" when accused of not supporting Bulgarian national interests, to underline his belief in a Balkan Federation that would supersede national identities. After gaining power he took Bulgaria into the League of Nations and "in an attempt to enhance the international standing of the country took comprehensive measures to cater to the needs of minorities in Bulgaria" (Karadjov 2011, 49). He was also involved in founding the International Agrarian Bureau. Stamboliiski was overthrown (tortured and killed) by a coalition of fascists and nationalists still smarting from Bulgaria's massive loss of territory after World War I, especially Macedonian lands. The party continued to function and was in fact one of the few parties allowed to operate under the Communist government, although not independently.

In Hungary, the "népi movement" emerged in the interwar period to challenge the government in the name of landless and land-poor agrarian workers and sharecroppers and the proletarianizing stratum of servants who emerged from this group and made up a third of the population of Hungary, and 67 percent of the peasant population (Borbándi 1989, 58).[8] The way the term was used reflected Hungary's recent history. The Hungarian Republic, established upon the collapse of the Hapsburg Empire at the end of World War I with only a third of the Kingdom of Hungary's prior territory, soon fell victim to associated border issues. The subsequent and brief Soviet Republic (which espoused a policy of land collectivization) was followed by a reentrenchment of neofeudal rule by successive Christian National governments representing the former nobility and military officers, under regent Miklos Horthy.

Hoping to avert attention from severe class distinctions, the Horthy governments focused on regaining lost territories and instituted anti-Semitic policies in the name of developing a modern and professionally qualified "Magyar" bourgeoisie out of members of the ruling "middle class." Two groups with competing visions of progress, népi (of the people) and urbánus (urban), fought for land reform and the franchise for those unrepresented by this regime. The népi movement expounded a vision of an agrarian Hungary of small producers, potentially in federation with other small peoples of the Danubian basin, while urbanists sought a path of modernization and industrialization according to a Western model.[9]

Népi was a blanket term that covered an array of personalities and efforts with a diversity of opinions about ethnicity/race and Hungarianness, including anti-Semitic expression by some, as well as varied positions on capitalism, socialism, and communism. Following the March Front (1937–1938), and tied closely with the movement to found People's Colleges, the National Peasant Party emerged in 1939, with the goal of attracting poor peasants away from fascist and national socialist formations.

In both these cases the "populists" in question challenged the predominant definitions/uses of nationalism. Dictatorial when in power, Stamboliiski was an antiwar and anti-imperial federalist and internationalist. These characteristics have interesting through lines in the Hungarian populists. Both lay emphasis on the poorest agrarian strata in countries without a significant industrial working class and flirted with regional political forms inconsistent with the nation-state, under conditions in which nation-state borders were in flux.[10] These kinds of emphases on the people remain central in contemporary historical consciousness and are not easily reducible to the pursuit of a Western-style ethnonational state.

Another layer in the history of narod/nép shared across eastern Europe is the explicit and pervasive use of these terms by socialists and communists, from the widespread and varied movements across Europe, to the Russian revolutions, the Hungarian Soviet Republic of 1919, and the practices of the

Bulgarian and Hungarian state socialist governments after World War II. This people/elite binary was rooted in a Marxist analysis of capitalist society in which owners of the means of production were contrasted with those who, dispossessed from the means of production, were forced to sell their labor. The communist governments ruling Hungary and Bulgaria after 1948 used the terms *nép* and *narod*, as their political movements had before gaining power, identifying the people as the working class.[11] Here "the people" referred explicitly to the supposedly undifferentiated masses of (erstwhile) peasants and workers committed to the building of socialism (as well as the vanguard leading them in the effort), thus, the naming of the polities after 1948 as the People's Republic of Bulgaria, and the Hungarian People's Republic. On the one hand, this built upon and furthered the class-based connotations of narod/nép expounded by the interwar movements, but on the other, it confounded the relevant class distinctions. The term became ubiquitous in designating institutions or units of these socialist states: the people's army, the people's police, house of the people, and so forth.[12] This recent and pervasive useage likely informs the contemporary resonance of the term. Certainly the increase in so-called socialist nostalgia maps nicely onto contemporary receptivity to appeals to a people with class overtones.

Given the association of narod/nép in these agrarian societies with the peasantry, it is no surprise that the terms also became entwined with the development of romantic nationalism in the nineteenth century. In its Herderian formulation, the peasantry/folk (older layer of society) carried the unique characteristics—language and other social practices—that made up the treasury of any national culture (and deserved protection by its own state). The narod/nép and the nation could thus become metonyms, and sometimes synonyms, even while alternative notions of nation existed and competed. The narod and nép of those interwar movements described previously then, might variously signify ethnic as well as class connotations, even while defying certain kinds of nationalist agendas. Similarly, the term was nevertheless used in the state socialist period, both colloquially and officially, in ways that also pointed to the ethnos (Taylor 2008, 2009). Indeed, the Bulgarian socialist state often seemed to use narod and nation interchangeably (Buchanan 2006) and was notorious for trying to make them synonymous through ethnic homogenization policies.

The fact that the major legislative body in Bulgaria has been called the Narodno Subranie since the nineteenth century (with different connotations in different political regimes) perhaps puts this in perspective, as does the fact that the object of those who identified as népi in interwar Hungary were agrarian workers, while today the object of the népi movement tends to be ethnic Hungarians over the borders (although particularly those who live in the countryside) (Taylor 2008).[13] An appeal to "the people" resonates differently, but likely deeply and symbolically to most members of these societies. "The people" may interpolate members of the struggling working or middle classes, or summon the idea of an ethnic group, a nation under threat, agrarian workers, "traditional peasants," sometimes in combination, or all at once. The point is not simply that appeals to the people have been alternatively either ethnic or class, but that many connotations have coexisted in a mixture that makes the term resonate powerfully across multiple meanings and also makes it extremely slippery. So-called populists in this region today work to produce its meaning via a series of cascading oppositions that rely upon and reinforce this. The people becomes equated with ethnonation (while still connoting class) when it is contrasted repeatedly with "foreigners" (whether elite or parasitic) who are also contrasted with nation.

While "the people" has not always equated with the ethnos, and alternate understandings of the nation have also existed, the idea of the ethnonation has been a central one in the region since the nineteenth century. Nonetheless, as late as the 1920s, Judith Irvine and Susan Gal write, Western (elite) observers were disturbed by the fact that "Macedonian linguistic diversity failed to correspond to social and ethnic boundaries in the ways Western ideologies led them to expect" (2000, 64). In other words, the work that has gone into making seemingly straightforward "homogenous nation-states" is heavily influenced by what Gal calls "Herdarian standardizing," which posits "a unity among language, national essence, and territory" (2006, 164). Since their emergence as nation-states (rather than other political forms) from the Austro-Hungarian and Ottoman empires, governments and political actors in Hungary and Bulgaria, as in most other countries of the region, have appealed regularly to a nationalism based in this ideology.

In Bulgaria the constitution of the modern state was in part a nationalist liberation project against the Ottoman Empire, so modern conception of the Bulgarian nation has been defined against Turks. But the history of Western intervention in the fate of eastern Europe has made it clear that ethnonational identity matters, as the Great Powers have drawn and redrawn boundaries multiple times justified by ethnic unification. The rounds of population exchange and border enforcement were most often under the tutelage of the Great Powers, including the United States (Woodrow Wilson). There is plenty of historical precedent to justify agitating for more territory with an ethnonational argument and for making sure that populations within state boundaries are homogeneous enough to deny this argument to other polities angling for territory. In a system of nations to which this region came late and with few resources, ethnonationalism was established as an imperative for political security and sovereignty.

In the state socialist period, the idea of the nation was also mobilized in different ways in different polities. Leninism had put a focus on the nation as the scale of self-determination/development and unit of internationalism. The Soviet-informed policy of "socialist in content but nationalist in form" had quite different results when there was no territorial autonomy or even distinctions for ethnic minorities as provided in the USSR. The pervasive use of a national idea in Romania ended up instantiating ethnonational identity as primary, even for those who did not think of themselves as Romanian nationalists (Verdery 1991). The long-time Bulgarian leader Todor Zhivkov may have been less identified with the nationalist strategy than Romanian leader Nicolae Ceausescu, but he still deployed it extensively (especially in a notorious assimilation campaign against Roma and Turks).

Hungary's leaders had to perform a relatively nonethnonational position and give up an irredentism focused on its vast former territory and the millions of ethnic Hungarians living there. In Hungary, as in Poland and some republics of Yugoslavia, the nation became one terrain of dissidents, in contrast to the communist state and its leaders, seen by many as oppressing the nation(s) (although in different ways). The ethical civil society, or antipolitical politics that "central European" dissidents became famous for, relied on ethical positions often in contrast to the state and/or politics proper. The community so defined was a vision of the national gemeinschaft in contrast to the gesellschaft ("society") of the socialist state (Žižek 1993). When the first Hungarian prime minister of the postsocialist era, József Antall, stated "I am in spirit the Prime Minister of 15 million Hungarians," he included the five million ethnic Hungarians in neighboring countries along with ten million Hungarian citizens (Fox 2003, 455).[14]

(Ethno)nationalist motivations and justifications have thus been present in the politics of the region since the nineteenth century and form part of a dynamic struggle around sovereignty, the form of the state, and the content of citizenship. Even when it is contested or resisted, as with the agrarian government in Bulgaria (or by the form of the neighboring Yugoslavia), an opposition tends to sustain the centrality of the (ethno)national via attacks and criticism. Since few major political actors eschew the national form, it can become, rather than an empty signifier, an ignorable one. While it is central to some actors, for others it is seen as the perfunctory requirement of political participation. This seems to be increasingly the case (as can be seen in some liberal parties' approach to migration). In short ethnonationalist pronouncements are expected in politics so they are hardly disqualifying for the majority of the populations, even for those who are not committed nationalists. This has rendered them somewhat less useful as a means for distinguishing and characterizing political parties. As ethnonationalism in some form has become political common sense, a nonnationalist rhetoric has become potentially disqualifying.

This means that Bulgarians and Hungarians who have not been motivated to support nationalist parties in the past may be willing to embrace the antineoliberal platforms of Ataka or Jobbik even if they come in an (ethno)nationalist package. This is not to deny that supporting those parties validates and promotes ethnonationalist policies and extremes, it is simply to point to another factor to explain why people might not see the nationalist discourse as disqualifying even though they do not condone its values. As Stanislav Dodov observes for Bulgaria, "nationalism is completely in the public's blind spot (allowing for it to be systemic). . . . In contrast with the recent US elections, here this narrative was not embodied in one particular subject, but was supported openly and in different ways by virtually all players" (2016). This is evidently even the case for Roma who are the target of much of the rabid nationalist rhetoric but still vote for parties with nationalist platforms, and the DPS, which has joined in coalitions with most successful parties over the years. It has become the baseline and thus cannot be the basis for disqualifying a politician or party. In postsocialist Hungary, while being ethnonationalist did not disqualify a party from being legitimate, the MSZP/SZDSZ coalition's insistence on civic nationalism, while also applying techniques of liberal diversity politics under the tutelage of the EU, played right into Fidesz's delegitimation strategy.[15] It reinforced Fidesz's ability to claim their continuity with the Communists and its own antisystem status and assured that over the border Hungarians who were finally granted dual citizenship would support the party that had ensured it. Today Roma in Hungary, themselves victims of such ethnonational rhetoric and policy, also report fear of migrants they have never encountered.

These factors help account for why ethnonational arguments (and appeals to the people) can resonate across the region but do not explain the recent peak in that reception in the form of the popularity of certain parties. We suggest that the ubiquitous language of the nation (and its mapping onto "the people") be considered alongside a number of factors that together contribute to the support of parties that position themselves as antisystemic. This positioning is achieved in part through use of the aforementioned oppositions (elite/people; foreign/Hungarian; unHungarian/Hungarian, Communist/Liberal; Socialist/Cosmopolitan; Jewish/Hungarian, in the Hungarian case) that make reference not just to the behavior of various actors, but essentialize the reasons for it. Here we point to some temporal provocations.

First is simply the exhaustion of options. After twenty years of experimenting and trying various options, frustration over the repeated failures, often seen as lies, reached a breaking point. In the recent past, the lack of real choices in elections had become graphically evident. While parties in Bulgaria array across the political spectrum, the different parties in power have not pursued significantly different programs, primarily because political leaders of all stripes share the primary agenda of enriching themselves and their clients/patrons (Ganev 2007), and secondarily because requirements for EU membership have dictated much domestic policy.

This lack of real choice in the electoral sphere combined with continuing disappointment also led to an increasing withdrawal from political participation. Political apathy set in soon after the first disappointments with democracy in the 1990s, but it has continued to increase in Bulgaria (see Novinite.com 2018). One could argue that as rational actors have thrown up their hands in exasperation and withdrawn from participation, political outcomes are shaped more by zealots, while those determined to participate are pushed further to the extremes in an effort to find a party that can deliver. The failure of MSZP to deliver a basic degree of equality certainly reduced its popularity. While voting numbers had become quite low in Hungary, the slightly over 70 percent turnout in the April 2018 elections (the highest in twenty years!) suggests that the exasperation thesis is insufficient. In addition, evidence continued to mount that the brunt of these failures was being visited on the masses while a minority actually benefits. As Kristin Ghodsee noted, "As radical income inequality becomes more and more visible, so too, may Ataka's nationalist economic appeal to ordinary Bulgarians" (2008, 36; see also Taylor 2008). She is referring to the early assent of Ataka, but the same principle would continue to operate, so that the more evident income inequality becomes, the more the disadvantaged find anti-elite or antisystemic arguments attractive.

An important question then, is how the few that benefit, the elite (or system), is defined. This is closely tied to the rhetorical fight against corruption. Transparency International's corruption perceptions index lists Bulgaria as the most corrupt country in the EU. This has justified holds on financial transfers from the EU and is considered by many to be the main reason Bulgaria remains excluded from the free travel agreement of the EU.[16] Borisov came to power with a strong anticorruption platform, buttressed by his reputation as a mafia buster while mayor. While observers have not been impressed with his success in this arena as prime minister, or even his efforts (Center for the Study of Democracy 2016), his pedigree plus his constant harping on corruption as the cause of contemporary problems allows Borisov to remain an outsider and antisystemic.

In Hungary, "stolen regime change" language points to how political capitalism distributed public resources into the hands of a few people poised to take advantage of it by their proximity to the late socialist state (Taylor 2008). Fidesz claimed to be outside those networks. While the party headed the government in 1998–2002, after its 2002 electoral defeat Orbán honed its position as antisystemic in relation to the ruling forces (MSZP and SZDSZ) in Parliament. Since Fidesz's 2010 ascent, Jobbik has used the same technique. Fidesz's thickening network of clients (which do attract claims of corruption by many) is now overtly framed as part of its project to bolster a national middle class, while the party has worked to construct itself as antisystemic vis-à-vis the EU government.

Another condition contributing to the political dynamics currently evident in eastern Europe is the continuing disqualification of leftist alternatives as a result of the experience with state socialism and the unsatisfactory performance of socialist parties since then. It's been taken as common sense that citizens of the former state socialist polities are anticommunist. After all, dominant accounts of a "velvet revolution" imply that "the people" had overthrown a tyrannical and dictatorial communism in order to join the West in a transition to democracy, which assumed a transition to capitalism in the moment when neoliberal globalization, characterized by a financialization that reduces nation-state sovereignty, was becoming dominant. Yet while something called communism may indeed have been rejected, some of its tenets were not. East Europeans have approved of extensive state control in providing social welfare and have considered equality important at much higher levels than Western Europeans. Fidesz plays upon this with its theater of redistribution.

Antisystemic parties on the right have seemed to offer an alternative to what appears now as the blatantly false promises of liberal democracy and those connected to it, as well as an alternative to the (self)-colonizing narratives of backwardness and catching up, central to the seemingly never-ending "transition." Moreover, with the left foreclosed, restricted, or "postpolitical," there seems nowhere for the dissatisfied citizen to go but further right. While the disqualification of communism and communists has kept leftist politics in the shadows, it has also required policing and a careful rearticulation of desires, with the right regularly reminding citizens of the horrors of the communist past.

While antisystem in the recent period has become increasingly appealing, it is not easily sustained once a party comes to power.[17] Orbán and Borisov have been able to do so. While some of their success can be attributed to authoritarian techniques, a specific incitement that appears to have helped Orbán and Borisov maintain popularity has been the production of an ongoing "migrant crisis." A dramatic increase in refugees into the region was evident by 2013 following the escalation of the Syrian conflict, with the number surging in 2015, including not only Syrians but Afghans, Iraqis, and others as well. In 2015, Hungary had 174,000 asylum applicants. Among European countries, only Germany had more. When adjusted for population size, Hungary had 1,770 per 100,000 population, the highest of any country (Connor 2016). The numbers for Bulgaria were much smaller, "but nevertheless migratory pressure reached a historic high over the past few years. A total of 58,034 [refugees] have applied for status since the first surge of the migrant crisis in 2013" (Novinite.com 2017).

Despite these scary numbers, both Hungary and Bulgaria are best conceived as "transit countries." In 2014, for example, Hungary granted asylum to only 9 percent of its applicants, and the vast majority of asylum seekers leave quickly (often after a few days) for points further west (Pardavi and Gyulai 2015). Most migrants prefer western Europe, where they see the possibility of work, and they regard learning eastern European languages as counter to their objective. Further, "in an Arabic language 'Refugee Handbook,' Bulgaria ranks first among countries asylum seekers should avoid. Refugees say xenophobia and Islamophobia are widespread and they try to skirt around the country.... Public opinion is clearly against accepting more refugees into the country, as seen by attacks on refugees as well as demonstrations and political rallies against them. The message is always the same: Bulgaria is poor and Christian; we don't want you!" (Andreev and Vaksberg 2015). As Creed (2011) has argued regarding relations between ethnic Bulgarians and Roma, there is a distinction between minorities who are considered part of the community (*nashiyat*, ours) and minority citizens who are not local.[18] Refugees, especially Muslim ones, are worse than minorities: they are outsiders. For a country unable to provide adequately for its own population in such graphic and widespread ways, indeed the poorest in Europe, they cannot afford to support needy outsiders. At the same time, outmigration to Europe is a key survival practice common in both countries, and these migrants face discrimination as well (Böröcz and Sarkar 2017).

While defiance of the EU's mandates regarding resettlement quotas signals resistance to the liberal hegemony, the Hungarian government's very aggressive antimigrant stances also work symbolically to place Hungary inside Europe. By virtue of cascading oppositions, Orbán can link the un-Hungarian left liberals, as well as Brussels, with migrants and Roma, whose liberties and rights the former support, while also insisting that his policies are in line with European (and Christian) values. Orbán's defiance of the EU regarding migrant settlement links with economic and symbolic concerns Hungarians have regarding EU citizenship and Europeanness, while also echoing the treatments East European migrants have faced in the core of Europe (the EU) (Böröcz and Sarkar 2017).

While its antisystem strategy seems to have helped Fidesz maintain power, Fidesz has had to work hard to cultivate antimigrant sentiment to the point that it appears to exist today.[19] In 2016, despite claims to have the mandate, the referendum on whether Hungary should reject the quota of migrants imposed by the EU failed to attract enough voters to make it valid. As in several cases before, the lack of turnout can be read as abstention (Taylor 2008). Examples abound of Hungarians helping migrants.

The "migrant crisis" solidified the alliance between Orbán and Borisov.[20] Both put up fences. Bulgaria began constructing a 201-kilometer fence on its border with Turkey in 2014, which was completed in 2017.[21] Hungary approved and completed a 175-kilometer fence along its Serbian and Croatian borders in 2015 and trained and deployed a border hunting force along it in the following years. Orbán visited the Bulgarian fence with Borisov in September 2016. Sounding increasingly like Orbán, "in January [2016] Borisov called on the EU to temporarily seal off its border to new arrivals" (Novinite.com 2016). This "crisis" has given Orbán and Borisov an ax to grind with the EU, positioning them as defenders of the people against the system administered from Brussels.

The "crisis" has also provided opportunities for Orbán to reinforce other foreign/national binaries. Centering on the figure of finance capitalist George Soros (a Hungarian of Jewish descent and founder of the Central European University, as well as foundations that fund a number of liberal and left organizations in the region), as a symbol of the "foreign-minded," Fidesz had used this binding trope for attacks on media, NGOs, academics, civil society writ large, and the university.[22] The government has also banned the "foreign-minded" discipline of gender studies from being taught in Hungary.

Both of these tropes are also evident in Bulgaria. Anti-Soros rhetoric targeting foreign funding, liberal media, and civil society was prominent in official responses to antigovernment demonstrations in 2013: "Pro-government media and politicians marked the protesters as paid 'Sorosoids'" (BalkanInsight 2017). In 2018 the Bulgarian Constitutional Court ruled that the EU's Istanbul Convention on the prevention of violence against women was incompatible with the Bulgarian constitution, and a proposal to UNESCO for a project addressing gender equality in schools was blocked by the Bulgarian Academy of Science and Ministry of Education. According to some feminist activists, "people who showed up at the anti-Istanbul Convention protests . . . see women's autonomy, as well as queer and gender–nonconforming people and practices, as a threat to the Bulgarian nation in the same way that they see migrants and refugees as a threat to national integrity (Schultes et al. 2019).

When the European Parliament voted in 2018 to sanction Hungary for "flouting EU standards on democracy, civil rights and corruption," Bulgaria joined Poland and the Czech Republic in promising to oppose any sanctions against Hungary (Tsolova 2018). In support of this decision a leader of Bulgaria's UP (GERB's coalition partner), said "central and eastern European countries should act in solidarity and help each other because they have common problems" (Tsolova 2018). It is hard to argue with that.

Conclusion: The Dangers of Antipopulism

Critical Hungarian scholars from the Helyzet (Position) Public Sociology Working Group argue that the binary at work in Hungary between a liberal-left elite block, which relies on democratic antipopulism and the national elite block, which employs antidemocractic populism, has become so hegemonic that it seems impossible to introduce other angles into the debate (Gagyi 2016). In Bulgaria this opposition is less categorical. In the final two weeks running up to Bulgaria's March 2017 parliamentary elections, GERB campaign chief Tsvetan Tsvetanov entreated citizens in the town of Dulovo to vote for GERB "to resist populism and the fear wrought by our opponents" (Leviev-Sawyer 2017). Here a party that has gained and retained power with populist ideas and rhetoric uses antipopulism against its opponents. The strategy may be an effort to deflect antipopulist opposition to the populist left or more extreme right wing, rather than at its own center-right variant, or it may simply reflect an audacious effort to court additional votes with contrary positions. Regardless, both cases underline the increasing role of liberal antipopulism in the political field.

Antipopulism, the dismissal of the opinions and preferences of ordinary people, was a shared characteristic of political elite across the spectrum in the early period of transition. Used by the liberals who have governed these polities for most of the period, as well as by the West, antipopulism functions to legitimate liberals as the apt inheritors of democracy, something that may not reflect the will of the people but must be imposed on them (at least for now). Antipopulism thus works much like how Lilith Mahmud (this volume) suggests neoliberal antifascism operates in Italy, where it empowers fascism by delegitimizing more serious and extensive antifascist projects. The pointing finger of antipopulism delegitimates with the force of a civilizing discourse both those political actors and parties labelled populist (right-wing authoritarians, at present, in this part of the world) as well as regular people who, following quite democratic impulses, feel silenced by neoliberal postsocialist democracy. As such, antipopulism, by misnaming and making commensurable (and dismissible) an array of critiques of liberal (and neoliberal) government and governance, works as an ideological device that reinforces the hegemonic binary, while distracting from growing disparity brought about by competing blocs of elites and their governments, the loss of a counterhegemonic socialist economic bloc, and this region's position within the EU and the global economy. In the name of democracy it conflates the popular with the populism it delegitimates and seeks to obscure the democratic deficit of (neo) liberalism and (neo)liberal governance under which these populations have experienced degrees of dispossession not seen since the 1930s. This delegitimizing trick can only work for so long in conjunction with postpolitical and technocratic governance that does not address equality and distribution on different scales. Yet how can any government of a peripheralizing country begin to address these issues when the rights of finance trump state sovereignty? With no substantive choices, politics is reduced to the rhetorical, which is the wellspring of populism *and* antipopulism.

Notes

1. See, for example, *East European Politics and Societies* 15, no. 1 (2000); *Problems of Post-Communism* 55, no. 3 (2008); *Slavic Review* 76, no. S1 (2017).

2. Kalb argues that eastern Europe was a pioneer in the now global political "populism" that rejects "the foundations of liberal rule" and marries ethnonational symbolism with "elements of the classical left" (2011, 5).

3. Chantal Mouffe (2005), who along with Ernesto LaClau can be said to be responsible for the centrality of the approach to populism that focuses on what we call rhetorical, argues that the widespread use of populist logic today is an effect of the postpolitical condition, marked by the tendency toward consensus at the middle and the diminution of the adversarial model of politics. This consensus can be seen, for example, in third-way social democracy or technocratic governance in the period characterized by neoliberalization.

4. In this it echoes interwar government attempts to replace Jews with "Hungarians" in various sectors.

5. Over 95 percent of these nearly 130,000 new citizens voted for Fidesz in 2014.

6. Unlike the traditional far right, Fabry argues, Jobbik built its popularity as a "counter-hegemonic bloc against the injustices wrought by neoliberal capitalism" (2015) not unlike Ataka in Bulgaria as described by Ganev (2017).

7. On the occasion of Borisov's 2017 reelection Orbán congratulated him and expressed his gratitude for the excellent cooperation between them (Standart 2017). After Bulgaria assumed the rotating presidency of the EU, Borisov invited Orbán to Sofia in an effort to defuse EU tensions with Hungary.

8. This movement is generally not mentioned in histories of agrarianism in the region because it was not party oriented. In fact after 1947 it was the Smallholders Party, not the party that emerged from this movement, that joined the International Agrarian Bureau's successor, the International Peasants Union.

9. The debate has often been reduced to anti-Semites (népi) vs. Jews (urbánus). We acknowledge that anti-Semites did exist in the former group, but the historical record shows that there were friendships (and shared underground political activity) that reached across this seemingly absolute divide, and that "conversions" occurred where people associated with one group moved to the other side (Jozsef Attila, for example). We do not wish to play down the presence of anti-Semitism, but in order to treat it properly we would also have to address the sociological conditions that distinguished the agrarian areas from the cities (particularly the capital, Budapest) that shaped the debate. We cannot do this justice here.

10. They shared the idea of a "third way" that would allow for a different kind of development for agrarian societies, perhaps between communism and capitalism.

11. Before national socialism, the term *volk* was also used by the international socialist parties in the German lands as a synonym for the proletariat.

12. While some suggest this may have rendered the term nearly meaningless we suggest it worked to make the term more flexible. Discussing the "normalization of language" in the case of the Soviet Union, Alexei Yurchak shows how "with increasing emphasis on the replication of form, what meanings or functions concrete texts and slogans had was becoming increasingly unpredictable; meaning was sliding in unprecedented directions" (2005, 53).

13. It should be noted that Orbán's politics are not referred to as népi, but rather as "populizmus/populista" in Hungary.

14. Already in the late 1980s, the Hungarian government had diplomatically intervened in Romania's "systemization" project, formally a village modernization project, but understood by many as a technique to break apart ethnic minority communities. But this intervention was after massive demonstrations, prompted by dissidents. The folk revival movement that had arisen in the 1970s partly from the institutional and organizational legacy of the interwar népi movement was responsible for much of the knowledge production and sentiment building behind this pressure on the government. Western observers generally lauded this "civil society" (Taylor 2008, 2009).

15. The MSZP /SZDSZ government was explicit about denying citizenship to over-the-border Hungarians and Fidesz (and others) then accused them of not being Hungarian. "Dissidents" of many stripes constructed the Communists as antinational already from 1956 onward, aligned as it was with the (occupying) USSR, and working against "Hungarian" culture (Taylor 2008).

16. At the time of their 2004 accession, East European states agreed to "transitional arrangements" that barred the free mobility of its citizens to work in other EU countries (a main motivator for EU membership for many).

17. This was the Achilles heel for Simeon II, who rode a wave of antisystemic

sentiment into the prime minister position and used his popular appeal to enact some liberal reforms, but that cost him his status as an outsider and his party lost the next election.

18. Ethnic Bulgarians are also vulnerable to being excluded from this category when used for village or regional inclusion, but they do not suffer the discrimination that minorities do as a result.

19. In the wake of the 2018 elections, the idea that Fidesz's excessive preelection antimigrant advertisements had swayed the vote was dominant in international news headlines. Certainly the media monopoly Fidesz enjoys may have done some work by now.

20. It was also a solid basis for the development of the Visegrad 4 as a counter bloc in the EU. Bulgaria did not join this bloc, perhaps because of its position as EU president at the height of the scandal.

21. Ironically, a prior fence and minefield built by the Communist government had been painstakingly removed two decades earlier.

22. The attack on Soros allows almost every set of oppositions to function simultaneously. Jew/Hungarian, foreigner/Hungarian, left/liberal;cosmopolitan/Hungarian, "foreign funded"/Hungarian, foreign minded/Hungarian and foreign bodied/Hungarian.

References

Andreev, Alexander, and Tatiana Vaksberg. 2015. "Why Do So Many Refugees Avoid Bulgaria?" *Deutsche Welle*, September 10. Accessed August 3, 2019. http://p.dw.com/p/1GUmH.

BalkanInsight. 2017. "Soros Foundation Blames Attacks on 'Illiberal Governments.'" Accessed May 5, 2019. http://www.balkaninsight.com/en/article/soros-foundation-rebuffs-balkan-governments-attacks-02-09-2017.

Borbándi, Gyula. 1989. *A Magyar Népi Mozgalom (The Hungarian Populist Movement)*. Budapest: Püski.

Böröcz, József. 2016. "An Incapacity to See Ourselves as Part of the Whole World, and the Insistence to See Ourselves as Part of Europe." *LeftEast*, December 14. http://www.criticatac.ro/lefteast/jozsef-Böröcz-interview-2016/.

Böröcz, József, and Mahua Sarkar. 2017. "The Unbearable Whiteness of the Polish Plumber and the Hungarian Peacock Dance around 'Race.'" *Slavic Review* 76 (2): 307–314.

Buchanan, Donna. 2006. *Performing Democracy: Bulgarian Music and Musicians in Transition*. Chicago: University of Chicago Press.

Center for the Study of Democracy. 2016. "State Capture Unplugged: Countering

Administrative and Political Corruption in Bulgaria." Accessed August 3, 2019. http://www.csd.bg/fileSrc.php?id=22925.

Connor, Phillip. 2016. "Number of Refugees to Europe Surges to Record 1.3 Million in 2015." Pew Research Center. Accessed March 22, 2018. http://www .pewglobal.org/2016/08/02/number-of-refugees-to-europe-surges-to -record-1-3-million-in-2015/.

Creed, Gerald W. 2010. "Strange Bedfellows: Socialist Nostalgia and Neoliberalism in Bulgaria." In *Post-Communist Nostalgia*, ed. Maria Todorova and Zsuzsa Gille, 29–45. New York: Berghahn.

Creed, Gerald W. 2011. *Masquerade and Postsocialim: Ritual and Cultural Disposses-sion in Bulgaria*. Bloomington: Indiana University Press.

D'Eramo, Marco. 2013. "Populism and the New Oligarchy." *New Left Review* 82: 5–28.

Dodov, Stanislav. 2016. "The Presidential Elections in Bulgaria between Systemic Nationalism and the Anti-system Vote." *LeftEast*, November 28. Accessed March 21, 2018. www.criticatac.ro/lefteast/the-presidential-elections-in-bulgaria -between-systemic-nationalism-and-the-anti-systemic-vote/.

Fabry, Adam. 2015. "The Far-Right as a Counter-Hegemonic Bloc to Neoliberalism: The Case of Jobbik (I)." *LeftEast*, August 10. Accessed August 3, 2019. http:// www.criticatac.ro/lefteast/the-far-right-as-a-counter-hegemonic-bloc-to -neoliberalism-the-case-of-jobbik/.

Fox, Jon E. 2003. "National Identities on the Move: Transylvanian Hungarian Labour Migrants in Hungary." *Journal of Ethnic and Migration Studies* 29(3): 449–466.

Gagyi, Agnes. 2016. "'Coloniality of Power' in East Central Europe: External Pene-trations as Internal Force in Post-Socialist Hungarian Politics." *Journal of World-Systems Research* 22 (2): 349–372.

Gal, Susan. 2006. "Contradictions of Standard Language in Europe: Implications for the Study of Practices and Publics." *Social Anthropology* 14 (2): 163–181.

Ganev, Venelin I. 2007. *Preying on the State: The Transformation of Bulgaria after 1989*. Ithaca, NY: Cornell University Press.

Ganev, Venelin I. 2017. "'Neoliberalism Is Fascism and Should Be Criminalized': Bulgarian Populism as Left-Wing Radicalism." *Slavic Review* 76 (S1): 9–17.

Ghodsee, Kristen. 2008. "Left Wing, Right Wing, Everything: Xenophobia, Neo-totalitarianism, and Populist Politics in Bulgaria." *Problems of Post-Communism* 55 (3): 26–39.

Hann, Chris. 2016. "Cucumbers and Courgettes: Rural Workfare and the New Dou-ble Movement." *Intersections: East European Journal of Society and Politics* 2 (2): 38–56.

Irvine, Judith T., and Susan Gal. 2000. "Language Ideology and Linguistic

Differentiation." In *Regimes of Language: Ideologies, Polities, and Identities*, ed. P. V. Kroskrity, 35–83. Santa Fe: School of American Research Press.

Kalb, Don. 2011. "Introduction." In *Headlines of Nation, Subtexts of* Class: *Working Class Populism and the Return of the Repressed in Neoliberal Europe*, ed. Don Kalb and Gábor Halmai, 1–36. New York: Berghahn Books.

Karadjov, Alexander. 2011. "The Turkish Minority in Bulgaria and the 'Revival Process': The Construction of a Political Minority." MA thesis, Budapest: Central European University, Department of Nationalism Studies.

King, Lawrence P. 2001. "Making Markets: A Comparative Study of Postcommunist Managerial Strategies in Central Europe." *Theory and Society* 30 (4): 493–538.

Leviev-Sawyer, Clive. 2017. "Bulgaria Elections 2017: From Populism to Polling Stations to Poverty and an Epilepsy Epidemic." *The Sofia Globe*, March 13. Accessed August 3, 2019. https://sofiaglobe.com/2017/03/13/bulgaria-elections-2017-from -populism-to-polling-stations-to-poverty-and-an-epilepsy-epidemic/.

Lyman, Rick. 2017. "In Bulgaria, a Tycoon who Talks (and Acts) like Trump," *The New York Times*. February 25, A9.

Martin, József Péter. 2017. "Continuity or Disruption?: Changing Elites and the Emergence of Cronyism after the Great Recession: The Case of Hungary." *Corvinus Journal of Sociology and Social Policy* 8 (3S): 255–281.

Mouffe, Chantal. 2005. "The 'End of Politics' and the Challenge of Right-Wing Populism." In *Populism and the Mirror of Democracy*, ed. Francisco Panizza, 50–71. New York: Verso.

Novinite.com. 2016. "Bulgaria's Borisov, Hungary's Orbán to Meet in Sofia on Friday." January 28. Accessed March 20, 2018. http://www.novinite.com/articles /172845/Bulgaria%27s+Borisov%2C+Hungary%27s+Orbán+to+Meet+in+Sofia +on+Friday.

Novinite.com. 2017. "Bulgaria and the Migrant Crisis in Numbers," January 16. Accessed March 18, 2018. http://www.novinite.com/articles/178377/Bulgaria +and+tje+Migrant+Crisis+in+Numbers.

Novinite.com. 2018. "Proportion of the Apolitical People in Bulgaria Is Increasing." February 21. Accessed March 21, 2018. www.novinite.com/articles/188110 /Proportion+of+the+Apolitical+People+in+Bulgaria+is+Increasing.

Pardavi, Márta, and Gábor Gyulai. 2015. "What You Need to Know about the Refugee Crisis in Hungary." Open Society Foundations, September 30. Accessed August 3, 2019. https://www.opensocietyfoundations.org/voices/what-you -need-know-about-refugee-crisis-hungary.

Ries, Nancy. 1997. *Russian Talk: Culture and Conversation during Perestroika*. Ithaca, NY: Cornell University Press.

Schultes, Hannah, and LevFem. 2019. "Under Assault: Class and Gender in Bulgaria

and Europe Today." *LeftEast*, February 4. Accessed August 4, 2019. http://www
.criticatac.ro/lefteast/levfem-interview/.

Standart. 2017. "Orbán to Borisov: I Owe You Lots of Respect." *Standart*, February
10. Accessed March 20, 2018. http://www.standartnews.com/english/read
/Orbán_to_borisov_i_owe_you_lots_of_respect_-12643.html.

Szombati, Kristóf. 2018. *The Revolt of the Provinces: Anti-Gypsyism and Right-Wing
Politics in Hungary*. Oxford: Berghahn.

Taylor, Mary. 2008. *The Politics of Culture: Folk Critique and the Transformation of
the State in Hungary*. Ph.D. dissertation, City University of New York Graduate
Center.

Taylor, Mary. 2008. "Does Folk Dancing Make Hungarians? Táncház, Folk Dance as
Mother Tongue, and Folk National Cultivation." *Journal of Hungarian Studies* 22
(1–2): 9–28.

Taylor, Mary 2009 "Intangible Heritage Governance, Cultural Diversity, Ethnonationalism" *Focaal—European Journal of Anthropology* 55:41–58.

Tsolova, Tsvetelia. 2018. "Bulgaria Pledges Solidarity with Hungary in Rights Stand-
off with EU." Reuters, September 19. Accessed May 5, 2019. https://www.reuters
.com/article/us-eu-hungary-bulgaria/bulgaria-pledges-solidarity-with-hungary
-in-rights-standoff-with-eu-idUSKCN1LZ2BF.

Verdery, Katherine. 1991. *National Ideology under Socialism: Identity and Cultural
Politics in Ceausescu's Romania*. Berkeley: University of California Press.

Williams, Raymond. 1976. *Keywords: A Vocabulary of Culture and Society*. New York:
Oxford University Press.

Yurchak, Alexei. 2005. *Everything Was Forever, until It Was No More: The Last Soviet
Generation*. Princeton, NJ: Princeton University Press.

Žižek, Slavoj. 1993. *Tarrying with the Negative: Kant, Hegel, and the Critique of Ideology*. Durham, NC: Duke University Press.

Fascism, a Haunting

Spectral Politics and Antifascist Resistance in Twenty-First-Century Italy

Fascism by Any Other Name

The year 2016 made fascism popular again. In the *Merriam-Webster American English Dictionary*'s annual tally of the most frequently searched terms, *fascism* came dangerously close to winning the title of "word of the year"—an honor ultimately bestowed upon the word "surreal," but only after the dictionary editors issued a passionate appeal to readers in November urging them "to stop fascism's rise" (Pengelly 2016).

Turning to the dictionary is what students of social phenomena do when at a loss for words. When world events defy available nomenclatures, the dictionary promises answers. In an interview with the *Guardian*, the Merriam-Webster editors explained that there are marked patterns in the words people search for. "Surreal," for instance, had already spiked in searches after September 11, 2001, whereas "fascism" rose in 2016 after Brexit and throughout Donald Trump's presidential campaign (Pengelly 2016). But if the allure of the dictionary is the promise of clarity, what one actually finds there is also an absence of meaning, a set of definitional exclusions that raise further doubts.

Take, for instance, the first definition of fascism in the Merriam-Webster Online:

> **Fascism:** *often capitalized*: a political philosophy, movement, or regime (such as that of the Fascisti) that exalts nation and often race above the individual and that stands for a centralized autocratic government headed by a dictatorial leader, severe economic and social regimentation, and forcible suppression of opposition.

Interestingly, this definition makes no mention of *populism* (one of the terms most frequently associated with fascism in contemporary political discourse), nor does it include the possibility that fascism might very well exist within, rather than without, the boundaries of a democratic society, as scholars of fascism and authoritarianism have noted (Hall 1985; Mann 2004; Sternhell 1986). In fact, the *Merriam-Webster*'s entry for fascism does not contemplate its rise without a dictatorial leader, or any leader at all, as a mass movement festering within democracy's own underbelly. Does this mean that it is not fascism, if "it" is democratically elected, just as Benito Mussolini was in 1921? Or does it mean that "it" can only become fascism later, only in retrospect, when it is too late to stop its rise? Can fascism be named, before it *is*?

My central concern in this essay is with the symbolic meaning of fascism in twenty-first-century politics. Focusing on the specific case of Italy in the broader context of global populisms that this volume attempts to explain, I will analyze the deployment of fascism in order to analyze the term's resurgence and its effects across the political spectrum. The year 2016 (re)activated a dormant semantic field, bringing to the fore of mainstream political debates in Europe and North America not only fascism, but also populism, nationalism, authoritarianism, and the right (Edwards, Haugerud, and Parikh 2017; Gusterson 2017; Scoones et al. 2018). Although these terms remain ambiguous and imprecise in everyday lay usage, their growing relevance to global politics is symptomatic of shifting configurations of power for which fascism often becomes a catchall organizing category. The fact that the word "fascism" can so easily attach to a vague and contradictory political lexicon needs not be surprising. According to semiotician Umberto Eco, fascism's own definitional "fuzziness" and philosophical "discombobulation" allowed it to become a "synecdoche" for different totalitarian movements throughout the world. Unlike Nazism, which did not adapt as easily to other contexts and times, "fascism became an all-purpose term because one can eliminate from a fascist regime one or more features, and it will still be recognizable as fascist" (Eco 1995).

The ground for my analysis of the discursive rise of fascism is the case of the Italian constitutional referendum of December 4, 2016. Held in the immediate aftermath of Trump's election and in the wake of Brexit, the referendum sent shockwaves through Europe, as the EU braced itself for yet another populist, Euroskeptic victory. The reform that the referendum put to popular vote and ultimately defeated was the brainchild of then–prime minister Matteo Renzi and of his center-left Democratic Party (PD). It would have been the first major reform of the Italian constitution since it was written in 1946. The reform, which I will review in detail later in this essay, would have completely overhauled the electoral system and governing bodies of the country in the name of more efficient governance. The "yes" campaign received the support of liberal democratic EU leaders, who valued its promise of modernizing Italy's notoriously slow legislative processes (Ansa 2016). By contrast, the reform's opponents were overwhelmingly depicted as Euroskeptics, isolationists, and fascists, especially in the foreign press, which, routinely represented the "no" vote as a threat to European liberal values analogous to Brexit. Taking issue with what I argue are profound mischaracterizations of the "no" side, I explore what the case of the Italian referendum can teach us about the spectral life of fascism and about its invocations to animate what are ultimately (neo) liberal policies.

The kind of fascism that is on the rise, I argue, is not only incarnate, embodied in a wide range of far-right parties and hate groups, whose violent actions and words, though not new, have certainly entered parliaments in greater numbers over the last two decades. Fascism is also spectral. It can haunt, possess, and manipulate mainstream politics even in the absence of actual fascists. It is this second meaning that interests me here. To be clear, the difference between fascism incarnate and spectral fascism is not to be found in a metric of the real. Both are "real" in the sense that social constructs and ideologies are real. Rather, the distinction matters tactically and analytically, if there is any hope of understanding contemporary manifestations of fascism in order to mount an effective resistance against them.

As a spectral force, fascism can be invoked through practices of fear that enliven political engagements across the spectrum. For instance, when fascism is conjured as a specter against which "we" must rise, a particular political subjectivity is called into being through the construction of an oppositional stance. The "we" that is animated in opposition to fascism could be an antifascist subject, and sometimes it is. However, since the 1990s it has been primarily neoliberal centrist parties in Europe that have mobilized fascism's spectral power by invoking it as an imminent threat to political life. The political subjectivity animated in contrast to fascism, therefore, has more often than not been a liberal one, rather than an antifascist one—and that is a crucial distinction. Although liberalism is in theory and in rhetoric staunchly opposed to everything fascism stands for, its own values of moderation, rationality, and freedom have at times displaced to the margins of legitimate political discourse not only fascist positions but also antifascist ones. Far-left political parties and activist groups, such as those that opposed the constitutional reform in Italy, and which have historically been in the front line of the militant fight against fascism, have often been accused by centrist parties of being as extremist as fascists themselves. One of the greatest dangers of spectral fascism, therefore, lies in its power to stupefy a normative liberal subjectivity into disarming antifascist resistance, thus abetting fascism's rise.

In pursuing a political anthropology of spectral fascism, I will ask two questions about the Italian constitutional referendum that could also be asked of a number of other political events of recent times. First, what kinds of political configurations did the referendum bring about? The poll-defying surprise that the victory of the "no" generated would appear to mark a departure from preexisting and predictable voting patterns based on operationalized identity categories. What novel political subjects did the referendum, therefore, represent? Second, why was the referendum so widely (mis)read as another Brexit—another right-wing, anti-European victory—by otherwise intelligent commentators? To put it differently, what is it that makes complex, alternative political configurations of resistance against dominant political parties legible only through a narrow binary logic of left and right sides, and, worst yet, through an invocation of fascism?

My argument is that the Italian constitutional referendum, which many dubbed Italy's Brexit, could just as easily have been celebrated as an antifascist victory in 2016. I build that alternative reading of the referendum by paying attention to both local activism and statistical results, which together paint a far more contradictory picture than headlines would suggest. Ultimately, though, I do not claim that my reading is necessarily more accurate than the official narrative of the triumph of fascist populism. I simply note that the erasure of antifascism from dominant accounts of the Italian constitutional referendum came at a high cost, and it is illustrative of the epistemic violence that liberalism continues to perpetuate against antifascist positions. I conclude, therefore, by reflecting on what it would take to turn the liberal project of anthropology into an antifascist endeavor, and what an antifascist anthropology could contribute to the analysis of the formidable politics of our time. While we may not be able to stop fascism's rise by simply limiting our dictionary searches, we can trace its spectral appearances across the body politic to discover the unexpected sites where fascism takes hold, the different shapes it shifts into, and the many dialects in which it speaks. And in each instance we can ask—to echo Sophie Bjork-James's intervention in this volume—if fascism is any kind of "answer" here, then what was the question?

Italy's Phantom Brexit

Between 2015 and 2016, Italian prime minister Renzi and his center-left Democratic Party (PD) put forth a complex package of legislative changes known collectively as the Renzi-Boschi constitutional reform. Parliament approved the reform package in early 2016, and a confirmatory referendum was called to take place by the end of the year to allow citizens, in accordance with Italian law, to either approve ("yes") or veto ("no") those constitutional changes before they could take effect.

According to its proponents, the reform would modernize Italy's governing bureaucracy. Its most significant proposal was a complete overhaul of the Senate as we know it, which would have been demoted to a consultative body made not of nationally elected senators but, rather, of a much smaller number of local politicians (regional presidents and city mayors) serving ex officio. For supporters of the reform, such a reconfigured Senate would have better represented local governments. Moreover, turning the Senate into a consultative organ would have given the Chamber of Deputies, the other half of Italy's bicameral Parliament, virtually unlimited authority to pass laws, making the legislative process overall more expedient. For detractors of the constitutional reform, the demotion of the Senate was the main point of contention. Whereas the idea of streamlining a long-winded and ineffective government could easily gather wide consensus, the legal and political risks of de facto reducing Parliament to a single chamber were frightening to those concerned about losing existing checks and balances. Such concerns were amplified by the simultaneous debates taking place throughout 2016 about another reform proposed by Prime Minister Renzi: a sweeping electoral reform known as "Italicum." The Italicum reform would have altered Italy's proportional electoral system by allotting a majority bonus to winning parties, and it would have made it much more difficult for small parties to hold any seats in Parliament. Unlike the constitutional reform, Italicum was not technically included in the referendum. However, the two were explicitly designed to complement each other. They were almost always discussed together in both political debates and informal conversations about the referendum. As the two pillars in what would have been Italy's "Third Republic," the Italicum and constitutional reforms promised to make the country easier to govern by effectively limiting the number of political parties and reducing Parliament to a single legislative chamber.

Throughout 2016, talk of the referendum was everywhere in Italy. The technical and legal complexity of the proposed reform package, however, made it unintelligible to the vast majority of voters, including educated audiences. In the months leading up to the vote, news outlets dedicated special segments to unpacking the details of the reform with the help of expert talking heads, while a number of online courses offered to teach people the details of the reform for a fee. Despite those educational campaigns, the only consensus on the ground seemed to be that the reform was incomprehensible. Discussing it with old friends and acquaintances in Italy, trying to tell fact from fiction in a sea of misinformation (e.g., would mayors-turned-senators earn two pensions?), I too initially struggled to educate myself about the elusive details of the reform. But if the content was fuzzy, the amount of public chatter and debate that the reform engendered was indicative of its high stakes. It may not have been fully clear to most citizens of Italy how exactly the reform was going to work or what its impact might be, but high voter turnout for the referendum suggests that most people cared deeply about what Prime Minister Renzi dubbed "the mother of all political battles" (La Stampa 2016).

To add to the generalized sense of confusion, endorsements of the reform were all over the political map. Its main proponent was the ruling center-left PD, joined in the "yes" by a choir of other left-wing parties and labor unions. The "no" side, on the contrary, included the entire right-wing coalition: Berlusconi's party, the League, and all the smaller far-right parties. Moreover, the "no" side also included the populist Five Star Movement (M5S), a left-leaning protest party founded in 2009 by a comedian, but which has since acquired xenophobic and anti-EU positions in line with the far right. At first sight, therefore, the mother of all political battles looked like a straightforward battle of the left and the right. However, right wingers and M5S populists were joined in voting "no" by the smaller far-left parties, as well as by a faction of the old communist leadership now housed inside the PD itself. The Communist labor union (CGIL) defected from other labor unions and voted no. Perhaps most important, the National Association of Italian Partisans (ANPI) also endorsed the "no" vote.[1] The Partisans (*partigiani*) were the antifascist militants who organized an armed resistance during World War II to liberate the country from Nazi-Fascism. The moral status of the Partisans in postwar Italy cannot be overestimated.[2] When it came to opposing the constitutional reform, therefore, it is highly remarkable that Partisans, Communists, populists, right wingers, and fascists all found themselves on the same side, although for very different reasons, against the establishment center left.

Despite the diverse makeup of the "no" camp, the referendum was widely misreported as a battle between progressives and those "integralist," counter-Enlightenment movements (Holmes 2000) that increasingly threaten European imaginaries of modernity and which are often summed up as "fascist," for short. Leading up to the vote, the sensationalist headlines of op-eds and news stories in the international press drew explicit continuities between the upcoming Italian referendum and the preceding cases of Brexit and Donald Trump's election. The *Guardian*, for instance, called the referendum "a test of populism" in the aftermath of Trump, while both CNN and the *Washington Post* emphasized the magnitude of the "shockwaves" that would "rock" Europe. To be fair, those articles did offer somewhat more nuanced analyses past the headlines. For instance, the *Guardian* admitted that voters were skeptical of whether the "mother of all battles" would ultimately make any difference at all and conceded that the prospect of giving Prime Minister Renzi a mandate through a "yes" vote was just as troubling to some people as the idea that a "no" vote would legitimize the populist M5S party (Kirchgaessner 2016). CNN even acknowledged that "while the foreign media is alarmed about the prospect of a 'No' victory, many Italians are surprisingly blasé about the potential consequences" (Wedeman 2016). And the *Washington Post* answered its own rhetorical title question—whether this was "Italy's Brexit moment"—by equivocating, several paragraphs down, "not exactly" (Taylor 2016). However, by consistently analogizing the Italian referendum to Brexit and to Trump's election, experts and news media inevitably limited their own analytical scope, while reinforcing the PD's narrative of progress (Brusini 2017). Given the complex and contradictory implications of both the "yes" and the "no," as well as the strong possibility that neither would in fact make much of a difference to Italian and European politics, it is astonishing that the reform could be so systematically misrepresented (even by ostensibly neutral news outlets) as a battle of apocalyptic proportions between progressive reformers and illiberal populists. Out of all possible readings of these events, why did this one become so compelling? How did fascism become the referendum's answer, despite all evidence to the contrary?

The initial terms of the debate, set by the PD, framed the reform as "progress" and boasted that it would bring Italy up to European standards of governance. The framework of the debate preemptively cast any opposition as antimodern, anti-European, and reactionary. The logical slippage is especially worth noting in comparison to Brexit, where the equivalent of a "yes" vote ("leave") had brought about significant anti-European change, whereas the equivalent of a "no" vote ("remain") would have simply maintained the status quo of the UK within the EU. In the Italian constitutional referendum a "no" vote would have kept the constitution as it was. Two assaults on logic had to occur, therefore, to transform the Italian referendum into another Brexit. First, the notion of "change" had to be redefined as necessarily progressive (despite the fact that Brexit reminded everyone that change is not always progressive). Second, the "no" option, which would have maintained the status quo, had to be recast as ushering in novel danger, with prophecies of financial collapse and democratic ruin to follow (La Repubblica 2016). Couched as it was in the language of neoliberalism, the reform therefore unleashed the discursive power of EU modernity to normativize its ideological positions, while simultaneously invoking the spectral power of an increasingly populist and xenophobic fascism to stigmatize any competing notions of change (and any refusals to change).

Who Won?

As Jonathan Rosa and Yarimar Bonilla wrote about Donald Trump, "there is just as much to be learned from the *reactions* to the election as there is from the results" (2017, 201). In the aftermath of the Italian referendum, the far-from-obvious questions of who won and who lost drove political debates. The striking defeat of the reform caught the ruling party by surprise. Prime Minister Renzi had repeatedly promised to resign if his constitutional reform was rejected by voters, and he kept his word. That ill-fated promise was indicative of the overconfidence with which the "yes" side had approached the vote, but also of its political identification of the "yes" with the center-left coalition in power. It was Renzi who personalized a rather dull referendum on legislative bureaucracy into a plebiscite on him (Matteucci 2016). By attaching his political mandate to the outcome of the referendum, Renzi's loss handed over to the right a victory they had not necessarily earned, but which they were happy to claim. In the wake of the referendum, populist and right-wing parties, all of which had unanimously opposed the reform, pounced at the chance to demand new elections—which they won in 2018.

The referendum results, however, paint a far more complex picture of the vote. Although it seems clear that Renzi lost, it is not as clear that the right won. Results show that voters did not always follow party lines. Instead, age, class, and highest level of education turned out to be the variables most highly correlated with the vote. Although the "no" side won 59.1 percent of the total votes, that percentage spiked among those aged forty-four and under (69 percent of whom voted no), as well as among the unemployed and underemployed (73 percent), and among those with advanced degrees. Demographic differences in voting were found even among registered PD members, among whom those making less than 18,000 euros per year broke away from Prime Minister Renzi and voted against the reform at a rate of 51 percent (Feltri 2016). Finally, the "no" side won by a higher margin in the south, showing the ongoing significance of regional differences to contemporary Italian politics.[3] Therefore, the statistical results paint a revealing picture of "no" voters as younger people, the unemployed or underemployed, the highly educated, and many southerners: categories that are very often one and the same in Italy.

While polling metrics may fail to capture the intersectionality of these variables, an ethnographically informed analysis of the vote suggests that a new political subject emerged outside political taxonomies of old. For anyone who has spent any time in Italy in the last few decades, the political subject of the highly educated but underemployed youth, especially from the south, should be immediately recognizable. Although certain parties might appeal more or less explicitly to any of its constituting categories, the intersectional subject that defeated the reform is found across the political spectrum. Like any other legitimate political subject, this one too appears genderless in the data, as mainstream polls in Italy typically do not account for gender differences. Its unmarked masculinity is further entrenched through highly gendered accounts of this subject's "anger." But unlike legitimate political subjects, measured by party affiliations, this one can only result from a recuperation of missing pieces, lost in the cracks of recognizable categories, at the intersection of metrics that were not designed to account for its existence and its outrage. As a subject, it amounts to an unaccounted multitude, an entire generation (or two, depending on how one counts it), lost to structural adjustment programs, systemic defunding of the welfare state, and neoliberal reforms in the country that used to have the most powerful Communist Party in the West (Kertzer 1996; Molé 2012; Muehlebach 2012). "Youth" in this context is a cultural category, which in Italian allows the words for girl or boy ("ragazza/o") to refer to people well into their forties. The prolonging of the status of youth is precisely the collective condition experienced by generations of Italians for whom the socioeconomic markers of adulthood that had applied to their parents became unattainable: a permanent job contract in the public sector; a mortgage; marriage and children.

How such a multitude could go unseen in Italian political surveys, how its compact actions *as a class* could elicit surprise even to a self-described left-wing party like the PD, is the mystification that needs to be unraveled. Renzi himself took office at the age of thirty-nine, becoming the youngest prime minister Italy had ever had since Mussolini. Renzi was often condescendingly referred to as the "bravo ragazzo" ("good boy"), who had attempted to move Italy forward but failed with his signature "Jobs Act" of EU-driven austerity policies dispensed in cool global English to an increasingly globalized European underclass (Jones 2015). Fed up and angry, but not unsophisticated, the highly educated unemployed "youth" of Italy lived on their skin the demystification of neoliberal ideologies, either succumbing to a "brain drain" and leaving the country in search of better career opportunities, or staying behind to work in a gig economy for which they are often overqualified (Alderman 2013).

Over the last decade, the anger and energy of this dispossessed youth has been channeled by new political parties and, most notably, by the M5S, which strongly opposed Renzi's constitutional reform. Although technically on the left, M5S is a populist movement of "young" people drawn from various sides of the political spectrum to form a protest party. In its championing of young, angry, disenfranchised Italians, the positions of M5S, such as increased welfare for citizens and critiques of the Euro currency, reflect a nationalist socialist stance on par with the far-right League in its racist, anti-immigrant statements. As Gerald Creed and Mary Taylor elucidated in their essay in this volume, liberal antipopulism has too often obscured and delegitimized reasonable and valid sources of popular discontent, with the result that the latter have found listening ears among the right. The political influence of M5S might have been underestimated by Renzi leading up to the referendum, but a mere fifteen months later, when new elections took place in March 2018, M5S rose to become the country's first party, joining forces with the League to form an ultrapopulist government and leaving no doubt about the need to take seriously the angry, underemployed, highly educated youth that M5S represented. Just like right-wing parties, M5S claimed victory too, after the referendum, confirming fears that populism and fascism had won indeed.

Whereas both M5S and right-wing parties were named as possible "winners" in news coverage of the referendum, there is another potentially victorious formation that I argue remained largely unseen: the antifascist left. Both numerically and morally, the far left shaped the referendum's results and the debates around it. One of the most illustrious voices of the "no" camp belonged to former Supreme Court justice and former Communist Party senator, Domenico Gallo. He was among the first to sound the alarm as soon as the constitutional reform was approved by Parliament in January 2016. As a constitutional scholar, and as a member of the committee that called for a confirmatory referendum, Gallo warned against the fascist echoes of Renzi's ostensibly progressive proposals: the Italicum electoral reform and the constitutional reform. By concentrating power within a few large parties and by abrogating the system of checks and balances built into Parliament, the two reforms bore a dangerous resemblance to Mussolini's infamous 1923 electoral reform, the "Acerbo law." Historically, the Acerbo law marked the turning point in the transformation of Mussolini's rule from a "democratically" elected government into a "dictatorship."[4] The Acerbo law awarded a huge majority bonus to the winning party. It enabled the National Fascist Party to gain full control of Parliament, which Mussolini then used to pass the "extraordinary laws" of 1925–28, which abolished democratic institutions piece by piece, until eventually Parliament itself was abolished. In Gallo's words, "only the erasure of historical memory can make a set of institutional reforms pass for innovative when they attempt to restore autocratic forms of power that history had left behind" (2016).

To call the Italian fascist regime a dictatorship, as people commonly do, is to simplify by way of misnaming it what was an internal weakness of liberal democracy—perhaps its own litmus test—which Italian fascists seized upon and carried to a dictatorial conclusion. To put it differently, characterizing Mussolini's regime as *simply* a dictatorship mystifies by means of historical amnesia the complicity of liberal democracy in authorizing, enabling, and disseminating fascism as a dictatorial regime. In postwar Italy, this mystification persisted through nationalist ideologies that retroactively construed fascism as a historical aberration (Del Boca 2003). However, any definition of fascism that posits it outside of democracy or in contrast to it (as the dictionary does) is not only historically untenable but ultimately dangerous in its failure to name fascism before it is too late.

That was the contribution of antifascist critics to the referendum's debate in

2016: the willingness to name as fascist even seemingly progressive, left-wing reforms like the Italicum and the constitutional reform. There is therefore an equally plausible reading of the referendum's outcome as an antifascist victory. In the remaining pages, I pursue that alternative reading not to declare the far left the "true" winner, but to examine what its significant absence from official victory narratives can reveal about the spectral work of fascism. In the case of the Italian constitutional referendum, and increasingly across Euro-American politics, the notions of crisis and progress have been deployed by ruling parties as they invoked fascism to explain their own defeats. This case serves as a reminder, then, that any notion of "progress" that conjures up the specter of fascism in order to pit itself against it ought to look suspect if it forecloses the actual lived politics of antifascist resistance.

No, We Won

A few days after the referendum, while I was in Bologna conducting research on a project about the intertwining crises of labor and migration, I came across an enormous mural. As a "native" anthropologist of Italy, I had walked by that same spot in Piazza Verdi countless times before, in the heart of the old city, by the Alma Mater Studiorum, the oldest university in Europe, and I had been greeted by the same scene that since the early 1980s has been indicted as the icon of social degradation in one of the wealthiest cities in Italy. A sea of bodies in clouds of smoke, consuming and transacting ill-disguised drugs, occupied the public space of the urine-reeking piazza with dogs, guitars, and bottles of alcohol, just as they had been doing for decades, under the gaze of police forces surrounding them from a safe distance. Despite repeated "cleansing" campaigns over the years, and not infrequent clashes with the authorities, Piazza Verdi has resisted gentrifying efforts waged in the name of safety and legality, seamlessly incorporating into its ranks of white students and drug addicts increasing numbers of black and brown immigrants, many of whom now not only populate the square and partake in its underground economy, but also own the convenience stores and kebab shops that feed its habitual hustlers.

With the surreptitiousness of street art, the approximately twenty-meter-long mural had appeared suddenly overnight a few months earlier, in September 2016. At the center of the image, in all capital letters, the words "STORIA PARTIGIANA" ("Partisan history") sat triumphantly and defiantly against a backdrop of red and yellow rays reminiscent of communist esthetics, while life-size police forces in riot gear were depicted as unsuccessfully trying to mount an assault against it from one side. In small letters, right under "STO-RIA PARTIGIANA," the mural quoted in Italian some verses by the socialist Turkish poet Nazim Hikmet: "To walk toward what is just and true. To fight for what is true, just. To seize what is just, true."[5]

The mural was claimed by the Collettivo Universitario Autonomo (CUA), an anarchist group that has engaged in a battle of street art with the city on multiple occasions (Zic.it 2016). Even without that knowledge, the mural's nostalgic iconography of resistance made clear the political leanings of the artists. "Partisan history" was an explicit reference to the antifascist national heroes of World War II, and to their political legacy. The figure of the Partisan was invoked in the mural in the service of a transhistorical and romanticized imagery of resistance, as it so often is in Italian politics. The Partisans' famous battle song, "Bella Ciao," for instance, continues to serve as the soundtrack to rallies and protests even today. But instead of celebrating the Partisans of the past or the far-left militants of the present, the mural recentered an antifascist historicity and reclaimed its centrality both to Italian liberation during World War II and to contemporary politics.

In the mural's transhistorical representation, fascism figured as the spectral nemesis of Partisan history. Here, however, fascism was not embodied by militants in black shirts but, rather, by police in riot gear. The uncanny life-size image of police forces attacking "Partisan history" could recall any number of police-led assaults that took place in that very piazza in recent years and which were rebuked by members of CUA and other far-left *collettivi*. On the right side of the mural, the imagery of hay balls (which also looked like gunpowder barrels) recalled the real-life hay balls that CUA had used a few months earlier, in June 2016, to barricade Piazza Verdi when the leader of the far-right League, Matteo Salvini, had tried to lead a march through it on Italy's Republic Day (Del Prete 2016). Spectral fascism was therefore present in the image, but it assumed contemporary, neoliberal, political, and militarized forms, whereas "Partisan history" figured as a timeless source of righteousness and truth, as written in Hikmet's verses, for present-day antifascists.

When I walked by the mural, a few days after the referendum in early December, a makeshift banner was hanging above it. Its message written in black marker on a white sheet read: "We are the ones who won the referendum. Now we are taking to the streets again to reclaim social rights and dignity."[6] In Italian the message contained a play on words. The pronoun *noi* means "we."

However, in the first sentence of the banner the word "NOi" stood out in all red letters, the first two of which ("NO") were capitalized to spell out a second word within the word: a resounding NO inside the *noi*. The political subject of the "we" animated in the sign was therefore rhetorically enjoined to a refusal. Literally, the NO won, WE won, WE are the NO. The handwritten protest banner about the constitutional referendum was added on later, but it mobilized the mural's timeless iconography of resistance in the service of a specific cause. The banner resignified the mural as a proud statement of victory of the "no." Just as Prime Minister Renzi had identified the "yes" with himself, here the dissenters—the CUA and other far-left groups that have long occupied Piazza Verdi—identified their own subject positions with the "no"—both sides personifying the referendum's stakes. In the center of Bologna, moreover, the victory sign and the "Partisan history" mural acquired heightened local meanings. During World War II, Bologna was the epicenter of Partisan resistance, but that communist history, which had earned it the nickname of "the red city," had slowly but steadily given way to political compromises. Bologna was now headquarters of the center-left PD establishment, and the "yes" therefore won in the city (with 52 percent of the votes), even though it lost nationally. In Piazza Verdi, however, a class-based and antiracist form of resistance had long been brewing, and it found in the referendum a new opportunity for expression. Although it predated the referendum by three months, the mural could easily become legible as a powerful critique of Renzi's proposed reform and as a broader critique of the neoliberal left for betraying its Partisan history even in the red city.

Italy's constitution of 1946 is sometimes affectionately referred to as the "partisan constitution" (*costituzione partigiana*). Even though the Partisans, most of whom had been communists, socialists, and anarchists, did not gain control of Italy's postwar Catholic and centrist government, the new constitution they helped bring to life was imprinted with their utopian visions. In addition to guaranteeing fundamental rights to work, healthcare, and education, Italy's 1946 constitution also outlawed fascism and the Fascist Party. The partisan constitution, therefore, did not simply reinstate a liberal democracy after the war. It established an antifascist democracy, setting up legal and institutional mechanisms meant to prevent the return of fascism. That was the antifascist constitution that the referendum proposed to change. That was the "Partisan history" that the ruling center-left party attempted to revision, but which new antifascists fought to protect.

Conclusion: Conjuring an Antifascist Anthropology

Nevertheless, even though political regimes can be overthrown, and
ideologies can be criticized and disowned, behind a regime and its ideology there is always a way of thinking and feeling, a group of cultural
habits, of obscure instincts and unfathomable drives. Is there still another ghost stalking Europe (not to speak of other parts of the world)?
— Umberto Eco. 1995. Ur-Fascism

The year 2016 changed the terms of engagement. When existing metrics failed
to capture the complexity of political life on the ground, in Brexit's case, in
Trump's case, and again in the Italian referendum's case, "fascism" was animated as a convenient answer to fill the gaps of knowledge. Perhaps that is
because fascism *can* be an answer to virtually any political question. Michael
Mann (2004) noted that "fascist" works as an insult against any opponent, and
the invective itself therefore tells us little about its recipients. It is far more telling to consider who is doing the name calling. In each of the 2016 cases, *mutata
mutandis*, a ruling centrist neoliberal party deployed fascism preemptively, as a
threat against which "we" must guard, and retroactively, as an explanation for
what happened, ousting any alternative interpretations from public discourse.
If we acknowledge that Partisans and far-left groups in Italy strongly endorsed
the "no" vote, however, the official reading of the referendum as a fascist and
populist victory becomes not only tendentious but perverse.

My aim in this essay has been to show that against the grain of dominant political analyses there is an equally plausible reading of the Italian constitutional
reform's defeat as an antifascist victory. The point is not that one reading is
better than the other, but that one reading—the one espoused by the party in
power—eclipsed the other with serious repercussions for Italian politics. The
invocation of fascism by the Italian PD not only elided the antifascist activism
that contributed to the reform's defeat but also bolstered far-right claims to
victory that may not have been entirely merited. A little over a year later, the
League and M5S went on to win the 2018 national elections, forming the most
populist government in Italy since Mussolini. It is possible, of course, that the
referendum results simply foreshadowed the victory of a populist right that
was to come. But it is also possible that the story of fascism's victory became
a self-fulfilling prophecy. When the PD attributed its referendum's loss to the
specter of fascism, rather than to the antifascist far left, or simply to its own
shortcomings, it lent credibility to a previously doubtful far-right and populist

alliance. Ironically, the erasure of antifascism from the official narrative of Italy's constitutional referendum was perpetuated in the name of fighting against fascism.

I suggest that it is both possible and necessary to recover an antifascist perspective from the rubble of 2016—in fact, it might even be possible to refuse to concede 2016 to fascism at all. For such a reading to be plausible, however, a new definition of fascism is needed, one that can reconcile it with history and locate it firmly within, rather than in opposition to, the liberal democratic model from which it came. In other words, we need a definition of fascism capacious enough to name it both in its evident incarnate forms and in its insidious spectral forms. Fortunately, the masterminds of Italian fascism have already provided the world with such a definition. In the Treccani encyclopedia entry that Mussolini himself co-authored, fascism is described not merely as a party or a political doctrine but as a "fundamental conception of life: . . . an organic conception of the world" (Mussolini and Volpe 1932). Fascists have already told us what fascism is in their own emic terms. We just need to take them seriously.

Understandably, much of the early critical scholarship, especially coming out of an Italian Marxist lens, dismissed and ridiculed fascism's capacity to engender meaningful worldviews and social systems, reducing its ensnaring influence to captive forms of brainwashing or to acquiescence to Nazi Germany.[7] As the historian of fascism Zeev Sternhell cautioned, however, "the official Marxist interpretation of the history of the interwar period, whereby fascism is alleged to have been merely the tool of monopolistic capitalism and its ideology a mere rationalization of imperialist interests, was a major obstacle to a comprehensive understanding of the phenomenon" (1986, 4). In addition to dismissing fascism's lack of a coherent philosophy, much work on Italian fascism has also foregrounded the class politics of the movement (Poulantzas 2018) at the expense of any serious analysis of its racial and white supremacist roots. To put it simply, fascism has been mythologized as Nazism's "lesser evil." In order to support the untenable claim that fascism was not really about race, postwar scholars had to exclude Italy's genocidal racial regimes in the African colonies from their studies, as though the lives of Eritreans, Ethiopians, Libyans, and Somalis under fascism did not matter to the argument (Ben-Ghiat and Fuller 2005; Burgio 1999; Palumbo 2003). They also had to downplay the 1938 racial laws against Italian Jews, looking at them as Mussolini's last-minute favor to Hitler rather than the culmination of a long anti-Semitic campaign that the duce had started in the 1920s and which led to the systematic obliteration of Italian Jews' rights and life (Sarfatti 1994).[8] Italian historiography since at least the 1980s has moved away from the "lie" (Raspanti 1994) of fascism's less virulent racism (Capristo and Ialongo 2019; Traverso 2008), but the fact that it took so long to get here is a reminder of the insidiousness of fascism: its ability to pass for something more benign than what it is. As Antonio Gramsci warned in 1925, when he was still a member of Parliament and the democratically elected National Fascist Party held the majority of seats, we underestimate fascism at our own peril (Gramsci and Mussolini 1997).

If we believe what fascists told us about fascism—that it is a total conception of life, a quasireligious worldview with spiritual, social, economic, and political dimensions, then anthropologists are uniquely well positioned to study it. A robust anthropology of fascism, however, cannot be merely *about* the right, though more ethnographic research on conservative and far-right movements is certainly called for.[9] It must also understand the deployment of fascism by the left, by the center, or in sites that may not appear "political" at all. Fascism is everywhere. In the wake of 2016, there is an urgent need for a renewed anthropological approach to the political that could deliver what polls and political commentaries could not: a way to foresee and to resist fascism's rise before it is too late. What is needed, I suggest, is an *antifascist* anthropology.

In *Antifa: The Anti-Fascist Handbook*, Mark Bray has defined antifascism broadly as "an *illiberal* politics of social revolutionism applied to fighting the far right, not only literal fascists" (2017, xv; emphasis added). While the methods and ideologies of various antifascist groups have differed widely, Bray has suggested that "it is vital to understand antifascism as a solitary component of a larger legacy of resistance to white supremacy in all its forms" (2017, xvii). There are two distinctive elements to Bray's definition that I find especially useful for anthropology. First, Bray subtended antifascism to antiracism. Given that an overemphasis on class analysis has too often obscured the deep roots of Italian fascism in white supremacy—a mistake seldom made about German Nazism—Bray's ideological framing of antifascist resistance squarely within the legacy of antiracist resistance leaves no doubt about the political stakes of such a project. Second, Bray characterized antifascism as an illiberal movement. Given liberalism's historical complicity with the rise of fascism, and its sometimes hostile relationship to antifascist movements, Bray's definition signals the need to untether a project of antifascist resistance from the constraints of a liberal worldview. This is not to say that antifascism must necessarily be antiliberal, nor to suggest a false equivalence between liberalism and fascism. It is merely to recognize that antifascism must be willing to resist liberalism, too, whenever the latter hinders an antiracist project of social justice centered on the principled rejection of fascism in all its forms.[10]

I recognize this is a tall order for anthropology—the liberal discipline par excellence, born from the marriage of colonial biopolitics and Eurocentric Orientalism. Elsewhere I have argued that liberalism is a cosmology, rather than merely an ideology (Mahmud 2016, 2018), and its worldviews and origin stories occupy a dominant place both in anthropology's assumptions and in what Michael Herzfeld (2004) termed the "global hierarchy of values." Some antifascist positions, especially around the use of violence, or the refusal to dialogue with fascists, can seem antithetical to anthropological ethics of relativism and engagement. Those ethics, however, are not neutral. They are steeped in an unreflexive acceptance of liberal premises and of all their attending power dynamics, which have proven resilient even to decades of decolonial, feminist, "native," queer, and indigenous critiques coming from within anthropology itself.

The mural at the center of my analysis, for instance, was an act of vandalism committed by members of a militant far-left collective and publicly condemned by city and university officials alike. On multiple occasions CUA members have destroyed private property and resorted to physical violence to stop *leghisti* and fascists from marching through the piazza, just as they have fought back the state police forces deployed against them by a center-left democratic government. Engaging in such actions, members of the CUA have lived up to the most stereotypical depictions of groups like antifa. Within a liberal system of morality, which values private property and condemns physical violence when it is not state-sponsored, it is easy to dismiss such groups as extremist. However, much of the CUA's less visible activism has been nonviolent, satirical, and artistic. In his ethnography of antiglobalization activists in the former Yugoslavia, Maple Razsa (2015) has shown that the violent practices attributed to far-left militant groups (e.g., the trope of "punching Nazis") are often exaggerated in mainstream representations precisely to discredit far-left collectives and social centers, all of which actually engage in a far wider range of direct action practices. Given the uncomfortable fact that liberalism often does more violence to antifascist positions than to fascist ones, an anti-fascist anthropology would have to become reflexive about those Eurocentric liberal values of progress, freedom, and rights, which overwhelmingly shape our etic categories.

Ultimately, it is true that antifascist militant actions rest on a fundamentally illiberal premise: that fascist speech is not a legitimate viewpoint in the marketplace of ideas but a violent assault on bodies and democracy to be rebuked by any means. The Italian "partisan" constitution of 1946 recognized as much when it outlawed the Fascist Party, and Italy's postwar government went even further in criminalizing both "fascist propaganda" and the "apology" of fascism.[11] Despite such lofty principles, (neo)fascist parties have nonetheless ascended to power in Italy simply by changing their names, and the constitutional reform that promised to make Italy more modern bore a dangerous resemblance to fascist ideals of governance. To call out those liberal practices that aid and abet fascism's rise, anthropology would need to become *partisan* in a political context where neutrality was never an option.

An important lesson offered by the ethnography of the right is that the study of conservative movements can make visible the shared cosmologies and hegemonic assumptions that are otherwise difficult to see about one's own social world. For instance, there are significant continuities between socially acceptable liberal beliefs and their inflammatory far-right counterparts with regard to Islamophobia (Fernando 2014), xenophobia (Cabot 2014), and workers' dispossession (Muehlebach 2012). Rather than taking 2016 as an aberration of apocalyptic proportions, then, an antifascist anthropology could have seen it coming (Mahmud 2016). It could have recognized the work of spectral fascism across various domains of life, including among liberal and democratic groups.

Regardless of whether the victory of the "no" in Italy should be attributed to the far left, as the CUA and others claimed, or to populism and neofascism, as both the PD and the right decreed, there is a populist lesson that gets lost if the analysis is blinded by liberal politics. That is, that the people of contemporary populisms are no longer captured by existing socioeconomic or party-centered taxonomies (if they ever were). Just as it turns out that the "white working class" did not elect Trump (Walley 2017), it was not just the far right that won Italy's constitutional referendum. The "no" vote in Italy was the vote of the highly educated and of the poorest. It was the young vote. It was driven as much by a distrust of neoliberal notions of "progress" as it was by nationalist sentiments. And because nationalism is not confined to the right or the left of the political spectrum (Anderson [1983] 1991), young nationalists could fight Renzi's reform out of allegiance to a romanticized partisan history or out of neofascist xenophobia. To be sure, many may have been Euroskeptics, as the international press decried, but what that actually means should not be taken for granted. As I wrote elsewhere, Euroskepticism has become a shared rubric of dissent for widely different political actors (Mahmud 2018). On the far left, anti-EU sentiments typically emerge from a critique of "fortress Europe," of its unwelcoming and inhumane immigration policies, of its neoliberal austerity economics that have eroded workers' rights and the public sector—a radically different set of considerations from those that motivate right-wing Euroskepticism. But it is the fact that such strange bedfellows can vote alike that is worth pondering. We are witnessing a populism of strangers united not by a shared class or identity as a "people," nor by shared concerns, but, rather, by a shared oppositional stance against a real or imagined common enemy. Historians have suggested that in the 1930s it was the ideological rejection of materialism and of the civilization it represented—"that is, of the essence of the European intellectual heritage from the seventeenth century onward" (Sternhell 1986, 268)—that allied a strain of socialism of the time with the antiliberal and antibourgeois nationalism of fascists. In 2016 that perceived common enemy of the people might have been liberalism.

To resist fascism, therefore, an antiracist and antifascist anthropology of the contemporary must be willing to take liberalism to task. White supremacy is at the core of fascism, despite revisionist amnesia. But white supremacy also lives deeply and paradoxically within liberalism itself, despite all its inclusionary promises. There cannot be a genuine critique of fascism without recognizing the complicity of a liberal system of values in the historical production of racism and in the rise of fascist regimes. An antifascist, illiberal anthropology must be ready and willing to name fascism even when it haunts democratic sites, when it latches onto liberal thought, when it sounds civilized and reasonable, when it incarnates in police uniforms rather than black shirts. There *is* another ghost stalking Europe, as Eco feared. And as any exorcist knows, the only way to vanquish a demonic being is to call it by its true name.

Notes

1. While some local ANPI chapters publicly dissented from the organization's national leadership and joined the Democratic Party in voting "yes," the association as a whole strongly endorsed the "no."

2. Even in the present, affirming one's grandparent's role as a *partigiano* (a militant fighter) or a *staffetta* (a messenger and carrier of weapons) is a claim to virtue in Italy. Well into the late twentieth century, when many partisans were still alive, they would routinely be invited to speak to schoolchildren, and they would be celebrated as the national freedom fighters who defeated fascism (see Krause 2009).

3. Perhaps as an indication of the international coverage, the "yes" prevailed among Italians residing abroad, whose votes are collected at embassies and counted separately.

4. At the time of Mussolini's election, Italy was a constitutional monarchy. Women did not gain the right to vote until 1945, and the monarchy was replaced by a republic in 1946.

5. On the mural, the verses read: "Camminare verso il giusto e il vero. Combattere per il vero, il giusto. Conquistare il giusto, il vero." The English version is my translation.

6. "Il referendum l'abbiamo vinto NOi. Ora torniamo in piazza per riprenderci diritti sociali e dignità." I translated the original "piazza" as "streets" rather than "square" to preserve the idiomatic connotation of protest that "going down to the piazza" and "taking to the streets" have, respectively, in Italian and English. In this context, "piazza" could also be a literal reference to Piazza Verdi.

7. The scholarship has been especially dismissive of women's active participation in Italian fascism. Save a few exceptions (De Grazia 1992; Macciocchi 1976), fascist women have been largely understood as either brainwashed or unwitting accomplices of fascism's masculine and statist project of racial supremacy.

8. Even an otherwise astute thinker like George Mosse wrote that, unlike for Nazism, "[r]acism and anti-Semitism were not a necessary component of fascism" (1999, 35). This failure to recognize the constitutive racism of Italian fascism has undoubtedly multiple causes, including Italy's successful postwar efforts to erase its colonial past from national memory, and its nationalist trope of Italians as "*brava gente*" (good people), who could not possibly have committed those atrocities on purpose.

9. For ethnographic research on the right, see Bacchetta and Power (2002); Ginsburg (1998); Harding (1991, 2000); Holmes (2000); Mahmud (2014); and Shoshan (2016).

10. For recent anthropological work on liberalism, see Boyer (2016) and Dzenovska and Kurtović (2018).

11. Constitution of the Italian Republic (1946), transitional and final provisions XII; Law 645 "legge Scelba" (1952).

References

Alderman, Liz. 2013. "Young and Educated in Europe, but Desperate for Jobs." *New York Times*, November 15. Accessed April 30, 2018. https://www.nytimes.com/2013/11/16/world/europe/youth-unemployement-in-europe.html.

Anderson, Benedict R. [1983] 1991. *Imagined Communities: Reflections on the Origin and Spread of Nationalism*. London: Verso.

Ansa. 2016. "Referendum Costituzionale, Merkel Appoggia Renzi." *Ansa*, September 15. Accessed April 30, 2018. http://www.ansa.it/sito/notizie/politica/2016/09/14/referendum-mattarella-sovranita-rimane-agli-elettori_f50dc019-2a68-406f-a16c-8a36896d8728.html.

Bacchetta, Paola, and Margaret Power, eds. 2002. *Right-Wing Women: From Conservatives to Extremists around the World*. New York: Routledge.

Ben-Ghiat, Ruth, and Mia Fuller, eds. 2005. *Italian Colonialism*. 1st ed., *Italian and Italian American Studies*. New York: Palgrave Macmillan.

Boyer, Dominic. 2016. Crisis of Liberalism. *Cultural Anthropology* Hot Spots, Fieldsights, October 27. Accessed April 15, 2019. https://culanth.org/fieldsights/989-crisis-of-liberalism.

Bray, Mark. 2017. *Antifa: The Anti-Fascist Handbook*. Brooklyn: Melville House.

Brusini, Chiara. 2017. "Referendum Costituzionale: Quando i Gufi Erano Renzi, Confindustria e Fitch: Dopo il No L'Apocalisse Non C'È Stata." *Il Fatto Quotidiano*, December 3. Accessed April 30, 2018. https://www.ilfattoquotidiano.it/2017/12/03/referendum-costituzionale-quando-i-gufi-erano-renzi-confindustria-e-fitch-dopo-il-no-lapocalisse-non-ce-stata/4009257/.

Burgio, Alberto, ed. 1999. *Nel Nome della Razza: Il Razzismo nella Storia d'Italia 1870–1945, Percorsi*. Bologna: Il Mulino.

Cabot, Heath. 2014. *On the Doorstep of Europe: Asylum and Citizenship in Greece*. Philadelphia: University of Pennsylvania Press.

Capristo, Annalisa, and Ernest Ialongo. 2019. "On the 80th Anniversary of the Racial Laws: Articles Reflecting the Current Scholarship on Italian Fascist Anti-Semitism in Honour of Michele Sarfatti." *Journal of Modern Italian Studies* 24 (1): 1–13.

Constitution of the Italian Republic. 1946.

De Grazia, Victoria. 1992. *How Fascism Ruled Women: Italy, 1922–1945*. Berkeley: University of California Press.

Del Boca, Angelo. 2003. "The Myths, Suppressions, Denials, and Defaults of Italian Colonialism." In *A Place in the Sun: Africa in Italian Colonial Culture from Post-Unification to the Present*, ed. Patrizia Palumbo, 17–36. Berkeley: University of California Press.

Del Prete, Federico. 2016. "Salvini a Bologna, Blitz a Sorpresa e Alta Tensione." *Il*

Resto del Carlino, June 2. Accessed April 30, 2018.https://www.ilrestodelcarlino
.it/bologna/politica/salvini-contestazione-2-giugno-1.2216420.

Dzenovska, Dace, and Larisa Kurtović. 2018. Lessons for Liberalism from the
"Illiberal East." *Cultural Anthropology* Hot Spots, Fieldsights, April 25. Accessed
April 15, 2019. https://culanth.org/fieldsights/introduction-lessons-for-liberalism
-from-the-illiberal-east.

Eco, Umberto. 1995. "Ur-Fascism." *The New York Review of Books*, June 22. Accessed
April 30, 2018. http://www.nybooks.com/articles/1995/06/22/ur-fascism/.

Edwards, Jeanette, Angelique Haugerud, and Shanti Parikh. 2017. "Introduction: The
2016 Brexit Referendum and Trump Election." *American Ethnologist* 44 (2): 195–200.

Fascism. n.d. In *Merriam-Webster.com*. Retrieved from https://www.merriam
-webster.com/dictionary/fascism.

Feltri, Stefano. 2016. "Referendum Costituzionale: Sì o No, Un Voto (Anche) di
Classe e di Partito." *Il Fatto Quotidiano*, December 5. Accessed August 2, 2019.
https://www.ilfattoquotidiano.it/2016/12/05/referendum-costituzionale-si-o
-no-un-voto-anche-di-classe-e-di-partito/3240285/.

Fernando, Mayanthi L. 2014. *The Republic Unsettled: Muslim French and the Contradictions of Secularism*. Durham, NC: Duke University Press.

Gallo, Domenico. 2016. "La Riforma Costituzionale È la Madre di Tutte le
Battaglie." *Micromega Online*, January 12. Accessed April 30, 2018. http://temi
.repubblica.it/micromega-online/la-riforma-costituzionale-e-la-madre-di
-tutte-le-battaglie/.

Ginsburg, Faye D. 1998. *Contested Lives: The Abortion Debate in an American Community*. Berkeley: University of California Press.

Gramsci, Antonio, and Benito Mussolini. 1997. *Contro la Legge sulle Associazioni Segrete, I Grandi Discorsi*. Roma: Manifestolibri.

Gusterson, Hugh. 2017. "From Brexit to Trump: Anthropology and the Rise of Nationalist Populism." *American Ethnologist* 44 (2): 209–214.

Hall, Stuart. 1985. "Authoritarian Populism: A Reply to Jessop et al." *New Left Review*
151: 115–124.

Harding, Susan. 1991. "Representing Fundamentalism: The Problem of the Repugnant Cultural Other." *Social Research: An International Quarterly* 58 (3): 373–393.

Harding, Susan. 2000. *The Book of Jerry Falwell: Fundamentalist Language and Politics*. Princeton, NJ: Princeton University Press.

Herzfeld, Michael. 2004. *The Body Impolitic: Artisans and Artifice in the Global Hierarchy of Value*. Chicago: University of Chicago Press.

Holmes, Douglas R. 2000. *Integral Europe: Fast-Capitalism, Multiculturalism, Neofascism*. Princeton, NJ: Princeton University Press.

Jones, Gavin. 2015. "Renzi's Jobs Act Isn't Getting Italy to Work." *Reuters*, December
14. Accessed August 2, 2019. https://www.reuters.com/article/us-italy

-employment-analysis/renzis-jobs-act-isnt-getting-italy-to-work
-idUSKBN0TX1WA20151214.

Kertzer, David I. 1996. *Politics and Symbols: The Italian Communist Party and the Fall of Communism*. New Haven, CT: Yale University Press.

Kirchgaessner, Stephanie. 2016. "After Trump Victory, Italy Referendum Is Seen as Test of Populism's Rise." *The Guardian*, November 24. Accessed April 30, 2018. https://www.theguardian.com/world/2016/nov/24/after-trump-victory-italy -referendum-is-seen-as-test-of-populisms-rise.

Krause, Elizabeth L. 2009. *Unraveled: A Weaver's Tale of Life Gone Modern*. Berkeley: University of California Press.

La Repubblica. 2016. "Referendum, Nuovo Affondo del Financial Times: 'Con il No a Rischio Fino a 8 Banche Italiane.'" November 27. Accessed April 30, 2018. http://www.repubblica.it/economia/2016/11/27/news/referendum_nuovo _affondo_del_financial_times_con_il_no_a_rischio_fino_a_8_banche _italiane_-152978861/.

La Stampa. 2016. "Renzi: 'La Riforma Costituzionale È la Madre di Tutte le Battaglie.'" *La Stampa*, January 10. Accessed April 30, 2018. http://www.lastampa .it/2016/01/10/italia/politica/renzi-la-riforma-costituzionale-la-madre-di-tutte -le-battaglie-sjDL4JAKwh5nsXUKulSCcJ/pagina.html.

"*Legge Scelba*." Law 645. June 20, 1952.

Macciocchi, Maria Antonietta. 1976. *La Donna Nera: Consenso Femminile e Fascismo*. Milano: Feltrinelli.

Mahmud, Lilith. 2014. *The Brotherhood of Freemason Sisters: Gender, Secrecy, and Fraternity in Italian Masonic Lodges*. Chicago: University of Chicago Press.

Mahmud, Lilith. 2016. We Have Never Been Liberal: Occidentalist Myths and the Impending Fascist Apocalypse. *Cultural Anthropology* Hot Spots, Fieldsights, October 27. Accessed April 15, 2019. https://culanth.org/fieldsights/981-we-have -never-been-liberal-occidentalist-myths-and-the-impending-fascist-apocalypse.

Mahmud, Lilith. 2018. "#Eurostop: Toward a Feminist Decolonial Critical Theory of Europe." In *North Africa and the Making of Europe: Governance, Institutions and Culture*, ed. Thomas Serres and Muriam Haleh Davis, 265–283. London: Bloomsbury.

Mann, Michael. 2004. *Fascists*. New York: Cambridge University Press.

Matteucci, Piera. 2016. "Referendum, Vince il No. Renzi Si Dimette: 'Ho Perso Io, La Poltrona che Salta È la Mia.'" *La Repubblica*, December 4. Accessed April 30, 2018. http://www.repubblica.it/speciali/politica/referendum -costituzionale2016/2016/12/04/news/risultati_referendum_2016-153452780/.

Molé, Noelle J. 2012. *Labor Disorders in Neoliberal Italy: Mobbing, Well-Being, and the Workplace, New Anthropologies of Europe*. Bloomington: Indiana University Press.

Mosse, George L. 1999. *The Fascist Revolution: Toward a General Theory of Fascism.* 1st ed. New York: H. Fertig.

Muehlebach, Andrea. 2012. *The Moral Neoliberal: Welfare and Citizenship in Italy, Chicago Studies in Practices of Meaning.* Chicago: University of Chicago Press.

Mussolini, Benito, and Gioacchino Volpe. 1932. "Fascismo." In *Enciclopedia Italiana,* ed. Arturo Marpicati. Milan, Italy: Treccani.

Palumbo, Patrizia, ed. 2003. *A Place in the Sun: Africa in Italian Colonial Culture from Post-Unification to the Present.* Berkeley: University of California Press.

Pengelly, Martin. 2016. "Word of the Year 2016: For Merriam-Webster, 'Surreal' Trumps 'Fascism.'" *The Guardian,* December 19. Accessed January 15, 2018. https://www.theguardian.com/us-news/2016/dec/19/surreal-trump-fascism -merriam-webster-2016-word-of-the-year.

Poulantzas, Nicos. 2018. *Fascism and Dictatorship: The Third International and the Problem of Fascism.* New York: Verso.

Raspanti, Mauro. 1994. "I Razzismi del Fascismo." In *La Menzogna della Razza: Documenti e Immagini del Razzismo e dell'Antisemitismo Fascista,* ed. Jesi Centro Furio, 73–89. Bologna, Italy: Grafis.

Razsa, Maple. 2015. *Bastards of Utopia: Living Radical Politics after Socialism, Global Research Studies.* Bloomington: Indiana University Press.

Rosa, Jonathan, and Yarimar Bonilla. 2017. "Deprovincializing Trump, Decolonizing Diversity, and Unsettling Anthropology." *American Ethnologist* 44 (2): 201–208.

Sarfatti, Michele. 1994. *Mussolini Contro gli Ebrei: Cronaca dell'Elaborazione delle Leggi del 1938.* Turin, Italy: Zamorani.

Scoones, Ian, Marc Edelman, Saturnino M. Borras, Ruth Hall, Wendy Wolford, and Ben White. 2018. "Emancipatory Rural Politics: Confronting Authoritarian Populism." *Journal of Peasant Studies* 45 (1): 1–20.

Shoshan, Nitzan. 2016. *The Management of Hate: Nation, Affect, and the Governance of Right-Wing Extremism in Germany.* Princeton, NJ: Princeton University Press.

Sternhell, Zeev. 1986. *Neither Right nor Left: Fascist Ideology in France.* Berkeley: University of California Press.

Taylor, Adam. 2016. "Italy's Brexit Moment? The Complex Constitutional Referendum That Could Rock Europe." *The Washington Post,* November 30. Accessed April 30, 2018. https://www.washingtonpost.com/news/worldviews/wp /2016/11/30/italys-brexit-moment-the-complex-constitutional-referendum-that -could-rock-europe/?utm_term=.e7e37442bbee.

Traverso, Enzo. 2008. "Interpreting Fascism: Mosse, Sternhell and Gentile in Comparative Perspective." *Constellations* 15 (3): 303–319.

Walley, Christine J. 2017. "Trump's Election and the 'White Working Class': What We Missed." *American Ethnologist* 44 (2): 231–236.

Wedeman, Ben. 2016. "First Brexit, Then Trump, Now Italy Faces Its Political Shockwave." *CNN*, December 2. Accessed April 30, 2018. https://www.cnn.com /2016/12/02/opinions/italy-referendum-preview/index.html.

Zic.it. 2016. "Piazza Verdi, I Muri Tornano a Raccontare una 'Storia Partigiana.'" *Zero In Condotta: Quotidiano Online Autogestito*, September 8. Accessed April 30, 2018. http://www.zic.it/piazza-verdi-i-muri-tornano-a-raccontare-una -storia-partigiana/.

Other People's Race Problem

Trumpism and the Collapse of the Liberal Racial Consensus in the United States

C ommon wisdom tells us that the rise of Trumpism in the United States is a backlash against liberal centrists' globalist cosmopolitan dreams. These centrists were, as the story goes, part of a meritocratic global order of elite citizens, a small rich homogeneous caste, disconnected from their own nationals and nonnationals alike because of their elite educational and social backgrounds, their superficial investment in multicultural openness (for elites only), and their disdain for the small-minded provincialism of those who were "left behind" by neoliberal globalization. And it is this *excess* of technocratic elitism and closed-minded cosmopolitanism that has spurred the wave of ethnonationalist populism in the United States and across the globe. Different versions of this story abound. Christine Lagarde, managing director of the International Monetary Fund, advocated a retooled globalism that is more effective at "sharing" its benefits (Lagarde 2016). Tony Blaire and Hilary Clinton have admitted begrudgingly some of the limitations of centrist Third Way politics in their attempts to outflank and discredit the social democratic factions in the Labor and Democratic Parties (Glasser 2017). And Dalibor Rohac, a conservative writer from the American Enterprise Institute, calls for more cosmopolitanism, not nationalism, as an antidote to elitist globalization (Rohac 2016).

As with much common wisdom, there is just enough truth in this story to make it very misleading. It is easy to agree with the part about globalism's technocratic elitism; this is, after all, a point made by the global justice and alt globalization movements, by Occupy Wall Street and by Bernie Sanders. But Donald Trump did not ride the global wave of popular protest to power; nor is his political popularity explainable exclusively in terms of his admittedly deft manipulation of widely held anti-establishment political sentiments felt in the aftermath of the late 2000s global economic meltdown. Many politicians have tried to ride that wave of political disaffection, but they failed to capture popular or electoral support. The issue that is ignored or glossed over in many popular accounts of the globalist versus nationalist debate is race. For Trump's brutal political effectiveness can only be explained, I think, in terms of his white nationalist appeal, and in terms of the failure of liberal cosmopolites and economic nationalists to offer a compelling racial project of their own as an alternative.

In this essay, I want to argue for the centrality of racialized subjects in the making of Trump-era politics, and for the specific understanding of Trumpism as a form of white nationalist politics that has shattered the liberal racial consensus of the post–civil rights era. To insist on the centrality of race may seem unnecessary and even gratuitous as we contend with the increasingly explicit xenophobic and racist language that Trump and his supporters use. But my point here is not merely that Trump is a racist (he is, and this was well established long before his presidential run). In the following pages, I hope to show that an important reason for the effectiveness of Trump's political project is the way that it prioritizes white community resentments and grievances as *the* political foundation for elaborating popular disaffection, nationalism, gender politics, and class politics. This articulation, to use Stuart Hall's term (Hall et al., 2013 [1978]; Hall 1986, 1987, 1989; see also Clarke 2014), does a great deal of political work. By displacing neoconservative color blindness and neoliberal multiculturalism, the dominant racial projects of the liberal centrist political establishment, the politics of white resentment and grievance have energized disgruntled fractions of the white middle and working classes, accelerated the authoritarian turn in US politics and governance, and unsettled long-standing liberal centrist political orthodoxies around race, class, and gender.[23]

This essay proceeds in three parts. First, I explain briefly the history of the rise of Trumpism, which, I emphasize, must be understood as a form of white nationalism that is resonant with, but ultimately different from, white nationalism in past eras of US history. I then locate Trumpism as a political problematic in the current conjuncture. I end with a brief discussion of a key political impasse that has emerged alongside white nationalism: the propensity by cosmopolites and economic nationalists to see racism as someone else's problem and to therefore ignore the importance of antiracist projects to the development of an effective popular politics in the United States. Taken together, these parts form the basis for a conjunctural analysis of the rise of Trumpism in the United States in the twenty-first century. Conjunctural analysis (Clarke 2014) helps make connections between different kinds of racial politics and the multiplicity of political forces, projects, and desires that circulate in US politics and culture in the present.[24]

Trumpism as the New White Nationalism

Trump's political rise must be attributed first and foremost to the resurfacing of white nationalism in the post–civil rights era. Prevailing popular wisdom tends to treat white nationalism's recent rise as an outgrowth of a generalized white male youth crisis rooted in the absence of fathers in white working-class households (Farrell and Gray 2018; Kimmel 2018; Picciolini 2018; for a review of the literature, see Hochschild 2018). Or it is viewed as an expression of mounting class resentments by increasingly precarious fractions of the deindustrialized working and middle classes (Fraser 2019). The first explanation resonates very strongly with more than a century of scholarship on the crisis of the black family, though the political implications of these resonances could not be more different (Frazier 1939). The second resonates with Kalb and Halmai's (2011) "return of the repressed" argument by charting the rise of a "reactionary politics of recognition" (Fraser 2019) in the context of the collapse of the political center, in both its progressive (neoliberal) and reactionary (neoconservative) forms. This latter argument takes us far in understanding the US case, about which I will say more below. Yet it is essential as well to make clear the extent to which race politics shaped this political outcome. The majority of white college-educated men, white non-college-educated men, and white non-college-educated women voted for Trump; in the category of white voters, it was only white college-educated women who did not vote mostly for Trump (Schaffner et al. 2018). These data contradict the simplistic—and ultimately inaccurate—story, promoted popularly and politically in the immediate aftermath of the election, that Trump was voted in by the disgruntled, downwardly mobile fractions of the white working classes. This is only true so far as the election was "determined" by votes by a small part of the electorate, mostly in the Midwest, who had voted in the past election for Obama but who voted, in 2016, for Trump. But voting data more broadly affirms the political effectiveness of Trump's strategy to run his campaign within the broad currents of white nationalism. Acknowledging the role that race played in the 2016 election, and in US politics more generally, also has the additional advantage of taking race at least as seriously as Trump and white nationalists do themselves.

How should we characterize the new white nationalism that has resurfaced in the Trump era, and to what extent does it unsettle post–civil rights era race politics? Today, white nationalism is not a unified movement. It is a diverse set of political, social, and cultural projects, programs, organizations, and activities. The Southern Poverty Law Center estimates that there are approximately 100 white nationalist groups operating in the United States today (the number of groups has fluctuated between 95 and 146 since 2003) (SPLC 2017). Under the banner of white nationalism are what the Southern Poverty Law Center would call "extremist" groups that elaborate explicit racist ideologies rooted in long-standing ideas about white biological or cultural superiority and that seek to transform the United States into a white ethnostate through violent means. Some representatives from groups such as these were at the "Unite the Right" rally in Charlottesville, Virginia, in August 2017. Groups that make explicit claims about white superiority remain on the fringe politically, however. But other groups have moved to the mainstream. The media-savvy alt-right, for example, is careful to emphasize white racial grievances and resentments and the need for white community restoration over overt arguments for racial superiority. With this tactic, its leaders have found new audiences for their xenophobic and racist political projects, and its growth accounts in large measure for white nationalism's popular appeal in the twenty-first-century United States (Bjork-James and Maskovsky 2017).

White nationalism's resurgence has unsettled both neoconservatism and neoliberalism, the two competing forms of liberal centrist cosmopolitanism, which elaborate different and antagonistic racial projects even as they share a commitment to many classic liberal values and to globalist dreams of one sort or another. The racial projects of neoconservative and neoliberal variety— color blindness and multiculturalism respectively—eschew white supremacist ideologies, at least explicitly. Suffice it to say that neoconservatives have made a political art form out of the selective appropriation of civil rights era political discourses about enfranchisement and equality to justify the rollback of civil rights legislation and policies and advance color-blind policy and postracial ideology (Mullings 2005). For their part, neoliberals have countered neoconservatism's postracialism with multiculturalism. This framework recognizes and celebrates racial differences, though the extent to which this recognition is linked substantively to a robust vision of equal proprietorship of public institutions or to redress and eradicate racial inequalities is hotly debated. If there was one similarity between these two positions and one line that was not crossed in the culture wars from the 1980s to the 2000s, however, it was that whiteness was off the table as a project of national unification.

Yet race continued to haunt US politics despite this consensus, and white nationalists were eventually able to mount a grassroots rebuke of neoconservatism and neoliberalism from their location inside the Republican Party base. The story of how precisely this happened requires some fleshing out. In the 1970s, in the wake of the civil rights movement, Republicans put concerted effort into appealing to white southerners' racial resentments to gain their support. This was helped along in the 1970s and 1980s by the political valorization of the white ethnic community across the political spectrum (di Leonardo 1998; Steinberg 1981). Once vilified as ignorant, dangerous, and criminal in comparison to mainstream WASP culture, white ethnicity became politically legitimate and even fashionable as a white ethnic identity politics formed in direct reaction to Black Power and other militant protest movements of the 1960s and 1970s. In the 1980s and 1990s, the culture wars were effective in further linking the politics of white ethnic pride to white racial resentments. The neoconservative condemnation of "illiberal" causes such as affirmative action, multiculturalism, political correctness, and liberal immigration policy also helped to shift white ethnic politics to the right.

The neoliberal and neoconservative ascendancies from the 1980s to the 2000s further politicized race and gender in connection with questions of government dependency and the critique of "big government." During the Reagan era, the racialized and gendered attack on the welfare queen was crucial to new right anti–big government policy advances, the rise of supply side economics, the breaking of the Fordist social compact, the rollback on the social wage, the attack on affirmative action, and the rise of nonunionized postindustrialism. For their part, centrist Democrats under Bill Clinton's leadership responded to Reaganism with a technocratic politics rooted in the pragmatics of prosperity, freighting multiculturalism to individualism, productivity, efficiency, personal responsibility, market enfranchisement, and reinvented government (smaller but still of vital necessity).

The ideological assault against welfare dependency, multiculturalism, affirmative action, and big government widened considerably in the Bush era, especially after 9/11. In this period, the basis for popular compassion and political support for the poor, immigrants, and people of color all but vanished, except among a small group of antipoverty activists and their supporters, while new fractions of the middle classes (especially lower- and middle-class white suburbanites) came under fire and financial duress as the libertarian attack against government—any government, not just big government—gained traction. "Welfare queens," already vanquished in the 1990s by welfare "reform," were largely left alone in the 2012 presidential campaign cycle. But in 2012 teachers and pensioned government employees became the targets: "government-dependent" profligates living life too large off the government dime. Ultimately the attack on "government dependency" spread so wide as to encompass "the 47 percent of the US population" whom Republican presidential candidate Mitt Romney condemned for not paying federal income tax but taking government services anyway.

During the Obama era, the attack on dependency from the right intensified and was once again elaborated in explicitly racist terms. The Obama administrative was effective in enforcing civil rights laws, reforming immigration, expanding access to health care (though on terms set by the right in the 1980s), and reviving the economy after the 2007–8 financial crisis. But the right was outraged by Obama's soaring rhetoric about the audacity of hope and his ascent to the presidency itself was viewed by many as an affirmation of neoliberal triumph. Some on the left, however, were dismayed by Obama's political abandonment of "main street" in the housing market bail out. Importantly, #BLM and the Movement for Black Lives, with their critique of racialized state violence, also surfaced during the Obama era, posing an overt challenge to some of the institutions where white nationalism has festered, such as the criminal justice system (Mullings in press). Throughout all of this, neoliberal and neoconservative governance struggled to manage "race relations" or to substantively address racial inequalities or white grievances, and racial conflagrations continued to surface, as, for example, in the Henry Louis Gates arrest controversy, into which former president Obama avoided any serious engagement.

This brings me to Trumpism. Trump's excoriation of political correctness is the centerpiece to his political worldview and a cornerstone of his populist appeal. With it, he stokes white nationalist sentiments, mobilizing supporters to be outraged by PC-induced free speech violations and in defense of white cultural worlds that, in this formulation, are perceived to be under constant attack by liberal accusations of racial insensitivity. Freighted to his anti-PC stance is a politics of nostalgia for a fictitious industrial heyday when Americans were purportedly better off. Indeed, the solution for the precarious status of many Americans today is, for Trump, a return not to the 1970s and 1980s, when white ethnicity was celebrated across the political spectrum, or to the 1990s, when the culture wars were at their peak, but to the mid-twentieth century, and to the industrial economy and welfare statism of that era. And this is an explicit desire to return to that era as it actually existed, with its racist and sexist hierarchies wholly intact. Although Trump is often viewed as ideologically inconsistent to the point of incoherency, his call for a new "industrial revolution"—his denunciation of free trade, his emphasis on Rust Belt manufacturing jobs, his grandstanding as the savior of jobs at the Carrier's Indianapolis factory, and his imposition of tariffs—combines with his support for current levels of Social Security and Medicare spending in his first proposed budget (while slashing the rest of the federally funded safety net) to define white male workers as the virtuous majority whom Trump claims to represent. Accordingly, it is the welfare statism part of Trumpism that so offends neoconservative intellectuals, who are fully invested in its dismantling, while it is the racist and sexist parts of the equation that offend the liberal establishment, which was nonetheless unable to mount a successful electoral political campaign to defeat him. This is, of course, a politics that few nonwhite Americans can embrace and that offends many women. Indeed, it is a nostalgia for a time of legal segregation that existed prior to the women's movements of the 1960s and 1970s. The immediate postwar period was also a time when whiteness and masculinity worked as unmarked categories of privilege, when the maintenance of the social order was presumed to be one in which white men had political and economic power. And it is that era that Trump compares favorably to the present period of overt race talk, liberal multiculturalism, and liberal social policy.

Yet Trump is invested in a different kind of race talk. Take, for example, his talk about black America, which reflects a similar investment in white male resurrection. For black Americans, Trump expresses mostly pity for the harrowing, violent conditions of life in the inner city. He blames Democrats for decades of policy experimentation that locked black Americans in the inner city (again there is just enough truth in this claim to make it grossly misleading). Trump's prescription for change, ironically (given his current hostility to Democrats) is to suggest that the Bill Clinton–era welfare-to-work regime should be extended to all other safety net programs, so black inner-city residents will be forced to work, for instance, to get food stamps or subsidized housing or government health insurance. Of course, Trump's description of the plight of inner-city residents has very little to do with reality for most

African Americans. Most African Americans are not poor, and they do not live in the urban core. And by treating the black inner city as a metonym for black America, Trump alienated many African American voters. But this kind of race talk signals something else entirely to his white middle-class supporters, who see black Americans both as government dependents for whom they hold disdain and as preferred recipients of government largesse.

As repulsive as his xenophobic race-baiting is, Trump's embrace of many white nationalist ideological precepts undoubtedly enhances his popularity for a polity for which white racial grievances have been stoked, sub rosa, by Republican operatives for decades. Eventually, much of the Tea Party became Trump's political base. Controversial figures such as Steve Bannon and his allies on the alt-right also helped to popularize the politics of white racial resentment, as did Fox News. But white nationalism is a more broadly held worldview, crisscrossing red state/blue state divisions, and class and gender differences among whites. Furthermore, Trump was certainly not the only political figure to attempt to craft a populist political message in 2016. Rand Paul tried as a Libertarian, Ted Cruz tried as a religious Conservative, and Bernie Sanders tried as a socialist. All three challenged the liberal centrist globalists— but not with respect to racial politics. Indeed, Cruz's and Paul's records suggest strong adherence to new right postracial orthodoxy, though Paul did support some criminal justice reforms that were ideologically heterodox. For his part, Sanders sought to downplay issues of racial difference and inequality in order to build his left-liberal coalition, which was defeated by Hilary Clinton in the Democratic Party primaries. Trump was thus the most brazen in elaborating an antiglobalist, anti-immigrant, white nationalist stance. He also had an oftentimes-overlooked advantage over the other candidates in the Republican primary race. His foray into birtherism against former president Obama, which at the time was considered a fringe position, gave him early credibility in some white Republican quarters and firmly freighted his subsequent anti-immigrant, anti-Muslim positions to antiblack politics. This, alas, turned out to be a very compelling articulation.

The Politics of Resentment and the Crisis in Political Authority

The context for this fairly conventional narrative about racisms in popular culture and politics is an ongoing crisis at the level of political economy that is made visible by the unraveling of several unstable settlements that I wish to highlight here. First, and foremost, is the ongoing crisis in neoliberal capitalism in the United States and across the globe and its attendant crisis in political legitimacy. At the economic level, neoliberal capitalism has been prone to crisis since its inception in the 1970s, and it has failed to guarantee freedom or equality for most people. After the 2007–8 financial crisis, finance-led neoliberal capitalism has remained in place, but it has taken on an even more dispossessive and hyperexploitative form while at the same time its political arm has weakened. It has become clear that, from the global financial elite's perspective, the solution to the volatility and long-term crisis in political economy is the severe constraint of popular sovereignty, separating it from capitalist decision-making and giving almost dictatorial authority to the central banks. But a full-fledged political crisis emerged after 2007–8, when neoliberals and neoconservatives alike were exposed as corrupt, ineffectual, and beholden exclusively to economic elites. Political elites thus lost legitimacy long before Trump was elected president—and his election is best understood as an effect of this crisis, not its cause (Fraser 2019).

A second related context is the rise of popular sentiment in politics. In a situation where the reigning capitalist ideologies are unpopular, in which neoliberal technocracy and neoconservative moralizing can no longer persuade people, the politics of sentiment is filling people's hearts (Grossberg 2006). This combines with the fragmentation of the public sphere (di Leonardo 1998) such that facts, authority, and rationality are frequently associated with flawed, ineffectual, elitist, and punishing forms of liberal governance such as neoliberalism. Importantly, this has occurred across the political spectrum. The denunciation of the "fake news" of the mainstream media by Trump, his white nationalist supporters, and pundits on Fox News is but one example of popular suspicion of elite forms of expertise and knowledge. Other examples abound, from Black Lives Matter's condemnation of CompStat and other crime statistics as racist to the revolt against vaccinations in some quarters. Overall, passion has not replaced rationality in politics today, but in the current conjuncture, the politics of resentment, the rise of angry publics, and the crisis over authority and knowledge culminate in a situation in which rage and resentment has been taken to new levels of intensity in liberal democratic politics. Furthermore, political rhetoric is meant more to invoke sentiments than to pinpoint concrete policy proposals or coherent political ideologies. Trump's chronic lying and overall lack of presidential comportment does little in this context to undermine his popular support, since his followers are far too enraged at the political establishment and their media accomplices to trust their accounts or opinions.

Donald Trump's political ascent is rooted in these developments. The gradual fraying of long-standing political arrangements that freight rights and recognition with access to public resources, accompanied by a mad-dash scramble to formulate workable political programs in defense of an ever-ambiguous category of "the middle class" were strained to the breaking point by the early 2010s. Trump's signature move was to innovate an articulation of revanchist middle-class politics framed in largely racial—and racist—terms. This formulation undermined the liberal racial consensus of the post–civil rights era with a politics of white community resentment and grievance that diverged significantly from the neoconservative attempt to impose postracial color-blind politics and that treated liberal multiculturalism with contempt and ridicule in the name of a retrograde politics of nostalgia for a white supremacist and patriarchal past.

The Political Impasse of the Present Moment

In the current conjuncture, the politics of sentiment, the rise of affective publics, the crisis over authority and knowledge, and the turn to authoritarianism are all intertwined in ways that have helped to suture together Trumpism as a white nationalist political project for the post–civil rights era. What is to be done about this? Certainly, liberal tolerance, the progressive politics of recognition and redistribution, and the celebration of difference as an intrinsic social good are preferred alternatives to Trump's xenophobic nativism and racist attacks on black and brown America. But, as the analysis I provide above suggests, liberal race projects are also vulnerable to the critique, from both the left and the right, that they are elitist and indifferent to class dynamics and structural racism. White nationalism today may eschew overt calls for white supremacy and replace them with a purportedly kinder, gentler politics of racial resentment that seeks to assert white pride and the celebration of white heritage as antidotes to the purported tyrannies of political correctness and multiculturalism. Yet this kinder and gentler position is still a form of white supremacy. Ultimately, the white nationalist march in Charlottesville, Virginia, as political spectacle and event, is not separable from Trump's and the Republican Party's racist politics in the lead up to the 2018 midterm elections and beyond. But the widespread condemnation in response to Trump's racism actually reinforces the sense of grievance felt by many who hold white nationalist sensibilities and sentiments, because those who harbor these resentments frequently feel unfairly characterized as racists by the anti-Trump backlash, especially if it is launched from the liberal quarters of the political establishment and media. These are the same people who see confederate monuments as symbols of their cultural heritage, which, they are convinced, is under attack from liberal cosmopolitan elites.

Located alongside these two conflicting racial projects are also neoconservatives, who are quietly laying the groundwork for the reassertion of color blindness via their legal attacks on affirmative action. They appear to be waiting for the return of globalism too as a dominant political ideal once their own rank and file is burned by Trump, or so they hope. Yet this position too is vulnerable to accusations of elitism from the nationalist populist right, for color blindness cannot, by definition, restore white culture and community to a prominent public place in American political life even if it can advantage whites across institutions from politics to education to work. It is because of the limitations of political ideas such as color blindness that the rank and file of the alt-right remains deeply suspicious of the centrist Republican establishment, who are frequently referred to on alt-right blogs as "cuckservatives" because of their emasculated fealty to the liberal establishment, so their argument goes.

Finally, there is the social democratic left that seeks to counter the ethno-nationalism of Trumpism with an economic or progressive populism and civic nationalism of the left. These positions have gained ground recently in electoral struggles inside the Democratic Party, and Bernie Sanders popularized them in the 2016 Democratic primaries. Notably, many proponents of this position have long eschewed liberal race talk and identity politics, which has tended, across successive waves of left mobilization from the 1990s to the 2010s, to be seen as an impediment to a new alignment of the ranks of disposable people in a new movement from below (Brecher et al., 2000; Frank 2004; Fraser 2019). In the immediate aftermath of Trump's presidential election, criticism of "identity politics" once again gained traction, as a new push for a platform of economic populism was linked, once again, to disdain for cultural radicalism, which is viewed at best as a troublesome diversion from a new working-class politics and at worse as a factor contributing to the rise of economic inequality and to the Democratic Party's inability to win over white working-class voters (see, e.g., the widely influential *New York Times* op-ed by Mark Lilla [2016]; see also Michaels et al. 2016).

The strong advantage that white nationalism has over its alternatives is its willingness to take on racial politics more or less explicitly and to blame black and brown people for the woes and challenges affecting white people. This has been a national pastime since the founding of the United States, and it remains, in 2019, an amazingly effective, if horrendous, form of political affiliation and rule. For the other projects, racism's entrenched capacities to shape political and economic life in the United States are frequently disregarded and, more important, displaced onto political opponents, whose ways of managing "race relations" are criticized as ineffective, inadequate, or racist (Steinberg 2007). In this regard it is only groups on the left that are poised to respond to white nationalism with a critical race politics of their own that can hope to diminish white nationalism's popular and political influence, as the abolitionist and civil rights movements demonstrated against similar foes in past eras. Groups such as Black Lives Matter, which has a progressive economic program for all linked to its critique of antiblackness (Williams 2015; Mullings forthcoming), and similar movements such as Standing Rock and the immigrant rights movement, are seeking to make race and settler colonialism matter politically in the United States, though on entirely different terms than those that are elaborated, obviously, by white nationalist groups. It is hard to imagine how these movements will flourish, let alone survive, given Trump's law-and-order posturing and the illiberal policing tradition of our major metropolitan areas (which are ironically now touted as liberal cosmopolitan refuges from Trumpland). If they do not, we will in all likelihood be stuck in an impasse in which white nationalist populism continues to hold sway. In favor or out of favor, it will rule or haunt politics for decades to come. It is, of course, difficult to know where US politics will be in the near future, let alone in the long-term. We may end up with a progressive populism of the left, with Trumpian fascism, or, if restored, a liberal centrist globalism. A better idea would be putting our energies into the work of building, aligning with, supporting, and acting in solidarity with political projects that make race something other than someone else's problem.

Notes

This essay has benefited from the insights from participants in the workshop, Fed Up: Angry Publics, New Politics, October 12–13, 2017, at the CUNY Graduate Center. Workshop participants included the contributors to this volume and Allyson Cole,

Leith Mullings, Gary Wilder, and Ida Susser. For invaluable feedback on the written version, thanks especially to John Clarke, Ana Croegaert, Don Kalb, Roger Lancaster, Leith Mullings, Steven Steinberg, Paul Stubbs, as well as to my co-editor, Sophie Bjork-James, and to the three excellent reviewers.

1. This essay builds on a long tradition of critical anthropological research on the United States; for an overview of this tradition, see Maskovsky (2013); see also Brodkin (2000); Cattelino (2010); di Leonardo (199); Lamphere et al. (1993); and Susser (1996).

2. A useful account of Trump's rise can be found in Fountain (2018); for an important account of gender in right-wing politics, see Spruill (2017); for a brilliant analysis linking Trump's political effectiveness to late capitalist spectacle, see Hall et al. (2016); for a brief account that locates Trump's rise vis-à-vis white nationalism, see Maskovsky (2017).

References

Brecher, Jeremy, Tim Costello, and Brendan Smith. 2000. *Globalization from Below: The Power of Solidarity.* Cambridge, MA: South End Press.

Bjork-James, Sophie, and Jeff Maskovsky. 2017. "When White Nationalism Became Popular." *Anthropology News* 58 (3): e86–e91.

Brodkin, Karen. 2000. "Global Capitalism: What's Race Got to Do with It?" *American Ethnologist* 27: 237–256.

Cattelino, Jessica R. 2010. "Anthropologies of the United States." *Annual Review of Anthropology* 39: 275–292.

Clarke, John. 2014. "Conjunctures, Crises, and Cultures: Valuing Stuart Hall." *Focaal* 70: 113–122.

Di Leonardo, Micaela. 1998. *Exotics at Home: Anthropologies, Others, American Modernity.* Chicago: University of Chicago Press.

Farrell, Warren, and John Gray. 2018. *The Boy Crisis: Why Our Boys Are Struggling and What We Can Do about It.* Dallas, TX: BenBella Books.

Fountain, Ben. 2018. *Beautiful Country Burn Again: Democracy, Rebellion, and Revolution.* New York: HarperLuxe, an imprint of HarperCollins.

Frank, Thomas. 2004. *What's the Matter with Kansas? How Conservatives Won the Heart of America.* New York: Metropolitan Books.

Fraser, Nancy. 2019. *The Old Is Dying and the New Cannot Be Born.* New York: Verso.

Frazier, E. F. 1939. *The Negro Family in the United States.* Chicago: University of Chicago Press.

Glasser, Susan. 2017. "Tony Blair Says the Left Has Lost Its Way. Democrats and Labourites are Stuck in the Past, the Former British Prime Minister Warns—and

They're Getting Donald Trump All Wrong." *Politico Magazine*, September 25. Accessed May 21, 2019. https://www.politico.com/magazine/story/2017/09/25 /tony-blair-donald-trump-global-politico-215642.

Grossberg, L. 2006. "Does Cultural Studies Have Futures? Should It? (or What's the Matter with New York?): Cultural Studies, Contexts and Conjunctures." *Peace Research Abstracts Journal* 43 (3).

Hall, Kira, Donna M. Goldstein, and Matthew Bruce Ingram. 2016. "The Hands of Donald Trump: Entertainment, Gesture, Spectacle." *Hau: Journal of Ethnographic Theory* 6 (2): 71–100.

Hall, Stuart. 1986. "Gramsci's Relevance for the Study of Race and Ethnicity." *Journal of Communication Inquiry* 10 (5): 5–27.

Hall, Stuart. 1987. "Gramsci and Us." *Marxism Today* (June): 16–21.

Hall, Stuart. 1989. *The Hard Road to Renewal*. London: Verso.

Hall, Stuart, Chas Critcher, Tony Jefferson, John Clarke, and Brian Roberts. 2013. *Policing the Crisis: Mugging, the State and Law and Order*. New York: Palgrave Macmillan.

Harvey, David. 2007. *A Brief History of Neoliberalism*. Oxford: Oxford University Press.

Harvey, David. 2018. *Marx, Capital, and the Madness of Economic Reason*. New York: Oxford University Press.

Hochschild, Arlie Russell. 2018. "Male Trouble." *New York Review of Books* 65, 15.

Kalb, Don, and Gábor Halmai. 2011. *Headlines of Nation, Subtexts of Class: Working-Class Populism and the Return of the Repressed in Neoliberal Europe*. New York: Berghahn Books.

Kazin, Michael. 2016. "Trump and American Populism: Old Whine, New Bottles." *Foreign Affairs* 95 (6): 17–24.

Kimmel, Michael S. *Healing From Hate: How Young Men Get Into and Out of Violent Extremism*. Berkeley: University of California Press.

Lagarde, Christine. 2016. Making Globalization Work for All. International Monetary Fund Sylvia Ostry Lecture (September 13). Accessed August 14, 2018. https://www.imf.org/en/News/Articles/2016/09/13/sp09132016-Making -Globalization-Work-for-All.

Lamphere, Louise, Patricia Zavella, Felipe Gonzales, and Peter B. Evans. 1993. *Sunbelt Working Mothers: Reconciling Family and Factory*. Ithaca, NY: Cornell University Press.

Maskovsky, Jeff. 2013. "Critical Anthropologies of the United States." In *Handbook of Sociocultural Anthropology*, ed. James Carrier and Deborah Gewertz, 489–505. London: Berg.

Maskovsky Jeff. 2017. "Toward the Anthropology of White Nationalist Postracialism: Comments Inspired by Hall, Goldstein, and Ingram's 'The Hands of Donald Trump.'" *HAU: Journal of Ethnographic Theory* 7 (1): 433–440.

Maskovsky, Jeff, and Ida Susser. 2016. "Critical Anthropology for the Present." In *Anthropology in Crisis*, ed. James Carrier, 154–174. London: Berg.

Michaels, Walter Benn, Charles W. Mills, Linda Hirshman, and Carla Murphy. 2016. "What Is the Left without Identity Politics?" *The Nation*, December. Accessed May 22, 2019. https://www.thenation.com/article/what-is-the-left-without-identity-politics/.

Mishra, Pankaj. 2017. *Age of Anger: A History of the Present*. London: Allen Lane, an imprint of Penguin Books.

Mullings, Leith. 2005. "Interrogating Racism: Toward an Antiracist Anthropology." *Annual Review of Anthropology* 34 (1): 667–693.

Mullings, Leith, with Ishan Gordon. Forthcoming. Neoliberal Racism and the Movement for Black Lives. In *When Rights Ring Hollow*, ed. Juliet Hooker and Hector Nahuelpan.

Picciolini, Christian. 2017. *White American Youth: My Descent into America's Most Violent Hate Movement—and How I Got Out*. New York: Hachette Books.

Rohac, Dalibor. 2016. Who Will Stand Up for Cosmopolitanism? *CAPX*. July 11. Accessed July 15, 2018. https://capx.co/who-will-stand-up-for-cosmopolitanism/.

Schaffner, Brian F., Matthew MacWilliams, and Tatishe Nteta. 2018. "Understanding White Polarization in the 2016 Vote for President: The Sobering Role of Racism and Sexism." *Political Science Quarterly* 133 (1): 9–34.

Southern Poverty Law Center (SPLC). 2017. "White Nationalist." Accessed August 25, 2018. https://www.splcenter.org/fighting-hate/extremist-files/ideology/white-nationalist.

Spruill, Marjorie Julian. 2017. *Divided We Stand: The Battle over Women's Rights and Family Values That Polarized American Politics*. New York: Bloomsbury.

Steinberg, Stephen. 1981. *The Ethnic Myth: Race, Ethnicity, and Class in America*. New York: Atheneum.

Steinberg, Stephen. 2007. *Race Relations: A Critique*. Stanford, CA: Stanford Social Sciences.

Susser, Ida. 1996. "The Construction of Poverty and Homelessness in US Cities." *Annual Review of Anthropology* 25: 411–435.

Williams, Bianca C. 2015. Introduction: #Black Lives Matter. *Cultural Anthropology*, June 29.

Euphemisms We Die By

On Eco-Anxiety, Necropolitics,
and Green Authoritarianism in the Philippines

Death on the roads, no electricity, no food and water, and people walking on the streets like zombies, looking for food." This is how Rodrigo Duterte described the city of Tacloban to reporters on November 12, 2013, five days after it was devastated by Typhoon Haiyan, known as Yolanda in the Philippines (Lacorte 2013). Haiyan was, at the time, the most powerful land-falling tropical cyclone in recorded history. Its trajectory across the densely populated Visayas region left more than seven thousand dead, some four million displaced, and many millions more subjected to long-term hardship. At the time, Duterte was still mayor of Davao, a city nearly three hundred miles to the south, with no direct authority to intervene in recovery efforts. But it was surely his ambition rather than his authority that took him to Tacloban and led him to criticize then-president Benigno Aquino III's declaration of a State of Calamity. "It has to be a State of Emergency," Duterte proclaimed.

Like Hurricane Katrina in the United States a decade earlier, Haiyan would go on to haunt the Philippines's 2016 presidential election as a liability for the incumbent party. At a March 2016 campaign event in the northern Philippine city of Dagupan, then-candidate Duterte accused his opponent, Mar Roxas, of mismanaging Haiyan relief funds. Roxas, who had served as secretary of the Interior for President Aquino from 2012 to 2015, had overseen the government's initial disaster response and recovery efforts. From Aquino's naïve statements of preparedness before the storm to Roxas's perceived lack of urgency in its aftermath, the administration's poor handling of the disaster, Duterte alleged, stemmed from its broader corruption, incompetence, and indifference to the plight of ordinary people. Billions of pesos were unaccounted for, while thousands of survivors remained homeless. Mocking Aquino's *Daang Matuwid* or Straight Path reform program, Duterte asked his audience, "Where will you find the straight path? If you ride on a motorcycle, you will fall down within one meter because the road is not properly paved. If you don't know how to ride on a motorcycle, I think you are not a real man. If you can't handle 'Yolanda' well, you are not a real man" (Corrales 2016).

Duterte went on to win the election by relatively wide margins. Since then, he has continued to use Haiyan recovery efforts as an opening to demonstrate his executive efficacy and delegitimize the establishment embodied by his predecessor.[1] At an event marking the three-year anniversary of the storm's landfall in Tacloban, the president accused officials involved in the recovery of "indolence" and ordered them to fast-track the release of housing to displaced families. (This was, characteristically, also a speech in which he made rambling, sexist comments about Vice President Leni Robredo's legs.)

Even as a brutal antidrug campaign remains Duterte's signature policy, his response to Haiyan reveals more than his self-styled brand of nationalist, antiestablishment populism. To be sure, it reflects both the "strongman" authoritarian impulse that has returned with a vengeance to Philippine politics and the role that disasters can play in the broader legitimization of such impulses. But there is, I believe, more to the story.

Beyond the sort of disaster opportunism one might expect from any aspiring autocrat, Duterte's response to Haiyan dovetails with a broader set of rhetorical and policy interventions that serve to greenwash his authoritarian ambitions. The Duterte regime's "green" hue may appear anomalous or exceptional amid what is otherwise a sharp (re)turn toward authoritarianism, and perhaps this is why most attempts to account for and theorize his ascent have little to say about the matter. But in fact the environment figures quite centrally in the regime's consolidation, with climate adaptation, disaster management, and environmental enforcement all key to the promise of "real change" (*tunay na pagbabago*).

Duterte's engagements in ecopolitics have two principal effects. On one hand, they work to defuse opposition by performing a commitment to cleaning up the environment and punishing those who despoil it. On the other, they help to coordinate collective anxiety about environmental and climatic disruption in service to a broader authoritarian agenda. That such sentiments, in turn, resonate with and amplify the increasingly nihilistic and illiberal mood of global society suggests that perceptions of global ecological crisis may play a greater role in the current authoritarian resurgence than we typically acknowledge.

To understand the greenwashing of authoritarianism in the Philippines, we must first consider the societal context that brought Duterte to power and the ambivalent, on-again-off-again relationship he has had with the radical, anti-imperialist left. Although Duterte's agenda is not primarily environmental in focus—it is also revanchist, neoliberal, demagogic, and nationalist—we will see how his performative ecopolitics has sought to consolidate his populist, antiestablishment image amid a souring of his relationship with the left, mounting civil unrest, and rising inflation. Green authoritarianism, I will argue, also raises a larger question about how the necropolitical impulses that Duterte and his ilk embody are entangled with a deepening sense of epochal planetary crisis. This is a matter of global concern, but one that seems especially urgent in the current (political) climate of the Philippines, where intersecting socioenvironmental disasters have helped a so-called populist delegitimize democratic institutions and launch a brutal assault on civil rights.

(Neo)Liberalism and Its Discontents

Philippine president Rodrigo Duterte is among the current crop of populist, revanchist authoritarians to take power amid rising discontent with neoliberal policies, systemic corruption, and extreme inequality.[2] He is often compared to Donald Trump for his blatant misogyny and disregard for norms. But in fact Duterte comes from a political family and served as mayor of Davao, the Philippines's third largest city, for more than twenty years before he ran for president. In that role, he garnered notoriety—some would say infamy—for his brutal pursuit of "law and order," including his well-documented use of paramilitary "death squads" to target alleged criminals and his admitted direct involvement in extrajudicial executions (Curato 2017). Like Trump, Duterte knows the cynical power of rape jokes in the age of hypermediated politics-as-entertainment; he knows the power of social media to disseminate misinformation and intimidation; and he knows the power of dehumanizing marginalized populations and then scapegoating them for societal problems. Recall that his campaign promised to "fatten the fish" of Manila Bay with the corpses of criminals, even if it meant killing as many people as the Nazi regime had done (Gomez 2016).

Unlike Trump, however, Duterte has faced few constraints in a context where the president of the Republic wields considerable constitutional powers, controls vital patronage networks, and has so far faced limited political opposition. As a result, his administration has delivered on its promise of mass murder while projecting an image of strength in matters of governance, foreign policy, and national security.[3] Under Duterte's Operation Tokhang—"a Cebuano portmanteau for 'knock' and 'plead'" (Rafael 2019, 147)—the Philippine National Police have unleashed a reign of terror, primarily in impoverished slum communities, as they have confronted suspected drug users and dealers in their homes, places of work, and on the street. At the start of the campaign, so-called Tokhang boxes began to appear in municipal buildings. As if leaving feedback in a chain restaurant, citizens were encouraged to fill these blue fiberglass boxes with anonymous tips on suspected "drug personalities" so that the police could knock on their door.

Since 2016, Duterte's violent, deeply classist war on drug users has claimed by some estimates more than 20,000 lives, including some 5,000 who have been murdered in encounters with the police (Billing and Cabato 2019; Sadongdong 2018). Thousands more have been compelled to "surrender" themselves as addicts or dealers and enroll in dubious rehabilitation programs. Jail and prison populations have swelled and, given the prominent role that penal institutions often play in organized drug trafficking, there is reason to believe that this campaign will actually strengthen the criminal networks that Duterte claims to despise (Gaviria 2017).

Faced with growing opposition due in large part to outrage over the violent deaths of minors like seventeen-year-old Kian delos Santos, whose sadistic murder by police was recorded on CCTV footage, the administration announced in October 2017 that the Philippine Drug Enforcement Agency (PDEA) would take over control of narcotics investigations and enforcement from the Philippine National Police (PNP).[4] Since the PDEA had reported few violent encounters with suspects, this change was supposed to stem the tide of killings and mollify so-called bleeding hearts (Mogato and Morales 2017). Less than two months later, however, the PNP resumed Operation Tokhang under the guise of better oversight by and coordination with PDEA. The steady stream of bloody "encounters" and lurid headlines resumed accordingly, with thousands more killed by police, vigilantes, and unidentified assailants in the months since.[5]

How did we come to this moment in Philippines? What of the People Power Revolution that overthrew the Marcos regime in 1986 and what of its promises of reform? To make a long story short, the so-called EDSA Republic, named for Epifanio de los Santos Avenue, where the momentous but peaceful demonstrations were held in February 1986, did not result in a substantial redistribution of wealth or power. Even as spaces opened up for critical journalism and oppositional politics, most of the same oligarchic families remained in power and continued to violently suppress dissent through the use of state security forces and private paramilitaries. Rates of extrajudicial assassination have remained high year after year. Laying the groundwork for this continuity was a period of neoliberal restructuring that has exacerbated inequality and further weakened the redistributive powers of the state.

In the lead-up to the Marcos regime's collapse, the Philippines underwent one of the first rounds of structural adjustment and became a proving ground for a host of the fiscal, trade, and social policies that we shorthand as neoliberalism. Since then, efforts by successive governments to attract foreign capital and liberalize trade have further eroded domestic industries and increased reliance on the export of labor and raw materials (Bello 2016). Scholars have described neoliberal governance in the Philippines as the "anti-development state" in light of what often seems like an elite conspiracy to disrupt inclusive development of any kind in the interest of perpetuating social dependency (Bello et al. 2004). Rather than prioritizing investments in education, healthcare, or food security, successive governments have focused on debt servicing, on attracting extractive and offshore industries, and on promoting remittances through migrant labor.

After ups and downs in the 1970s, 1980s, and 1990s, growth has been more or less steady since 2000 and then quite rapid since 2010 as investors have grown increasingly confident in the Philippines's stability. As Don Robotham suggests (this volume), sustained macroeconomic growth has meant that rates of extreme poverty have declined in the Philippines and other parts of Asia, enabling an expansion of the middle class very different from what we see in most of the Global North. Lest we forget, however, this development remains deeply uneven and dispossessory. As in the Global North, neoliberal policies in the Philippines have further concentrated wealth and power in the hands of predatory elites, particularly but by no means exclusively in rural areas, where decades of failed agrarian reform perpetuate hardship and unrest (Lumibao 2018). Meanwhile, aspiring and actual members of the middle class remain fundamentally insecure about their prospects in the medium and long term—and increasingly frustrated with the failures of governance that underpin their insecurity. Aries Arugay offers a blunt summary: "Widespread discontent caused by predatory elites too lazy to build responsive institutions coupled with the inability of previous governments to address inequality and exclusion provided fertile ground for the rise of populists like Duterte" (Arugay 2018, 7).

Populist Diversions

Filipinos' disillusionment with the EDSA Republic dovetails with the global trajectory of neoliberal restructuring—and with a broader push to channel public resentment away from the oligarchs who have benefited from it. In her contribution to this volume, Preeti Sampat relates how the Modi regime in India uses Hindu nationalism to distract the public from a broader trajectory of "jobless growth" that has enriched elites at the expense of most everyone else. Similarly, the IBON Foundation has observed that, despite rapid GDP growth, real employment and income are declining in the Philippines, and the national debt is ballooning as a result of the "Build, Build, Build" infrastructure program (IBON 2019). Yet Duterte's enduring popularity suggests that his populist rhetoric has so far succeeded in diverting public attention away from the deeply uneven societal structures that remain intact.

In this respect, the Philippines is part of a global political-economic pattern. But there is also a political-ecological dimension to this pattern, as collective anxieties surrounding climate disruption, disaster risk, and environmental degradation stoke a larger sense of planetary crisis and thus help propel an authoritarian project cloaked in a performative shade of green.

Recall how, on the third anniversary of Typhoon Haiyan's landfall, Duterte ostentatiously ordered government agencies to expedite disaster recovery efforts. This coincided with a PR push reminding everyone that he had been the first Filipino official to arrive in storm-ravaged Tacloban and claiming that his order was already having a transformative impact on storm recovery. In a dramatic video produced by the Presidential Communications Operations Office, Duterte's return to Tacloban for the anniversary commemoration was presented as an act of "solidarity" by "the man who is willing to sacrifice his presidency, his honor, and his life to bring about genuine change in the country" (PCOO 2016b). An aide to the president even declared that the "problem besetting the Yolanda resettlement in three years is solved in just 18 days after President Duterte's 'tapang and malasakit' to the Yolanda victims made him to issue presidential directives to finish it without delay" (PCOO 2016a). "*Tapang at malasakit*"—which roughly translates as "courage and compassion"—was Duterte's campaign slogan and has since become the name of an "alliance" that supports the administration.

Not coincidentally, it was also in November 2016 that Duterte announced a reversal of his position on the Paris Climate Agreement: he was, he said, persuaded to sign it despite his concerns about its impacts on industrialization. In the years since, the administration has repeatedly invoked his efficacy in responding to disasters and his commitment to climate-change adaptation. This propaganda belies the ongoing struggles of Haiyan survivors who remain in temporary housing and/or have lost their land to investors (Uson 2017; Yee 2018a, 2018b). It is also at odds with the government's support for the expansion of coal-fired power plants and oil-palm plantations.

As I detail below, disasters and climate change are not the only domains in which Duterte has sought to add a green inflection to his *tapang at malasakit*. First, though, *why* do environmental concerns seem to feature so prominently in the particular brand of authoritarianism that Duterte embodies? After all, many of the revanchists who have arisen in recent years have adopted a decidedly hostile stance toward environmental regulation—take, for example, the ardently antienvironmentalist platform of Brazilian president Jair Bolsonaro (Sganzerla and Palatino 2018). Others, like Narendra Modi in India, have accepted UN awards for solar-power leadership while simultaneously working to dilute environmental regulations (DTE 2018). For his part, Duterte stands on even more ambiguous ground. He is often like Modi in his seemingly duplicitous embrace of environmentalism and aggressive development. But his positions on both social and environmental issues are in other instances in sync with those of progressives and even leftists. This ambiguity, I believe, reflects a broader set of competing impulses that have enabled Duterte to consolidate support from the left at key points in his career.

A Socialist, Neoliberal, "Fascist Original"

For those who know Duterte largely through the international media, it may come as a surprise to learn that he is a self-identified "socialist" who once declared that he wanted to be the Philippines's "first leftist president" (Palatino 2017). These statements are difficult to reconcile with his deeply classist assault on petty drug users and dealers. And yet, unlike most of the revanchist authoritarians currently ascendant around the world, Duterte has backed a number of progressive social policies over the course of his political career while at times enjoying considerable albeit far from unanimous support from the left.

Where do these purported leftist credentials originate? They begin with Duterte's mother, Soledad Roa Duterte, who participated actively in resistance to the Marcos regime and in advocacy on behalf of women's rights (Ranada 2017). Although Duterte himself has long expressed admiration for Ferdinand Marcos's authoritarian rule, he has also made many references to his mother's formative influence, no small part of which was her frequent recourse to corporal punishment (Paddock 2017). Second, as a university student, he studied under Jose Maria Sison, the founding chairman of the Communist Party of the Philippines (CPP), and belonged to CPP-affiliated activist groups (Palatino 2017). While Duterte has since disclaimed any affiliation with the CPP's armed wing, the New People's Army (NPA), his distinctly anti-imperialist brand of nationalism very much aligns with that of the Philippine radical left. Finally, during his tenure as a city prosecutor, he witnessed and likely participated in a bloody counterinsurgency campaign in the streets of Davao, where the Philippine Constabulary and armed vigilante squads known as the Alsa Masa pursued and summarily executed suspected members of the NPA (Weiss 2017). But then, as mayor, Duterte built a reputation for deescalating tensions with the NPA by allowing the collection of "revolutionary taxes" and shifting the focus of the so-called Davao death squads to the pursuit of "criminals." Some reports even claim that he helped the NPA "in its purge of urban revolutionaries who had deviated from the party's Maoist line" (McBeth 2016). What is clear is that he developed some kind of a symbiotic relationship with the NPA while overseeing a number of progressive social policies, including, for example, the provision of healthcare to sex workers.[6]

This history notwithstanding, the Philippines's sixteenth president is not by any conventional definition a leftist. So who then is he, politically speaking? It depends on whom you ask. Walden Bello, a prominent public intellectual and former member of the Philippine House of Representatives, describes Duterte as a "counterrevolutionary" and a "fascist original." "Duterte's charisma," Bello writes, "would probably be best described as cariño brutal, a Filipino-Spanish term that denotes a volatile mix of will to power, a commanding personality, and gangster charm that fulfills his followers' deep-seated yearning for a father figure who will finally end what they see as the 'national chaos'" (Bello 2017). According to sociologists Herbert Docena and Gabriel Hetland, Dutertism is simply a form of "populist neoliberalism" that recasts standard-fare neoliberal policies in a mold of federalism, nationalism, and debt-financed fiscal expansion (Docena and Hetland 2016). Historian Alfred McCoy (2017) has argued that while Duterte shares the diplomatic adeptness and cultural charisma of past Filipino populists (Quezon and Marcos), "[his] mix of machismo and narrow nationalism seems typical of this current crop of anti-globalization populists" (11). And political theorist Adele Webb (2017) puts the accent even more directly on nationalism, citing the rejection of US imperialism as Duterte's defining characteristic and as the source of his mass appeal. "He embodies," she writes, "the scrutinized Filipino 'native' subject of history, subordinated and looked down upon by the 'foreign' outsider; in standing up for 'the people,' he signifies a refusal to continue the indignity of the past" (139). But then again the president's rejection of foreign, especially Western, domination sits somewhat awkwardly alongside his toleration of Chinese military expansion in the South China Sea. As political scientist Richard Heyderian noted in the wake of a November 2018 state visit by Chinese president Xi Jinping, this selective nationalism "seems to have only exposed internal fault lines and widespread scepticism in the Philippines over Duterte's strategic flirtation with Beijing" (Heyderian 2019).

While to some extent these varying assessments represent a sort of disciplinary Rorschach test, they also evoke Duterte's own mercurial performativity. Duterte has himself proclaimed that only two out of his every five statements are true. The rest, he said, are *"kalokohan"*—a term that connotes jest, nonsense, and mischief (Romero 2017). This calculated kalokohan is what cultural historian Vicente Rafael (2018, see also 2019) underscores when he likens Duterte to a *pusong* or folkloric trickster:

> In taking on the role of the dissipator in chief, Mr. President thumbs his nose at bourgeois demands for discipline and decorum. Instead, he becomes a sort of trickster figure who entertains by veiling his aggression with jokes and obscenities. As a trickster, he plays the role of the pusong, a staple figure in traditional komedya and folktales. It is the pusong who makes fun of those in power, while managing through deceit or humor to gain power himself.

Indeed, there is a certain cunning if not outright duplicity to much of what Duterte and his advisors say and do, making it risky to impute any stable ideological framework onto his vision or actions. As noted above, I see Duterte and his counterparts as agents of revanchist authoritarianism, a term that centers the resoundingly vengeful if ideologically variable impulses that seem to unite them. But he is also at turns a populist, a proponent of neoliberal policies, and an anti-imperialist nationalist, and in that sense all of the assessments I cited above ring true. Duterte embodies competing forces at work in

Philippine society and in the world more broadly. Per McCoy (2017), he "mediate[s] the contradictions, the structural flaws if you will, in the Philippine polity"—"a recurring tension between a nominally strong central government, headed by an empowered executive, and local elites who control their provincial peripheries through economic assets, political office, and extralegal violence" (12).

Whatever the precise contours of Duterte's political identity, an important part of what has made him such a deft populist is his ability to consolidate support from state security forces while deferring opposition from the left. This he accomplishes in large part by offering a defiantly independent alternative to the perceived corruption, criminality, and chaos that result from submitting to the hypocrisy of Western liberalism. As he said when faced with US president Barack Obama's criticism: "You must be kidding. Who is he to confront me? America has one too many to answer for the misdeeds in this country. . . . As a matter of fact, we inherited this problem from the United States. Why? Because they invaded this country and made us their subjugated people" (quoted in Webb 2017, 130).

During the 2016 campaign, Duterte's personal history, anti-imperialist nationalism, commitment to federalism, and performative disdain for establishment elites all read favorably to many on the Philippine left. When he then appointed a number of prominent leftist and progressives to his inaugural cabinet, it seemed possible that his administration would coopt at least some elements of what would otherwise be his main opposition. Perhaps predictably, though, this prospect has since proven dead on arrival.

Losing the Red . . .

The first months of Duterte's presidency brought a long-awaited resumption of peace talks with the National Democratic Front and a "wait-and-see" attitude among many on the left. Since then, however, relations have soured. Several of his leftist appointees were rejected by Congress, and several have resigned, including one who was indicted on trumped-up murder charges. In May 2017, Duterte declared martial law on the island of Mindanao after the city of Marawi was seized by an Islamist rebel group, and six months later, the aforementioned peace talks were suspended following violations of the ceasefire agreement and Duterte's decision to declare the CPP and NPA terrorist groups. In February 2018, an array of more than six hundred activists, including the United Nations Special Rapporteur on the Rights of Indigenous Peoples, were included on a list of suspected CPP-NPA members and thus labeled terrorists, drawing widespread outrage and condemnation. In September of the same year, rumors began to spread about an alleged Communist coup plot known as "Red October," stoking fears of a return to a Marcos-style crackdown on dissidents. This was accompanied by calls from the military for a ban of "partisan political activity" on college campuses, said to be "hotbeds" of recruitment for the CPP. It is unclear to what extent Duterte has been pressured into shifting his approach, but as he comes to rely more and more on former military officers and other hardliners, it is likely that his estrangement with the left will continue.[7]

Meanwhile, of course, the drug war has proven bloodier and more indiscriminate than many Duterte agnostics had imagined, and it has fed a further escalation of extrajudicial killing in the realm of electoral and environmental politics. To cite but one grisly figure, forty-eight Filipino environmental activists were assassinated in 2017, according to the NGO Global Witness (AFP 2018).[8]

What is perhaps most troubling about the escalation of violence under Duterte is not its novelty, but its continuity with the past. From colonial times to the present, political power in the archipelago has relied heavily on an "informal devolution of coercive authority," resulting in what McCoy *pace* Weber calls "a virtual oligopoly on armed violence" (McCoy 2017, 13). And this state (of) terror, while fundamental to the maintenance of power, also works over time to undermine the legitimacy of the state and to engender collective resentment toward the elites who control it. The Duterte presidency increasingly reads as a reprise of Marcos, and this sense of déjà vu has not been lost on Filipino activists both in the country and abroad. As a result, resistance has intensified, most notably in the massive protests outside the State of the Nation Address in July 2018 and in the reported surge of rebel activity in Mindanao, as have the state's efforts to suppress it.

... but Keeping the Green?

But even as Duterte has failed in his attempts to consolidate support on the left, he has managed to maintain a certain degree of credibility among environmentalists. In fact, I would even argue that the environment has become a central dimension of his authoritarian program. It's not just that he has promised to "Build, Build, Build" massive quantities of infrastructure, a proposition with major consequences for the politics of land, labor, and the environment. It is, rather, that environmental protection and disaster management have become two of the most important ways in which Duterte performs his commitment to impose public order and discipline. Above I described how this performance operated in the context of Typhoon Haiyan, and it worth noting that this pattern has continued with subsequent disasters, including the one precipitated by Typhoon Mangkhut (Ompong) in September 2018.

Disaster response, though, is only part of the story. To understand the broader workings of this dynamic and their implications for our understanding of resurgent authoritarianism, let's return to the matter of Duterte's initial cabinet appointments. Among the appointees—alongside a smattering of military officers, businesspeople, neoliberal economists, and leftist activists—was a woman named Regina Lopez, a self-described "yoga missionary" and environmentalist who was tapped for secretary of the Department of Environment and Natural Resources (DENR) (AFP 2017). As heiress to one of the wealthiest and most powerful families in the country, Lopez was no radical, but she enacted some fairly radical policies.

Already known for her conservation work and antimining advocacy, Lopez expedited a mining audit initiated by the outgoing Aquino administration and then ordered the closure or suspension of more than two dozen active mining operations. Going beyond Aquino's Executive Order 79 (EO 79), which suspended the issuance of new mining permits pending the passage of updated legislation, this move against ongoing operations shocked the Philippine mining sector, provoked a backlash among those with vested interests, and led to the eventual rejection of Lopez's appointment by Congress. But her order also brought praise from environmentalists around the country and around the world, even as it coincided with the bloody initial months of the drug war. Since that time, Duterte has made statements linking mining to poverty and national dispossession, but his administration has moved to reconsider both Aquino's EO 79 and Lopez's order while he has claimed that his hands are tied by existing legislation. With the moratorium on mining lifted in July 2018, high-level efforts underway to amend EO 79, and assassinations of environmental activists continuing unabated, this episode seems unlikely to have a major impact on destructive mineral extraction in the long run.

If the status of mining remains somewhat unclear, the pollution of tourist destinations has provided a clearer read on the role of environmental politics in Duterte's authoritarian agenda. Upon Lopez's removal as DENR secretary, a retired general named Roy Cimatu was appointed to the post, and he has since found ways to enact a version of green authoritarianism that is less politically contentious but no less performative. For example, after describing the country's most popular tourist destination, Boracay, as a "cesspool," Duterte declared a State of Calamity on the island and ordered its closure to tourists for a period of six months (Ranada 2018). Backed by riot police, General Cimatu pursued the ensuing cleanup effort as a mission to "search and destroy" illegal sewers, unpermitted structures, and other regulatory violations. Hundreds of businesses were ordered closed or fined, and many buildings were demolished. As the demolitions unfolded, many speculated that the cleanup, particularly the newly opened beachfronts and widened roads, would ultimately benefit large developers (Tayona 2018). These suspicions were only reinforced when Duterte proposed using agrarian-reform measures to distribute land to Boracay residents so that they could then sell it to developers (Hutton 2018).

In addition to the closure of Boracay, a number of other popular tourist destinations have been subjected to regulatory crackdowns and threats of closure. While the long-term benefits of these operations remain to be seen, the short-term costs have been borne most acutely by the many low-wage workers who were displaced, while the short-term gains have accrued largely to Duterte's image as a decisive law enforcer and to the contractors hired to undertake the work. As Mark Thompson noted, "the shutdown [of Boracay] played well to his fan base as another demonstration of his iron will to cleanse the country of its social ills" (Thompson 2018).

Environments of Anxiety

Duterte is by no means the first revanchist authoritarian to show an interest in environmental regulation, nor are his interventions in environmental politics unprecedented in the Philippines.[9] As Kristian Saguin has shown, the administration's attempts to resolve conflicts between fishing communities and large-scale aquaculture in Laguna Lake echo those of Marcos, who also promised to "'return the lake to the people'" (Saguin 2019). Unlike Marcos, however, Duterte has approached the lake as a crisis of environmental quality as much as one of social distribution, and he has relied on it to shore up his environmental credentials even as his attempt to crack down on mining has faltered.

In the end, Duterte's environmentalism is like his socialism: performative, selective, and often contradicted in practice. From the highly controversial reclamation project in Manila Bay to China's exploits in the South China Sea to the expansion of monocrop plantations in Palawan, his administration has supported or tolerated many of the same ecologically destructive practices as its predecessors did. Even so and even as his relationship with the left has collapsed, spectacles of authoritarian environmental protection have become an important part of his approach. This makes political sense in a context where people feel profound anxiety and resentment not just about social inequality, corruption, and the legacies of colonialism but also about environmental degradation and climate change.

Put simply, the dispossession of working-class Filipinos has not been an exclusively political-economic process—it has also been a political-ecological one. The Philippines has undergone rapacious deforestation, resource extraction, and ecological degradation over the past century, and this has come at the expense of workers, peasants, and the environments that sustain them. Faced with what seems like a constant string of landslides, floods, typhoons, and other disasters, the Philippines is not just one of the most disaster-prone countries in the world, it is also one of the most vulnerable to the effects of climate change. Surveys have found that some 72 percent of Filipinos say they are "very concerned" about climate change, and some 85 percent report they are feeling its effects (Ranada 2015; Yeo 2013).[10]

Under these conditions, Duterte has channeled collective anxiety and resentment not just into a classist drug war and a nationalist assault on liberalism but also into a performative green authoritarianism that promises to punish polluters (especially poor "squatters") for subjecting the nation to environmental risk. Similarly, he has co-opted the rhetoric of the climate-justice movement, as, for example, when he said during an Al Jazeera interview: "'Who's responsible for the climate? Who's responsible for Haiyan? Who's responsible for the monsters of tornado? It's industrialized countries. We had nothing to do with it'" (Punzalan 2016).

By focusing on discrete, often remote places and "others," these moves serve to channel collective angst away from structural conditions. In typical reactionary fashion, Duterte claims that he alone can avenge the people's grievances while simultaneously embodying and amplifying the very forces that aggrieve them. Results from the May 2019 midterm elections suggest that this strategy is working: the President's allies now occupy a majority of seats in the

House of Representatives, Senate, and Supreme Court, suggesting that his administration may yet oversee a redrafting of the 1987 Constitution (Calonzo, Jiao, and Heijmans 2019).

Life or, Well, Death in the Necropocene

In his influential essay on necropolitics, Achille Mbembe (2003) offers a corrective to Michel Foucault's theory of biopower, which describes the sociopolitical forces that produce certain kinds of bodies in order to make them live and others in order to make or let them die. Biopower, Mbembe argues, "is insufficient to account for contemporary forms of subjugation of life to the power of death" (39). Examining enactments of indiscriminate violence, state terror, and collective punishment by (neo)colonial regimes, Mbembe develops the concept of necropower to describe how "in our contemporary world, weapons are deployed in the interest of maximum destruction of persons and the creation of *death-worlds*, new and unique forms of social existence in which vast populations are subjected to conditions of life conferring upon them the status of *living dead*" (40). In Mbembe's account, these weapons operate as technologies of rule in the hands of late-modern colonial regimes and as part of a larger "concatenation of multiple powers: disciplinary, biopolitical, and necropolitical" (29).

Necropower certainly seems to be at work in the indiscriminate terror and death that Duterte has unleashed and in the violent colonial foundations on which Philippine state power is built (more on this below).[11] But this is not the only form that necropower takes in the world today. In an essay titled "Haunted Geologies," Nils Bubandt (2017) argues that the operations of necropower are shifting amid the ecological upheavals and anxieties that we associate with the Anthropocene, a proposed new geologic epoch in which humans have become a dominant geophysical force on the planetary scale. Bubandt writes that "humans, animals, plants, fungi, and bacteria now live and die under conditions that may been critically shaped by human activity but that are also increasingly outside of human control. . . . In the Anthropocene, necropolitics operates under the sign of a metaphysical indeterminacy rather than certainty, unintended consequences rather than control" (G125).

I would add that any large-scale deployment of necropower raises the possibility of metaphysical indeterminacy and a loss of control. Regardless, this sense of uncontrolled necropolitical agency at the planetary scale is, I believe, part of what engenders collective anxiety and thus carves affective pathways for authoritarian consolidation. But of course not everyone experiences these times of metaphysical indeterminacy and epochal anxiety in the same way. Just as human societies bear vastly uneven levels of historical responsibility for bringing about Anthropocenic conditions, countries like the Philippines bear a vastly disproportionate share of the resulting risks.

Reinforcing this disparity are narratives that foretell an "apocalypse" as a result of climate chaos. Examples of these narratives abound, but one recent and especially clear example is David Wallace-Wells's viral essay, "The Uninhabitable Earth." Writing for *New York Magazine*, Wallace-Wells (2017) declares that "the mass extinction we are now living through has only just begun; so much more dying is coming." The essay, as Audra Mitchell and I have written elsewhere, goes on to "regale readers with graphic imagery of starvation and perpetual war in a coming climate apocalypse" (in press). While critically registering his concerns about human "dominion" over the earth, in the same breath Wallace-Wells embraces the idea that humans have weaponized the earth against ourselves, suggesting that we have "[engineered] first in ignorance and then in denial a climate system that will now go to war with us for many centuries, perhaps until it destroys us." The earth, he writes, is an "angry beast" or, better yet, a "war machine."

Perhaps it goes without saying, but the "we" in Wallace-Wells's account includes all of humanity only up to the point of salvation. Who, after all, would be doing all of the dying he envisions and who would have the means to engineer their survival? Paradoxically, the silences around race, class, gender, nationality, and colonial occupations speak volumes about who survives—and who does not—in the world envisioned by such narratives. It is no coincidence that the "living dead" of Duterte's deeply classist war on drugs are drawn largely from the same marginalized communities whose anonymous annihilation is foretold in climate apocalypse narratives and whose supposed deficits of "resilience" are the subject of neoliberal climate-adaptation schemes (Walch 2018).

And as speculative narratives of eco-apocalypse proliferate, so too do apocalyptic depictions of actual climate-related disasters. In the aftermath of Haiyan, reporters from around the world descended on Tacloban, telling heart-breaking tales of survivors' losses, of their attempts to secure food and medical care, of their psychological trauma. Many reports described survivors as "walking around like zombies," and as we saw above this was a term Duterte himself echoed in his account of what he encountered there. As one widely quoted witness put it, "it's like a movie" (Leon and Demick 2013). Keep in mind here that those most affected by Haiyan—and most likely to be destitute in its wake—were poor communities living in unprotected areas along the seashore. Although different words were used, we saw an analogical dehumanization of racialized survivors in the wake of Hurricane Katrina and, more recently, in Trump's baldly white supremacist response to the devastation of Puerto Rico. Such imagery resonates ominously with what Bubandt describes in "Haunted Geologies." What we have here is a planetary necropolitics for the Anthropocene.

Euphemisms We Die By

What, then, are we to make of the resonances between the necropolitics of authoritarian state terror as enacted by tyrants like Rodrigo Duterte and the necropolitics of the Anthropocene as envisioned by authors like David Wallace-Wells? Posing this question neither equates these actors nor diminishes the tremendous gravity, scale, and pace of planetary ecological change. My aim, rather, is to provoke critical reflection on how a growing sense of epochal planetary rupture might both reflect and augment the affective conditions that conduce revanchist authoritarianism. When so many authoritarian regimes take root in narcissism and feed on necropolitics, how might similar impulses shape our anxious fascination with the (necro)power of humans-as-planetary-force? Do eco-apocalyptic narratives, even critical ones, risk normalizing the greenwashed brand of authoritarianism that Duterte represents?

I offer these questions as a provocation about the potential effects of eco-apocalyptic anxiety in authoritarian projects, for which Duterte offers one compelling archetype. This essay's title—"Euphemisms We Die By"—riffs on George Lakoff and Mark Johnson's influential book *Metaphors We Live By* (1980), which traces how key metaphors (e.g., "time is money") structure our perceptions and actions in the world. It is my contention that performative environmentalism offers Duterte one relatively effective way to euphemize and thus normalize his administration's broader assault on democratic institutions and civil rights.[12] Duterte's environmental politics are not an exception to his revanchist authoritarian project—they are an integral part of it. Just as he exploits the legitimate anger and frustration that people feel about inequality and corruption, he exploits their legitimate fear and anxiety in the face of planetary ecological disruption. Both of these moves provide cover for the continuation of a necropolitical regime that, since colonial times, has directed state-backed violence at dissidents and other marginalized populations. At a larger scale, I submit, eco-apocalyptic narratives escalate our growing sense of desperation and powerlessness—and thus create an opening for the greenwashing of authoritarianism.[13]

Notes

1. Duterte has himself faced mounting criticism from Haiyan survivors. An advocacy group called Peoples' Surge described him as "inutile" in a statement released on the storm's fifth anniversary (LSDE 2018).

2. The term *revanchism* derives from the French *revanche* (revenge) and from a right-wing nationalist movement known as *revanchisme*, which formed in late-nineteenth-century France in reaction to the Paris Commune, the perceived decadence of the Second Republic, and the loss of territory in the Franco-German War. My use of revanchist authoritarianism refers to current political conditions around the world that favor demagogic and/or "strongman" figures—including Duterte in the Philippines, Trump in the United States, Putin in Russia, Xi in China, Erdoğan in Turkey, Modi in India, Orbán in Hungary, and Bolsonaro in Brazil, inter alia—who actively undermine democratic norms and institutions in the pursuit of power. What unites this trend, in my mind, are promises to repel, punish, and/or eliminate corrupting elements from society in order to (re)claim a lost or stolen greatness. These rhetorics and movements scale up and amplify the urban revanchism that Neil Smith (1996) and others have described in relation to the aggressive gentrification and policing of inner cities beginning in the 1960s.

3. This image has notably begun to fray due to the administration's apparent inability or unwillingness to confront high rates of inflation, China's occupation of Philippine maritime territory, rampant misconduct by security forces, and basic problems with infrastructure in Manila and other cities.

4. Another important factor was the scandal over PNP officers' abduction, murder, and posthumous ransoming of a South Korean businessman, Jee Ick-joo (PDI 2018).

5. What international media have largely overlooked is that this was also a test balloon for militarizing the police. Duterte has long speculated about reviving the Philippine Constabulary. As the American colonial regime's successor to the Spanish *Guardia Civil*, the Philippine Constabulary was a military police force that, until 1991, violently suppressed the radical left, Muslim autonomy movements, peasant resistance, and other internal "threats" to the US colonial regime and its neocolonial

successor. It is worth noting that the PDEA, which has played an increasingly prominent role in the drug war despite the PNP's dominance in street-level enforcement, is widely associated with former Constabulary officers.

6. His support for reproductive healthcare and healthcare for sex workers is especially ironic given his record of sexist and misogynistic remarks, including those calling for the sexual assault of women rebels (Rauhala 2018).

7. This crackdown on the left reflects a larger effort by the administration and its surrogates to suppress dissent. They have, for example, seen to the ouster of Chief Justice Maria Lourdes Sereno from the Supreme Court; they have criminally charged or jailed a number of prominent critics, including two senators and the head of Rappler, an independent news outlet; they have deployed online trolls to attack prominent activists and journalists; and they have made unsubstantiated criminal accusations against public officials who were later assassinated.

8. Although verified counts were not yet available at the time of writing, Mongabay reported that the Philippines and Brazil had the highest number of environmental activists murdered in 2018 (Volckhausen 2018).

9. Preserving "nature" was a central aim of German National Socialism and its vision of a racially and environmentally purified "homeland" (Staudenmaier 2011). And of course the roots of American environmentalism are entangled with those of white supremacism (Purdy 2015).

10. These numbers are from 2015 and 2013 respectively. It is likely they have increased in the years since. For perspective, consider that a "record number" of 22 percent of Americans were "very worried" about climate change in 2017 (Chow 2017).

11. Vicente Rafael (2019) makes a similar point in his remarkable new article, "The Sovereign Trickster." This essay was already in press when his article came out, so I have been unable to give it the attention it merits.

12. I am also thinking here of how terms like *extinction* and *the Anthropocene* euphemize the world-breaking violence of colonialism, capitalism, and white supremacism (Davis and Todd 2017; Mitchell, Todd, and Pfeifer 2017; Mitchell 2014).

13. I would like to thank Paul Eiss, Ema Grama, Jennifer Riggan, Kristian Saguin, Judith Schachter, and two anonymous reviewers for their insightful comments on drafts of this essay. I am also grateful to Jeff Maskovsky and Sophie Bjork-James for their patient editorial work and helpful feedback.

References

AFP. 2017. "Time to 'Do the Right Thing': Former Yoga Missionary Takes Aim at Philippine Miners." *South China Morning Post*, February 23. Accessed August 2, 2019. https://www.scmp.com/news/asia/southeast-asia/article/2073378/time-do-right-thing-former-yoga-missionary-takes-aim.

AFP. 2018. "Record 207 Environmental Activists Killed in 2017." *Rappler*, July 24. Accessed August 2, 2019. https://www.rappler.com/science-nature/environment /208069-number-environmental-activists-killed-2017-global-witness-report.

Arugay, Aries. 2018. "When Populists Perform Foreign Policy: Duterte and the Asia-Pacific Regional Order." *German Institute for International and Security Affairs Working Papers* 4: 1–9.

Bello, Walden. 2016. "How Neoliberalism Killed the Philippines' EDSA Republic." *Green Left Weekly*, June 24. Accessed August 2, 2019. https://www.greenleft.org .au/content/walden-bello-how-neoliberalism-killed-philippines-edsa-republic.

Bello, Walden. 2017. "Rodrigo Duterte: A Fascist Original." *Rappler*, January 2. Accessed August 2, 2019. https://www.rappler.com/thought-leaders/157166 -rodrigo-duterte-fascist-original.

Bello, Walden F., Herbert Docena, Marissa De Guzman, and Mary Lou Malig, eds. 2004. *The Anti-Development State: The Political Economy of Permanent Crisis in the Philippines*. Quezon City: University of the Philippines and Focus on the Global South.

Billing, Lynzy, and Regine Cabato. 2019. "'This Is Manila.'" *Washington Post*, February 22. Accessed August 2, 2019. https://www.washingtonpost.com/graphics /2019/world/philippines-manila-body/?utm_term=.44620d491747.

Bubandt, Nils Ole. 2017. "Haunted Geologies: Spirits, Stones, and the Necropolitics of the Anthropocene." In *Arts of Living on a Damaged Planet*, ed. Anna Lowenhaupt Tsing et al., 121–143. Minneapolis: University of Minnesota Press.

Calonzo, Andreo, Claire Jiao, and Philip Heijmans. 2019. "Opposition Crushed in Philippines Midterm Vote in Nod to Duterte." Bloomberg, May 13. Accessed August 22, 2019. https://www.bloomberg.com/news/articles/2019-05-13 /philippines-vote-count-stalls-as-duterte-allies-take-lead.

Chow, Lorraine. 2017. "Record Number of Americans 'Very Worried' about Climate Change." *EcoWatch*, November 20. Accessed August 2, 2019. https://www .ecowatch.com/climate-change-public-opinion-2511043076.html.

Corrales, Nestor. 2016. "Duterte Slams Roxas: Where Are Billions of 'Yolanda' Funds?" *Philippine Daily Inquirer*, March 3. Accessed August 2, 2019. https:// newsinfo.inquirer.net/770440/duterte-slams-roxas-where-are-billions-of -yolanda-funds.

Curato, Nicole. 2017. "Politics of Anxiety, Politics of Hope: Penal Populism and Duterte's Rise to Power." *Journal of Current Southeast Asian Affairs* 35 (3): 91–109.

Davis, Heather, and Zoe Todd. 2017. "On the Importance of a Date, or, Decolonizing the Anthropocene." *ACME: An International Journal for Critical Geographies* 16 (4): 761–780.

Docena, Herbert, and Gabriel Hetland. 2016. "Why Duterte Is Not—and Is Unlikely to Be—a Socialist." *Rappler*, June 29. Accessed August 2, 2019. https:// www.rappler.com/thought-leaders/137804-duterte-not-socialist.

DTE. 2018. "Is PM Modi Really a 'Champion of the Earth'?" *Down to Earth*, September 27. Accessed August 2, 2019. https://www.downtoearth.org.in/news/forests/is-pm-modi-really-a-champion-of-the-earth--61739.

Gaviria, César. 2017. "President Duterte Is Repeating My Mistakes." *New York Times*, February 7. Accessed August 2, 2019. https://www.nytimes.com/2017/02/07/opinion/president-duterte-is-repeating-my-mistakes.html.

Gomez, Jim. 2016. "Duterte 'Happy to Slaughter' Drug Suspects; Mentions Hitler." *Associated Press News*, September 30. Accessed August 2, 2019. https://www.apnews.com/1a8bd4625272423e9801bbcd447073e8.

Heyderian, Richard Javad. 2019. "Duterte's Pivot to China Less Than Meets the Eye." *East Asia Forum*, January 4. Accessed August 2, 2019. https://www.eastasiaforum.org/2019/01/04/dutertes-pivot-to-china-less-than-meets-the-eye/.

Hutton, Mercedes. 2018. "Duterte's 'Cesspool' Boracay Island Set for Closure. Or Is It?" *South China Morning Post*, March 20. Accessed August 2, 2019. https://www.scmp.com/magazines/post-magazine/travel/article/2138014/dutertes-cesspool-boracay-island-set-closure-or-it.

IBON. 2019. "Duterte's Midterm: Change for the Worse - Midyear Birdtalk Paper." IBON Foundation. Accessed October 18, 2019. https://www.ibon.org/2019-midyear-birdtalk-paper_dutertes-midterm-change-for-the-worse/.

Lacorte, Germelina. 2013. "God Was Away When 'Yolanda' Flattened Tacloban—Duterte." *Philippine Daily Inquirer*, November 12. Accessed August 2, 2019. https://newsinfo.inquirer.net/525771/god-was-away-when-yolanda-flattened-tacloban-duterte.

Lakoff, George, and Mark Johnson. 1980. *Metaphors We Live By*. Chicago: University of Chicago Press.

Leon, Sunshine de, and Barbara Demick. 2013. "Typhoon Haiyan: Thousands Feared Dead in Philippines." *Los Angeles Times*, November 10. Accessed August 2, 2019. http://articles.latimes.com/2013/nov/10/world/la-fg-wn-tyhpoon-haiyan-thousands-feared-dead-in-philippines-20131110.

LSDE. 2018. "'Yolanda' Survivors Call Pres. Duterte 'Inutile' as Rehab Projects Continue Unfinished." *Leyte-Samar Daily Express*, November 9. Accessed August 2, 2019. https://www.leytesamardailynews.com/yolanda-survivors-call-pres-duterte-inutile-as-rehab-projects-continue-unfinished/.

Lumibao, Ruth. 2018. "As Landlessness, Land Grabbing Intensifies, So Does Agrarian Unrest." *Bulatlat*, June 11. Accessed August 2, 2019. https://www.bulatlat.com/2018/06/11/landlessness-land-grabbing-intensifies-agrarian-unrest/.

Mbembe, Achille. 2003. "Necropolitics." *Public Culture* 15 (1): 11–40.

McBeth, John. 2016. "Duterte Always Loved Communists—Except When He Was Killing Them." *South China Morning Post*, October 19. Accessed August 2, 2019.

https://www.scmp.com/week-asia/geopolitics/article/2038320/duterte-always
-loved-communists-except-when-he-was-killing.

McCoy, Alfred W. 2017. "Global Populism: A Lineage of Filipino Strongmen from
Quezon to Marcos and Duterte." *Kasarinlan: Philippine Journal of Third World
Studies* 32 (1–2): 7–54.

Mitchell, Audra. 2014. "Only Human? A Worldly Approach to Security." *Security
Dialogue* 45 (1): 5–21. doi: 10.1177/0967010613515015.

Mitchell, Audra, Zoe Todd, and Pitseolak Pfeifer. 2017. "How Can Aboriginal
Knowledge Systems in Canada Contribute to Interdisciplinary Research on the
Global Extinction Crisis?" SSHRC Knowledge Synthesis Research Report.

Mogato, Manuel, and Neil Jerome Morales. 2017. "Philippines' Duterte Hopes
Drugs War Shift Will Satisfy 'Bleeding Hearts.'" *Reuters*, October 12. Accessed
August 2, 2019. https://www.reuters.com/article/us-philippines-drugs
/philippines-duterte-hopes-drugs-war-shift-will-satisfy-bleeding-hearts-id
USKBN1CH10Y.

Paddock, Richard. 2017. "Becoming Duterte: The Making of a Philippine Strongman."
New York Times, March 21. Accessed August 2, 2019. https://www.nytimes.com
/2017/03/21/world/asia/rodrigo-duterte-philippines-president-strongman.html.

Palatino, Mong. 2017. "Is the Philippines' Duterte Really a Leftist?" *The Diplomat*,
May 7. Accessed August 2, 2019. https://thediplomat.com/2017/05/is-the
-philippines-duterte-really-a-leftist/.

PCOO. 2016a. "Christmas Comes Early for 280 'Yolanda' Families, 28 Nov. 2016."
Presidential Communications Operations Office, Republic of the Philippines,
November 28. Accessed August 2, 2019. https://pcoo.gov.ph/christmas-comes
-early-280-yolanda-families-28-nov-2016/.

PCOO. 2016b. "President Duterte Visits Tacloban during Yolanda Commemoration." *Presidential Communiations Operations Office, Republic of the Philippines*. Accessed August 2, 2019. https://www.facebook.com/watch/?v=1502103039819352.

PDI. 2018. "What Went Before: Jee Ick-joo Slaying." *Philippine Daily Inquirer*, June 6.
Accessed August 2, 2019. https://globalnation.inquirer.net/167549/went-jee-ick
-joo-slaying.

Punzalan, Jamaine. 2016. "Duterte Blames Yolanda on Industrialized Nations,
Belittles US Aid." *ABS-CBN News*, October 17. Accessed August 2, 2019. https://
news.abs-cbn.com/news/10/17/16/duterte-blames-yolanda-on-industrialized
-nations-belittles-us-aid.

Purdy, Jedediah. 2015. "Environmentalism's Racist History." *New Yorker*, August 13.
Accessed August 2, 2019. https://www.newyorker.com/news/news-desk
/environmentalisms-racist-history.

Rafael, Vicente L. 2018. "Duterte, the Authoritarian Trickster." *Philippine Daily*

Inquirer, September 5. Accessed August 2, 2019. https://opinion.inquirer.net
/115861/duterte-authoritarian-trickster.

Rafael, Vicente L. 2019. "The Sovereign Trickster." *Journal of Asian Studies* 78 (1):
141–166. doi: 10.1017/S0021911818002656.

Ranada, Pia. 2015. "72% of Filipinos 'Very Concerned' about Climate Change—
Survey." *Rappler*, August 3. Accessed August 2, 2019. https://www.rappler.com
/science-nature/environment/101366-filipinos-very-concerned-climate-change.

Ranada, Pia. 2017. "Meet Davao's Foremost 'Yellow' Activist: Soledad Duterte."
Rappler, March 4. Accessed August 2, 2019. https://www.rappler.com/nation
/163130-davao-soledad-duterte-yellow-friday-movement.

Ranada, Pia. 2018. "Duterte: 'I Will Close Boracay.'" *Rappler*, February 10. https://
www.rappler.com/nation/195703-duterte-warning-close-boracay.

Rauhala, Emily. 2018. "Duterte Makes Lewd Threat to Female Rebels in Philippines."
Washington Post, February 12. Accessed August 2, 2019. https://www.washington
post.com/world/asia_pacific/duterte-tells-philippine-soldiers-to-shoot-female
-rebels-in-their-vaginas/2018/02/12/fd42c6ae-0fb0–11e8–827c-5150c6f3dc79
_story.html.

Romero, Alexis. 2017. "Duterte Admits Only 2 Out of 5 of His Statements Are
True." February 8. Accessed August 2, 2019. https://www.philstar.com/headlines
/2017/02/08/1670434/duterte-admits-only-2-out-5-his-statements-are-true.

Sadongdong, Martin. 2018. "Over 400 Died in One Month of Drug War;
Death Toll Now at 4,800—PNP." *Manila Bulletin*, September 26. Accessed
August 2, 2019. https://news.mb.com.ph/2018/09/26/over-400-died-in-one
-month-of-drug-war-death-toll-now-at-4800-pnp/.

Saguin, Kristian. 2019. "'Return the Lake to the People': Populist Political Rhetoric
and the Fate of a Resource Frontier in the Philippines." *Annals of the American
Association of Geographers* 109 (2): 434–442. doi: 10.1080/24694452.2018.1483815.

Sganzerla, Taisa, and Mong Palatino. 2018. "Is Jair Bolsonaro Another Rodrigo
Duterte? It's More Complicated Than You Think." *Global Voices*, November 10.
Accessed August 2, 2019. https://globalvoices.org/2018/11/10/is-jair-bolsonaro
-another-rodrigo-duterte-its-more-complicated-than-you-think/.

Smith, Neil. 1996. *The New Urban Frontier: Gentrification and the Revanchist City*.
London: Routledge.

Staudenmaier, Peter. 2011. "Right-Wing Ecology in Germany: Assessing the Historical Legacy." In *Ecofascism Revisited*, ed. Janet Biehl and Peter Staudenmaier,
89–132. Porsgrunn: New Compass Press.

Tayona, Glenda. 2018. "Grief and Anger: For Boracay's Poor Sectors, Closure
Worse Than 'Yolanda.'" *Panay News*, October 29. Accessed August 2, 2019.
https://www.panaynews.net/grief-and-anger-for-boracays-poor-sectors-closure
-worse-than-yolanda/.

Theriault, Noah, and Audra Mitchell. In press. "Extinction." In *The Anthropocene Unseen: A Lexicon*, ed. Cymene Howe and Anand Pandian. Goleta, CA: Punctum.

Thompson, Mark R. 2018. "Is There More to President Rodrigo Duterte's Boracay Closure and Drug War Than Meets the Eye?" *South China Morning Post*, May 1. Accessed August 2, 2019. https://www.scmp.com/comment/insight-opinion /article/2144058/there-more-dutertes-boracay-closure-and-drug-war-meets-eye.

Uson, Maria Angelina M. 2017. "Natural Disasters and Land Grabs: The Politics of Their Intersection in the Philippines Following Super Typhoon Haiyan." *Canadian Journal of Development Studies/Revue canadienne d'études du développement* 38 (3): 414–430. doi: 10.1080/02255189.2017.1308316.

Volckhausen, Taran. 2018. "For Embattled Environmental Defenders, a Reprieve of Sorts in 2018." *Mongabay*, December 24. Accessed August 2, 2019. https:// news.mongabay.com/2018/12/for-embattled-environmental-defenders-a -reprieve-of-sorts-in-2018/.

Walch, Colin. 2018. "Typhoon Haiyan: Pushing the Limits of Resilience? The Effect of Land Inequality on Resilience and Disaster Risk Reduction Policies in the Philippines." *Critical Asian Studies* 50 (1): 122–135.

Wallace-Wells, David. 2017. "The Uninhabitable Earth." *New York Magazine*, July. Accessed August 2, 2019. https://nymag.com/intelligencer/2017/07/climate -change-earth-too-hot-for-humans.html.

Webb, Adele. 2017. "Hide the Looking Glass: Duterte and the Legacy of American Imperialism." In *A Duterte Reader: Critical Essays on Rodrigo Duterte's Early Presidency*, ed. Nicole Curato, 127–144. Quezon Citry: Ateneo de Manila University Press.

Weiss, Brennan. 2017. "Duterte's Death Squads Were Born in America's Cold War." Foreign Policy, July 10. Accessed October 18, 2019. https://foreignpolicy.com /2017/07/10/dutertes-death-squads-were-born-in-americas-cold-war/.

Yee, Dakila Kim P. 2018a. "Constructing Reconstruction, Territorializing Risk: Imposing "No-Build Zones" in Post-Disaster Reconstruction in Tacloban City, Philippines." *Critical Asian Studies* 50 (1): 103–121. doi: 10.1080/14672715.2017.1407663.

Yee, Dakila Kim P. 2018b. "Violence and Disaster Capitalism in Post-Haiyan Philippines." *Peace Review* 30 (2): 160–167. doi: 10.1080/10402659.2018.1458943.

Yeo, Sophie. 2013. "85% of Filipinos Say They Are Feeling Effects of Climate Change." *Climate Home News*, July 14. Accessed August 2, 2019. http://www .climatechangenews.com/2013/07/17/85-of-filipinos-say-they-are-feeling -effects-of-climate-change/.

PART THREE

Unsettling Authoritarian Populisms

Left Populism in the Heart of South America

From Plurinational Promise
to a Renewed Extractive Nationalism

According to many analysts, popular exhaustion with neoliberal economic policies is responsible for the rise of right-wing populism in the Global North. The new populists of the right have capitalized on working-class disillusionment with an elite political consensus on a form of global economic integration that prioritizes transnational corporations over workers and local control. In South America, this exhaustion came over a decade earlier in the wake of the financial and debt crises of the late 1990s. Angry crowds from the left carried out a wave of disruptive protests beginning in 1999, toppling governments in Argentina, Bolivia, and Ecuador and leading to a nearly continent-wide electoral shift to the left, labeled the "pink tide." In Bolivia and Ecuador, antineoliberal governments also defined themselves as antiracist movements that put indigenous peoples and their rights at the center of new "plurinational" political orders. Alongside pink tide governments in Venezuela, Brazil, and Uruguay, they moved to dramatically renationalize and redistribute resource wealth to the poorest members of society.

Yet by the mid-2010s, the pink tide was receding, losing electoral strength, undergoing economic collapse in Venezuela, or falling before hostile political maneuvers in Paraguay and Brazil. By contrast, the continued political strength of Bolivia's Movement Towards Socialism and Ecuador's Alianza PAÍS seem much more secure, at least through the current terms of presidents Evo Morales and Lenín Moreno. A 2014 *Washington Post* profile of Ecuador's president Rafael Correa pointed to "a new model of Latin American leadership: economically populist, socially conservative, quasi-authoritarian—and seemingly unbeatable at election time" (Miroff 2014). This characterization, minus the social conservatism, increasingly applies to the Bolivian government led by Aymara coca growers' union leader Evo Morales. In both countries, left governments have maintained populist redistributive policies funded by accelerated exports of hydrocarbons, minerals, and industrial-scale agriculture. In so doing, they have traded their tight connections with radical movements of the poor and marginalized for working relationships with domestic economic elites and transnational investors. Beyond their borders, they have connected to capitalist economic circuits with new centers in the Global South, becoming part of the BRICS-led "neoliberalism with Southern characteristics" identified by Vijay Prashad (2013). In the process, these left populists have increasingly put the nation, centralized power, and limits on dissent ahead of the multicultural and decentralized principles they once championed. Those still frustrated with the national economic path are, for the moment, fragmented between visionary, but minority, tendencies on the left and a neoliberal and decidedly nonpopulist right.

This essay examines the consolidation of durable, if less transformative, left nationalism in South America by tracing the experience of Bolivia. The political experiment led by Morales's party, the Movement Towards Socialism–Political Instrument for the Sovereignty of the Peoples (MAS-IPSP) must be understood within a conjuncture of political, economic, and social movement factors that shaped its possibilities.[1] This essay surveys each of these in turn.

First, like the rest of the pink tide, the MAS-IPSP's rule emerged as part of a popular rejection of neoliberal globalization, the policy approach that dominated Latin America beginning in the 1980s. Both moderate social-democratic and radical socialist policies were conceivable responses, and the Morales government—together with its Ecuadorian and Venezuelan counterparts—foregrounded the more radical course in its early years. Significantly, it combined its leftism with a bold turn toward indigenous-led plurinationalism. However, the neoliberal model had itself been a counterpoint to so-called dangerous left populism, under whose aegis Bolivia had plunged into economic crisis in the mid-1980s. I show how the MAS-IPSP sought to demonstrate that its program was a *fiscally responsible* left populism. The essential basis for this program was export revenue from hydrocarbons, minerals, and agricultural commodities. This populist economic program led to concrete poverty reduction and material and symbolic rewards for the public, who ratified the MAS project, turning back a racially divisive opposition challenge in 2008 and 2009. However, this central commitment to resource-driven redistribution drew the government ever closer to conventional capitalist industries and away from social and communitarian economic experiments and from recognition of indigenous territorial rights.

As I address next, the collapse of commodity prices (in combination with the government's own power imperatives, which are beyond the scope of this essay) have led to a scaling back of the more transformative aspects of the MAS program. The result is a still populist, if somewhat less popular, unitary nationalism whose socialist and plurinational elements are increasingly hollow. The resulting left populism has an Andean indigenous face (in the symbols of state as well as the head of government) but is neither socialist nor plurinationalist. Indeed, since the end of the commodity boom, the government has increasingly worked in collaboration with multinational oil corporations and lowland agricultural barons, offering them incentive policies reminiscent of the neoliberal era.

My exploration of the Morales government's trajectory here parallels several other analyses. As the government's interest in radical "alternatives to development," indigenous re-territorialization, and the communal economy have proven ephemeral, Pablo Mamani and Fernanda Wanderley and colleagues have chronicled those shifts (Mamani Ramírez 2017; see also Wanderley, Sostres, and Farah 2015). Jeffrey Webber offers a synthetic read of the MAS government as what Antonio Gramsci called a "passive revolution": "a process of containment and redirection of a radical left–indigenous insurrectionary process ... into the consolidation of a state-capitalist process of modernization from above" (Webber 2016, 1860). Where Webber faults the class coalitions assembled by the MAS for this turn, Mamani contrasts the decolonial visions of indigenous movements with the long-run project of the Bolivian state and its colonial power relations (Mamani Ramírez 2017).[2] Similarly, Rebecca Hollender questions whether states enmeshed in global economic relations have the institutional latitude to carry out a radical questioning of capitalist and development paradigms (Hollender 2016). Writing this at a moment in which disappointment has replaced enthusiasm on many analyses of the current Bolivian government, I intend to highlight both the elements of transformation and restoration that, as Webber notes, coexist in a process of passive revolution (Webber 2016, 1860).

Popular Rejection of Neoliberalism in Latin America

One major theoretical approach for explaining the rise of right-wing populisms in the Global North has been a combination of economic anxiety and political exhaustion with a neoliberal policy consensus. But if we turn our geographical focus from North America and Europe to Latin America, the relationships among left and right, populism and technocratic neoliberalism, and nation and race all shift.

In the Global North, right-wing populists weave a narrative that charges educated and urban elites with embracing globalization policies that sent industrial jobs overseas while allegedly welcoming Third World immigrants in. They put a nationalist spin on opposition to neoliberal globalization and demand that government instead put "America [or Britain] first." In Latin America, by contrast, it is leftist movements that most directly challenge globalization. They portray governmental elites who embrace neoliberalism as prioritizing the needs of foreign capital over their own citizens, serving as *vendepatrías*, people who sell out their own country. Where northern right-wing populists cultivate fear of a foreign racial other, these southern left-wing populists may embody or embrace indigenous and mixed racial statuses as they call for multicultural or plurinational society. These distinctions reflect that—unlike the neoliberalisms of Ronald Reagan and Margaret Thatcher, the populisms of a domestic privileged class— neoliberalism in Latin America has always been the externally approved reaction to local populism (King and Wood 1999; Lowndes 2017; Peck and Tickell 2007).

Neoliberal policies arrived in South America a decade prior to the Reagan and Thatcher revolutions. Augusto Pinochet's coordination with the "[University of] Chicago Boys" on his economic policies was a test case of economic reform by a police state. Bolivia's 1985 shock therapy decree was imposed in response to a hyperinflation crisis under the left-leaning Democratic and Popular Union party (UDP), which ruled from 1982 to 1985. In Naomi Klein's *The Shock Doctrine* (2008), Bolivia is the leading example of the abrupt imposition of neoliberalism under quasidemocratic conditions. A state of siege was declared in August 1985, and prolonged detention of union and civil society leaders was used to break national strikes opposing Supreme Decree 21060. The end of hyperinflation in Bolivia and GDP growth in the Southern Cone justified a recipe of policy changes—the Washington Consensus— that would be promoted as essential to growth and imposed as a condition of international loans by the World Bank and International Monetary Fund. These institutions, along with the US Treasury Department and the Paris Club of private lenders, advised governments to compete for foreign investment, privatize state-run industries, avoid subsidizing commodities, and eliminate deficit spending, even if that meant cutting back public services (Williamson 1990). The goal was export-led growth and the means was increased foreign investment, which were facilitated by rapid leasing of natural resource concessions and construction of export infrastructure for raw materials (Hogenboom and Fernández Jilberto 2009).

By the end of the 1990s, however, numerous "star pupils" of this tutelage were caught up in crises of finance, political legitimacy, or both. Argentina's economy was devastated by capital flight during its 1999 to 2002 crisis. Overlapping debt, banking, and inflation crises in 1998 and 1999 led the Ecuadorian government to abandon its currency for the dollar in early 2000. Resulting civil unrest brought down governments in Ecuador (2000 and 2005), Argentina (2001), and Bolivia (2003 and 2005), and drove electoral shifts: eleven presidents in ten countries were voted in on the promise of rolling back neoliberalism between 2002 and 2010 (Coronil 2011).

By 2006, journalists and analysts were speaking of a pink tide of left-leaning electoral success across Latin America. But if "pink" was intended to imply a dilution of orthodox leftist red, then some rising political parties and the movements behind them went beyond that. In a 2011 analysis, Fernando Coronil pointed out two blocks: a more moderate stance in Brazil (led by Lula da Silva's Worker's Party), Argentina (headed by the Kirchners), and Chile (under Michelle Bachelet), and "the VEBo countries (typified by Venezuela, Ecuador, and Bolivia) [that] more openly endorse socialism and promote policies associated with it" (Coronil 2011, 251). Together with Sandinista-ruled Nicaragua, Cuba, and a half-dozen other Caribbean nations, the VEBo nations formed the Bolivarian Alliance for the Peoples of Our America (ALBA), a left-leaning trade and development bloc. Domestically, they made nationalization of resources and utilities, redistribution of wealth, and experiments with community-based economic alternatives the pillars of a "twenty-first-century socialism."

Meanwhile, even prominent proponents of the Washington Consensus began to theorize alternatives to it, among them future Peruvian president Pedro Pablo Kuczynski (Kuczynski and Williamson 2003; Serra and Stiglitz 2008). For many mainstream economists, the Wall Street–driven financial crisis of 2008 and the persistent rise of East Asian economies that disregarded the Washington Consensus demonstrated that more government intervention was necessary for growth. "Successful development," wrote Robert Stiglitz, "requires not the minimal role assigned to the state by the Washington Consensus, but a balanced role. . . . In the most successful countries, government has taken on the broader set of roles associated with the *developmental state*"

(Serra and Stiglitz 2008, 54). Eventually, even the core institutions behind neoliberal structural adjustment came to question these policies for leaving the poor behind. In 2016, the IMF issued a strategic reassessment, finding that "instead of delivering growth, some neoliberal policies have increased inequality, in turn jeopardizing durable expansion" (Ostry, Loungani, and Furceri 2016; see also Obstfeld 2016). This means that many pink tide initiatives, especially social democratic forms of redistribution, mesh with mainstream rethinking among capitalist development economists.

Left and Plurinational Promise

Evo Morales came to power in the wake of popular uprisings in 2003 and 2005, which capped a remarkable five-year period of social mobilization. The government inherited a dual mandate to nationalize and redistribute the country's natural wealth (principally its gas resources) and to redefine the country with the goal of ending the marginalization of its diverse indigenous majority. The twin ideologies of leftism and plurinationalism are expressed in the two-part title of Morales's political party, the Movement Towards Socialism–Political Instrument for the Sovereignty of the Peoples. Each represented a radical transformation of decades, if not generations, of Bolivian governance, and the government presented itself as a bold effort to redefine the state.

The new governments in Bolivia and Ecuador both held constituent assemblies to rewrite their constitutions, implemented partial nationalizations that increased government ownership of hydrocarbon and mineral resources, and devolved new powers to their indigenous and Afro-descendant communities. Along with these changes came renewed reliance on natural resource royalties to finance spending on antipoverty programs, a combination known as *neoextractivism* (Gudynas 2009). This strategy fulfilled longstanding leftist and anticolonial demands that Latin American countries should benefit from their natural resource wealth, even as it ran counter to some indigenous and environmentalist visions for a new relationship with the natural world.

At the heart of this radical visioning process was the 2006–7 Constituent Assembly, an extraordinary legislative body that wrote a bold governing document that redefined the Bolivian government as a plurinational state. Campesinos, teachers, miners, workers, and indigenous people all took their place among the body's 255 members. Half of them spoke an indigenous language; and one in five was a grassroots leader (Albó 2008). Many attendees saw the assembly as a place where bottom-up democracy could and should replace political parties, and where the unified and centralized Bolivian republic would be replaced by a new plurinational state that would guarantee indigenous and Afro-descendant peoples' rights to self-government, "to control their own institutions," and "to reconstitute their territories" (Programa Nina 2015).

The social movements represented in the Constituent Assembly demanded radical change along three fundamental axes: a leftist challenge to capitalism, a plurinationalist challenge to colonial hierarchies of culture and race, and an ethno-ecological critique of a distanced and destructive relationship with nature. While the third axis was peripheral to the largest Bolivian protest mobilizations, it was a core part of the radical ethical critique of the capitalist West. During its early years, the Morales government (like its Ecuadorian counterpart) was able to openly embrace the more radical versions of these visions, particularly in the lengthy constitutional text, presidential discourse, and international diplomacy.

A Fiscally Responsible Left Populism

A generation ago, neoliberal economists and policy makers defined themselves as rational opponents of populist economic policies. Populism, in the orthodox, neoliberal development literature, was "dangerous populism." This perspective was taught as development policy at the University of Chicago to upper-class Latin Americans in training to be the next generation of policy makers.[3] In this narration, political leaders offered populist economic policies — social spending, wage increases, commodity subsidies, or state-sponsored jobs — to attract votes. These policies were like candy, having an immediate appeal, but deviating from the necessities for long-term, healthy growth. Yet because they appealed to the public, they were incentivized by the democratic system. Hence democracy itself was seen as a paradox, a social good that tempted leaders (who should know better) to disregard the long-term best interests of their countries (Rodrik 2018).

Some dangers associated with populist economic policies were quite real, and none of them were more dramatic than runaway inflation, something indelibly marked in the historical memory of Bolivia. In 1982, the Bolivian military relinquished power to Hernán Siles Zuazo, who headed the breakaway left faction of the Nationalist Revolutionary Movement. (This was the last decisive left turn in Bolivian politics before Morales's election in 2005.) Siles faced pent-up demands from labor and rural movements that had endured years of dictatorship and massacre, frontal opposition from private enterprise, and closed doors from international creditors. Sharp increases in the cost of debt service and bailouts for state-run enterprises were not matched by new taxes, opening a yawning deficit that reached 30 percent of GNP in 1984 (Morales and Sachs 1989). Attempts to close the fiscal gap through wage freezes, subsidy cuts, or public-sector layoffs only aroused mass labor opposition in the form of strikes and direct action. Siles refused to use deadly force to suppress protests and instead used another state capacity: printing money to cover the state deficit.[4] Hyperinflation was the result. The Bolivian peso's value fell sharply in 1982 and 1983, and then cratered in 1984 and 1985, adding four extra zeroes to prices expressed in Bolivian pesos. Real incomes fell by 25 percent in the first half of the 1980s and continued their slide as the country's chief exports, tin and coca, lost their value. Despite mixed sources of responsibility, left governance has absorbed the historical blame for this economic catastrophe.[5] And in the international development literature, early 1980s Bolivia became an exhibit of the dangers of left populism.

To counter these dangerous impulses, neoliberal policy theorists proposed a variety of mechanisms to insulate economic policies from democratic interference. Fiscal discipline, dismantling of state enterprises, and openness to foreign investment were made into "conditionalities" of loans to stabilize and restructure foreign debt. Policy planners advised that central banks should be made independent of national governments, led by unelected officers whose terms are lengthier than those of heads of government. Regional blocs like the European Union unified currencies and subjected national budgets to coordinated limits. Increasingly broad trade agreements mandate certain policies and make deviations punishable by international tribunals. In essence, all of these neoliberal efforts push economic policy into technocratic domains, governed by experts, and out of democratic domains, subject to the popular will. In Bolivia, technocratic rule was accomplished through a consensus among major political parties, forged in 1985 and continued through 2003.[6] For an entire generation, the major political parties united behind the same economic policies, no matter who won. Each president built a coalition to lead the country rightward, prioritizing foreign investment over labor rights and social spending.

When Morales was elected president, international observers were shocked. The coca growers' leader had long been a bogeyman of demagogic populism.

He was vilified by American diplomats for the coca leaf's connection to narcotics and stereotyped domestically as an uninformed peasant ignorant of diplomatic protocol and economic realities. Moreover, Morales proposed a "twenty-first-century socialism" as his economic project. Everything that was an anathema to neoliberal technocrats seemed to be packaged together.

And yet, the new Morales government was far from ignorant of global economic or political realities. It still needed foreign credit, still lived in a hemisphere politically and militarily dominated by the United States, and still sought international investment. The specter of dangerous populism, and the historical shadow of the 1982–86 hyperinflation, threatened all of those relationships. The Bolivian government could not afford to be downgraded in international bond markets, isolated like a new Cuba, or spurned by transnational corporate investors. And so, the government sent clear signals to global powers about just what its brand of populism would entail. One unlikely emissary was Vice President Álvaro García Linera, a Marxist intellectual and former guerrilla, who spoke at the Washington-based Center for Strategic and International Studies in 2006.

"We are not," the vice president pledged, "a populist government with easily opened pockets and cheap promises."[7] He highlighted the government's "austerity" with its officials, who would no longer put money in offshore accounts (unlike their notoriously corrupt predecessors), and its "responsible management of macroeconomics." Speaking directly to the narrative of electorally driven populism, he observed that when facing elections, "The temptation to accede to every demand, to raise salaries 50%, 70%, 100%, to say 'yes' and 'yes' and 'yes' to everyone using the state's money, indebting ourselves, was very strong. In fact, other governments have done so. Not us." Over the next decade, Bolivian government officials became experts at playing against type, contrasting their moderate polices with their radical reputation. They maintained small fiscal deficits, large currency reserves, and a high growth rate in GDP. Accordingly, the international capital markets have provided Bolivia with financing, while gradually upgrading its bond rating. As Carlos Ivan Lopez, head of Bank of America Merrill Lynch's debt brokerage sector, explained, "You have to separate the headlines from the fundamentals and in the case of Bolivia it was very easy to do because the numbers are there. . . . That's why the investors could see and dissociate Bolivia from some other countries in the region that also have very strong social agendas, but with less discipline on the fiscal side."[8]

So, the Morales–Garcia Linera government has been intent on offering the world a fiscally responsible left populism. The essential foundation of this plan is the partial nationalization of resource rents, principally natural gas exports, and high commodity prices: "The will of this government," García Linera had told the CSIS in 2006, "is to produce, produce, and produce. Bring resources into the productive arena. Because only by generating wealth do you bring poverty to an end." They wouldn't print money. They would pump it out of the ground.

The Defeat of the Right and the Establishment of the Plurinational State

The election of Morales in 2005 capped five years of defiant protests with a dramatic political victory. Even the dramatic 53.8 to 28.6 percent margin of victory understates its significance. No political party had crossed the 40 percent mark in the quarter century since the last military dictator. The neoliberal parties found their fractions of the electorate suddenly inadequate at the national level. From 2004 to 2009, right-wing forces regrouped to mount a serious challenge from the departmental governments of the east and center. This spirited effort, backed by the urban and agribusiness elite, pursued a separatist challenge that counterposed the entrepreneurial agrarian lowlands to the supposedly backward and intransigent (and indigenous-dominated) Andean highlands. They rallied a "camba nation" centered on the four lowland departments of Santa Cruz, Beni, Pando, and Tarija (the "media luna"), where midcentury mestizo migration and European immigration had coalesced in an elite that saw itself as racially distinct from Bolivia's highland indigenous ("colla") plurality.

Media luna separatism drew on deeply rooted racism, past frictions between the regional elite and national government, and class antagonisms between the self-identified cambas and the large numbers of colla workers and peasants who had arrived in the previous quarter century. The region's representatives formed an opposition front in the Constituent Assembly, built ties to urban mestizo politicians in Chuquisaca and Cochabamba, and held autonomy referendums that the Morales government termed illegal in May and June 2008. However, the tide then began to turn. The five right-leaning prefects demanded Morales face a recall referendum, and he agreed on the condition that their mandates also appear on the ballot. Morales received a 67.41 percent vote of confidence, while Manfred Reyes Villa, the opposition prefect of Cochabamba, lost his seat. The other four right-wing prefects survived, but many voters in their departments also offered support for Morales. Doubling down, the right wing mobilized to implement de facto "autonomy," taking over national government buildings and looting the offices of left grassroots movements in four eastern departments. Rural organizations quickly organized marches on the eastern capitals, one of which was attacked with gunfire on September 11, 2008, killing eleven campesinos and educators in Pando department. This proved to be the turning point after which all stars aligned against the separatists: the Union of South American Nations condemned their movement and foreclosed any possibility they could take over the lucrative export of gas to Brazil and Argentina. Meanwhile, the national government finally deployed its security forces to arrest Pando's prefect Leopoldo Fernandez. Subjected to a trial by fire, separatism had failed.

Perhaps more important, the countermobilization against separatism brought the grassroots left back into the street. Morales's government redirected this mobilization from further confrontation around the eastern capitals to supporting his negotiations with the opposition in Cochabamba, and finally on a cross-country march from Caracollo, Oruro, to La Paz. Thousands of marchers filled the capital's Plaza Murillo and camped out there, surrounding the Bolivian National Congress on the night of October 20, 2008, to demand a referendum to approve the new constitution. Months of political deadlock finally ended the next day, and the January 2009 vote went decisively (61.4 percent) in favor of the constitution. From December 2005, the grassroots left remained mobilized "in defense of the process of change," in the drafting of the constitution, and in contests with the right. Amid these years of stalemate, their support of the government was vital, while the MAS-IPSP was spared hard choices by the perpetual deadlock with the right over legislation.

Jorge Komadina and Céline Geffroy argue that the MAS-IPSP innovated a form of political action that put the tactics of social movement action behind the electoral advance of a party.[9] In its initial incarnation, largely rural and indigenous organizations directly endorsed the creation of the MAS-IPSP as a *political instrument* that would return power and sovereignty to them. Mass mobilizations challenging neoliberal politicians alternated with the party's electoral takeover of local governments. At the local level, in places like the

Villa Tunari (the municipality at the center of the Chapare), MAS-IPSP officials were expected to subordinate their decisions to grassroots organizations.
Once in power nationally, however, the MAS-IPSP embarked on a major and
conventional party-building effort. As it expanded rapidly to compete in four
elections from 2008 to 2010, many of its new candidates and local efforts lacked
the kind of organic connections to local organizations that once defined the
MAS-IPSP. The party recruited local politicians, activists, and celebrities in
its effort to secure a parliamentary majority and a local presence nationwide.
Meanwhile, a substantial number of long-time high-profile leaders, ministers,
and intellectuals were pushed out of, or broke with, the party and became
critics of the government.

The plurinational state came into reality in 2010 with the seating of the first
Plurinational Legislative Assembly. The MAS-IPSP had won 64 percent of
the vote and two-thirds supermajority in the legislature. The party dominated
the highland indigenous vote (with an estimated 80 percent of the Aymara
vote and 66 percent of the Quechua vote) and even won 47 percent backing
among the nonindigenous.[10] Morales proclaimed January 22, 2010, the day of
his second inauguration, to be a holiday celebrating the foundation of the
plurinational state. Symbolically, the plurinational state positioned itself as
both the continuation of a centralized Bolivian republic and the embodiment
of indigenous emergence. The immediate job of the Plurinational Legislative
Assembly was to formalize the rules of the new government, its electoral and
judicial mechanism, the meaning of autonomy, the protection for the environment, and the ownership of natural resources.

Shifting Priorities of the MAS-IPSP

The economic and political project of the MAS-IPSP government has a shifting set of components drawn from the social democratic and syndicalist left,
visions of plurinationalism that center either on social inclusion or radical
decentralization/decolonization, and on either rethinking or deepening the
country's extractivist economic model. This diverse collection of ideas all
found early expression the Morales government's rhetoric, international diplomacy, and self-image, and in the text of the 2009 constitution. Over time,
however, the centralizing tendencies of the state and economy have displaced
the more radical and transformative elements of this mix. The following section considers the continuing and the discarded elements of this left populism.

Leftism

Morales and García Linera proposed a twenty-first-century socialism and an "Andean-Amazonian socialism" that would recover control over natural resources, industrialize them domestically, redistribute the proceeds, and begin a transition to a more diverse, community-centered economy.

LEFTISM AS REDISTRIBUTION

The core of left populist economic policies is the redistribution of wealth to the poorest sectors of society. In Bolivia, the primary means for this has been three cash-grant programs targeting demographic sectors of the public: the Dignity Pension (*Renta Dignidad*) offers a monthly payment to citizens over the age of sixty; the Juana de Azurduy Bonus provides cash payments to pregnant women and new mothers, conditional on receiving prenatal care; and the Juancito Pinto Bonus provides cash payments to families with small children attending school. These programs, combined with a rapidly rising minimum wage, reduced extreme poverty in Bolivia from 38.6 percent of the population to 16.8 percent over ten years.[11] They parallel efforts in the softer end of the pink tide, notably Zero Hunger (*Fome Zero*) in Workers' Party–led Brazil.

LEFTISM AS NATIONALIZATION AND INDUSTRIALIZATION

In the first five years of Morales's presidency, Bolivia renationalized its gas fields and infrastructure (under the state-owned YPFB), electrical grid (ENDE), telephone company (ENTEL), the Huanuni and Vinto tin mines (COMIBOL), major airports (SABSA), and the Vinto smelter (Empresa Metalúrgica de Vinto). It also created a new national airline, BoA, and a series of light manufacturing enterprises producing cardboard (CartonBol), packaged milk (LacteosBol), cement (ECEBOL), paper (PapelBol), clothing (Enatex), and refined sugar and alcohol (San Buenaventura). Employment in state-owned enterprises skyrocketed from 673 to 16,366 in the ten years from 2005 to 2015, although the latter total is little more than half the number that the mining giant COMIBOL once employed.[12]

Theoretically, the new economic model of Bolivia positioned the government as the redistributor of profits from the extractive sector to "Sectors that generate income and employment," such as manufacturing and public services. In reality, however, resource extraction generated more jobs than the manufacturing sector, and aside from the successful airline, the service sector consisted largely of legacy employment in declining utilities. The government also promised to redistribute surplus funds to the "communitarian economy," that is, the 18 percent of the population involved in rural production (Rodríguez 2015, 30).[13] However, a 2015 Fundación Tierra report found "an enormous breach between what is declared in [government] proposals and the reality that small-scale agriculturalists . . . realize an ever less import share of national economic production" (Rodríguez 2015, 73). The numerous experiments in productive employment, urban and rural, have not achieved self-sustaining growth.

After the 2014 crash in oil and gas prices, which marked the end of an extended commodity boom, the already shaky economic model faced a fundamental crisis. As commodity prices ebbed, the government sought to compensate for lower prices with increased volume. As older gas fields began to decline in production, they sought out corporations willing to invest in new fields. And, with limited gas reserves, the government is seeking to generate a new source of revenue by exporting electricity. There was no longer enough of a surplus for experiments in a diverse economy. At the peak of the "plural" model, gas producer YPFB had received 86 percent of the state enterprise budget. Now, the extractive sector needed all the investment it could get, just when revenues were shrinking.

Accordingly, the government shifted toward more traditional policies for attracting investment, while discarding its socialist experiments. "The era of nationalization has already finished," Development Planning Minister Rene Orellana told prospective investors in 2015. "Now we are looking for, and we are working on, agreements and associations with private investors and private operators." In an interview with Santa Cruz's ultraconservative *El Deber*, Vice President García Linera declared, "The MAS is no longer the MAS of 2005, it has been changing its proposal, it is not as communitarian anymore, now it has embraced the Santa Cruz model, which is capitalist." Santa Cruz elites had spearheaded the resistance to the Morales government in its early years, but the socialist government now moved to work with Cruceño elites to expand large-scale export agriculture. In its ten-year development plan, the Patriotic Plan 2025, the government proposed quadrupling the land under cultivation in the next decade, mostly by expanding mechanized monoculture. In the same interview, the vice president termed the light industrial enterprises a mistake, the result of overestimating "the associative maturity of the unions, and of the community of producers" (García Linera 2014). By 2015, the government announced that it would begin to shut down state enterprises that had yet to produce a profit, leading to struggles over layoffs at clothing maker Enatex and the Ecobol postal service.

The heart of the plan, however, is developing Bolivia's energy resources under the aegis of the largest state enterprises, YPFB and ENDE. The government envisions a dramatic increase in hydrocarbon production: from 56 to 103 million cubic meters per day of gas and from 59 to 135 million barrels of oil per day.[14] However, the gas sector has been hard hit by falling prices and state-owned gas producer YPFB has not found a major new field since the 1990s. Accordingly, the government has sought to make more of the country available for drilling and has begun to incentivize new private investment in the sector (Krommes-Ravnsmed 2019). New laws passed in 2015 and 2016 allocate government funds to subsidize private corporate investment in oil and gas and to customize the legal environment to attract companies like Repsol, Total, Pluspetrol, and Petrobras. Meanwhile debt-financed public investment is planned to build thirty-five hydroelectric dams at a cost of US$27 billion, providing 9.9 to 11 gigawatts of power by 2025.[15] Among the largest is the El Bala/El Chepete complex, which is set to flood parts of the Amazon basin in northern La Paz, including in the Madidi National Park. This energy is not needed within Bolivia, whose peak electricity consumption is well under 2 gigawatts. Instead, the government hopes to make electricity into a major export commodity, sent overland to Brazil, Argentina, Chile, and Peru.

Not only have these initiatives crowded out government support for socialist experiments, they have begun to reverse the much-vaunted leftward shifts of the early Morales years. Under concessionary contracts, the always-partial nationalization of the gas sector is undermined by effective partial ownership of new fields by YPFB's foreign corporate partners. And in the agricultural sector, a hard-fought 5,000-hectare constitutional cap on the size of estates has been bypassed by landholding families (Brabazon and Webber 2014). The proposed expansion of the agrarian frontier will accelerate that trend, indefinitely postponing the promised "end of the era of the latifundio." Finally, investment in pharaonic public infrastructure projects, of which the dams are only the most visible element, have already reversed the trend toward declining public debt the government had promoted as a symbol of economic autonomy.

Plurinationalism

Similarly, only some of initial meanings of plurinationalism have become defining features of the Morales government, while others have been discarded.

The incorporation of indigenous individuals into state and citizenship has proved more durable than the corresponding transformation of governance toward indigenous perspectives and norms. Along the way, those indigenous social movements that held firm to a more expansive vision of autonomy have become the targets of its direct ire.

PLURINATIONALISM AS MASS ENFRANCHISEMENT

From the beginning, the government worked to make indigenous people legible as citizens and eligible as voters. At Morales's inauguration, he lamented the prevalence of illiteracy and the existence of Bolivians without identity documents (unlike Europe "where even the dogs have passports") (Morales 2006). Mass literacy campaigns, structured by Venezuelan and Cuban aid workers, and a new cost-free identity registration program made hundreds of thousands of Bolivians into literate voters. The electoral rolls exploded from 3.6 million in 2005 to 6.5 million in 2016.[16] There is no doubt that indigenous and poor Bolivians had been underrepresented in the pre-2006 electorate, and these initiatives built up a powerful defense for the MAS-IPSP in future electoral contests.

Enfranchisement also describes the new relationship between indigenous Bolivians and government offices. Many indigenous Bolivians had previously felt unwelcome to conduct official business before national and regional agencies, particularly if they appeared in traditional indigenous dress or spoke their native language. The MAS-IPSP mandated that government officials each learn an indigenous language and make services available to all. In ten years, public administration grew from 23,158 to 54,224 workers (Mamani 2016), and the face of this growth was often indigenous. At higher levels of the civil service, initiatives like the Diplomatic Academy diversified government service in gradual, but effective ways.[17]

PLURINATIONALISM AS RADICAL DECENTRALIZATION

Plurinationalism was supposed to be about redefining governance in a way that centered indigenous autonomy. A longstanding effort to title indigenous territories continued under the Morales government. By 2009, 20.7 million hectares or 19 percent of Bolivia's land area had been included in "Native Community Lands" (TCOs) soon to be renamed "Indigenous/Native/Peasant Territories" (TIOCs) (Fundación Tierra 2011). This figure would inch up to 23.9 million hectares by 2016.[18] Indigenous representatives at the Constituent Assembly proposed these territorial units as the basis for a decentralized government in which executive and judicial functions would be retaken by the preexisting nations of Bolivia.

But once the constitution was in place, the MAS-IPSP proved unenthusiastic about decentralizing power away from the national government it now controlled. The new laws reflected this: in the 2010 Framework Law on Autonomies, devolved powers were limited and a central authority oversaw them. In 2011, the government undertook a major effort to build a road through the Isiboro-Sécure National Park and Indigenous Territory (TIPNIS) despite the objections of the territory's indigenous organizations. The 2012 Mother Earth Law made the planet and its ecosystems into "a collective subject of public interest" with quasi-legal rights, but reserved to the executive all rights to sue on her behalf (Bjork-James 2012a). During the 2010–15 term, seven indigenous deputies (chosen independently of the MAS-IPSP) critiqued all of these moves (Bjork-James 2012b). In the 2014 elections, however, the government brought indigenous representation into the party system and imposed harder discipline on its legislators, declaring there was no room for "free thinkers" in the party. The two indigenous organizations that spearheaded protests over the TIPNIS highway, CIDOB and CONAMAQ, were torn apart by pro-government representatives who formed parallel leaderships for the organizations, while the government refused to provide services or even meetings for its critics within these organizations (Bjork-James 2019; Apaza 2014). According to Pablo Mamani these are "the old forms of colonial power, such as dividing social organizations, cosmetic discourse, violently attacking and criminalizing [indigenous] movements with the police and the judicial system" (Mamani Ramírez 2016).

The current extractive push has further limited indigenous self-governance. The constitution provides for "free, prior, and informed" consultation over "the exploitation of natural resources," to be conducted through indigenous norms and procedures within indigenous territories. In 2015, Morales moved to "streamline" this process, explaining, "It's not possible for so much time to be lost in the so-called consultations, that is the great weakness of our state . . . we will modify some of the rules with the sole objective of accelerating investment and obtaining more natural resources."[19] Among these modifications is the declaration of the national strategic need to drill for oil and gas in protected national parks and biosphere reserves, limiting the consultation period to forty-five days, and capping the amount of compensation to indigenous communities harmed by extraction activities.[20]

Gender and Sexuality

While redistribution of economic power and increased representation in Bolivia's long-excluded indigenous plurality have been the central axes of the government's approach, the prospect of a new Bolivia has raised hopes for gaining similar ground in struggles against patriarchy, homophobia, and transphobia. For example, feminists have astutely put forward the claim that "there can be no decolonization without de-patriarchalization." The results on this front are similarly split.

The government instituted an electoral parity law requiring all candidate lists to alternate between men and women. Through this mechanism Bolivia and Rwanda are the only two countries with a female majority in their national legislatures. The government has fallen short of promised parity in the cabinet, but an unprecedented 35 percent of the first ninety-seven cabinet members were women.[21] If gender parity can be glossed as an Andean tradition, women's reproductive rights and freedom from violence and LGBT equality cannot. The government charted a moderate course on these issues in the constitution, prohibiting discrimination on the basis of sexual orientation or gender identity but defining marriage as exclusively heterosexual. The government backed limited legislation to decriminalize abortion in the first eight weeks of pregnancy in 2017, and Morales signed it in December 2017, only to repeal it in January 2018 to resolve an unrelated dispute over the penal code. More significant legal reforms include the 2013 Violence Against Women Law and the 2016 Gender Identity Law, but gender violence remains common and lethal.

The MAS-IPSP government's gender policies distinguish it sharply from the conservative path taken by other Latin American leftist governments, notably Correa's Ecuador and Daniel Ortega's Nicaragua (in its post-2007 incarnation). As president, Morales has been a fraught messenger for this gender progressivism since his public persona involves a comedic performance of an understated but insistent machismo in his daily speeches before constituents. ("I define myself as a feminist, although with *machista* jokes," Morales told a radio audience in 2015.) These performances have sparked a continuing series of gender controversies in the media, sometimes followed by progressive policy moves.

Bolivia's New Left Populism: Extractivist, Centralizing, and Nationalist

Plurinational Bolivia has made a major turn from the country I came to know from 2008 to 2011. Bolivia under Morales had distinguished itself as one of the most enthusiastic proponents of indigenous and environmental rights. Foreign Minister Choquehuanca led that effort, pledging, "We have begun the process of recovering our identity, our dignity, our codes and symbols. We have begun to recover our own forms of organization and administration of natural resources."[22] It blocked consensus at the 2009 Copenhagen climate summit, demanding deeper emissions cuts, and then hosted over twenty thousand activists in Cochabamba to back up its demands. There, President Morales delivered an extended speech condemning how "capitalism kidnaps Mother Earth to loot her resources, to exploit her sons and daughters, to poison her rivers and lakes."[23] Despite this engagement with environmental radicals, however, the government has always been a vocal proponent of getting oil and gas out of the ground, so long as natural resource wealth is redirected by the nation-state to fund an ambitious social agenda. The Morales government combined ethnoecological rhetoric taken from the transnational indigenous movement with leftist policies of nationalization and redistribution. In this early period, there was room for every vision, for social democratic and socialist economic policies, for enfranchising and decentralizing plurinationalism.

Beginning in 2011, however, the government moved from an aspirational constitution to drafting and executing its laws. It began to face growing pressure from left, indigenous, and environmentalist protest mobilizations. And, in 2014, the commodity boom collapsed. Choices had to be made.

Since then, the government has not wavered from its commitment to the macroeconomic fundamentals and has doubled down on extractivism as the basis for perpetuating its redistributionist economic agenda. The pillars of this approach—a small number of public enterprises and social welfare programs—are centralized around the nation-state, but they are branded as plurinational initiatives. A quick survey of how this is done symbolically is vital to understand how the practical centrality of the state is reconciled with the plural impulses of the movements that brought it to power.

Consider the Juana Azurduy maternal bonus program, which provides cash assistance and medical services to expectant mothers. The mestiza patriot Azurduy is honored as a speaker of Quechua and Aymara, a bearer of four sons who fought for independence, and a soldier in her own right. By naming the bonus after her, the government identifies giving birth as a form of national loyalty. And by honoring indigenous and poor women, it inverts the stigma around their fecundity into a service to the nation. Rather than welfare, it is framed as a well-deserved right that symbolically and materially includes them in the country's prosperity.

Similarly, the Tupac Katari telecommunications satellite is an example of *pluri*-branded national progress. Indigenous rebel Túpac Katari laid siege to La Paz in the ultimately unsuccessful indigenous rebellion of 1781 and 1782. Prophetically, these were the last words before his execution by Spanish authorities: "I die, but I will return as millions." In December 2013, a Chinese rocket launched the Túpac Katari 1 into orbit over Bolivia. A government propaganda mural promoting the satellite pictures Katari alongside Morales, while declaring, "The future is ours. The past is present." The satellite serves a as bridge between Bolivia's indigenous rebel past and its technological future, a talisman of the kind of Sputnik leftism that figures technological progress as a socialist achievement.

Indeed, much of the state sector of the economy—particularly the gas company YPFB, Entel telecommunications, and BoA airline—serves as part of the image-making apparatus of the state, promoting a combined image of inclusive progress, modernity, and economic accessibility. Advertising spots from YPFB narrate the protests for nationalization and interplay images of Bolivian tricolors and industrial equipment. The affordability of domestic BoA flights dovetails with government investment in opening dozens of airports to connect far-flung corners of Bolivia to modern transportation. Entel's by-the-second cell phone pricing plans are uniquely geared to the needs of poor urbanites, a MAS-IPSP constituency overlooked by its private competitors. Meanwhile, its advertising depicts rural Bolivians speaking Aymara as they discuss watching the Copa America football tournament via Katari satellite in their dusty Altiplano homes. Through its state-owned corporations, the MAS-IPSP has renationalized political struggle in a way that may not radically redefine the economy but does offer material and symbolic rewards to a broad sector of the public.

Winning by Retreating?

Unexpectedly, the central state and the president himself have become the prominent center of a new governing project. As the MAS-IPSP has come into its own, it has become more party and less movement, altering the balance between movement and state. The experiments promised in 2006—a movement-controlled party, a decolonizing government, and a revolution through the ballot box—have softened into something else, while retaining some of the color of those promises in both their rhetoric and substantive advances. This process has not (despite persistent narratives alleging this) demobilized the movements, but it has generally deterred them from direct repudiation of the Morales government and simply conceded some movement demands at moments of greatest vulnerability (Bjork-James 2020).[24]

For now, the Bolivian government has found a winning combination of new and old elements, of indigenous participation but limited territorial rights, of social democratic redistribution and macroeconomic stability, of nationalized resource revenues and large-scale capitalism. With each passing year, it becomes more difficult to call this combination either socialism or plurinationalism. It is, however, populist and nationalist. It offers leftists material advancement and offers indigenous peoples dignity. It binds these material changes to a symbolic realm where modernity, freedom from foreign domination, and indigenous glory all play a role.

The Bolivian right has been unable to regroup from either of its recent defeats at the ballot in 2005 or in the streets in 2008. The roster of right-of-center presidential candidates for the past decade is relatively static: businessman Samuel Doria Medina and ex-president Jorge Quiroga have run repeatedly, and a one-time regional alliance was led by two deposed prefects Manfred Reyes Villa and Leopoldo Fernández (the latter still awaiting trial in jail). Meanwhile, the independent left parties—the Without Fear Movement (MSM) led by Juan del Granado, and the Green Party, which put TIPNIS indigenous leader Fernando Vargas atop its 2014 ticket—have failed to attract a significant vote share at the national level. These two forces, which made similar criticisms of the MAS, failed to unify in 2014, dooming both to disqualification as they narrowly missed the 3 percent threshold to retain eligibility for national elections. However, the nucleus of the Without Fear Movement reconstituted itself as Sovereignty and Freedom (SOL.bo), allied with indigenous dissident Felix Patzi, and defeated the MAS in La Paz governor and mayor's races.

There are cracks in the MAS-IPSP's incredible electoral dominance, but the party continues to hold a remarkable share of elected offices. It barely slipped in terms of municipalities under its control, from 231 to 225 in the 2015 election. Between 2010 and 2014, the party made a major push for middle-class and Santa Cruz voters, which nearly offset its declining dominance among Aymara voters and in the highland cities (Bonifaz Moreno 2016; Pedraza 2016). But its influence in the capital cities, regional governments, and national votes is weakening. Opposition parties govern three departments and major parts of the left grassroots defected from the MAS in two more: the peasant federation in Chuquisaca and lowland indigenous movement in Beni. To make the leap from local opponents to national challengers, however, requires a single candidate to get within a 10 percent striking distance of Morales, an extreme challenge given the enduring hostility between left and right political forces.

The alignment between a massive indigenous electoral block and the MAS-IPSP government is highly dependent on the personal role of Evo Morales, who has been able to "embody the people" through his biography and presentation (Harten 2016). A 2015 *Financial Times* profile of the country quoted a "senior MAS member" as saying that the president "is the only element of cohesion of indigenous, peasant and social movements, and there is a strong belief that he is the only one who could manage this country" (Schipani 2015). The profile continued, "Not a few capitalists believe that too. 'We should be thankful we have Evo. Marginalisation was a time-bomb and he has forced us to share the pie,' says a businessman who did not want to be named" (Schipani 2015, 12). In the eyes of many capitalists, Morales has clearly moved from a threat to stability to its guarantor.

The governing party's confidence in Morales, and the lack of a highly visible figure who could substitute for him at the top of the ballot, have led to three consecutive nominations for him as president. Rather than groom a successor, the party and its closest movement allies are now preparing to put him forward for a fourth term. This required breaking earlier promises and the term limits stated in the 2009 constitution. A February 2016 referendum to amend that term limit failed narrowly, with 51.3 percent opposed. The "no" vote was the first national electoral defeat for the MAS-IPSP in its twelve-year rule. Undeterred, the government challenged the provision before the Plurinational Constitutional Tribunal, which, in December 2017, struck down term limits as a violation of the president's civil and political rights. The question of Morales's fourth term has brought together dissident indigenous and civic movements, numerous left dissidents who have become critical of the government's direction, and political parties on the left and right. The events of late 2019, still unfolding at the time of this writing, reflect both the attraction and the brittleness of Morales's extractive left populism. In the run up to the October 20 presidential election, former president Carlos Mesa mounted the first serious electoral challenge by adopting major components of the MAS-IPSP political program, including public investment, redistribution bonuses, and other social programs: "We won't adopt any measure that affects people in need," Mesa pledged (Manetto 2019). The disastrous fires in August through October 2019, which blazed on 5 percent of Bolivian land and burned over two million hectares of forest, proved a major embarrassment for the president and a rallying point for his opponents in hard-hit Santa Cruz department. While none of the candidates genuinely challenged the extractive agribusiness model that has propelled deforestation, Mesa spoke of a "post-extractivist" economy.

In the official October 20 election results, Morales obtained 47 percent of the vote, outpacing the strong 36.5 percent showing by Carlos Mesa. This margin would have allowed Morales to narrowly avoid a December runoff. But these results were immediately thrown into doubt by irregularities in the counting process, and ultimately rejected by Organization of American States auditors on November 10. In the intervening three weeks, mass protest rallies, blockades, and finally a bottom-up police mutiny shook the nine departments of Bolivia. The apparent vote fraud proved a more unifying force among left and right critics of Morales than anything up to this point. Following the auditors' report, Morales first offered new elections and then resigned the presidency at the urging of the military high command. This inaugurated a political transition in which the political and economic model established by the Morales years will be subject to new and uncertain winds.

Notes

1. Other recent analyses of the trajectory of the Evo Morales government include the following: Hollender (2016); Mamani Ramírez (2017); and Webber (2016).

2. For an argument that the MAS already represented the subordination of a more expansive movement vision in 2003, see Gutiérrez Aguilar (2008).

3. I know this because I studied alongside such students at the Harris School of Public Policy from 1996 to 1998.

4. The choice to print money domestically rather than borrow it abroad—usually

treated as a foolish decision—was forced upon the Siles government, as Juan Antonio Morales and Jeffrey Sachs acknowledged, "a key condition for the eventual outbreak of hyperinflation was the cutoff in access to foreign borrowing in 1982: only a credit-constrained government would choose to finance current expenditures with a hyper-inflation rather than with more foreign borrowing." (Morales and Sachs 1989, 187).

5. The more detailed accounting by Morales and Sachs (1989) shows that service on the debt (accumulated during the dictatorship), rather than new spending was the primary cause of the deficit. Likewise, the public payroll had increased 92 percent during the Banzer years. The left mobilized to defend public sector employees (in both the government and the state-run companies) from layoffs and wage cuts, but its demands were essentially defensive and not about creating new services or entitlements.

6. Vice President Carlos Mesa and president of the Supreme Court Eduardo Rodríguez came to be presidents from October 2003 to January 2006 without representing any political parties.

7. This and the following quotes are from my transcription and translation of Álvaro García Linera's speech at Center for Strategic and International Studies, July 21, 2006. Accessed August 4, 2019. https://www.csis.org/events/%C3%A1lvaro-garc%C3%ADa-linera-vice-president-bolivia.

8. Speech at "Investing in the New Bolivia," 2015.

9. Their term for this is a "political movement" rather than a "social movement" (Komadina and Geffroy 2017).

10. The corresponding election was the 2009 general election. Ethnic analysis appears in Hirseland and Strijbis (2018, 13).

11. 2005 versus 2015 figures found in Morales (2017, 100).

12. *Página Siete*, May 21, 2017. Accessed February 20, 2018. http://www.paginasiete.bo/economia/2017/5/21/ende-mayor-utilidad-mejores-ventas-138381.html/.

13. The 18 percent estimate is from Tellería (2014, 30).

14. From slide 2 of Ministerio de Economía y Finanzas Públicas de Bolivia. Presentation. Nacionalización e Industrialización de Hidrocarburos, January 22, 2014. Accessed August 4, 2019. https://es.slideshare.net/EconomiaBo/rea-econmica.

15. "ENDE: Bolivia Generará 11.000 MW de Energía Por Medio de Hidroeléctricas Hasta 2025." *La Razón*. October 20, 2016. Accessed August 4, 2019. http://www.la-razon.com/economia/ENDE-Bolivia-generara-MW-hidroelectricas_0_2585741478.html.

16. The growth prompted an opposition polemic against "fraudulent" registration in 2009, leading the Congress to mandate a biometric electoral database. In a two-and-a-half-month marathon campaign, the government re-registered 5,138,583 voters, 27 percent more than in the January 2009 election. Misión de Observación Electoral de La Unión Europea en Bolivia. Elecciones Generales y Referendos Autonómicos, 2009. Accessed August 4, 2019. http://www.eods.eu/library/FR%20BOLIVIA%202009_es.pdf.

17. See interview with Esteban Ticona in Svampa, Stefanoni, and Fornillo (2010).

18. Diario Pagina Siete. 2017. "Volver al campo: historias de lucha y reconquista de la tierra." January 3. Accessed August 4, 2019. https://www.paginasiete.bo/sociedad /2017/1/3/volver-campo-historias-lucha-reconquista-tierra-122414.html.

19. "Evo dice en consulta previa se pierde mucho tiempo," *Erbol Digital*, July 12, 2015. https://correodelsur.com/politica/20150713_evo-en-la-consulta-previa-se-pierde -mucho-tiempo.html.

20. Via Supreme Decree 2195 (issued November 28, 2014); Supreme Decree 2298 (issued March 18, 2015); and Supreme Decree 2366 (issued May 20, 2015).

21. At 35 percent, Bolivia would have ranked fifteenth out of 189 nations in women's cabinet representation in 2015, but the six ministers out of twenty-one serving then placed it twenty-fourth, slightly ahead of Barack Obama's 2015 cabinet. Inter-Parliamentary Union and UN Women. "Women in Politics: 2015," 2015. https://www .scribd.com/document/289065476/Women-in-politics-2015.

22. "Indígenas de 138 Países Del Mundo Inician Lucha Para Consolidar Su Auto-determinación." *Agencia Boliviana de Información*, October 2007. Accessed August 4, 2019. http://www.katari.org/articulos/2007/oct/mundo.html.

23. Bolivia. Ministerio de Relaciones Exteriores, 2010. *Conferencia Mundial de Los Pueblos Sobre El Cambio Climático y Los Derechos de La Madre Tierra: Tiquipaya, Cochabamba, 20 Al 22 de Abril 2010, Discursos y Documentos Seleccionados*. Diplomacia Por La Vida 8 (La Paz, Bolivia: Ministerio de Relaciones Exteriores), 24.

24. While beyond the scope of this essay, these retreats include the reversed Gasolinazo (December 2010), temporarily abandoned TIPNIS highway (October 2011), and repealed Penal Code reform (January 2018).

References

Albó, Xavier. 2008. "Datos de Una Encuesta: El Perfil de Los Constituyentes." *T'inkazos: Revista Boliviana de Ciencias Sociales* 11 (23–24): 60.

Apaza, Ana. 2014. "El movimiento indígena está en crisis, pero no destruido." Erbol Digital, January 27. http://www.erbol.com.bo/noticia/indigenas/27012014/el _movimiento_indigena_esta_en_crisis_pero_no_destruido.

Bjork-James, Carwil. 2020. *The Sovereign Street: Making Revolution in Urban Bolivia*. Tucson: University of Arizona Press.

Bjork-James, Carwil. 2019. "When 'Plurinational' States Undermine Indigenous Territories: TIPNIS in Bolivia." In *Landscapes of Inequity: The Quest for Environmental Justice in the Andes/Amazon Region*. Lincoln, NE: University of Nebraska Press.

Bjork-James, Carwil. 2012a. "Bolivia's New Mother Earth Law to Sideline Indigenous Rights." Carwil without Borders (blog), August 24. Accessed August 7,

2019. https://woborders.blog/2012/08/24/new-mother-earth-law-sidelines
-indigenous/.

Bjork-James, Carwil. 2012b. "Indigenous Bloc in Bolivian Parliament Now a Reality." Carwil without Borders (blog), January 18. Accessed August 7, 2019. https://woborders.blog/2012/01/18/indigenous-bloc/.

Brabazon, Honor, and Jeffery R. Webber. 2014. "Evo Morales and the MST in B Olivia: Continuities and Discontinuities in Agrarian Reform." *Journal of Agrarian Change* 14 (3): 435–465.

Constitución Política Del Estado: Sistematización de La Experiencia. 2010. ed. Fernando Garcés. La Paz: Programa NINA, Anexo 9.

Coronil, Fernando. 2011. "The Future in Question: History and Utopia in Latin America (1989–2010)." In *Business as Usual: The Roots of the Global Financial Meltdown*, ed. Craig J. Calhoun and Georgi M. Derluguian, 240–241. Possible Futures Series 1. New York: New York University Press.

Gudynas, Eduardo. 2009. "Diez tesis urgentes sobre el nuevo extractivismo." In *Extractivismo política y sociedad*, ed. Jürgen Schuldt and Centro Latino Americano de Ecología Social, 187–225. Quito: Centro Andino de Acción Popular and Centro Latino American de Ecología Social.

Gutiérrez Aguilar, Raquel. 2008. *Los Ritmos Del Pachakuti: Movimiento y Levantamiento Indígena-Popular En Bolivia.* La Paz, Bolivia: Ediciones Yachaywasi.

Harten, Sven. *The Rise of Evo Morales and the MAS.* London: Zed Books, 2011.

Hirseland, Aline-Sophia, and Oliver Strijbis. 2018. "'We Were Forgotten': Explaining Ethnic Voting in Bolivia's Highlands and Lowlands." *Journal of Ethnic and Migration Studies* 45, no. 11 (October 6): 13. doi.org/10.1080/1369183X.2018.1492371.

Hogenboom, Barbara, and Alex E. Fernández Jilberto. "The New Left and Mineral Politics: What's New?" *European Review of Latin American and Caribbean Studies* 87: 93–102.

Hollender, Rebecca. 2016. "Capitalizing on Public Discourse in Bolivia–Evo Morales and Twenty-First Century Capitalism." *Consilience: The Journal of Sustainable Development* 15 (1): 50–76.

Jimenez P., Georgina. 2011. "Trasfondo Del Gasolinazo," *PetroPress*, February.

King, Desmond, and Stewart Wood. 1999. "The Political Economy of Neoliberalism: Britain and the United States in the 1980s." *Continuity and Change in Contemporary Capitalism* 13: 371–397.

Klein, Naomi. 2008. *The Shock Doctrine: The Rise of Disaster Capitalism.* New York: Picador.

Komadina, Jorge, and Céline Geffroy. 2007. *El Poder Del Movimiento Político: Estrategia, Tramas Organizativas e Identidad Del MAS En Cochabamba (1999–2005).* La Paz: Fundación PIEB.

Krommes-Ravnsmed, Jeppe. 2019. "The Frustrated Nationalization of Hydrocarbons

and the Plunder of Bolivia," *Latin American Perspectives* 46 (2): 72–74. doi.org
/10.1177/0094582X18820294.

Linera, Álvaro García. 2014. "'Sáquense El Chip de Que El Gobierno va a Dar El
Golpe y a Estatizar Todo' (Entrevista)." *El Deber*, November 18. Accessed August
7, 2019. http://www.eldeber.com.bo/bolivia/saquense-chip-gobierno-dar-golpe
.html.

Lowndes, Joseph. 2017. "Populism in the United States." In *The Oxford Handbook of
Populism*, ed. Cristóbal Rovira Kaltwasser et al., 232–247. Oxford: Oxford University Press.

Mamani, Lidia. 2016. "Los empleos en empresas públicas crecieron 23 veces en una
década." *Página Siete*, May 1.

Mamani Ramírez, Pablo. 2017. "'Estado Plurinacional' Autoritario Del Siglo XXI."
Religación 2 (6).

Manetto, Francesco. 2019. "Carlos Mesa, el expresidente que se presenta como
opción de cambio en Bolivia." *El País*, October 20, sec. America. https://elpais
.com/internacional/2019/10/19/america/1571519446_507697.html.

Miroff, Nick. 2014. "Ecuador's Popular, Powerful President Rafael Correa Is a Study
in Contradictions." *Washington Post*, March 15. Accessed August 7, 2019. https://
www.washingtonpost.com/world/ecuadors-popular-powerful-president-rafael
-correa-is-a-study-in-contradictions/2014/03/15/452111fc-3eaa-401b-b2c8
-cc4e85fccb40_story.html.

Morales, Evo. 2017. Informe de Gestión 2016, January 22. https://bolivianembassy
.ca/2017/01/23/informe-gestion-2016/

Morales, Evo. 2006. *Discurso Inaugural Del Presidente Evo Morales Ayma*. Publicaciones Cancillería.

Morales, Juan Antonio, and Jeffrey D. Sachs. 1989. "Bolivia's Economic Crisis." In
Developing Country Debt and Economic Performance, ed. Jeffrey D. Sachs, vol. 2. A
National Bureau of Economic Research Project Report, 200. Chicago: University
of Chicago Press.

Moreno, Gustavo Bonifaz. 2016. "La Emergencia y Desarrollo de un Sistema Político
Subnacional en el Departamento de La Paz (2009–2015)." In *La Reconfiguración
Del Estado En Bolivia*, ed. Moira Zuazo, 65–136. La Paz, Bolivia: Friedrich Ebert
Stiftung-Bolivia.

Obstfeld, Maurice. 2016. "IMF Survey: Evolution Not Revolution: Rethinking Policy at the IMF (Interview)." IMF Survey, June 2. Accessed August 2, 2019. http://
www.imf.org/en/News/Articles/2015/09/28/04/53/sopol060216a.

Ostry, Jonathan D., Prakash Loungani, and Davide Furceri. 2007. "Neoliberalism:
Oversold?," *Finance and Development*.

Peck, Jamie, and Adam Tickell. 2007. "Conceptualizing Neoliberalism, Thinking
Thatcherism." *Contesting Neoliberalism: Urban Frontiers* 26: 50.

Pedraza, Gustavo. 2016. "Recomposición Política En Santa Cruz." In *La Reconfiguración Del Estado en Bolivia*, ed. Moira Zuazo, 33–64. La Paz, Bolivia: Friedrich Ebert Stiftung-Bolivia.

Prashad, Vijay. 2013. *Neoliberalism with Southern Characteristics: The Rise of the BRICS*. New York: Rosa Luxemburg Stiftung. Accessed August 7, 2019. http://www.rosalux-nyc.org/wp-content/files_mf/prashad_brics.pdf.

Programa NINA. *El Pacto de Unidad y El Proceso de Construcción de Una Propuesta de Constitución Política Del Estado: Sistematización de La Experiencia*. Edited by Fernando Garcés. La Paz: Programa NINA, 2010.

Ramírez, Mamani. "'Estado Plurinacional' Autoritario Del Siglo XXI," 72.

Rodríguez, José Luis Eyzaguirre. 2015. *Importancia Socioeconómica de La Agricultura Familiar En Bolivia*. La Paz, Bolivia: Fundación Tierra, 73. Accessed August 1, 2019. http://www.ftierra.org/index.php?option=com_mtree&task=att_download&link_id=152&cf_id=.

Rodrik, Dani. 2018. "Is Populism Necessarily Bad Economics?" AEA Papers and Proceedings 108 (May): 196–99. https://doi.org/10.1257/pandp.20181122.

Schipani, Andres. 2015. "President or Patron." *Financial Times*, October 27, sec. The New Bolivia, 12.

Stiglitz, Joseph E. "Is There a Post-Washington Consensus Consensus?" In *The Washington Consensus Reconsidered: Towards a New Global Governance*, edited by Narcís Serra and Joseph. E. Stiglitz, 57–62. Oxford: Oxford University Press, 2008.

Svampa, Maristella, Pablo Stefanoni, and Bruno Fornillo. 2010. *Balance y Perspectivas: Intelectuales en el Primer Gobierno de Evo Morales*. La Paz: Le Monde Diplomatique, edicion boliviana, 199–211.

Tellería, Gabriel Loza. 2014. "El Modelo de Economía Plural En Bolivia: Una Evaluación de Su Implementación." In *Memoria Del Segundo Foro Andino Amazónico de Desarrollo Rural: Bolivia, Perú, Ecuador, Brasil, Colombia, Argentina, Inglaterra*, 30. La Paz, Bolivia: Centro de Investigación y Promoción del Campesinado (CIPCA). http://www.cipca.org.bo/docs/publications/es/15_memoria-segundo-foro-andino-amazonico-de-desarrollo-rural-1.pdf.

Wanderley, Fernanda, Fernanda Sostres, and Ivonne Farah. *La economía solidaria en la economía plural: Discursos, prácticas y resultados en Bolivia*. La Paz: Plural, 2015.

Webber, Jeffery R. 2016. "Evo Morales and the Political Economy of Passive Revolution in Bolivia, 2006–15." *Third World Quarterly* 3710 (10): 1855–1876. doi.org/10.1080/01436597.2016.1175296.

Williamson, John. 1990. "The Progress of Policy Reform in Latin America." Washington, DC: Institute for International Economics.

"Fed Up" in Ethiopia

Emotions and Antiauthoritarian Protest

Two thousand sixteen was a turbulent year around the world. Through the latter part of 2016, just as the Trump candidacy was gaining ascendancy and Britain was voting to exit the European union, Ethiopia was also embroiled in populist uprisings. Ethnically based protests targeting businesses (particularly foreign-owned) surrounded the capital city and were met by staunch government crackdown, which often became violent. The government oscillated between declaring wide-sweeping states of emergency (first in October 2016 and again in February 2018) and, when these failed to quell popular anger, acceding to protestor demands. Although initially these events were analyzed as indicative of distinctly Ethiopian political cycles of everyday repression, unrest, and violent state crackdown, there are paralells with antiauthoritarian, populist uprisings elsewhere.

These protests ultimately resulted in Prime Minister Abiy Ahmed taking power in April 2018. Although Prime Minister Abiy is a leader in the Ethiopian People's Revolutionary Democratic Federation (EPRDF) that has ruled Ethiopia since 1991, he is regarded as a reformer within the party and his taking leadership is often referred to as a coup made possible by populist uprisings from outside of the party. Abiy Ahmed is also the first leader in Ethiopia's centuries-long history to come from the marginalized, but majority, Oromo ethnic group. Thus, Abiy Ahmed's leadership simultaneously represents internal reform of a ruling party that many believe had grown corrupt, antiauthoritarian struggle in a country that has never had democracy, and an ethnically based liberation movement. Thus, events in Ethiopia bring together the elements discussed in many of the essays in this volume—angry politics that emanate from frustration with the nexus of neoliberal globalization and authoritarian governance but effervescently coalesce around identities: racial, ethnic, and religious. The case of Ethiopian angry politics discussed in this essay complicates our understanding of these global populisms in several interlocking ways.

First, the case of Ethiopia helps us distinguish between antiauthoritarian movements in places where authoritarianism is not rising but is well established and, perhaps, in decline. While populist movements that appear to support a rightward moving state have come to dominate angry politics in Europe, the United States, and elsewhere, this is not the case everywhere in the world. Across the African continent popular protests have brought down several longstanding dictators, challenged the long-term reign of autocratic governments, and demanded more accountable forms of democracy. In Ethiopia, ire at a longstanding authoritarian regime that was increasingly willing to use force against its people sparked this new wave of angry politics. The presence of a longstanding authoritarian state may configure angry politics in different ways than it does in places where authoritarianism is on the rise. Authoritarianisms that have already established the capacity of the state to use force with impunity yield a different emotional response than those where this is a new phenomenon (see also Noah Theriault, this volume). One of the key differences is in the emotional response to established authoritarianism and the utility of emotion to unravel it. However, these processes are multifaceted and their ultimate outcomes are far from predictable as mass protests entangle in complex ways with entrenched power structures and the powerful forces exerted by processes of identity formation.

Second, exploring the crises of neoliberalism from the vantage point of Ethiopia challenges the relationship between neoliberalism and our conventional understandings of the right-left spectrum in politics. Policies of both the previous and the current leadership in Ethiopia elide placement on this spectrum. While the previous leadership in Ethiopia merged right and left positions by courting investment and embracing the Asian model of neoliberal developmentalism and echoing long-held Marxist ideology, the new prime minister simultaneously privatizes state-held businesses, courts the industrial sector, and promotes the development of a regional economic block, on one hand, while moving in directions that might be thought of as socially progressive on the other, for example, by promoting the concerns of women, minority groups, and refugees. In some ways this resonates with the "pink tide" in South America in which political positions hybridize in order to adapt to the exigencies of global neoliberal economics (see Carwil Bjork-James, this volume) and also with the case of "green authoritarianism" in the Phillippines (see Noah Theriault, this volume). One might characterize Prime Minister Abiy Ahmed's approach to governance not as oriented toward the right or left, but around a principle of *openness*—open hearts, open borders, open politics, open opportunities for women and marginalized groups, and also open for business. However, it is unclear how Prime Minister Abiy will balance this principle of openness with regulation, rule of law, and protection of vulnerable populations. One of the questions around which this volume circulates is why right-wing populisms seem to have surpassed the left. But current developments in Ethiopia may indicate the emergence of hybridization of leftist ideologies and neoliberal governance practices.

Finally, the case of Ethiopia raises the question of why it is that when popular uprisings confront the nexus of authoritarianism and neoliberalism, long-standing identity-based grievances seem to provide the emotional charge needed to fuel mass outrage. I suggest that to understand the role that identity plays in populist politics, an ethnography that dissects an array of emotional states is called for. As noted elsewhere in this volume, racial, ethnic, or religious identities seem to be the point around which angry politics coalesce even if neoliberalism and frustrations with the enduring or emergent authoritarianism are the underlying grievances (see Sophie Bjork-James; Jeff Maskovsy, this volume).

In this brief essay, I cannot fully address these issues, which continue to unfold and transform at the time of this writing. But I will begin to unravel the question of why political effervescence coalesces around identity politics rather than neoliberal economics or the authoritarian state. I suggest that we need to explore outrage at the cool rationality of liberalism, a rationality that is belied by the everyday experiences of political violence and economic precarity. This essay explores this outrage from a somewhat odd vantage point—an analysis of civics education in Ethiopia in the wake of the declaration of the state of emergency there in 2016. The Civic and Ethical Education (CEE) curriculum finds itself centrally situated in debates about the plight of youth; economic and political marginalization; the nature of citizenship and inclusive belonging for different groups; and the appropriateness of forms of civic participation, such as protests.

CEE in Ethiopia was the blueprint for the ruling party's ideal model citizen and calls for good patriots to behave in a calm, cool manner, to be tolerant peacemakers, and to uphold the core tenets of the constitution. However, the previous leadership also flouted their own ideals. The CEE curriculum teaches students that the constitution upholds standards of democracy and human rights and yet the previous leadership was known for excessive use of violence, mass arrests, and allocating sweeping powers to police under repeatedly declared states of emergency. This contradiction between the taught ideals of democracy and human rights and lived experiences under the state of emergency evoked tremendous anger. This contradiction also challenges the legitimacy of Ethiopia's previous leadership; however, interestingly, Ethiopians are less critical of the ruling Ethiopian People's Revolutionary Democratic Federation (EPRDF), which continues to rule the country, than of the Tigrayan ethnic group, which was perceived to control the party until the recent prime minister was put in place.

Analyzing civics teaching and learning in light of populist political unrest in Ethiopia and the ensuing authoritarian state crackdown reveals a complex and multifaceted national dialogue and a complex range of emotions that we often don't consider when we think of antiauthoritarian uprisings. The debate over civics critiques both rising authoritarianism *and* populist, ethnically based nationalisms while also expressing anxieties about how youth will navigate their future in Ethiopia and how Ethiopia will manage its restive youth. The debates over the civics curriculum, in particular, and Ethiopia's populist political protests more broadly, complicate our understanding of this moment of global political "crisis" by illuminating the relationship between authoritarianism, growing concerns about economic disparity and youth unemployment, and the emotions of populist nationalism. This essay is organized around a series of different emotions related to the political climate in Ethiopia. I discuss each one and then conclude with some general thoughts on the political power and unwieldy nature of emotions in countering stable authoritarian regimes. I conclude with some brief thoughts on how Ethiopia's Prime Minister Abiy Ahmed, who came to power in April 2018, elicits and choreographs emotions, particularly sentiments of love. He seems to move away from both the cool, intellectual citizenship laid out in the civics curriculum and the narrow outrage of ethnonationalisms instead evoking passions in all Ethiopians. It remains to be seen, however, if these passions will converge or diverge.

Authoritarianism, Ethnic Federalism, and Impotence

Ethiopia has either a long or less long history as a state, depending on how one wants to define a nation-state. Since Ethiopia began a process of modern state consolidation in the mid- to late 1800s, the country has been a lot of things—a prenational set of kingdoms and fiefdoms vying and fighting for the power to consolidate ever larger territories; a feudal empire, transitioning to a modern empire that attempted to consolidate control and exert sovereignty over populations within more or less fixed boundaries that would eventually become a nation-state; a communist autocracy; and, since the mid-1990s, a system of democratic federalism in which decentralized ethnically based states are ostensibly self-governing within the larger country. More accurately, I think the regime can be categorized as a neoliberal, competitive, or hybrid authoritarian regime (Brownlee 2007; Levitsky and Way 2010), but one that is both built on the vestiges of earlier forms of authoritarianism (imperial, communist) and wrapped in the combined ideology of developmentalism, democracy, and the ruling party's diverse ideological lineages. Ethiopia's leaders and many of its people still believe that the country is a burgeoning democracy despite often-violent centralizing tendencies and strategies used by the ruling party to maintain single-party control, which it has done effectively since 1991. One thing that is important to note about Ethiopia is that throughout its history it has always had some form of authoritarian governance. I think this raises an important question for looking at cases like Ethiopia—what can we learn about this particular historical moment from places where authoritarianism is not *rising* but really has never gone away and yet is changing, and perhaps declining, in light of shifting assemblages of governance, politics, and resistance to forms of governance?

One of the byproducts of longstanding authoritarian regimes is often an affective state referred to as *anomie*. In their work on Eritrea, Nicole Hirt and Abdulkader Saleh Mohammed draw on Durkheim's concept of anomie to explore how pervasive authoritarianism results in a sort of societal malaise and inability to move forward (Durkheim 1965; Hirt and Mohammad 2013). Anomie, indeed, is characteristic of the affective state of a number of authoritarian regimes in which extremes of surveillance, control, coercion, arbitrary state harassment, and the ever-present threat of state violence immobilizes the population. Although in-depth ethnographic accounts of lived experiences under conditions of authoritarianism are few and far between, anomie as an affective characteristic has been described in several authoritarian regimes, including Burma (Skidmore 2004), Syria (Wedeen 1999), and a variety of African countries (Mbembe 2001). In order to depict a similar condition of "stuckness" in my own work in Eritrea, I prefer Achille Mbembe's concept of impotence to explore the ways in which authoritarianism and the response to it renders both ruler and ruled "impotent" and incapable of political progress (Mbembe 2001; Riggan 2013, 2016, 2018).

Interestingly, Ethiopia does not seem to be permanently stuck in this condition as is its northern neighbor, Eritrea. Beginning with student movements in the late 1960s that eventually led to the overthrow of Haile Selassie in the mid-1970s, Ethiopia has oscillated between periods of outraged street protests (and at times armed uprisings) followed by brutal government crackdowns and periods of calm and anomie in which authoritarianism seems to be widely accepted (Kebede 2006; Milkias 2006). This suggests that Ethiopia may be an interesting place in which to explore the capacity of public anger and outrage to shake off anomie and the capacity of governments to restore authoritarian order by culling this anger.

In 1991, Ethiopia began to reconfigure itself as an ethnic federation. Ethiopia, a country long noted for its centralized, hegemonic, Amhara-dominated national narrative, reorganized the country into ethnic "nations" (James et al. 2002). Although the central state has notably still retained a great deal of power, the redesigning of the country allows for a great deal of autonomy in several ethnic regions (Bariagaber 1998; Mains 2004). In Ethiopia and elsewhere, there has been an increased tendency to articulate belonging to the nation through belonging to a narrowly defined place or people (Dorman, Hammett, and Nugent 2007; Geschiere 2009; Geschiere and Jackson 2006). Whereas the tendency of previous Ethiopian regimes was to impose a hegemonic nationalism on all the nation's people (including those who did not feel it represented them), with the implementation of the 1995 constitution, the current ruling party requires diverse people to define their positions in the nation and lay claim to being authentically national by virtue of their attachment to the blood and soil of a particular ethnic state. Unlike the earlier phase of nation-building that was intent on creating a synthetic, cohesive nationalism, the system of ethnic federalism in Ethiopia was designed to avoid co-opting identity. And yet, while ethnic federalism seems to have organized political subjectivities in Ethiopia quite intentionally around ethnicity, the countervailing forces of both authoritarian single-party rule and the illusion of constitutional democratic citizenship (promoted in no small part through the civics curriculum) have prevented ethnic fragmentation. Instead of truly devolving state power to these ethnic states, the party has retained centralized power, leaving Ethiopia with a centralized state, a decentralized nation, and a frustrated citizenry turning toward ethnic organization to shake off anomie and impotence.

From Anomie to Anger: A Brief History of a Multifaceted Uprising

In May 2014 protests in Ethiopia began in the Oromia state, the ethnic state of Ethiopia's most populous, and most historically disenfranchised, ethnic group. Protests began with the announcement of a new master plan for the capital city, Addis Ababa, which is entirely surrounded by Oromia. According to the master plan, Addis Ababa would expand into Oromo sovereign territory. Security forces used excessive force against protestors at this time, resulting in many deaths throughout the years of protest (Human Rights Watch 2014). Despite the government cancelling the Addis Ababa master plan in early 2016, the protests continued, becoming bolder as they pushed back against a pattern of central government repression and gaining greater support (Fasil and Lemma 2015).

A surprising alliance was forged between Oromo and Amhara opposition (Dahir 2016). The Amhara, Ethiopia's second largest ethnic group and the ethnicity from which the majority of Ethiopia's leaders have hailed, including Ethiopia's last emperor, Haile Selassie, and the brutal communist military commander who deposed him, Mengistu Haile Mariam. The flashpoint for protests in the Amhara region also related to incursions into their ethnic state, this time over a border dispute in the Wolkait region, a region that the Amhara accuse the Tigray ethnic group (the group reputed to control the countries ruling party, military, and economy) of taking from them in 1995 (Zelalem 2018). Eventually, in the wake of growing protests, the government declared a wide-sweeping six-month state of emergency in the fall of 2016, which was then extended for an additional three months. During the state of emergency tens of thousands of people were arrested and protests halted.

In July 2017, before the state of emergency was lifted in early August of that year, protests once again emerged (Al Jazeera 2017). The flashpoint for protests this time was the passage of a new tax law, which particularly targeted small businesses and farmers. As with the Addis Ababa master plan, in the wake of protests, the government quickly recanted on the tax law. However, protests continued through the fall of 2017, intensifying and demanding, among other things, the release of political prisoners. Ethiopia also witnessed a rise in ethnic violence through this time period as protests acquired an increasingly ethnic slant. Tigrayan students were killed in university protests in the Amhara region and in retaliation Amhara students were targeted in protests in the Tigray region (Addis Standard 2017a, 2017b).

This cycle of protest, unrest, government concessions, and crackdown continued. Following a stream of increasingly violent and ethnically motivated protests though the fall of 2017, the government announced the release of tens of thousands of political prisoners. Prisoners were released in January 2018, but days later the prime minister resigned and two key moderate opposition leaders were promptly rearrested. The government then declared another, even more restrictive, state of emergency, which fueled, rather than quelled, protests. The government, in turn, responded to those protests with more violence. Emotion, in general, and anger, in particular, are central to these protests. Newspaper articles from Ethiopian and international sources used words like "outrage," and "anger" (Shaban 2018). Government efforts to clamp down on protests through declaration of another state of emergency and through intensifying violence failed to quell the anger.

As I mentioned above, Ethiopia has never had an operable democracy. One of the weaknesses of entrenched authoritarian regimes is that through the same strategies that they consolidate their power, they also consolidate the ire of their opponents. They become a repository for imaginaries of all that is wrong with the country. Additionally, rather than organizing around policies and political platforms, these movements have organized around ethnic grievances in response to the authoritarian rule of a party perceived as controlled by one ethnic group.[1] Thus, identity becomes the modality through which authoritarianism is challenged leaving the economic issues unaddressed.

Second, a causal factor of the protests is arguably economic frustrations and particularly a large number of unemployed youth. Despite Ethiopia's impressive levels of economic growth in recent years, youth unemployment, including unemployment among educated youth, remains a tremendous problem fueling allegations of corruption. Concerns about youth unemployment are often bundled together with concerns about corruption, forming a sense that an elite, ethnically based core has been pulling the economic strings of the country, and benefiting from doing so, while the majority of youth are left out in the cold.

Finally, longstanding ethnic grievances also fuel the diffuse protests occurring in different parts of Oromia and Amhara. While outrage against the regime forged a coalition between the Amhara and Oromo ethnicities, that coalition seems to be weakening. Meanwhile ethnic tensions abound around the country. Not only have there been ethnically motivated killings, as well as a border dispute between the Amhara and Tigray states, but during the same time period, ethnic tensions between the Somali and Oromo states in Ethiopia were also amplified. While there have been longstanding conflicts between Oromo farmers and Somali pastoralists along the fluid border between the two Ethiopian states, many date the origins of this violence to the creation of the Liyu (special) forces. The Liyu are an ethnically Somali paramilitary group that evolved out of Ethiopian government-supported efforts to squash the Ogaden National Liberation Front in 2008 (ONLF). While there is debate as to whether the Liyu acted in the Ethiopian government's interest, if the government was merely drawing a blind eye to their actions, or if the government opposed these actions, there is agreement that the Liyu forces make use of egregious violence and that this violence accelerated dramatically in 2017 (BBC 2017; Zelalem 2017). These and other more recent trends toward ethnic violence in several regions may suggest an alignment of politics around ethnicity and ethnic borders. Thus, just as the ruling party seems to become a repository for multifaceted outrage and frustration, emotions also coalesce around ethnicity.

Ethnicity in Ethiopia seems to be the vehicle to move populations from anomie to anger. As in many other places, identity seems to be more effective at organizing political emotion than political ideology, economic grievances, or anger at authoritarian state violence. As political participation is increasingly attached to ethnic or regional affiliations, citizens are categorized on the basis of belonging not only to a nation but to a place and a people. Additionally, notions of national belonging are increasingly articulated through one's autochthonous ties to a particular place (Geschiere 2009). A growing literature notes that when politics is organized around rigid identity categories, such as ethnicity, political struggles over who belongs and who does not are exacerbated. The stakes are raised around questions of who belongs to what polity, who can run for office, and who gets a share of scarce resources (see, for example, Dorman, Hammett, and Nugent 2007; Geschiere 2009; Geschiere and Jackson 2006). Protestor demands to depose the ruling party and demands for rights for ethnically marginalized groups may be on a collision course as protestor emotions coalesce around antiauthoritarianism, on one hand, and ethnic identity, on the other.

Cool Patriotism: Civic and Ethical Education

Ethiopia's Civic and Ethical Education (CEE) curriculum is often considered the blueprint for the country's post-1991 nation-making process. The curriculum, which garners a great deal of public and policy attention, has been revised three times since 1991, is taught at the primary, secondary, and tertiary levels, and is not only a required subject from elementary school through university but a mandatory subject on the university entrance exams, meaning students have to not only take the civics course, but master the material if they wish to go to the university. The curriculum promotes liberal democratic political values and a form of neoliberal developmental economic personhood laced with echoes of earlier leftist developmentalism. Key themes that emerge across units are constitutionalism, federalism, multiculturalism, and rule of law. The themes of "constitutional democracy" undergird a sense of patriotism, government accountability, and individual responsibility, tightly linking it with living peacefully in a multiethnic country. On the one hand, the curriculum is intent on moving Ethiopia forward and away from past political oppressions and toward democracy, and, on the other, lays on the individual citizen the responsibility for being peaceful, tolerant, and economically disciplined. CEE educates citizens about human rights and democratic governance and peacebuilding (Smith 2013; Wondimu 2008) and also promotes qualities of hard work, industriousness, and savings as well as self-reliance and avoidance of dependency. It suggests that young people should engage with and embrace the global economy by engaging these personal characteristics and not spending frivolously on expensive cultural traditions. Thus CEE outlines the duties, rights, and responsibilities of a politically liberal, tolerant, democratic citizen poised to respect rule of law and work on behalf of the neoliberal, developmental state.

If the written curriculum clearly details the kind of citizen that youth should be and become, the "hidden curriculum" of CEE specifies what their role in politics should, and should not, be. Teachers, in their teaching of civics, make it clear that the passions of political protest are inappropriate for students whose main patriotic duty is to study hard. They cautioned that the time to become involved in politics would be later in life when they had matured. For example, in a ninth-grade civics class, the teacher defined patriotism as follows: "If you work for democracy and human rights, you are a patriot. If you are a student, you should study. If you get an "A" you are a patriot. Patriotism is working hard. Patriots work for the community." The lesson went on to further detail the attributes of a patriot as defined by the textbook as including:

- Maintaining internal peace and security
- Tolerating diversity
- Fighting against terrorism, poverty, and corruption
- Keeping state secrets
- Working hard
- Promoting the common good
- Respecting the rights of others
- Respecting the laws of the country

After going through the entire lesson and detailing each of these points, the teacher differentiated between patriotism and chauvinism, further setting the affective tone for Ethiopian patriotism. "Chauvinism is blind love," he told them, "Patriotism is a quality of loyalty and being peaceful." A few minutes later, in the class, the teacher again encouraged students toward peace and cautioned against "selfish groups," saying, "A community can be disturbed because of many things, because of selfish groups. We are patriots if we restore peace to the community." Patriotism, thus, was characterized as cool, rational, and peaceful in contrast to the blind passions of chauvinism and the "selfish" desires of some communities.

The suggestion here is that selfish groups and chauvinism would result in disruptive activities, such as protests. These so-called selfish, chauvinistic, disruptive activities are not well defined in the teachers' comments, but if one understands the context of Ethiopian politics it seems clear that this is a reference to ethnically based protest movements. Two Amharic words *neftegna* and *tabab* began to circulate more broadly during this time period to critique narrow, ethnically based nationalisms. *Naftegna*, which literally translates as "one who carries a gun," refers to chauvinistic nationalism that considers one group superior to another. *Tabab*, a related but distinct term, references narrow, selfish, nationalism, which is only concerned with one's own community's concerns and issues. The civics teacher's reference, which was in English, to chauvinism and selfishness appears to be a reference to these terms. These "selfish" groups and their disruptive, emotional, attitudes and actions toward the nation are contrasted with the ideal student patriotic behavior—studying hard and getting "A's."

After observing the entire lesson, I probed the teacher to tell me more about the patriotic work of students particularly with regard to human rights and democracy. He clarified and expanded on what he had said to the students earlier, repeating again that students' patriotic duty was only to study: "Students should work hard and get good results. That is patriotism. If they score 'A.' Working hard in school is patriotism. At the grassroots level if they work hard they are patriots. When they grow up, their roles will be diverse. But right now we don't expect them to do other roles." The idea that students' duty was to study, nothing more, was a common theme that I heard among many CEE teachers who seemed to fear encouraging students to take an active political stance.

The teaching of cool, liberal nationalism is particularly problematic in Ethiopia given the passions that emerged in the time of protests, giving rise to a number of critiques of CEE and its teachers. CEE was depicted as politically neutral and cool; however, many Ethiopians regarded it as anything but neutral.

Beyond Impotence:
From Teacher Fear to Student Frustration with CEE

In many ways the CEE curriculum became a centralized repository for complaints about the party's vision for the country itself, and, particularly in the wake of mass protests, a repository for anger and frustration with the ongoing control of the ruling party. There were widespread frustrations with the CEE curriculum and the teaching of it. One critique was that the curriculum was "too political," meaning that it not only supported and promoted the ruling party but also the values and beliefs of the ethnic clique within the ruling party that held the reigns of power until the current prime minister was put in place. Another critique was that it was belied by the on-the-ground experience of joblessness and state repression. Below, I explore both of these critiques and then show how student frustration with the curriculum challenged teachers' ability to teach it, particularly under increased conditions of repression and states of emergency.

In everyday conversations, Ethiopians would comment to me that the CEE curriculum promoted the ruling party's vision of the country. They complained that it demonized previous leaders, notably Emperor Haile Selassie and Mengistu Haile Mariam, both of whom hailed from the Amhara ethnic group, as brutal and authoritarian, while depicting the current regime as demo-cratic and tolerant. The Ministry of Education officials' concerns about this critique led to a 2006 assessment of the CEE curriculum. The assessment found that there were a number of widespread critiques of the curriculum, namely that it was too political. One Ministry of Education official said to me that this critique was confusing and misguided because the curriculum was not political, but rather, based on the constitution. What is missing in this comment, however, is the fact that constitution itself is politically con-tentious (Smith 2013). Particularly controversial in the constitution is Article 39, which guarantees ethnic states the right to self-determination up to and including the right to secession. Rights allocation to ethnically based states works against centuries of Amhara ethnic hegemony over Ethiopia but also challenges notions of a unified, centralized nation instead promoting ethnic identity over national identity. The efforts of the curriculum to promote multi-cultural tolerance were also often interpreted as an attempt to remake, or un-ravel, the nation. However, another critique of the promotion of ethnic rights, self-determination, and multiculturalism was that it failed to work in practice. Indeed there were a number of frustrations with the curriculum because it failed practically on a number of fronts.

People also critiqued the curriculum for imposing a sense of economic per-sonhood while structural barriers to economic success were never addressed. Even more egregious was that values and practices promoted in the curric-ulum were perceived as contrary to Ethiopian culture, particularly the units that told students to save money and avoid spending on expensive cultural celebrations. Meanwhile, youth unemployment was the norm, good jobs for educated youth were increasingly scarce, costs of living were skyrocketing, and large swathes of the capital city were being sold off, displacing urban pop-ulations to condominiums built in previously rural areas and rural farmers elsewhere. The evidence of modernization and progress abounded but so too did the evidence that these youth were being left off that path.

Many of the CEE teachers I spoke with described a strong feeling of be-ing caught in the middle of the political system. They believed in the values enshrined in the text and believed in the importance of continuing to teach those values but were also aware that many Ethiopians' experiences belied those values. The conflict this created for teachers was amplified in the face of increased student frustration for a few reasons. First, teachers were under increased pressure under the state of emergency and could face very real

consequences, including imprisonment. Second, frustrated students challenged teachers with greater frequency.

Most CEE teachers were initially attracted to teaching civics because they
genuinely liked the subject matter and believed in its importance. When I
asked whether they thought the CEE curriculum was successful, many teachers expressed a belief in the value of the subject: "CEE is a multidisciplinary
subject. There is nothing that it doesn't touch. It is important to make students interactive in their society and its political aspects. It is a laboratory to
enhance their education level and participation in their country." However, in
the current political climate, CEE teachers found themselves labeled "political
teachers" by students and other teachers even though CEE teachers didn't see
themselves that way. One teacher stated that, "Other teachers perceive us as
instruments of the government. We are perceived as political missionaries. But
we are citizenship missionaries."

CEE teachers knew that one of the reasons they were labeled as "political
teachers" was because they were required to teach things that did not reflect
what students saw and experienced outside of school and therefore were often
regarded as spreading propaganda. One teacher noted, "The book is good.
The written part is good. The curriculum is good. The challenge is with the
practical application." Teachers themselves saw the contradictions between
the ideals presented in the curriculum and the realities on the ground: "I have
a mission to transmit civics values. When students understand their rights,
some use them, some abuse them. Some have no understanding of them. You
have to model character. But they laugh at you because they observe corruption. Honesty is the best policy, but they don't see this in society, so they
laugh at you. There are contradictions." Another teacher explained how this
contradiction resulted in the curriculum losing its credibility: "Initially it was
successful but it has lost its credibility. People see corruption. And the government is deceiving people through media. Through time it has lost its honesty.
But initially we were very interested but through time it deteriorated. Now
there is rampant corruption."

Another teacher explained that the moment when perceptions about curriculum began to change was in 2005, the year many Ethiopians lost hope in
democracy:

> Another problem is that the subject has not been changing the attitude
> and behavior of the students. They consider students as political subjects.

The government has been using the curriculum as an instrument of propaganda.

Students do not have a good outlook toward CEE teachers because they think they are political. Students think the country has not been building democracy and peace. Since 1997 in the Ethiopian calendar [2005], the attitude of students toward building a democracy has declined so we can say subject has no contribution.

In parliamentary elections in 2005, opposition parties enjoyed unprecedented support, threatening the ruling EPRDF and leading to a crackdown on political openness. The year 2005 is typically regarded as when the ruling party firmly staunched political opposition, consolidated its rule, and began the country's progress toward authoritarianism. We also might think of 2005 as the year many Ethiopians began to regard the party not as the legitimate governing power in Ethiopia but as something to be feared.

As if it was not hard enough to teach civics values to students who regarded them as government propaganda, teachers were also under political pressures from the government and the party. Many teachers noted that it was not only the perception of other teachers and students that CEE teachers were "political" but that the government itself exerted a good deal of pressure on CEE teachers:

The perception of people in Ethiopia is that CEE is a means to propagate the political agenda of the government. In some cases it may be true. The government interferes in schools. When I was teaching in rural areas, the *woreda* [local government] tried to ask me to join the party. "How can you teach CEE without belonging to the party?" they asked. People think that we are members of the party. The government should not intervene in school affairs. But the government is blaming some teachers and can fire teachers.

Many teachers had stories about teachers being coerced into joining the party, being threatened, having their pay docked, or even being stopped from working. As one teacher told me: "A teacher was teaching civics. And he raised students' political consciousness to the highest level and they removed the person. They denied him to teach CEE because he raised the consciousness of the students. They stopped him from teaching." Given the political pressures teachers were under, they often recounted feeling afraid of students' challenging questions. One teacher noted, "the students are not afraid, but the teachers are afraid." Another teacher noted: "What they are learning in the school and what they observe is not the same, so they ask us, 'what you are teaching us is not what they are doing.' This is a challenge for the teacher. To say this is very hard." And another teacher said, "Students ask about what they see outside: 'Why are police harassing people rather than being peacekeepers?'"

There could be very real repercussions for teachers who identified too strongly with students. In May 2018, I had been observing CEE classes for over a month and the state of emergency had ended a few months prior. On my second day in the school, I observed a class taught by a young, dynamic woman. She was teaching a class on the topic of the value of saving. The students were reasonably engaged and she seemed far more energetic than many of the teachers. She had a good rapport with her students who seemed to enjoy her class. As we walked back to the staff room where I was to hold a focus group with her and some other teachers, she told me rather off-handedly that she was a bit behind in the curriculum because she had been in jail for four months. I asked her why she was arrested. She told me that just after the state of emergency was declared, one of her students asked her why the government was arresting people who were protesting given that, as they had learned in their civics class, it was their right to protest. The teacher explained to me that in her answer to the student, she tried to distinguish between nonviolent protests, which are allowed, and violent protests, which are not. Shortly after that two police officers came to the school and told the teacher they wanted to ask some questions. She was subsequently arrested without trial and released four months later. She suspected that some of her students reported the exchange she had in response to the student's question about the protests.

Despite teachers' best intentions of instilling democratic, liberal citizenship values in students, teachers were coerced and coopted by the authoritarian apparatus of the state. They were forced to join the party, punished for engaging seriously with student critiques, and even arrested. All of this fueled student beliefs that the curriculum was a tool of propaganda and stripped the curriculum, and the regime that put it in place, of legitimacy. Because the curriculum also promoted liberal, democratic constitutionalism as the modality through which to effect change, I would argue that the delegitimation of the CEE curriculum also unraveled liberal, democratic constitutionalism as a legitimate modality of change paving the way for a violent ethnic politics that is rampant in Ethiopia as of the time of this writing.

Many teachers noted that they responded to challenging questions by sticking close to the text and teaching in theoretical, rather than practical, ways. As one teacher noted, "In general, what we teach theoretically is different in practice. In the living standard, there is a difference between theory and practice." Another teacher expanded on these thoughts noting the importance of teaching theoretically in order to stay safe. When asked how he addressed challenging questions, he responded as follows:

> You go back to what you are taught. Look at yourself by these instruments. They know it very well. Teachers don't react to the students. The teacher fears that if they answer that question there will be a problem. So the teacher refers back to what is written. The teacher does not judge. They never say that is wrong. In order for the students to accept them, they have observed what is wrong. The instrument is what is written here.

But young people, instead of heeding their teachers, have increasingly taken to the streets and instead of cohering around multicultural tolerance and constitutional democracy, they increasingly organize around ethnicity.

Conclusion: Love in a Time of Anger?

Ethiopia's newly appointed Prime Minister Abiy Ahmed is a master at eliciting, choreographing, and channeling emotions. Emerging from within the ruling EPRDF, he has not yet dismantled Ethiopia's sole party's hold on power. But as the first prime minister to come from Ethiopia's majority Oromo ethnic group, he identifies as a reformer. His critics argue that he is merely paying lip service to reform and intends to consolidate power for his own ethnic group as every Ethiopian leader has done; however, since he took power in April 2018, he has welcomed armed opposition groups back to Ethiopia, erased the designation of "terrorist group" from opposition political parties, and released political prisoners by the tens of thousands. He announced publicly that multiparty democracy is the only way forward for Ethiopia.

He preaches a powerful and effervescent message of love and unity. For example, in a speech on June 23, 2018, he stated, "We will win with love. I asked each one of you brothers and sisters to turn to the next person on this 'Day of Love and Forgiveness' and embrace them and tell them you love them and forgive them. I ask you to do so in love" (Mariam 2018). A popular slogan "*demeregn*" meaning "add us in" has appeared on t-shirts in response to his message. He speaks of erasing borders, both between ethnic states within Ethiopia and international borders, and replacing them with love.

At the same time ethnically based violence has proliferated and the prime minister seems to be doing little to stem it. He has rolled back the coerciveness and use of violence by the state, but, at the same time, Ethiopians complain that rule of law is also eroded. His critics and intellectuals are wary of Prime Minister Abiy's populist appeal and the way he evokes the emotions of the masses. But his turn toward feelings counteracts the cool, liberal package that masked the authoritarianism of his predecessors, a package that had become the object of anger. The direction in which these passions will ultimately turn remains to be seen. As of this writing, estimates suggest that ethnic violence resulted in the displacement of up to 2.9 million people in 2018 and 2019. Meanwhile, the government seems to be ignoring the severity of the crisis, insisting that displaced people return home and denying them aid in IDP camps even if they are afraid to return (Gardner 2019).

It is tempting in these moments of political volatility to attempt to create comprehensive explanatory frameworks that analyze and tie things up in a neat package. I would argue that in the current moment of ongoing political volatility, we are left with more questions than answers. The case of Ethiopia, which fits the script of things going on elsewhere, in many ways also challenges many of our assumptions about what, precisely, *is* going on. In this exploratory essay, I have argued that Ethiopia shows us what the rejection of liberalism looks like. Why liberalism is so roundly rejected is a question that requires further analysis—is it because it was seen as disingenuous in the face of a party that, while preaching liberalism, was actually the opposite of liberal? Is it because the promises of liberalism are belied by the dystopian inequalities produced by neoliberalism, particularly in the developing world? Is it because ethnic marginalization and discrimination were ignored for centuries while the imposition of ethnic federalism in the 1990s provided the pretense of equality but also the mechanism to forge a new form of violent politics around the maintenance of ethnic boundaries?

Here I have used the teaching of civics during a particularly volatile period in Ethiopia to explore the intersections of liberalism, neoliberalism, authoritarianism, and the capacity of emotion and identity to mobilize populations that have been immobilized by the coercive capacity of the authoritarian state. In Ethiopia neoliberalism is made manifest through relative and actual deprivation and the visceral presence of wealth, on one hand, and mass un-employment and underemployment, on the other. Although the root cause of what troubles youth is arguably rooted in these economic disparities, state authoritarianism, violence, and disenfranchisement has been the target of people's anger, not economic factors. But increasingly, the state is no longer the target. Rather, people, turning inward toward ethnically based factions, blame each other for their marginalization.

In an array of interviews and casual conversations I had in Ethiopia while studying civics, I became aware that the CEE curriculum was being blamed for the political unrest in the country. I wondered if the protests reflected the success rather than the failures of the curriculum. The response when I posed this question was usually that students, and the curriculum itself, were too fixated on political rights and not enough on duties to the nation. Protest, not surprisingly, was seen as an exercise of demanding rights rather than as a patriotic duty. As I made clear in my discussion of civics above, there was a widespread attitude that students' duty was to work hard, study, and serve the nation quietly. But whether one sees the protests as a result of the success or failures of the CEE curriculum is dependent largely on one's stance toward emotion in the construction of national subjectivity. Should citizens be ratio-nale and patient? Or passionate and demanding?

Emotions create a contradiction for nationalism—in order for national subjects to be willing to sacrifice for their nation, the nation needs to evoke passions in its citizens, but the liberal state, in theory, also needs to be able to temper these passions. In Ethiopia, the Civic and Ethical Education curric-ulum detailed and disseminated a vision that required citizens to be calmly tolerant of diversity, to form themselves into a subject of developmentalism, and to accept the government's timeline for democratization. However, the curriculum perhaps also got out ahead of the ruling party itself by teach-ing students about human and democratic rights, for example, the right to protest. It would seem that frustration with these contradictions and with the failure of the government to bring to fruition its own vision of peaceful multiculturalism, development, and democracy initially led to protest, but that the violent and authoritarian response to protests turned frustration into an outrage. This outrage has found a vehicle in ethnonationalism and ethnic violence despite the current prime minister's best efforts to preach love, peace, and unity.

Note

1. Ethiopia's ruling EPRDF (Ethiopian Peoples' Revolutionary Democratic Front) is a coalition of four parties that represent Ethiopia's most populous and influential states—the TPLF (Tigrayan People's Liberation Front), the OPDO (Oromo Peoples' Democratic Organization), the ANDM (Amhara National Democratic Movement), and the SEPDM (Southern Ethiopian Peoples' Democratic Movement). All of these parties are ethnically based with the exception of the SEPDM representing the vastly multiethnic Southern Nations Nationalities and Peoples (SNNP) state. Most Ethiopians and observers of Ethiopia contend that the TPLF has enjoyed economic and military dominance and has exerted disproportionate political control over the party, even though the recently resigned prime minister hailed from the SEPDM. The ruling EPRDF has exerted very strong party discipline among its four member parties, but in the wake of protests at times it seemed that there may have been rifts between reformers and hard-liners in the party as well as between the ethnically based parties.

References

Addis Standard. 2017a. "At Least 10 Killed, 20 Wounded When Security Fired Live Shots at Fresh Protests in Ambo," October 26. Accessed August 2, 2019. http://addisstandard.com/news-least-10-killed-amidst-fresh-protests-ambo/.

Addis Standard. 2017b. "Three People Killed, Properties Damaged in Nekemte, Western Ethiopia," October 30. Accessed August 2, 2019. http://addisstandard.com/news-three-people-killed-properties-damaged-nekemt-western-ethiopia/.

Al Jazeera. 2017. "Ethiopia Lifts State of Emergency Imposed in October," *Al Jazeera*, August 5. Accessed August 2, 2019. https://www.aljazeera.com/news/2017/08/ethiopia-lifts-state-emergency-imposed-october-170805044440548.html.

Bariagaber, Assefaw. 1998. "The Politics of Cultural Pluralism in Eritrea: Trajectories of Ethnicity and Constitutional Experiments." *Ethnic and Racial Studies* 21 (6): 1057–1073.

BBC. 2017. "What Is Behind Clashes in Ethiopia's Oromia and Somali Regions?" September 18. Accessed August 2, 2019. http://www.bbc.com/news/world-africa-41278618.

Brownlee, Jason. 2007. *Authoritarianism in an Age of Democracy*. Cambridge: Cambridge University Press.

Dahir, Abdi Latif. 2016. "Ethiopia's Previously Divided Ethnic Groups Are Unifying to Protest against the Government." *Quartz*, August 9. Accessed August 2, 2019. https://qz.com/753252/ethiopias-previously-divided-ethnic-groups-are-unifying-to-protest-against-the-government/.

Dorman, Sarah, Daniel Hammett, and Paul Nugent, eds. 2007. *Making Nations, Creating Strangers: States and Citizenship in Africa.* Leiden: Brill.

Durkheim, Emile. 1965. *Elementary Forms of the Religious Life.* New York: Free Press.

"Ethiopia: Brutal Crackdown on Protests." 2014. Human Rights Watch, May 5. Accessed August 2, 2019. https://www.hrw.org/news/2014/05/05/ethiopia-brutal-crackdown-protests.

Fasil, Mahlet, and Tsedale Lemma. 2015. "Oromo Protests: Defiance amidst Pain and Suffering." *Addis Standard,* December 16. Accessed March 5, 2018. https://addisstandard.com/oromo-protests-defiance-amidst-pain-and-suffering/.

Gardner, Tom. 2019. "'Go and We Die, Stay and We Starve': The Ethiopians Facing a Deadly Dilemma. *The Guardian,* May 15. Accessed May 25, 2019. https://www.theguardian.com/global-development/2019/may/15/go-and-we-die-stay-and-we-starve-the-ethiopians-facing-a-deadly-dilemma.

Geschiere, Peter. 2009. *The Perils of Belonging: Autochthony, Citizenship, and Exclusion in Africa and Europe.* Chicago: University of Chicago Press.

Geschiere, Peter, and Stephen Jackson, eds. 2006. "Autochthony and the Crisis of Citizenship," Special Issue, *African Studies Review* 49 (2): 1–7.

Hirt, Nicole, and Abdulkader Saleh Mohammad. 2013. "'Dreams Don't Come True in Eritrea': Anomie and Family Disintegration Due to the Structural Militarisation of Society." *Journal of Modern African Studies* 51 (1): 139–168.

James, Wendy, et al. 2002. "Introduction." In *Remapping Ethiopia: Socialism and After,* ed. Wendy James, Donald Donham, Eisei Kurimoto, and Alessandro Triulzi, 1–7. Oxford: James Curry.

Kebede, Messay. 2006. "The Roots and Fallouts of Haile Selassie's Educational Policy." Philosophy Faculty Publications. Paper 113. Accessed August 2, 2019, http://ecommons.udayton.edu/phl_fac_pub/113.

Levitsky, Steven, and Lucan Way. 2010. *Competitive Authoritarianism: Hybrid Regimes after the Cold War.* Cambridge: Cambridge University Press.

Mains, Daniel. 2004. "Drinking, Rumour, and Ethnicity in Jimma, Ethiopia." *Africa* 74 (3): 341–360.

Mariam, Alemayehu. 2018. "Prime Minister Abiy Ahmed of Ethiopia, We Must Separate the Thorns from the Roses." Ethiopian Media Forum. Accessed July 30, 2018. http://ethioforum.org/prime-minister-abiy-ahmed-of-ethiopia-we-must-separate-the-thorns-from-the-roses-by-prof-al-mariam/.

Mbembe, Achille. 2001. *On the Postcolony.* Berkeley: University of California Press.

Milkias, Paulos. 2006. *Haile Selassie, Western Education and Political Revolution in Ethiopia.* Amherst, MA: Cambria Press.

Riggan, Jennifer. 2018. "The Teacher State: Navigating the Fusion of Education and

Militarization in Eritrea and Elsewhere." *Compare: A Journal of International and Comparative Education.*

Riggan, Jennifer. 2016. *The Struggling State: Nationalism, Mass Militarization, and the Education of Eritrea.* Philadelphia: Temple University Press.

Riggan, Jennifer. 2013. "'It Seemed Like a Punishment': Teacher Transfers, Hollow Nationalism and the Intimate State in Eritrea." *American Ethnologist* 40 (4): 749–763.

Shaban, Abdur Rahman Alfa. 2018. "Ethiopia Crisis Needs Reforms Not Emergency Rule—E.U. Warns Govt." *Africa News*, February 19. Accessed August 2, 2019. http://www.africanews.com/2018/02/19/ethiopia-crisis-needs-reforms-not -emergency-rule-eu-warns-govt/.

Skidmore, Monique. 2004. *Karaoke Fascism: Burma and the Politics of Fear.* Philadelphia: University of Pennsylvania Press.

Smith, Lahra. 2013. *Making Citizens in Africa: Ethnicity, Gender and National Identity in Ethiopia.* Cambridge: Cambridge University Press.

Wedeen, Lisa. 1999. *Ambiguities of Domination: Politics, Rhetoric, and Symbols in Contemporary Syria.* Chicago: University of Chicago Press.

Wondimu, Habtamu. 2008. *Handbook of Peace and Human Rights Education in Ethiopia.* Addis Ababa: Organization for Social Science Research in Eastern and Southern Africa.

Zelalem, Zecharias. 2018. Amhara Protest Stalwarts Released but Government Remains Mum on Welkait Issue. *OPride*, February 23. Accessed March 5, 2018. https://www.opride.com/2018/02/23/amhara-protest-stalwarts-released -government-remains-mum-welkait-issue/.

Zelalem, Zecharias. 2017. Oromo-Somali Conundrum: Can Ethiopia Tame the Liyu Police? *OPride*, September 26. Accessed August 2, 2019. https://www.opride.com /2017/09/26/oromo-somali-conundrum-can-ethiopia-tame-liyu-police/.

Islamophobic Nationalism and Attitudinal Islamophilia

The election victory of Donald Trump at once marked a continuity of and an intensification in a longstanding Islamophobic reality in the United States. Shortly after the inauguration of Trump, the country would be rocked by the executive order that came to be known as the "Muslim ban," ostensibly institutionalizing the anti-Muslim rhetoric that had been a cornerstone of the 2016 election cycle (including in the campaign strategies of Ted Cruz, Hillary Clinton, and other candidates). After several legal challenges and social movement energy challenging the ban, it would ultimately be upheld by the Supreme Court in a ruling that was crushing to Muslims around the world. At the time I wrote this essay, the Muslim ban was the law of the land. Trump's victory seemed to herald a preponderance of Islamophobia. Yet in many ways, it fit neatly within the decades-old existence of anti-Muslim sentiment and policy: a vicious media campaign that has smeared Arabs and Muslims as greedy oil barons, barbarians, or terrorists (Shaheen 2001); the existence of the Guantanamo Bay detention camp that has incarcerated many Muslims without due process, even those cleared for release (Bayoumi 2015); and the institutionalization of surveillance of Muslim spaces of worship and culture (Bakalian and Mehdi 2009; Bayoumi 2015; Cainkar 2009; Kumar 2012; Lean 2012; Marable 2003).

Nearly a decade before Trump's victory, when I had first begun my fieldwork with congregants of Muslim American advocacy groups, I found many of them making claims about the relative invisibility of Islamophobia in "mainstream" US racial discourse. Lina, a major interlocutor in my ethnographic work, told me some years ago, "When people talk about race or American racism, it's always about the struggles of African Americans or Mexican Americans. What about the struggles of Muslims though? Why don't we get to be a part of the conversation on race?" That was 2011. In a matter of just five years, Lina's statement would lose all relevance. Islamophobia undoubtedly entered the national conversation on race and tolerance. In the weeks following Trump's inauguration, a *Saturday Night Live* monologue delivered by Muslim American comedian Aziz Ansari explicitly took Islamophobia as its central theme. CNN roundtables were devoted to the subject of anti-Muslim bigotry, and op-eds appeared in major newspapers dealing with the new racial landscape faced by US Muslims. Islamophobia had undeniably gone from the margins of US racial discourse to front and center, and all it seems to have taken was one election cycle.

Of course, this ushering-in of Islamophobia to public conversations about race and difference should come as no surprise. The lead-up to the 2016 presidential elections had seen Muslims placed explicitly on the political menu, so to speak. The "Muslim problem" surfaced in the campaign strategies of all major candidates, including Democrats. Most infamously, Trump called for a "total and complete" shutdown of Muslims entering the United States—a statement that somewhat mysteriously vanished from his website after coming under attack. Yet shortly after his election, he would issue the notorious Muslim ban, a piece of legislation so jarring that tens of thousands of protestors descended upon US airports in defiance of the executive order. On January 29, 2017, I stood inside the airport terminal in Philadelphia, absolutely stunned at the breadth of the outrage and solidarity that emerged in response to the Muslim ban. After reaching seventeen, I stopped counting how many protest signs contained the word "Islamophobia." Muslims had become hypervisible long ago (Alsultany 2006; Aretxaga 2002; Salaita 2006), many might say in the aftermath of the 9/11 attacks.[1] Now, in the wake of the Trump election, so too had Islamophobia.

There is a growing body of literature connecting US Islamophobia to both the politics of empire and the longstanding history of white supremacy. In other words, Islamophobia in the United States is inextricable from US foreign policy practices that have both demonized and instrumentalized global Muslim populations, stretching well before 9/11/2001, and a longstanding American history of racialized xenophobia. Deepa Kumar, for instance, traces the history of anti-Muslim violence alongside the legacies of the Crusades, the Cold War, and the newest instantiation of post-9/11 imperialist violence (Kumar 2012). As such, she extends the argument made by Mahmood Mamdani, who considers the geopolitical machinations that neatly divided the so-called Muslim world according to the dictates of global superpowers (Mamdani 2005). Such considerations of global politics are a necessary backdrop to the richly documented rise of US Islamophobia that we see in the work of Erik

Love (2017), Stephen Sheehi (2011), and Sunaina Marr Maira (2009). Like Love and Bakalian and Bozorgmehr (2009), I find a discussion of US Muslims' responses to an overarching and intensifying climate of Islamophobia to be especially edifying. In understanding not only the nature of anti-Muslim violence, but the agentive capacity of those who experience it, a more nuanced understanding of Islamophobia is possible.

In this essay, I will begin to consider both the continuities and ruptures in US Islamophobia marked by the dawn of the Trump era. Under Trump, it seems dog-whistle politics are gone, replaced by a megaphone (Blades 2016). Critiques of colorblind racism seem now an ancient preoccupation; antiracist activists must now contend with Nazi chants shouted through the streets of Charlottesville, Virginia. Yet, as Islamophobia was certainly not born after Trump's inauguration, I also interrogate the fact that the Trump victory has disarmed many anti-Islamophobia advocates, several of whom have been attempting to combat anti-Muslim sentiment for well over a decade. How, I ask, do the valences of anti-Islamophobic engagement before the rise of Trump explain why so many Muslim organizations were caught off guard, unprepared to handle what clearly seems to be an inevitable, almost predictable outgrowth of a longstanding and already-intensifying American Islamophobia? (Aretxaga 2002). I suggest that the strategies that anti-Islamophobia advocates have been using bypassed a necessary confrontation with the systemic, state-based practices of anti-Muslim racism.

I begin by exploring the dominant ways Islamophobia has been contested in the United States, suggesting that a focus on diversity, tolerance, and cultural understanding has often stood in for a more militant, anti-imperialist framework. From this, I move on to discuss the rifts among politically vocal Muslims in the United States who, we will see, are quite divided regarding these approaches. These rifts, I argue, offer insight into the antiauthoritarian and anti-imperialist impulses that serve to upend the dominant modes of anti-Islamophobia advocacy.

Culture Talk against Islamophobia

There have been arduous, extensive efforts to fight anti-Muslim sentiment in the United States for well over a decade. Indeed, in my research I found that many of these efforts stretch well before the aftermath of 9/11. National-level Muslim organizations have been combatting Islamophobia well before

Islamophobia entered the national lexicon on race. The post-9/11 moment and the election victory of Donald Trump are but two moments of intensification of an already-simmering anti-Muslim US social imaginary.

In the summer of 2017, Linda Sarsour spoke at the annual convention for the Islamic Society of North America (ISNA). Sarsour has become increasingly well known as a civil rights activist, a Muslim American spokesperson, and as one of the central planners for the massive Women's March in Washington, DC, the day after Trump's inauguration. ISNA was one of the organizations I focused on in my ethnography; it is the largest Muslim American organization. The annual convention in July brings together tens of thousands of attendees and features fundraising events, panel discussions, keynotes, plenaries, a bazaar, and even matrimonial events. As Sarsour addressed thousands of ISNA attendees that July, she implored them to remain steadfast in what she called a jihad against tyranny. Sarsour, who has sued the Trump administration and has been quite vocal in her resistance to this new instantiation of Islamophobia, caused an uproar with these words:

> I hope when we stand up to those who oppress our communities, that Allah accepts from us that as a form of jihad, that we are struggling against tyrants and rulers not only abroad in the Middle East or the other side of the world, but here in the United States of America, where you have fascists and white supremacists and Islamophobes reigning in the White House.

The outrage triggered in Sarsour's opponents by her ISNA speech was overwhelming. Conservative commentators were aghast. They saw in Sarsour's words a call for insurgency, holy war, or violence against the state. The kerfuffle even prompted a tweet from Donald Trump Jr., who wrote, "Who in the DNC will denounce this activist and democrat leader calling for jihad against Trump?" Liberal commentators and left activists were exasperated at the conservative outcry. They were quick to rush to Sarsour's defense. These aggravated defenders of Sarsour were clear about the *true* meaning of jihad: quite simply, an Islamic principle that asks Muslims to struggle against injustice, of which holy war is but one of many interpretations.

For well over a decade, Muslim spokespeople have been tirelessly explaining jihad's meaning to the general public. At cultural awareness events on college campuses, at interfaith panels, in Introduction to Islam classes for undergraduate students, and in earnest op-eds, Muslims have been consistently, patiently reminding America that jihad does *not* mean "holy war." This type of cultural production was indeed the focus of much of my ethnographic analysis: the ways in which Muslim American spokespeople's energies have been directed at campaigns of awareness and religiocultural literacy among ordinary Americans regarding Islam. Such explanations were offered in an attempt to deflate Islamophobia. Muslims are certainly not the only ones expending energy on "clearing up misconceptions about Islam," as one of my interlocutors put it. *National Geographic* and CNN have featured pieces trying to correct the widespread misunderstanding of jihad-as-holy-war, and popular books have been devoted to the subject. The Council on American-Islamic Relations (CAIR) took out a series of billboard-sized ads in public transportation to tackle the misunderstanding directly. Each poster featured a Muslim American, along with a caption "my jihad is to build bridges through friendship," for example, or "my jihad is to stay fit despite my busy schedule." (That last one prompted more than a few eye rolls from critics of the billboard campaign.) CAIR's billboard campaign would never have existed had it not been for another series of billboards that had similarly popped up in US cities. An organization called Stop Islamization of America (SIoA) had placed billboards on city buses and subway platforms across the country. SIoA, formerly known as the American Freedom Defense Initiative, is an overtly anti-Muslim extremist group, deemed a hate group by the Southern Poverty Law Center. SIoA's ads asked Americans to "oppose Jihad" and referred to Muslims as savages and as uncivilized. CAIR's "My Jihad is . . ." billboard series was thus a response, a defensive posture existing only as a counterattack to the vicious hate speech espoused by the SIoA billboards.

If we are to properly understand why the public conversation on Islamophobia has reached a seeming impasse, why "the Islamophobes won," we must take seriously the poles of this debate, encapsulated in the billboard wars and the conversation about jihad. This is a fight in which, on the one hand, Islamophobes unleash vitriol on Muslims and, on the other, Muslims and their allies often respond by generously explaining away misconceptions about the Islamic faith or Muslim cultures. Often, my fieldwork was replete with examples of Muslims responding to Islamophobia by waging what Mamdani calls "culture talk" (Mamdani 2005). In what Lila Abu-Lughod (2013) calls the "persistent resort to the cultural," we see how mainstream media, terrorism "experts," and policy makers themselves have turned to understanding *Islam*—Muslim practices, customs, and ideologies—as a means to understanding global politics in general, and terrorism more specifically. (Perhaps tellingly, neither pole of the jihad-billboard debates pointed out that the most expensive CIA operation in the 1970s and 1980s was the extensive US sponsorship of jihadist ideology as a critical part of the proxy warfare in Afghanistan against the Soviet Union.) That the public conversation on Islamophobia is rooted in these shallow understandings of culture should come as no surprise: anthropologists have long documented the shape-shifting forms of Western xenophobia that have, increasingly over past decades, relied upon notions of a *culturally* inassimilable other (Stolcke 1995).

Understanding the institutionalization of Islamophobia as a cornerstone of the US war on terror requires us to grasp the centrality of culture talk as not only a social- but policy-level preoccupation. For instance, the NYPD demographics unit sought to detect terror plots by deploying informants to spend time at Arabic bookstores, coffee shops in Muslim enclaves, and college student groups. This Orwellian program dubbed all spaces of Muslim life potential terrorist hubs. The Demographics Unit, now disbanded and deemed racist, collected data on how Muslims dressed, what shows they watched, and which preachers they listened to—Muslim culture, essentially—all as a purported means to detect terrorism. Clearly, the assumptions Mamdani calls "culture talk" led terrorism prevention measures drastically awry, epitomized by the ineffective demographics unit (an initiative that detected and thwarted no terror plots). Under institutionalized culture talk, questions about Ramadan, hijab, or the various theological interpretations of jihad are rendered serious investigations into the nature of global terrorism.

Yet what often falls out of these necessary critiques of culture talk are the myriad ways Muslim Americans themselves, or anti-Islamophobia advocates in general, have also taken this route as a way to combat Islamophobia. Culture talk is not the property of the Islamophobes alone; my research unearths the many ways well-intentioned Muslim American organizations and other allies in the fight against Islamophobia have turned to it as a defensive posture, an attempt to represent Islam and Muslims in the best possible light. In their work on post-9/11 Muslim advocacy work, Bakalian and Bozorgmehr (2009) note that these organizations have often opted for an integrationist approach. I have suggested that this integrationist approach has been a counternarrative offered by Muslim organizations attempting to topple anti-Muslim racism (Kazi 2014). Grewal writes of the "triumphalism" that underlies these narratives of Muslim American inclusion and the "mainstreaming" of Muslims in the United States for the purposes of inclusion (Grewal 2013, 156–157).

In my research, I noticed mainstream Muslim advocacy groups focusing on demanding prayer spaces, hijab days, and Islam awareness events. This, while there was a striking silence on topics including that of growing militarism in Muslim majority countries, the mobilization of police presence as counter-terrorism forces, and government infiltration of mosques and community spaces. When I spoke to my interlocutors about this glaring imbalance, many of them said Muslims *can't* make these critiques in this political moment. A common refrain was "it's just not the right time for us to talk about this." Compulsory patriotism has become, in the years since 9/11/2001, a prerequisite for Good Muslim status. With the now-infamous post-9/11 presidential declaration "either you are with us, or you are with the terrorists," the tendentious position of Muslims who expressed anything other than wholesale support for the war on terror became clear. This might be why many can recall with clarity Gold Star father Khizr Khan waving the Constitution in defiance of Donald Trump at the Democratic National Convention in 2016, yet few know that Khan has also been a vocal critic of US militarism in Muslim majority countries.

The limited spectrum of engagement, with both Islamophobes and their detractors often resorting to tactics shaped by eerily similar contours, is itself contested and provocative. Within Muslim American organizations, dissenting voices make clear their exasperation with representational politics that eschew the political and favor the cultural. These rifts reveal what I call the representational impasse, a sense of being "stuck" in the types of demands the congregants of these groups feel empowered to make. These coexisting realities reveal a deep tension inherent in these advocacy efforts: members of these organizations aim for counterhegemonic, anti-imperialist social transformation that exists *alongside* a deeply entrenched neoliberal multiculturalism or a commitment to cooperating with the mechanisms of the state.

These internal rifts surface without fail even in the work of smaller organizations, such as Muslim Student Associations (MSA) on college campuses across the country. These tensions are essentially a microcosm of those I encountered in my fieldwork with larger, national-level organizations. At one small MSA in New England, the organization was neatly divided into two camps in 2016. There were those Muslim students who felt the MSA's duty is to be a cultural organization, not a political one. This camp believed that, as Amani told me, "if the MSA hosts the best damn campus bake sale, there will be no room for Islamophobia anymore." They organized an annual hijab solidarity day to allow non-Muslim women to build sympathy with Muslims by sampling a headscarf, and they agitated for halal food options and Eid as an observed campus holiday. Yet a vocal subset in the MSA consistently brings up BDS—the boycott, divest, and sanctions movement aimed at drawing national attention to the humanitarian crisis in occupied Palestine. This contingent wants to force a campus conversation about anti-Muslim hostilities students face from the growing population of veteran students; they wish to host events on topics about the military industrial complex and Guantanamo and the war on terror, on what one alumni dubbed "the inherent Islamophobia of the US military." These efforts are often shut down by the former, larger contingent. Some MSA members left the organization due to what they perceived to be an "apolitical" stance of the organization.

What this discussion illuminates is that the very divisions we see existing among the highest seats of power exist in equal magnitude among marginalized populations. With politicians debating whether or not to criminalize, for instance, the BDS movement, we also see Muslim student groups debating whether or not it is appropriate to talk about Palestine. If the seats of power are debating whether or not religiocultural traits are predictors of terrorism, as with the NYPD demographics unit, Muslim organizations also mirror these assumptions, with certain members eager to demonstrate that their religious and cultural traits are evidence of peacefulness or patriotism. Having demonstrated the range of forms that anti-Islamophobia advocacy has taken, we turn now to a discussion of the larger climate in which these efforts exist.

Contesting Islamophobic Nationalism

Contemporary conversations on Islamophobia must be situated in the larger global context of the resurgence of an authoritarian right. Others in this volume have suggested that to understand the angry nationalism of today, we must consider the central role of racism and white supremacy and their undeniable connection to the economic failures of neoliberalism. For Don Robotham, these failures are transformed into an angry politics of racial resentment, acted out upon an outsider-other. Sophie Bjork-James similarly points to class resentment as part of a much broader conservative agenda that rests foundationally on the notion of a besieged and imperiled whiteness, the resurgence of white nationalism highlighted by Jeff Maskovsky. In other words, many in this volume are suggesting a racist blame game is a constitutive element of today's politics. In the United States, we see migrants—ambiguously Latino or Muslim—posing a nebulous threat to national security. Perhaps this is why, facing accusations of child cruelty and illegal border violence, the Trump administration responded with unfounded claims that the 2018 migrant caravan had "Middle Easterners" in it. Any whispers of sympathy and solidarity with these Latino migrants could easily be dissolved by Islamicizing them.

Today's Islamophobic nationalism has crystallized since the Trump campaign made explicit the anti-Muslim assumptions long embedded in US racism. For my interlocutors, there is no denying the reality of Islamophobic nationalism's intensification under a Trump presidency. In my conversations with members of these organizations in the days, weeks, and months following the Trump victory, the awareness of American Islamophobia was undeniable. Often, this awareness surfaces in a crude type of humor, the "who's *your* white friend who'd hide you in their attic?" joke. When Hasan Minhaj took the stage at the 2017 White House Press Correspondent's Dinner, he opened with, "My name is Hasan Minhaj, or, as I will be known in a few weeks, Number 830287."

This nascent Islamophobic nationalism is angry nationalism. Two weeks after the Trump election, a visibly Muslim student sat in my office, telling me that classmates sat near her, turning the text on their "Make America Great Again" hats to face her in class. Another one of my students in a hijab was denied service at a local pizza place the week after the inauguration. She was told, "Now that Trump is president, you won't even be here in two years." A man in Michigan, Quadir, told me of cars filled with white teens who ride past his local mosque, yelling "Allahu akbar, ragheads," as they screech past. Quadir says he has never seen anything like this in his twenty years of attending that mosque. I spoke to a sixty-year-old Muslim woman who was attending her first-ever protest recently, rallying in support of the Rohingya Muslim minority who had been facing a genocide in Myanmar. She told me the rally was interrupted by a car full of people who rolled down the window and chanted "build the wall!" at the protestors. This is indeed an angry nationalism, just as it was angry nationalism in 2016 when two white men were killed and a third stabbed after coming to the defense of a black Muslim woman on a Portland train who was being verbally assaulted by a knife-wielding white supremacist. It was angry nationalism that saw a Hindu Indian man in Olathe, Kansas, killed, perceived by his assailant to be Iranian. Or consider the case of Robert Doggart, the man who, just a few short years after an unsuccessful run for a congressional seat, began stockpiling weapons to fulfill his plan to massacre Muslim Americans in a town in upstate New York. He called this a holy war and attempted to recruit others in this effort online. He was caught before he was able to carry out his terror plot. At his sentencing hearing, Judge Curtis Collier said to him, "You, sir, are no monster. In many respects, you lived a life of honor." The egregiousness of Doggart's case is only outdone by its relative invisibility in mainstream media and political discourse, indicating just how taken for granted an Islamophobic nationalism has become.

In beginning to make sense of Islamophobic nationalism and the immense momentum it carries, first, I'd like to suggest that we consider carefully what Khaled Beydoun (2016a) calls the dialectical relationship between state-sponsored Islamophobia and personal Islamophobia. I refer to these as systemic Islamophobia and attitudinal Islamophobia. Systemic Islamophobia refers to the institutional apparatuses (for instance, the NYPD demographics unit, the USA Patriot Act, or the Executive Order Travel Ban) that single out Muslims for profiling, surveillance, or policing. Beydoun shows how these apparatuses are not to be seen as separate from individual animus (i.e., personal or attitudinal Islamophobia), but rather that the two have a uniquely dialectical relationship. Understanding dialectical Islamophobia will require us to look well past Trump as a singular figure in American racial history and think instead about the steady expansion of executive power (emblematic of both Bush and Obama presidencies). As such, Islamophobia follows well-documented forms of racism in which racial formations and animosities are closely imbricated with persistent social structures (Balibar and Wallerstein, 1991).

Let us return for a moment to the Philadelphia airport protest of 2017. A spontaneous action that was mirrored in protests across the country, it is more appropriate to think of it as two separate protests. Outside of the international arrivals terminal, a police barricade had been set up. One set of protestors was gathered behind these barricades, some of them wearing the pink hats that had become emblematic of the Women's March just weeks before. Inside the terminal, by the baggage claim, was a second set of protestors. These were people who had defied the police instructions to remain behind the barricades and, with chants such as "The Fraternal Order of Police Endorsed Donald Trump!," risked arrest to hold a sit-in inside the terminal. At this sit-in, a whole range of people of color took the microphone to share stories of migration, warfare, and brutality at the hands of both Border Patrol and Philadelphia police. They were surrounded by a ring of police, poised to make arrests. They also made very clear that the obedient liberal masses outside the terminal were not "here for true liberation," as one young protestor put it. The militant antistate stance of the sit-in stood in clear contrast to the law-abiding protest energy outside the terminal. In a sense, the divisiveness among the airport protestors reflected the pivotal rift among the anti-Trump resistance in general and anti-Islamophobia organizing more specifically. It reveals a crucial tension among organizers themselves, with more militant/systemic forms of protest clashing with those forms that focus on diversity, tolerance, and inclusion.

The Contested Fight against Islamophobia

With this in mind, I'd like to think about the ways in which attitudinal or personal Islamophobia has dominated the realm of anti-Islamophobia organizing on the part of large Muslim organizations. In so doing, we can begin to see how systemic manifestations of Islamophobia have remained largely unaddressed in much of the public conversation on Islamophobia. We may also understand the failures of these approaches as part of the undermining of cosmopolitan liberalism described by Jeff Maskovsky and Sophie Bjork-James in the introduction to this volume.

The immense effort to combat anti-Muslim racism on the part of well-funded Muslim American organizations and coalitions spans well over a decade. Yet the bulk of the representational strategies of an organization like ISNA has been focused on presenting Muslims as patriotic, peaceful, and compatible with a quintessential Americanness, a strategy I refer to as Islamophilia. It has been, in short, a concerted effort to show the general public that Muslims are not terrorists, backward, or intolerant. All too often, this focus has left the fundamental realities of systemic Islamophobia intact. I do not delve into the motivations of these organizations in this piece, nor do I discuss here the relative privilege that spokespeople of these organizations enjoy along lines of class, immigration status, or educational attainment. Instead, I focus here on how these representational strategies have led to a deep impasse, a foreclosure of engagement around material and geopolitical realities in favor of a particular brand of 'good Muslim' multiculturalism.

While I was conducting my fieldwork with large, national-level Muslim American organizations, they deployed vast resources to host events that fostered interfaith dialogue. They invited Congresspeople to Ramadan dinners and offered op-eds in local papers that explained the tenets of Islam. During this era of abundant "Muslimsplaining" (as one of my interlocutors, Samar, termed it), there was a striking intensification of institutional apparatuses that criminalized Muslim life. In an eerie precursor to Trump's Muslim ban, the National Security Entry-Exit Registry System, or NSEERS, spanned the administrations of both George W. Bush and Barack Obama. Also known as Special Registration, NSEERS was established shortly after 9/11/2001, and its legal framework was only repealed during Obama's lame duck window, many felt in anticipation of the undeniable anti-Muslim wave that loomed in a Trump presidency. In other words, the figure of Trump was not to be trusted with the Islamophobia that had been somewhat unchecked in the hands of Obama and Bush. The aforementioned NYPD demographics unit also formed and disbanded during the era of Muslim American culture talk, and, of course, the notorious USA PATRIOT Act was established, renewed, and expanded during the bipartisan "terror age."

It is noteworthy that each of these measures prompted outcry from civil rights advocates and Muslim Americans, yet nothing on the scale of the wholesale uprising against Trump's travel ban. Perhaps it was the outlandishness of Trump's Islamophobia that was being protested by thousands who gathered at airports and on city streets in the weeks following the inauguration, not the fact of it. Instead, Trump stands out not as a singular Islamophobe, but as the most *overt* Islamophobe in such high political office. With 2016 presidential candidates Ted Cruz calling for greater surveillance and profiling of Muslims, Bobby Jindal saying "let's be real, Islam has an America problem," and Hillary Clinton asking Muslims to be the "eyes and ears on the front lines against terrorism" (assuming Muslims possess some special knowledge of terrorist activities), it is clear that Islamophobia is a sine qua non of American political culture (Kazi 2017). While dog-whistle politics have been part and parcel of the US racial landscape (López 2015), this "resistance" energy reveals that overt Islamophobia is roundly rejected by wide swaths of the American population. Many of my interlocutors expressed to me a sense that perhaps Trump-era Islamophobia would force the hand of civil rights advocates to abandon a futile project of culture talk, grappling head-on with the institutional foundation for Islamophobia instead.

With Muslim American advocacy groups generally poised to deem Islamophobia a matter of prejudice, bigotry, and intolerance, I turn now to the Countering Violent Extremism (CVE) programs that were established in 2014 and continue today. Under CVE, the government promotes collaboration between law enforcement, religious leaders, schoolteachers, health professionals, and social service workers to detect and deter threats to extremist violence. Under former president Obama, CVE disproportionately focused on Muslim extremism, drawing criticism from civil rights advocates and legal experts who saw this discriminatory focus as obfuscating a very real threat—often from extreme Christian white nationalists. Regardless, Obama's CVE program was race neutral, at least de jure. Now, the Trump administration is poised to change the name from Countering Violent Extremism to Countering Islamic Extremism. This would eliminate all funding except to that countering the Muslim threat. Almost seamlessly, the dog whistle becomes a megaphone (Beydoun 2016b; Dahi, 2017). CVE has been another reminder of the deep rift carved through Muslim American advocacy spaces. Indeed, many imams, Islamic schoolteachers, and other Muslims have themselves accepted CVE funding. This collaboration has upset those who regard CVE as an expansion of Islamophobia, a way of recruiting ad-hoc homeland security agents from the Muslim community itself. As Sahar Aziz put it, it serves as a "guise for deputizing well-intentioned Muslim leaders to gather intelligence on their constituents that places their civil liberties at risk" (Aziz 2015).

The CVE programs are a useful example for understanding the impassive position of Muslim American spokesmanship. On the one hand, many Muslim activists are eager to demonstrate Muslims' willingness to cooperate with authorities and be pliant with state processes. Yet, on the other hand, many understand the dangers and injustices of the inherently Islamophobic practices of the Department of Homeland Security, Immigration and Customs Enforcement, and local law enforcement. For those who choose to collaborate with CVE or accept CVE funds, they see it as a chance to expose Islam's "true" character (virtuous, peaceful, with nothing to hide) to a state that seeks to eradicate terrorism and extremist violence. It is, in a sense, the endgame of culture talk, the MSA bake sale in its final iteration. It rests on an assumption that "showing" Islam to potential Islamophobes will deflate Islamophobia. Perhaps the quest for legitimacy in an Islamophobic racial context necessitates this collaboration. The defeated realization among many Muslim Americans that certain Muslim community leaders, imams, and teachers would cooperate with the state's own project of Islamophobia is a recognition of the futility of such inclusionary ambitions.

With such vast Muslim American representational energy aimed at shifting *perceptions* and explaining the tenets of Islam, Islamophobia's institutional tentacles have remained firmly intact, even grown stronger. As such, Muslim advocacy groups are disarmed by the rising tide of Islamophobic nationalism, repeating clichés about Islam as a religion of peace, Thomas Jefferson's ownership of a Quran (Kazi 2014), or other banalities that do little to mobilize a far-flung population of Muslims against the impending wave of a dialectical Islamophobia that leaves Muslims vulnerable—vulnerable to the state, their neighbors, even their very own Muslim community leaders. It remains to be seen what happens not only to Islamophobic nationalism under Trump, but whether and how the tactics meant to fight anti-Muslim animus shift.

Conclusion

We have seen in this essay that, in the face of an upsurge in the type of angry nationalism that is emblematic of the Trump administration's overt Islamophobia, the shape of resistance itself is disputed. Those who proclaim themselves adversaries of the newest instantiation of American white nationalism are divided, often viciously, on questions of what shape this resistance should take and how it ought to relate to the state apparatus itself.

The election victories of two Muslims, Ilhan Omar, a Somali American congresswoman from Minnesota, and Rashida Tlaib, an Arab American representative from Michigan, have reignited the conversation about the potential for elected officials to fight racist and authoritarian impulses. It has also brought a sense of hope to many Muslims in the United States, who see their presence in Congress as a direct response to the Islamophobia of the Trump administration. With Omar speaking out, at great personal risk, against the influence of the AIPAC lobby and questioning Elliott Abrams about his role in Latin American "dirty wars," she sparked a sense of hope that, perhaps, a hollow identitarian "good Muslim" trope would not be the only route available for Muslims to claim space in the United States. For Tlaib, her invocation of her Palestinian roots and her words in defense of the BDS movement had a similar effect. The two have galvanized a sense of possibility for many anti-Islamophobia advocates. Leading up to their elections, debates flooded the left: Would these candidates be co-opted by an establishment that has all-too-often capitalized upon identitarian impulses (as have, for instance, the "black faces in high places" described vividly in Taylor [2016]) to distract from the political impulses of the elected officials themselves? Or would they pose a substantive threat to not just the Islamophobic impulses of the Trump administration, but the deeper threat of a bipartisan Islamophobia, a consistently anti-Palestinian state apparatus, and a hawkish militarism that gets eager support from both major political parties? It remains to be seen.

Yet what we might take away from this is an emergent shift in the age of angry nationalism. No longer can weak-kneed and hollow appeals to identity politics sustain momentum. Instead, the very public debates around how best to confront the new authoritarian right have brought into light the possibility that what is needed is likely much deeper than a narrow critique of the Trump administration or appeals to diversity and inclusion. Electoral politics are not leading toward this; rather they are a reflection of a sea change among Americans ready to accept that the tried (and perhaps tired) mechanisms of a liberal incrementalism have indeed failed.

Note

1. I hesitate to use the phrase 9/11 as shorthand for the events in New York City, in Pennsylvania, and at the Pentagon on September 11, 2001, which problematically erases the historical and political relevance of other events that took place on that date in other times and places. I do this for the sake of readability.

References

Abu-Lughod, Lila. 2013. *Do Muslim Women Need Saving?* Cambridge, MA: Harvard University Press.

Alsultany, Evelyn. 2006. "Introduction: Arab Americans and US Racial Formations." In *Race and Arab Americans Before and After 9/11: From Invisible Citizens to Visible Subjects*, ed. Amaney Jamal and Nadine Naber, 1–45. Syracuse, NY: Syracuse University Press.

Aretxaga, Begoña. 2002. "Terror as Thrill: First Thoughts on the 'War on Terrorism.'" *Anthropological Quarterly* 75 (1): 138–150.

Aziz, Sahar. 2015. "Opening Statement." Islamic Monthly Debate—CVE—June 27. Accessed August 3, 2019. http://theislamicmonthly.com/tim-debate-cve.

Bakalian, Anny P., and Mehdi Bozorgmehr. 2009. *Backlash 9/11: Middle Eastern and Muslim Americans Respond*. Berkeley: University of California Press.

Balibar, Etienne, and Immanuel Maurice Wallerstein. 1991. *Race, Nation, Class: Ambiguous Identities*. New York: Verso.

Bayoumi, Moustafa. 2015. *This Muslim American Life: Dispatches from the War on Terror*. New York: New York University Press.

Beydoun, Khaled A. 2016a. "Islamophobia: Toward a Legal Definition and Framework." *Columbia Law Review* 116.

Beydoun, Khaled A. 2016b. "Between Indigence, Islamophobia, and Erasure: Poor and Muslim in War on Terror America." *California Law Review* 104: 1463.

Blades, Lincoln. 2016. "Trump Won by Turning Bigoted Dog Whistles into Megaphones." *Rolling Stone*, May 4. Accessed August 3, 2019. https://www.rollingstone.com/politics/news/trump-won-by-turning-bigoted-dog-whistles-into-megaphones-20160504.

Cainkar, Louise. 2009. *Homeland Insecurity: The Arab American and Muslim American Experience after 9/11*. New York: Russell Sage.

Dahir, Zeinab A. 2017. "Blurred Intersections: The Anti-Black, Islamophobic Dimensions of CVE Surveillance." *All Theses, Dissertations, and Other Capstone Projects*. Minnesota State University, Mankato.

Grewal, Zareena. 2013. *Islam Is a Foreign Country: American Muslims and the Global Crisis of Authority*. New York: New York University Press.

Kazi, Nazia. 2014. "Thomas Jefferson Owned a Quran: Cultural Citizenship and Muslim American Representational Politics." *North American Dialogue* 172: 53–63.

Kazi, Nazia. 2017. "Voting to Belong: The Inevitability of Systemic Islamophobia." *Identities* 1–19.

Kumar, Deepa. 2012. *Islamophobia and the Politics of Empire*. Chicago: Haymarket Books.

Lean, Nathan Chapman. 2012. *The Islamophobia Industry: How the Right Manufactures Fear of Muslims*. London: Pluto Press.

López, Ian Haney. 2015. *Dog Whistle Politics: How Coded Racial Appeals Have Reinvented Racism and Wrecked the Middle Class*. Oxford: Oxford University Press.

Love, Erik. 2017. *Islamophobia and Racism in America*. New York: New York University Press.

Maira, Sunaina Marr. 2009. *Missing: Youth, Citizenship, and Empire after 9/11*. Durham, NC: Duke University Press.

Mamdani, Mahmood. 2005. *Good Muslim, Bad Muslim: The US, the Cold War, and the Roots of Terror*. New York: Harmony Books.

Marable, Manning. 2003. "9/11 Racism in a Time of Terror." In *Implicating Empire: Globalization and Resistance in the 21st-Century World Order*, ed. Stanley Aronowitz and Heather Gautney. New York: Basic Books.

Salaita, Steven. 2006. *Anti-Arab Racism in the USA: Where It Comes From and What It Means for Politics Today*. London: Pluto Press.

Shaheen, Jack G. 2001. *Reel Bad Arabs: How Hollywood Vilifies a People*. Ithaca, NY: Olive Branch Press.

Sheehi, Stephen. 2011. *Islamophobia: The Ideological Campaign against Muslims*. Atlanta, GA: Clarity Press.

Stolcke, Verena. 1995. "Talking Culture: New Boundaries, New Rhetorics of Exclusion in Europe." *Current Anthropology* 36 (1): 1–24.

Taylor, Keeanga-Yamahtta. 2016. *From# BlackLivesMatter to Black Liberation*. Chicago: Haymarket Books.

Afterword

The Future of Angry Politics

In the world today, anger saturates the political scene, seemingly operating as an overwhelming, undirected force. Yet struggling to make some sense of the politics of anger, even if its ends are never fully legible or clear, seems vital if we are to play our part, as academics ought, in imagining, and helping to bring about, a more positive future. In this afterword, we reflect on the perils and possibilities of angry politics, building on the essays anthologized in this volume, to consider what might be needed to transform anger from a reactionary to an emancipatory force.

Let us start with the perils.

In the introduction to this anthology, we make four main points about the nature and scope of angry politics in the world today. First, we argue that neoliberalism's recent failures, faults, and retreats have opened up new political spaces that have been filled in many instances by new destructive projects of resentment. We are not saying that neoliberalism as a governing project has been vanquished or that it will not continue to hold sway in various forms in many, or even most, contexts. Our argument, instead, is that its hegemonic powers are decisively on the wane, as vastly different people from vastly different social, political, and geographical backgrounds experience the disruptions, disappointments, and dilemmas that came about in the name of neoliberalism, despite its promises of wealth, security, and prosperity. In this context, retrograde politics around race, class, gender, sex, ethnicity, migration, and inclusion have surfaced, as has the unsettling of longstanding governing and political arrangements that freighted representative democracy and cosmopolitan liberalism with capitalism and replaced them with *more* illiberal forms of governance. (We say more because representative democracy and liberalism have always had illiberal features.)

Our second point is that the term *populism* is of limited use in characterizing the kinds of political antagonism that we see as in urgent need of critical attention and exploration. We eschew approaches that attempt to characterize these antagonisms in simplistic terms as, say, the unified expression of a global populist wave. Instead, we emphasize the importance of locating the roots of angry politics in specific cultural, political, and economic contexts.

This leads in part to our third point, which is about the importance of conjunctural analysis in enabling a nuanced understanding of the emergent political forms of the present. We embrace a conjunctural approach not out of a clannish politico-theoretical fealty to Antonio Gramsci, Stuart Hall, and other theorists who have pioneered and embraced it. Rather, we see it as vital to tease out the multiplicity of forces, antagonisms, and conflicts that shape politics. These multiplicities matter. And an urgent task of the moment is to explain how they matter so that we have a better understanding of the dismaying political scenes we are observing, enduring, and implicated in.

Our fourth point is to identify three kinds of anger that we see as essential in shaping politics today: *neoliberal disenchantment, racialized resentments*, and the *rage of the downtrodden and repressed*. We think these kinds of anger are widespread, though they are felt differently in different contexts. Although they are not intrinsically reactionary in their political orientation, they seem better articulated in the current conjuncture by the right than by the left. Indeed, the right has been very effective at articulating anger to the forms of violence, fear, desperation, and other affects and atmospherics that have surfaced as neoliberalism falters.

Ultimately, we see angry politics as playing a decisive role in the consolidation of harder edged forms of authoritarian populism. As the global political polarity shifts from the post–Cold War period to the present, and as neoliberalism wears itself out, authoritarian regimes are surfacing, being pitted against each other, and traveling from place to place. Emancipatory alternatives appear at the moment to have been largely vanquished, or, at the very least, to have disappeared from national political scenes.

Most of the essays gathered in this volume illustrate these dynamics, locating the roots of new angry politics in shifting global and regional capitalist political economy and in the disenchantment with, and disaffection from, neoliberalism. They also trace the multiple and complex political forces that converge to forge new toxic political alignments and outcomes. An important line of argument informing these assertions is that racialization is essential to the elaboration of right-wing populist rage and toxic politics. Don Robotham, for example, shows how this works on a global scale, as whites in the Global

North lash out at the prospects, true or not, that they may no longer be able to take their global hegemonic positionality for granted, especially in the context of a rising China. This sentiment is not disconnected from the entrenched racial ideologies that inform common sense about political and economic power, a thematic that Sophie Bjork-James explores in great detail in her analysis of the cultural roots of white supremacist rationality in the United States. She shows how stories about imperiled white families and communities work to shore up alliances between the religious right and white nationalists. (She also shows its fragility and the ideological limits of this rationality as the basis for forging connections between far-right groups.)

It is important also to trace the role of political elites in stoking the flames of political resentment, and in channeling rage into particular political projects and directions. Preeti Sampat and Lesley Gill provide concrete case studies of precisely these dynamics, demonstrating, in the cases of India and Colombia respectively, what happens when elites are successful in exploiting widespread racialized disillusionment. Political economic realignments and widespread repression are two important and interconnected consequences. Sampat shows how Modi in India focused the disillusionment that many people felt as India's economy liberalized into Hindu nationalist politics. Gill shows how a far-right coalition in Colombia exploited public frustrations with a long-term guerilla insurgency and middle-class disdain for popular social movements to outflank these movements and gain political control. Taken together, these four pieces help us to understand why the anger of the dispossessed and repressed so frequently is channeled to the right. They show the kind of political work that is necessary to channel popular resentments into nationalist, xenophobic, homophobic, sexist, and racist projects.

It is also important to emphasize anger's multiple sources and to trace how they converge in the making of political antagonisms. John Clarke shows how the Brexit vote in Britain was multiply motivated by frustrations with politics as usual, antiglobalism, anti-immigration, and anti-European sentiments. Lilith Mahmud describes the multiple social and political bases of opposition to a constitutional referendum of 2016 in Italy. Some Italians opposed it out of nationalist and xenophobic fervor while others were rooted in concerns over mounting inequality and the elitism of technocratic rule. Ironically, these nuances were, much like those in the Brexit vote, politically illegible. One reason for this, Mahmud explains, was the Italian left's propensity to label their opponents crudely as fascists. By doing this, they ironically obscure the new roots of nationalist sentiment and anti-immigrant rage.

The ability of far-right protagonists to exploit historical senses of grievance and racialized resentment is crucial to their political success in these multiply motivated political scenes, as is their capacity to invoke a public image of themselves as "strongmen" who are uniquely capable of rescuing feminized nations from their enemies. Gerald Creed and Mary Taylor use the case of eastern Europe to show how antidemocratic and anti-immigrant populists succeed by pitting themselves against a variety of political alternatives including liberals whose postsocialist privatization schemes produced a widespread sense of resentment and political disaffection and socialists whose critique of the unequal distribution of resources has been discredited by their own political struggles and failures in the postsocialist period. Jeff Maskovsky shows how Trump exploited widespread white nationalist political sentiments and frustrations with color blindness and multiculturalism to smash the liberal racial consensus that has dominated in the United States in the post–civil rights era. And Noah Theriault shows how in the Philippines, Rodrigo Duterte exploited ecopolitics—specifically popular frustrations with climate-change adaptation, disaster management, and environmental enforcement—to consolidate his authoritarian rule. Taken together, these essays point to the various ways that right-wing leaders use anger—at multiculturalism, privatization, immigration, environmental destruction, and so forth—to move politics toward more illiberal and authoritarian ends.

And now finally to the promises.

The critique of unequal power relations and of new forms of authoritarianism is important, but it is not sufficient. We must consider also what might be needed to transform anger from a reactionary to an emancipatory force. In our view, the last three essays included in this anthology are the ones that point most clearly in this direction. Carwil Bjork-James looks at the case of Bolivia, where Evo Morales came to political prominence as part of a leftist antiglobalization movement that demanded material advances and symbolic power for the formerly marginalized indigenous majority. Morales has put off his socialist and plurinational goals but Bolivia remains one of the more durable pink-tide regimes in a region that is moving rapidly to the right. The politically mobilized indigenous majority's rage against its treatment by right-wing governments in the past is not easily dissipated. In a discussion of populist politics in Ethiopia, Jennifer Riggan shows how political anger works against an authoritarian regime. Riggan describes a case in which public anger and protests forced the regime to roll back its unpopular policies. And, in the final essay in the volume, Nazia Kazi highlights the political effectiveness of the militant forms of popular pro-immigrant activism that erupted spontaneously in reaction to Trump's travel ban in February 2017. In all three cases, we see the deployment of a deeply entrenched kind of anger, popularly felt or at least very familiar to a significant segment of a democratic polity or by the subjects of an authoritarian regime, and animated either spontaneously or by a charismatic leader who can remind their followers of what they have to lose.

The sense of loss in all three cases seems significant to us. The articulation of loss to anger and fear has been an essential feature in contemporary forms of reactionary politics. But loss has also been articulated to righteous and emancipatory forms of anger as well, as, for example, with radical AIDS activism in the United States and worldwide. In this movement, the sense of loss of community, health, lovers, and friends helped to motivate a radical politics of health (see, for example, Gould 2009; Maskovsky 2018; Susser 2011; see also Eng and Kazanjian 2003). As in the past, we think that the accounting of what has been lost, what remains, and what still could be lost, is crucial to the current-day pursuit of justice, equality, egalitarianism, and freedom. Durable political transformations have never relied on anger alone. It has certainly catalyzed the movements that won progressive changes across the world in the twentieth century. But other affects or feelings such as joy or hope were needed to transform insurgent action into durable change. Emancipatory and transformative work may also require a defense of some aspects of liberalism despite its significant limitations.

But we should not embrace liberalism too much. In an important set of articles, Nancy Fraser (2017a, 2017b; Fraser and Sunkara 2019) argues that neoliberalism is not the solution to the rise of right-wing populism but the root of the problem. We could not agree more. Indeed, it is this position, our sense of the importance of anger in the enactment of xenophobic, racist, and ethnonationalist forms of politics, and our concerns about growing economic inequality and the persistence of inequalities around sex and gender, that has motivated us to work collectively to put this anthology together and to use conjunctural analysis in our reading of different cases. We concur with Fraser's comment, "The sort of change we require can only come from elsewhere, from a project that is at the very least anti-neoliberal, if not anti-capitalist"

(Fraser 2017b, 64). And we, like Fraser, refuse to limit our political imaginations to the depressing choice between neoliberalism and a more dangerous and exclusionary form of authoritarian rule. For Fraser, the path toward such a project is progressive populism. We see a broader set of political possibilities, including those that are elaborated as antiracist, queer, and antisexist projects. It is essential to consider what it might take to advance durable forms of more positive, emancipatory politics and to help create and sustain spaces of political experimentation, even in increasingly illiberal or postpolitical environments (Swyngedouw 2018). Keeping in mind the lessons learned from the essays collected here, we have a sense that anger will be key to these endeavors. An angry new global order is not necessarily one sutured together through increasingly hard-edged authoritarian populism, though this is a distinct possibility. We hope that anger can be put to positive political uses.

Acknowledgments

For invaluable feedback on this afterword, we thank John Clarke, Gerald Creed, Lesley Gil, and Don Robotham.

References

Eng, David L., and David Kazanjian. 2003. *Loss: The Politics of Mourning*. Berkeley: University of California Press.

Fraser, Nancy. 2017. "The End of Progressive Neoliberalism." *Dissent Magazine*. January 2. Accessed May 14, 2019. https://www.dissentmagazine.org/online_articles/progressive-neoliberalism-reactionary-populism-nancy-fraser.

Fraser, Nancy. 2017b. "From Progressive Neoliberalism to Trump—and Beyond." *American Affairs* 1 (4) (Winter): 46–64.

Fraser, Nancy, and Bhaskar Sunkara. 2019. *The Old Is Dying and the New Cannot Be Born: From Progressive Neoliberalism to Trump and Beyond*. London: Verso.

Gould, Deborah Bejosa. 2009. *Moving Politics: Emotion and ACT UP's Fight against AIDS*. Chicago: University of Chicago Press.

Maskovsky, Jeff. 2018. "Staying Alive: AIDS Activism as Relational Poverty Politics." In *Relational Poverty Politics: Forms, Struggles, and Possibilities*, ed. Victoria Lawson and Sarah Elwood, 77–94. Athens: University of Georgia Press.

Susser, Ida. 2011. *AIDS, Sex, and Culture: Global Politics and Survival in Southern Africa*. Hoboken, NJ: John Wiley & Sons.

Swyngedouw, Erik. 2018. *Promises of the Political: Insurgent Cities in a Post-Political Environment*. Cambridge, MA: MIT Press.

Carwil Bjork-James is assistant professor of anthropology at Vanderbilt University and the author of *The Sovereign Street: Making Revolution in Urban Bolivia* (forthcoming). His research—both ethnographic and historical—concerns disruptive protest, grassroots autonomy, state violence, and indigenous collective rights in South America. This work draws on his experience as an environmental and human rights advocate and as a participant in direct action protest movements. He holds a PhD in anthropology (from the Graduate Center, City University of New York) and a masters in Environmental and Human Rights Policy (University of Chicago).

Sophie Bjork-James has over ten years of experience researching both the US-based religious right and the white nationalist movements. She is finalizing a book manuscript titled "The Divine Institution: The Racial Politics of White Evangelicalism's Theology of the Family," on race and evangelical politics in the United States. Her work has appeared in *American Anthropologist, Oxford Bibliographies, Sex Roles: A Journal of Research,* and *The Ethnic Studies Review.* Her work has been featured on the NBC *Nightly News,* NPR's *All Things Considered,* the *New York Times,* and BBC Radio 4's *Today.*

John Clarke is an emeritus professor at the UK's Open University and is also a recurrent visiting professor at Central European University. He has been working on the politics and policies of austerity and the rise of nationalist, populist, and authoritarian politics. Recent publications include: *Making Policy Move: Towards a Politics of Translation and Assemblage* (with Dave Bainton, Noémi Lendvai, and Paul Stubbs, 2015) and *Critical Dialogues: Thinking Together in Turbulent Times,* based on a series of conversations with people who have made him think (2019).

Gerald W. Creed is professor of anthropology at Hunter College and the Graduate Center, City University of New York. He has conducted research in rural Bulgaria since 1987 on diverse topics including political economy, ritual, nationalism, socialist nostalgia, and gender. His first book, *Domesticating Revolution: From Socialist Reform to Ambivalent Transition in a Bulgarian Village* (1998) examines the impact of collectivization, socialist agrarian reforms, and subsequent privatization efforts on village and household economies. His subsequent project, entitled *Masquerade and Postsocialism: Ritual and Cultural Dispossession in Bulgaria* (2011) uses ancient fertility rites still popular in Bulgaria to challenge standard orthodoxies of postsocialist studies.

Lesley Gill teaches anthropology at Vanderbilt University. Her research focuses on political violence, labor, class, and state formation in Latin America and the United States. Her most recent book is *A Century of Violence in a Red City: Popular Struggle, Counterinsurgency,* *and Human Rights in Colombia* (2016), and she is the co-editor of *Fifty Years of Peasant Wars in Latin America* (in press).

Nazia Kazi is an anthropologist specializing in Islamophobia, racism, and the global war on terror. Her public-facing scholarship has been featured on *TedX, Democracy Now!,* and the *Chronicle of Higher Education.* Her book, *Islamophobia, Race, and Global Politics,* explores the relationship between empire-building and American racism. She lives in Philadelphia and is assistant professor of Anthropology at Stockton University, where she is also affiliated with the American Studies and Africana Studies programs.

Lilith Mahmud is associate professor of anthropology at the University of California, Irvine. She specializes in feminist anthropology and critical European studies with research interests in secrecy, transparency, migration, nationalism, liberalism, and the right. Her first book, *The Brotherhood of Freemason Sisters: Gender, Secrecy, and Fraternity in Italian Masonic Lodges* (2014), was awarded the William A. Douglass Prize for best ethnography in Europeanist anthropology. Mahmud has served on the executive board of the Society for the Anthropology of Europe (2017–19), and as book review editor for *American Anthropologist* (2010–13).

Jeff Maskovsky is executive officer (chair) and professor of anthropology at the Graduate Center, and professor of urban studies at Queens College, City University of New York. His research and writing focus on poverty, politics, welfare, health, security, and governance in the United States. His publications include *The New Poverty Studies: Ethnographies of Power, Politics and Impoverished People in the United States* (2001) and *Rethinking America: The Imperial Homeland in the 21st Century* (2010).

Jennifer Riggan is professor of international studies in the Department of Historical and Political Studies at Arcadia University. A political anthropologist whose ethnographic research focuses on political identities and state formation, she has published on the changing relationship between citizenship and nationalism, the decoupling of the nation and the state, and the relationship between militarization, education, and development. Her current research explores the effects of new paradigms in global migration management on Ethiopian refugee policy and Eritrean refugees in Ethiopia. She is the author of *The Struggling State: Nationalism, Mass Militarization and the Education of Eritrea* (2016). She has been awarded the Georg Arnhold Professorship in Education for Sustainable Peace (2019), a Fulbright Scholar Award for Ethiopia (2016–17), a Spencer/National Academy of Education Postdoctoral Fellowship (2012–14), and a Social Science Research Council International Dissertation Field Research Fellowship.

Don Robotham is professor of anthropology at the CUNY Graduate Center and director of the Advanced Research Collaborative. His fieldwork has been in the gold mines of Ghana and in various countries in the English-Speaking Caribbean. He is the author of *Militants or Proletarians? The Economic Culture of Underground Goldminers in Southern Ghana* (Cambridge African Studies Center Monographs 1989), and *Culture, Society,*

Economy: Globalization and Its Alternatives (2007). He has published extensively on anthropological theory, economic anthropology, and political economy as well as on issues of development in the Caribbean and West Africa. His work has appeared in the *American Ethnologist, Identities, South Atlantic Quarterly, Social and Economic Studies, Transforming Anthropology*, and various book collections. His most recent article is "Interrogating Post-Plantation Caribbean Society," *Journal of Latin American and Caribbean Anthropology* 23, 2 (July 2018). He sits on the editorial board of the *Critique of Anthropology*.

Preeti Sampat teaches sociology in the School of Liberal Studies in Ambedkar University Delhi. Trained as an anthropologist, she works on urbanization, infrastructure, and land rights in India and is currently developing a manuscript that analyzes India's land impasse in the context of India's growing rentier economy; struggles against dispossession; and the current historical conjuncture of the rise of Hindutva (Hindu nationalism). Her research interests include legal anthropology, the anthropology of infrastructure, urbanization, capital, nature, state, social movements, democracy, and authoritarianism.

Mary N. Taylor's praxis sits at the intersection of anthropology, dialogical art, and urbanism. Her research focuses on overlapping sites, techniques and politics of civic cultivation, social movement, and cultural management; the ethico-aesthetics of nationalism, cultural differentiation, and people's movements; and the politics of solidarity. Her publications have appeared in *Focaal, Bajo al Volcan, Nationalism and Ethnic Politics*, and the *Journal of Hungarian Studies*, among others. Her books include *Co-Revolutionary Praxis; Accompaniment as a Strategy for Working Together* (with Charlotte Huddleston, Abby Cunnane, and Sakiko Sugawa, 2015) and *Movement of the People: Populism, Folk Dance, and Citizenship in Hungary* (forthcoming). She is a member of the editorial collective of LeftEast and is a key organizer of annual LeftEast summer encounters convened in movement spaces in Budapest, Sofia, Istanbul, Kaunas, and Skopje. The work of Brooklyn Laundry Social Club, which she cofounded in 2012, has been exhibited in the Living Gallery and the Office for Urban Disturbances (Mitchell Innes and Nash Gallery). Taylor has taught anthropology at Hunter College and the Cooper Union for the Advancement of Science and Art, and urban theory and methods at Parsons, The New School. She is currently assistant director of the Center for Place, Culture and Politics at the Graduate Center of the City University of New York.

Noah Theriault is assistant professor of anthropology in the Department of History at Carnegie Mellon University, where he offers courses on Southeast Asia, environmental justice, and social theory. His research uses ethnographic methods to trace how global-scale forces of social and environmental change shape the lives of rural and urban communities in the Philippines, with particular attention to the everyday practices through which those forces are enacted, contested, and potentially transformed. This includes a long-term study of indigeneity and biodiversity conservation in Palawan and more recently a political ecology of transportation infrastructure in Manila. Theriault's other primary interests include antiauthoritarian theory/practice and decolonial approaches to global ecological crisis.

CPSIA information can be obtained
at www.ICGtesting.com
Printed in the USA
FSHW021545051219

9 781949 199468